TAKING SIDES

Clashing Views on
African Issues
THIRD EDITION

TAKING SIDES

Clashing Views on
African Issues
THIRD EDITION

Selected, Edited, and with Introductions by

William G. Moseley
Macalester College

 Higher Education

Boston   Burr Ridge, IL   Dubuque, IA   New York   San Francisco   St. Louis
Bangkok   Bogotá   Caracas   Kuala Lumpur   Lisbon   London   Madrid   Mexico City
Milan   Montreal   New Delhi   Santiago   Seoul   Singapore   Sydney   Taipei   Toronto

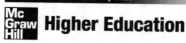

Higher Education

TAKING SIDES: CLASHING VIEWS ON AFRICAN ISSUES, THIRD EDITION

Published by McGraw-Hill, a business unit of The McGraw-Hill Companies, Inc., 1221 Avenue of the Americas, New York, NY 10020. Copyright © 2009 by The McGraw-Hill Companies, Inc. All rights reserved. Previous edition(s) 2004–2007. No part of this publication may be reproduced or distributed in any form or by any means, or stored in a database or retrieval system, without the prior written consent of The McGraw-Hill Companies, Inc., including, but not limited to, in any network or other electronic storage or transmission, or broadcast for distance learning.

Some ancillaries, including electronic and print components, may not be available to customers outside the United States.

Taking Sides® is a registered trademark of the McGraw-Hill Companies, Inc.
Taking Sides is published by the **Contemporary Learning Series** group within the McGraw-Hill Higher Education division.

1 2 3 4 5 6 7 8 9 0 DOC/DOC 0 9 8

MHID: 0-07-351518-3
ISBN: 978-0-07-351518-2
ISSN: 1545-5327

Managing Editor: *Larry Loeppke*
Production Manager: *Faye Schilling*
Developmental Editor: *Jade Benedict*
Editorial Assistant: *Nancy Meissner*
Production Service Assistant: *Rita Hingtgen*
Permissions Coordinator: *Leonard J. Behnke*
Senior Marketing Manager: *Julie Keck*
Marketing Communications Specialist: *Mary Klein*
Marketing Coordinator: *Alice Link*
Project Manager: *Jane Mohr*
Design Specialist: *Tara McDermott*
Senior Administrative Assistant: *DeAnna Dausener*
Cover Graphics: *Kristine Jubeck*

Compositor: Hurix Systems Private Limited
Cover Image: William Moseley

Library of Congress Cataloging-in-Publication Data
Main entry under title:
Taking sides: clashing views on African issues/selected, edited, and with introductions by William G. Moseley.—2nd ed.

Includes bibliographical references.
I. Africa—Politics and government—1989– II. Africa—Social conditions—1989–
III. Africa—Economic conditions—1989– IV. Africa—Civilization—21st century.
1. Moseley, William G. ed. 2 Series.

916

www.mhhe.com

Preface

This volume's cover photo features three women who I met in the gardens of a village in southern Mali about four years ago. They had been working in their plots that morning, but had subsequently slipped into some nicer clothes as they were headed to their area's once weekly market (a major commercial and social event for the surrounding communities). This image, and the story of the women and place behind it, offers some interesting insights about Africa that are rarely covered in the popular media. As is the case for women in other parts of the world, African women suffer from discrimination and inequality. Yet, despite these disadvantages, African women are actively shaping the future of their continent. They form the backbone of the rural economy in many African settings where it is estimated that they produce 70 percent of the food supply. Women are also significant commercial players in many West African market places. Even though Mali is a predominantly Muslim country (and Western perceptions of Islam are largely negative), the religion here is generally tolerant and pragmatic, with little to no prohibition on female participation in the public sphere. The community from which these women hail is also multiethnic, predominantly by Bamanan agriculturalists and Fulani agropastoralists. Despite all the stories of ethnic strife in Africa, these groups peacefully coexist.

I find studying Africa so exciting and captivating in part due to the types of issues discussed above. I have been working and conducting research in Africa for over 20 years now, originally as a development professional and currently as an academic. My applied work and research have led to extended stays in several African countries (Mali, Zimbabwe, South Africa, Malawi, Niger, and Lesotho) and to travel in many others. This firsthand experience with nuts-and-bolts development issues, as well as vital research questions, has led me to care deeply about Africa as a region and to grapple intellectually with many of the issues presented in this volume.

I have been fortunate to share my fascination for the African continent with (and learn from) some incredibly bright, insightful, and engaged students. Like other academics who have been bitten by the Africa bug, it is during my Africa course each spring that I find my own and my students' enthusiasm for the subject to be most infectious. I hope this volume will serve as a useful platform for discussions in courses offered in a variety of departments dealing with contemporary African issues, including anthropology, African studies, development studies, economics, geography, history, international studies, political science, and sociology. I find that the best way to encourage students to grapple with their preconceptions about Africa is to offer readings that both support and contradict their initial leanings. Through the process of reviewing different arguments and discussing them with their classmates, individual students continually surprise me by the degree to which their positions may change during the course of a semester (far more than if I had tried to convince them of the validity of a certain perspective). Of course, there is no obvious right or wrong to many of these issues, and some of the most rewarding class discussions occur when there is no clear majority of students for one position or the other.

Changes to this edition The third edition has been extensively revised and updated. Based on the feedback of reviews of the second edition, six new issues have been added. These include: Issue 3 (*Is European Subjugation of Africans Ultimately Explained by Differences in Land, Plant, and Animal Resources?*), Issue 7 (*Is Increasing Chinese Investment Good for African Development?*), Issue 8 (*Does the Conflict in the Darfur Region of Sudan Have Environmental Causes?*), Issue 10 (*Does African Agriculture Need a Green Revolution?*), Issue 14 (*Is the International Community Focusing on HIV/AIDS Treatment at the Expense of Prevention in Africa?*), and Issue 19 (*Are African-Led Peacekeeping Missions More Effective than International Peacekeeping Efforts in Africa?*). In all, 12 of the 38 selections, or 30 percent of the material, has been changed. Additional revisions include fine-tuning the questions, reordering the material in the book, and rewriting the introductions and postscripts.

A word to the instructor An *Instructor's Resource Guide with Test Questions* (multiple choice and essay) is available through the publisher for the instructor using *Taking Sides* in the classroom. Also available is a general guidebook, *Using Taking Sides in the Classroom*, which offers suggestions for adapting the pro-con approach in the classroom setting. An online version of *Using Taking Sides in the Classroom* and a correspondence service for *Taking Sides* adopters can be found at http://www.mhcls.com/usingts/.

    Taking Sides: Clashing Views on African Issues is only one title in the *Taking Sides* series. If you are interested in seeing the table of contents for any of the other titles, please visit the *Taking Sides* Web site at http://www.mhcls.com/takingsides/.

Acknowledgements I am grateful to several students at Macalester College, especially Elyse Gordon, who helped me with various aspects of this text. I wish to acknowledge members of the editorial board for this text (listed below) and several anonymous reviewers who provided me with invaluable feedback during the first, second, or third editions of this volume. I thank my spouse, Julia, and children, Ben and Sophie, for their shared enthusiasm for Africa. I finally wish to acknowledge the editorial staff at McGraw-Hill, especially Susan Brusch, for her copyediting, insight, and encouragement.

William G. Moseley
Macalester College

Clashing Views on African Issues

THIRD EDITION

William G. Moseley
Macalester College

Advisory Board

Abigail Amissah-Arthur
Slippery Rock University

Misty L. Bastian
Franklin and Marshall College

Simon Batterbury
University of Melbourne

James Burns
Clemson University

Padraig R. Carmody
Dublin City University

Simeon Chilungu
Buffalo State College

Chris Duvall
Michigan State University

Raymond Hopkins
Swarthmore College

Ezekiel Kalipeni
*University of Illinois,
Urbana-Champagne*

Howard Lehman
University of Utah

B. Ikubolajeh Logan
Penn State University

Jamie Monson
Carleton College

David Newbury
Smith College

Maano Ramutsindela
University of Cape Town

David Simon
University of London

Stephen Wooten
University of Oregon

Aguibou Y. Yansane
San Francisco State University

Contents In Brief

Contents

Paul E. Lovejoy, professor of history at York University, argues that the trans-Atlantic slave trade significantly transformed African society. It led to an absolute loss of population on the continent and a large increase in the enslaved population that was retained in Africa. The economic advantages of exporting slaves did not offset the social and political costs of participation, there were disastrous demographic impacts, and Africa's relative position in world trade declined. John Thornton is a professor of history at Boston University. He notes that slavery was widespread and indigenous in African society. Europeans simply worked with this existing market and African merchants, who were not dominated by Europeans, responded by providing more slaves. African leaders who allowed the slave trade to continue were neither forced to do so against their will, nor did they make irrational decisions. As such, the preexisting institution of slavery in Africa is as much responsible as any external force for the development of the trans-Atlantic slave trade.

Duncan Clinch Heyward, a former Carolina rice planter writing in the middle of the last century, represents the mainstream view that Europeans were primarily responsible for developing South Carolina's remarkable rice plantations in the eighteenth century. In his own accounting of the rise of rice cultivation in the Carolinas, Duncan suggests that the techniques and approaches must have been derived from those observed in China. Judith Carney, a professor of geography at UCLA, explains that slaves from rice-producing areas in West Africa have only recently been recognized for their intellectual contributions to the development of rice cultivation in the New World. Carney describes how her work, and that of others, challenged the view that slaves were mere field hands, "showing that they contributed agronomic expertise as well as skilled labor to the emergent plantation economy."

Jared Diamond, professor of physiology and biogeography at UCLA, argues that Europeans were able to colonize Africa (rather than vice versa) because of the advantages of guns, widespread literacy, and political organization. These advantages stem ultimately from different historical trajectories that are linked to "differences in real estate" (or differences in physical geography). Lucy Jarosz, associate professor of geography at the University of Washington, is troubled by Diamond's narrow conception of geography and asserts that explaining differences in wealth and power between regions must also take account of social, political, and economic connections. She focuses on the specific case of Madagascar and argues that the intentions of the colonizer are as or more important than their military power for determining the nature of the colonial relationship.

Marcus Colchester, director of the Forest Peoples Programme of the World Rainforest Movement, argues that rural communities in equatorial Africa are today on the point of collapse because they have been weakened by centuries of outside intervention. In Gabon, the Congo, and the Central African Republic, an enduring colonial legacy of the French are lands and forests controlled by state institutions that operate as patron-client networks to enrich indigenous elite and outside commercial interests. Robin M. Grier, associate professor of economics at the University of Oklahoma, contends that African colonies that were held for longer periods of time tend to have performed better, on average, after independence.

UNIT 2   DEVELOPMENT   71

Gerald Scott, an economist at Florida Atlantic University, argues that structural adjustment programs are the most promising option for promoting economic growth in Africa. He disputes the evidence used to suggest that these programs have a deleterious effect on economic growth in Africa. Thandika Mkandawire, director of the UN Research Institute for Social Development, counters that, even though African governments have reshaped domestic policies to make their economies more open, growth has faltered. Mkandawire assesses structural adjustment from a developmental perspective, judging its effects on economic development and the eradication of poverty. He suggests that structural adjustment policies designed to integrate Africa into the global economy have failed because "they have completely sidestepped the developmental needs of the continent and the strategic questions on the form of integration appropriate to addressing these needs."

Oliver Maponga, Economic Affairs Officer in the Southern Africa Office of the United Nations Economic Commission for Africa, and Philip Maxwell, professor at the Western Australian School of Mines at Curtin University of Technology, describe a resurgence in the African mining industry in the 1990s after several lackluster decades. They assert that mineral and energy mining can make a positive contribution to economic development in Africa. Sunday Dare, a Nigerian journalist, describes how "much sorrow has flowed" from Africa's resource blessing. While Dare blames African leaders for corruption and resource mismanagement, he also implicates transnational corporations (TNCs) as key contributors to this problem. He states that TNCs have acted as economic predators that support repressive African leaders in order to garner uninterrupted access to resources. The result, Dare suggests, is that Africa's "raw materials are still being depleted without general development."

Ali Zafar, a macroeconomist with the World Bank, acknowledges the downside of increasing Chinese economic interests in Africa, but foresees more potential winners than losers. Among the big winners of increasing Chinese trade are oil exporters (Angola, Gabon, and Sudan) and resource-rich countries (Mauritania, South Africa, Mozambique, and Zambia). Chinese foreign direct investment is also increasing rapidly in those countries where it has trade interests. Padraig R. Carmody of Trinity College Dublin and Francis Y. Owusu of Iowa State University are less sanguine about Chinese involvement in Africa. Even though they also perceive potential benefits from increasing trade with China, they describe how increasing resource flows are strengthening authoritarian states and fuelling conflict.

UNIT 3   AGRICULTURE, FOOD, AND THE ENVIRONMENT   139

The UN Environment Programme argues that there is a strong link between land degradation, desertification, and conflict in Darfur, Sudan. It suggests that declining rainfall in Darfur, ecological collapse, and population growth have triggered social disintegration and the conditions for conflict that are then sustained by political, tribal, or ethnic differences. Lydia Polgreen, reporter for the *New York Times*, questions whether environmental degradation is at the root of the Darfur Crisis. Making such a causal link leads to the faulty conclusion that the conflict may be resolved by improving environmental conditions. An alternative explanation for the conflict lies in the land-use patterns promoted by the government of Sudan and the development policies of the World Bank and the IMF.

Michael Mortimore, a geographer, and Mary Tiffen, a historian and socio-economist, both with Drylands Research, investigate population and food production trajectories in Machakos, Kenya. They determine that increasing population density has a positive influence on environmental management and crop production. Furthermore, they found that food production kept up with population growth from 1930 to 1987. John Murton, with the Foreign and Commonwealth Office of the British government, uses household-level data to show that the changes in Machakos described by Mortimore and Tiffen "have been accompanied by a polarization of land holdings, differential trends in agricultural productivity, and a decline in food self-sufficiency." As such, he argues that the "Machakos experience" of population growth and positive environmental transformation is neither homogenous nor fully unproblematic.

Kofi A. Annan, former UN Secretary General, deplores the fact that Sub-Saharan Africa is the only region where per capita food production has declined. Annan is now leading a new organization that answers the call of many African leaders to build on the achievements and lessons learned from the Green Revolution in Asia and Latin America that began several decades earlier. He is spearheading an African Green Revolution that aims to increase African food production. Carol B. Thompson, professor of political economy at Northern Arizona University, suggests that increasing yields of a few targeted crops will not solve Africa's food problems. Rather, she argues that sustaining Africa's food crop diversity and indigenous ecological knowledge is the key to reducing hunger. She further eschews food security built on global market dependence in favor of food sovereignty.

World Bank economists Kevin M. Cleaver and Götz A. Schreiber argue that Africa is engaged in a downward spiral of population growth, poor agricultural performance, and environmental degradation. Academic geographers Thomas J. Bassett and Koli Bi Zuéli counter that it is dominant perceptions of environmental change, rather than concrete evidence that lie behind the widely held belief that Africa is engaged in an "environmental crisis of staggering proportions."

Fuambai Ahmadu, an anthropologist at the London School of Economics, finds it increasingly challenging to reconcile her own experiences with female initiation and circumcision and prevailing (largely negative) global discourses on these practices. Her main concern with most studies on female initiation is the insistence that the practice is necessarily harmful or that there is an urgent need to stop female genital mutilation in communities where it is done. She suggests that "the aversion of some writers to the practice of female circumcision has more to do with deeply imbedded western cultural assumptions regarding women's bodies and their sexuality than with disputable health effects of genital operations on African women." Liz Creel, senior policy analyst at the Population Reference Bureau, and her colleagues argue that female genital cutting (FGC), while it must be dealt with in a culturally sensitive manner, is a practice that is detrimental to the health of girls and women, as well as a violation of human rights in most instances. Creel et al. recommend that African governments pass anti-FGC laws, and that programs be expanded to educate communities about FGC and human rights.

Richard A. Schroeder, an associate professor of geography at Rutgers University, presents a case study of a group of female gardeners in The Gambia who, because of their growing economic clout, began to challenge male power structures. Women, who were the traditional gardeners in the community studied, came to have greater income-earning capacity than men as the urban market for garden produce grew. Furthermore, women could meet their needs and wants without recourse to their husbands because of this newly found economic power. Human Rights Watch, a nonprofit organization, describes how women in Kenya have property rights unequal to those of men, and how even these limited rights are frequently violated. It is further explained how women have little awareness of their rights, that those "who try to fight back are often beaten, raped, or ostracized," and how the Kenyan government has done little to address the situation.

Andrew Creese and his colleagues, who work for the World Health Organization (WHO) and European Universities, suggest that cost-effectiveness is an important criterion for deciding how to allocate scarce health care funding. A case of HIV/AIDS can be prevented for $11 by selective blood safety measures and targeted condom distribution with treatment of sexually transmitted diseases. In contrast, antiretroviral treatment for adults can cost several thousand dollars. They argue that a strong economic case exists for prioritizing preventive interventions and TB treatment. Philip Hilts, who teaches journalism at Boston University, describes a comprehensive HIV/AIDS program in Botswana. This program not only offered preventive care, but sophisticated triple drug AIDS treatments to all people of the nation, free of charge. By 2005, the program was treating 43,000 people and the cost of treatment is one-tenth of what it is in the United States.

Dorothy Logie, a general practitioner and active member of Medact, and Michael Rowson, assistant director of Medact, argue that debt is a human rights issue because debt and related structural adjustment policies reduce the state's ability to address discrimination, vulnerability, and inequality. Debt relief, if channeled in the right direction, could help reduce poverty and promote health. Robert Snyder, faculty in the department of biology at the College of the Ozarks, counters that debt cancellation will only work if the factors that created debt in the first place are addressed. He uses a case study of Rwanda to demonstrate why political and social change must occur for debt forgiveness to work.

Michael Bratton, professor of political science at Michigan State University, and Robert Mattes, associate professor of political studies and director of the Democracy in Africa Research Unit at the University of Cape Town, find as much popular support for democracy in Zambia, South Africa, and Ghana as in other regions of the developing world, despite the fact that the citizens of these countries tend to be less satisfied with the economic performance of their elected governments. Joel D. Barkan, professor of political science at the University of Iowa and senior consultant on governance at the World Bank, takes a less sanguine view of the situation in Africa. He suggests that one can be cautiously optimistic about the situation in roughly one-third of the states on the African continent, nations he classifies as consolidated democracies and as aspiring democracies. He asserts that one must be realistic about the possibilities for the remainder of African nations, countries he classifies into three groups: stalled democracies, those that are not free, and those that are mired in civil war.

Arthur A. Goldsmith, professor of management at the University of Massachusetts in Boston, examines the relationship between the amount of development assistance given to sub-Saharan African countries in the 1990s and the evolution of their political systems. He suggests that there is a positive, but small, correlation between donor assistance and democratization during this period. He views aid as insurance to prevent countries from sliding back into one-party or military rule. Julie Hearn, with the department of politics and international relations at Lancaster University, investigates democracy assistance in South Africa. She critically examines the role assigned to civil society by donors, questioning the "emancipatory potential" of the kind of democracy being promoted.

Robert I. Rotberg, director of the Program on Intrastate Conflict and Conflict Resolution at Harvard University's John F. Kennedy School of Government, holds African leaders responsible for the plight of their continent. He laments the large number of corrupt African leaders, seeing South Africa's Mandela and Botswana's Khama as notable exceptions. According to Rotberg, the problem is that "African leaders and their followers largely believe that the people are there to serve their rulers, rather than the other way around." Arthur A. Goldsmith, professor of management at the University of Massachusetts–Boston, suggests that African leaders are not innately corrupt but are responding rationally to incentives created by their environment. He argues that high levels of risk encourage leaders to pursue short-term, economically destructive policies. In countries where leaders face less risk, there is less perceived political corruption.

Issue 19   Are African-Led Peacekeeping Missions More Effective than International Peacekeeping Efforts in Africa?   354

David C. Gompert, an adviser to Refugees International and a senior fellow at the RAND Corporation, believes that the African Union could be effective in Sudan if adequately supported. He believes that Africans are willing to commit combat forces to stop the killing in Darfur because they are more deeply affected by such abuses than Europe or North America. In fact, the unwillingness of the great powers to create a standing UN peacekeeping force is illustrative of a weak commitment of the West to intervene in Africa. Nsonurua Udombana of Central European University is more critical of the African Union peacekeeping mission in Sudan. He believes this mission has failed in Darfur because it suffers from several weaknesses, including problems of command and control, logistical support, operational practice, and lack of funds.

Introduction

Understanding African Issues in Context: The Global and the Local as Interpreted by the Media, Scholars, and Policymakers

William G. Moseley

People go to Africa and confirm what they already have in their heads and so they fail to see what is there in front of them.

Chinua Achebe, Nigerian author

When the missionaries came to Africa they had the Bible and we had the land. They said "Let us pray." We closed our eyes. When we opened them we had the Bible and they had the land.

Bishop Desmond Tutu, South African spiritual leader and novelist

As the quotes above suggest, African issues cannot be fully appreciated without a deep knowledge of the region and a broad understanding of its connections to the rest of the world. Every place, country, and region in Africa has its own environmental conditions, cultural dynamics, politics, and history. Yet these African places do not exist in a vacuum. They almost always have a history of connections to other areas of the continent and the world. As such, serious students, scholars, and policymakers with an interest in Africa must both seek to understand the specific geographic milieu in which an issue is being debated, as well as the extent to which a local level problem is connected to broader scale dynamics at the national, regional, or global level. The mere act of growing food crops, for example, is a deeply local process that relates to site-specific environmental conditions, agricultural practices, and cultural preferences. But what and where certain crops are grown often has been influenced by cultural exchange, colonialism, and global markets.

Scholars and policymakers seeking to understand the synergy of global and local forces that imbue most African issues often privilege one set of causes over another. This privileging of more global or local causes is often described in terms of externalist versus internalist explanations. Scholars evoking externalist (or structuralist) explanations suggest that contemporary development patterns cannot be properly understood without an understanding of historical patterns of resource extraction and political control, as well as the position of Africa within the global economic system. In particular, these explanations often look to problematic colonial legacies to elucidate contemporary economic distortions. Scholars emphasizing internalist explanations tend to look to local factors to explain an issue or problem. These local phenomena may be negative (corruption, mismanagement, incompetence, nepotism, ethnic allegiances, regional ties, obligations to the extended family, and patron-client relationships) or positive (local cultural practices, indigenous knowledge, family support networks).

Externalist or structuralist critiques of internalist positions range from accusations of spatial and temporal myopia to "blaming the victim." Internalist leaning critics suggest that the structuralists are apologists who deny Africans' "agency" (i.e., the ability to influence contemporary events) and responsibility, thereby fostering a sense of victimization, helplessness, and further mismanagement. The reality, of course, is that good scholarship must equally explore both sets of factors. In some instances, both types of explanations will be equally critical for understanding an issue, in other cases either internal or external factors may rightly be seen to be more important. The rest of this introductory chapter explores the key actors who often interpret African issues and provides an introduction to the major themes explored in the reader.

Interpreting African Issues: Journalists, Scholars, Policymakers

Our impressions of Africa, our understanding of African issues, and the actions organizations take on the ground and in the policy sphere vis à vis Africa are filtered and articulated by a number of key players. Most notable among these are the popular press, the academy, and policymakers.

The Popular Press

Images and descriptions in the popular press suggest that the African continent is a troubled land where corruption, ethnic warfare, poverty, hunger, environmental destruction, and pestilence prevail. Some have even suggested that Africa is a lost cause, asserting that the continent be "written off" by international development organizations. Meanwhile, commercial tour operators also hawk the region as a place of high adventure and exoticism. Even quasi-scholarly publications such *National Geographic Magazine* often promote a vision of a primitive or wild Africa. What these popular and commercial descriptions hold in common is level of superficiality and one-sidedness. Yes, bad things do happen in Africa and there is beautiful scenery to be seen, but this is only one side of a complex and highly varied picture. It is the apparent unwillingness (or laziness) of popular commentators to provide a more nuanced view of an enormous continent that is often frustrating to scholars of Africa (or Africanists).

Africa is, after all, a place of extraordinarily diverse, vibrant, and dynamic cultures. Since the early 1990s, no other continent has seen more dramatic improvements in human rights, political freedom, and economic development—from the overthrowing of apartheid in South Africa to the revitalization of economies in countries such as Ghana and Uganda. Although environmental threats are real, African societies have proven their capacity, when given a chance, to use resources sustainably. Some conservation efforts in Africa even have become models for progressive community-based resource management in Western societies. The importance of human relations, family, and good neighborliness in many African societies also stands in stark contrast to the more closed and individualistic tendencies in a number of Western settings.

The Academy

For the past century, the Western academy has been organized largely along disciplinary lines. The disciplinary approach encourages focused investigations from one perspective across a range of geographies. Area studies complement disciplinary inquiry by promoting multiperspective investigations of focused regions. In other words, the region or area represents a different framework around which to organize knowledge. Recent world events have revealed that there is a dearth of regional experts within the academy, government, and the private sector. The ideal scholar-practitioner may therefore be someone who not only has a firm grasp of the methods and theories of a particular discipline, but who also has a broader understanding of the issues and challenges (cutting across several disciplines) facing a particular region of the world.

While a variety of disciplinary departments offer courses that deal with contemporary African issues, it is notable that there are now a number of interdisciplinary programs and departments devoted to African and Afro-American studies. In the United States, the first African studies programs were established at Northwestern University (1946) and Boston University (1953). A number of other large programs were started in the early 1960s at places like Michigan State, Wisconsin, UCLA, Indiana, and Ohio University [*African Studies and the Undergraduate Curriculum*, Patricia Alden, David Lloyd, and Ahmed Samatar (eds), Lynne Rienner, 1994]. By the mid-1990s there were approximately 330 programs of African and Afro-American studies in the United States (*Directory of African and Afro-American Studies in the United States*, African Studies Association, 1993). African studies is as or more developed at institutions in other areas of the world. Although the names of these organizations are too numerous to list, there are over 1,800 academic institutions, research bodies, and international organizations involved in African studies research in all parts of the world [*International Directory of African Studies Research*, 3rd edition, Philip Baker (ed), Hans Zell Publishers, 1994]. In the United States, over 1,300 scholars from a broad array of disciplines meet each year at the annual meeting of the African Studies Association to present their research findings and debate key African issues. African studies associations and societies also exist in a number of other countries (e.g., Australia, Canada, France,

Germany, India, Japan, Netherlands, South Africa, Spain, Sweden, Switzerland, United Kingdom).

Prior to the establishment of African studies as a recognized interdisciplinary field of study, some scholars encountered resistance from quarters of the academic establishment who perceived Africa to be lacking in history or otherwise unworthy of academic investigation. African studies has grown to be a dynamic realm of inquiry that regularly contributes to the broader academic discourse. Africanist scholars have tested the validity of widely accepted notions in the African context. They also have developed new theories that have influenced thinking in other regional contexts. Those disciplines contributing to African studies may roughly be divided between the humanities (mainly history and literature), the social sciences (anthropology, archeology, education, geography, political science, sociology), and the physical sciences (physical geography, ecology, botany). In the North American context, African studies meetings tend to be dominated by the humanities and social sciences, with historians and political scientists attending in the largest numbers (perhaps due to the sheer size of their disciplines). This volume largely deals with controversial African issues in the social sciences, although some of the questions have a significant historical or environmental dimension that pulls on literature from the humanities or physical sciences.

The burgeoning field of African studies has spawned a number of academic journals, examples of which include: *Africa, Africa Today, African Affairs, African Studies Review, Cahiers d'Etudes Africaines, African Geographical Review, South African Geographical Journal, Canadian Journal of African Studies, Journal of African History, Journal of Modern African Studies, Journal of Southern African Studies,* and *Review of African Political Economy.* There are also a number of more policy related or popular media magazines that focus on Africa including, for example, *Africa Analysis, Africa Confidential, Africa Now, Afrique Express* (French), and *Jeune Afrique* (French).

Policymakers and Development Professionals

In addition to the press and the academy, the other major sphere where African issues are framed and examined is in the offices of government bureaucrats, global policymakers, and nongovernmental organizations. These include individuals within the bilateral development agencies (e.g., U.S. Agency for International Development, British Department for International Development, Cooperation Française, or Canadian International Development Agency), international financial institutions (e.g., World Bank, International Monetary Fund, World Trade Organization), UN agencies (e.g., Food and Agricultural Organization, World Health Organization), and nonprofit community (e.g., CARE, Oxfam, Save the Children). While these organizations contribute to and influence discourse, their role is slightly different than the media and the academy in that this is where rhetoric is transformed into programmatic reality.

Even though I present the media, the academy, and development institutions as separate spheres of debate on Africa, there is, in fact, a considerable amount of crossover in thinking, not to mention personnel, between each realm. Policymakers and development professionals do not make decisions in a vacuum, but are influenced by public opinion (shaped by the media) and the latest academic research. Academics and policymakers attempt to influence public opinion through the media (via op-eds and interviews with the press). Governments may seek to shape academic findings by funding research projects or hiring scholars as consultants. Scholars may agree to consult on development issues because they believe this is a way for them to influence decision making. There also is a certain amount of personnel exchange between the different sectors (e.g., it is to think tanks, multilateral development agencies, and universities that a number of foreign service and aid advisors flee each time the party in power changes in Washington, Ottawa, or London). Despite these exchanges, significant differences exist in tone, timeliness, depth and emphasis in analysis, and standards of knowledge production. The distribution of power (i.e., the power to have one's ideas heard) also differs within each group.

Major Themes

If this book has one overarching theme it is African development. I interpret development in the broadest sense of the term, going beyond conventional measures of economic progress, to embrace processes occurring at a variety of spatial and temporal scales that allow people to meet their full potential. When viewed in this manner, nearly all of the issues presented in this volume pertain in one way or another to development. In order to give the volume a more accessible format, it has been organized into five thematic categories of African issues that are most often debated by Africanists in the academy, as well as by policymakers and media commentators. These thematic categories are: (1) history; (2) development; (3) agriculture, food, and the environment; (4) social issues; and (5) politics, governance, and conflict resolution. Although I present these themes as distinct, the reader should understand that there are often a number of connections that exist between issues in different parts of the book.

History

The number of historical debates pertaining to Africa are so numerous that they easily could constitute a separate volume. There are, however, a few issues that stand out as they highlight the connections between Africa and the rest of the world, and because these questions impinge on contemporary development patterns. First, understanding the impact of the trans-Atlantic slave trade on African development patterns is critical. Was this a significant historical moment with lasting impacts or was it consistent with existing practices and effectively managed by Africans? Given that so many Africans departed to the New World, it is also crucial to understand the active role they played in shaping and developing the Americas. What led the Europeans to colonize Africa, rather than vice versa? Was it something about the continents' different natural endowments that made this possible (as some have argued), or was it more a question of intent and political economy? Finally, to what extent has colonialism shaped contemporary development patterns? Some find that this led to huge and lasting distortions in African economies, whereas others argue that this was beneficial for economic development.

Development

The nature of and approach to development in the African context is highly contentious. Commentators, scholars, and policymakers argue, for example, over the perceived failure of Africa to develop, the impact of the colonial experience on contemporary events, the influence of global economic structures on African development patterns, and the role of the state versus the private and nonprofit sectors in the development process.

Closely related to the externalist/internalist debate is one concerning the most appropriate approach to development in Africa. The structuralists evoke dependency theory and world systems theory to suggest that, even though the colonial era has ended, historical patterns of resource extraction persist. In many instances, African nations are supplying cheap commodities (minerals, oil, lumber, cotton, coffee, cocoa, tea, and sugar) to Europe and North America in exchange for relatively expensive manufactured goods. As such, the participation of African nations in the global economy under current conditions leads to a process of underdevelopment. The best way to avoid this trap, according to the structuralists, is to diversify the national economy by producing imported goods at home, an approach also known as import substitution.

The general failure of import substitution, and the related Third World debt crisis, led the international financial institutions (especially the World Bank and International Monetary Fund) to begin pushing for the structural adjustment of African economies beginning in the early 1980s. With the basic aim of balancing the national budget and spurring economic growth, these programs obliged African government to privatize state-owned enterprises, devalue local currencies, cut government programs, and expand exports. The uneven success and social costs of these free-market policies have led to bitter debates in academic and policy circles. Many contend that the role of the state in the development process has been underestimated by neoclassical economists.

Another key aspect of African development is the rise in the number and prominence of non-governmental organizations (NGOs) since the 1980s. Bilateral and multilateral donors increasingly bypass the African state by providing funds to NGOs for project and program implementation. NGOs (both local and international) are perceived to be more efficient and more in tune with the needs of the local population. Critics argue that NGOs can be equally autocratic, patronizing, and detached from the local population.

Finally, what is the role of mineral and energy resources in African development? The notion that a rich natural resource base may play a key part in the development of some African nations is hotly contested. Critics contend that bountiful resources may actually be a "curse" because they tend to inhibit economic diversification, fall under the control of unscrupulous government officials, and attract predatory multinational corporations. Proponents of mineral and energy resource development point to the positive contributions of mining in several developed country economies. This topic has become more important in recent years as the United States and China increasingly look to African nations for their energy and mineral needs (the United States because of unstable supplies in other parts of the world, and China because of its rapidly expanding economy).

Agriculture, Food, and the Environment

Since the global media focused attention on large-scale droughts in the early 1970s and mid-1980s, famine and environmental destruction in Africa have loomed large in the public imagination. Key debates have centered on whether or not environmental deterioration is a cause of ethnic conflict, if the continent's population is growing too quickly for its agricultural base, whether or not a new "African Green Revolution" is needed, and if the continent is facing a deforestation crisis.

The idea that resource scarcity and environmental degradation may lead to ethnic conflict has captured the imagination of policymakers since the early 1990s. This position, known as the environmental security argument (developed by the political scientist Tad Homer-Dixon (1994), was popularized and applied to Africa in journalist Robert Kaplan's 1994 article "The Coming Anarchy." This causal framework has most recently been applied to the conflict in Darfur, Sudan. In contrast, others suggest that climate change and environmental degradation do not, in and of themselves, cause conflict. In many ways, Sudan is rich in environmental resources. It is often the battle to control these riches, and local people around them, that is the real reason for oppression and strife.

A fundamental debate persists as to whether or not famine and food insecurity in Africa is the result of underproduction or the maldistribution of food. Many development assistance programs, including the international network of crop development institutes under the aegis of the Consultative Group on International Agricultural Research (CGIAR), are predicated on the assumption that Africa's food problems will be resolved by increases in food production. Economist and Nobel laureate, Amartya Sen, has argued that famine rarely results from an absolute shortage of food, but the inability of poor households to access available supplies.

Related to the aforementioned debate are two long-standing discussions. The first concerns the relationship between food production and population growth. The eighteenth-century parson, Thomas Malthus, asserted that human populations would inevitably grow more quickly than food production, ultimately leading to famine. Contemporary neo-Malthusians, such as Paul Ehrlich, have similarly argued that urgent measures are needed to control population in order to avert disaster. Ester Boserup has countered that Malthus had it all wrong because it is population density that controls the level of food production, rather than food production quantities setting population thresholds. In recent years, some of the best case studies (both pro-Boserupian and pro-Malthusian) on the relationship between population growth and food production have come out of Africa. The second debate concerns a recent push for a new "African Green Revolution," an attempt to increase yields through improved seeds and inputs. This initiative has received prominent support from former UN secretary general Kofi Annan and Columbia University economist Jeffrey Sachs. Critics are skeptical on two fronts. First, and as discussed above, they wonder if hunger in Africa is really a supply-side problem that improving yields can resolve. They argue for more locally appropriate technologies. Second, they are concerned about repeating the costly social and environmental errors of the Green Revolution in Asia where packages of improved seeds and inputs led to pesticide problems and increasing economic differentiation in rural areas.

The "tragedy of the commons" is another prominent paradigm that has been used to explain resource problems in Africa. According to this theory, commonly held natural resources will tend to be overexploited by individuals seeking to maximize personal gain. The solution advocated by economists is to privatize common resources, as it is believed that the private owner will more carefully husband environmental resources over the long term. The commons is actually a misnomer in the African context because many African communities effectively have managed commonly held natural resources through traditional mechanisms of control and enforcement. It is when these traditional mechanisms break down, and the commons become "open access resources" (or resources where there is no effective management authority) that problems develop. Deforestation in Africa has been characterized as an open access resource problem. Environmentalists argue that drastic measures are needed to protect the continent's dwindling forest resources from overuse by poor households. Critics suggest that the assertion of widespread deforestation is based on bad science and a historical misreading of environmental change in many instances.

Social Issues

Perhaps more than any other set of contested African issues, those pertaining to the social sphere tend to provoke deep-seated emotional responses. Different aspects of the AIDS crisis in Africa, female genital cutting, the position of women in African societies, and debt relief all have attracted considerable media attention and scrutiny in recent years.

Many of these issues get at a deeper debate between those who assert there are certain universal rights and wrongs, and cultural pluralists who believe we need to evaluate practices within their own cultural context. Advocates of the universality of norms disparage defenders of certain African practices as cultural relativists. Cultural relativism is cast as problematic because it may be used as an excuse to say that anything goes. In contrast, cultural pluralists assert that there are separate and valid cultural and moral systems, which may involve social mores that are not easily reconcilable with one another. Cultural pluralists are not necessarily cultural relativists as many would argue that everything does not go, for example, murder is wrong.

The challenge for cultural pluralists is to determine if a practice violates a universal norm when it is viewed in its proper cultural context (rather than in the cultural context of another). The result of this deep philosophical divide is that we often see Western feminists pitted against multiculturalists (two groups that frequently function as intellectual allies in the North American context) over some of the issues addressed in this section of the book. No issue better exemplifies this divide than the debate over female genital cutting.

If one does want to work for change, how should this be approached? In the case of empowering women, some argue that fundamental legal changes must be made whereas others suggest that the creation of economic opportunities is key.

Certain aspect of the HIV/AIDS policy debate in Africa also involve the question of human rights. Should all people be eligible for more expensive HIV/AIDS treatments because it is their basic human right, or do we need to consider the fact that some rationing may need to occur so that governments may adequately invest in more cost-effective prevention strategies? Foreign debt may also be considered a human rights issue because it, and related structural adjustment policies, reduce the state's ability to address discrimination, vulnerability, and inequality. Debt relief could help reduce poverty and promote health. Others argue that such relief may only promote irresponsibility and stop any attempts to address the factors that created the debt in the first place.

Politics, Governance, and Conflict Resolution

The terrain of politics, governance, and conflict resolution is simultaneously one of the most hopeful and distressing realms in contemporary African studies. Even though more contested elections have been held in the last 10 years than at any other time in the postcolonial period, the African continent also suffers from more instances of civil strife than other world regions. Key debates have focused on the success or nonsuccess of multiparty democracy in the African context, the role of foreign assistance in promoting democracy, reasons for corruption among African officials, and the role of African states in their own peacekeeping efforts.

An underlying theme related to several of these questions concerns the most appropriate form of governance in the African context. Proponents of multiparty democracy assert that this form of government will promote economic growth and minimize ethnic tensions. They also believe that a healthy civil society will serve as a check on corruption and other government excesses. Increasingly, foreign assistance for a variety of projects is conditional upon certain types of democratic reform.

Other scholars and African leaders see the imposition of democracy in Africa as a form of neo-imperialism. They suggest that the problem with multiparty democracy in many African countries is that it leads to the formation of too many political parties, each with a regional or ethnic outlook, and none representing the interests of the country as a whole. Furthermore, some Afro-centrists assert that the one-party state is more consistent with traditional consensus decision making that occurs at the village level. They maintain that the process of competitive elections is a foreign notion that is divisive in the African context. They also have also argued that democracy may actually inhibit economic growth. According to this argument, the problem with democracy is that it does not allow leaders to make tough economic decisions, such as the austerity measures required under structural adjustment.

Finally, what is the role of African peacekeeping forces on the continent? Some argue that international peacekeepers are critical for resolving some ethnic conflicts, whereas others suggest that Africans must play a central role in resolving their own conflicts.

Internet References . . .

H-Africa

H-Africa encourages discussion of Africa's history and culture. It offers a variety of listserves related to specific themes and regions of the continent. The site also allows one to search past discussions, link to other sites that deal with continent, and examine reviews of books on the region.

http://www.h-net.org/~africa/

African Studies Association

The African Studies Association is the largest African Studies organization in North America. It coordinates a meeting each year where scholarly presentation takes place, and publishes several Africa-related journals.

http://www.africanstudies.org/

Columbia University's African Studies Internet Resources

A catalog of links to African Studies programs, resources by region and country, electronic journals and newspapers, and resources by topic. It also has a directory of African Studies scholars.

http://www.columbia.edu/cu/lweb/indiv/africa/cuvl/

The University of Pennsylvania's African Studies Center, History Section

The history page of this website offers links to several other reputable sites dealing with African history and archival resources.

http://www.africa.upenn.edu/About_African/ww_hist.html

History

It is important for students of Africa to place the continent in its historical and global context. Sub-Saharan Africa has long-standing connections with other areas of the world. Debates rage over the nature of these connections, their persistence and impact on the future of Africa, why and how Africa was colonized, and how African ideas influenced development in other regions of the world.

- Did the Trans-Atlantic Slave Trade Underdevelop Africa?
- Have the Contributions of Africans Been Recognized for Developing New World Agriculture?
- Is European Subjugation of Africans Ultimately Explained by Differences in Land, Plant, and Animal Resources?
- Did Colonialism Distort Contemporary African Development?

ISSUE 1

Did the Trans-Atlantic Slave Trade Underdevelop Africa?

YES: Paul E. Lovejoy, from "The Impact of the Atlantic Slave Trade on Africa: A Review of the Literature," *Journal of African History* (1989)

NO: John Thornton, from *Africa and the Africans in the Making of the Atlantic World, 1400–1680* (Cambridge University Press, 1992)

ISSUE SUMMARY

YES: Paul E. Lovejoy, professor of history at York University, argues that the trans-Atlantic slave trade significantly transformed African society. It led to an absolute loss of population on the continent and a large increase in the enslaved population that was retained in Africa. The economic advantages of exporting slaves did not offset the social and political costs of participation, there were disastrous demographic impacts, and Africa's relative position in world trade declined.

NO: John Thornton is a professor of history at Boston University. He notes that slavery was widespread and indigenous in African society. Europeans simply worked with this existing market and African merchants, who were not dominated by Europeans, responded by providing more slaves. African leaders who allowed the slave trade to continue were neither forced to do so against their will, nor did they make irrational decisions. As such, the preexisting institution of slavery in Africa is as much responsible as any external force for the development of the trans-Atlantic slave trade.

The debate about the impact of the trans-Atlantic slave trade on Africa, and related discussions concerning the role that African elites played in this process dates back to at least the time period leading up to the abolition of the slave trade within the British Empire in 1807. During this time frame, some were arguing that the majority of Africans were already slaves in Africa, and consequently their situation would not be improved by ending the trans-Atlantic slave trade.

Apologists seeking to justify slavery in the American South also pointed to the existence of slavery in Africa and the role of African elites in the trans-Atlantic trade. Many academics (who would not have considered themselves apologists) writing in the 1950s and 1960s also made similar observations. Walter Rodney is probably the scholar most widely known for challenging these views about the nature of slavery in Africa prior to the arrival of Europeans. For an example of Rodney's writing in this vein, see his 1966 article in the *Journal of African History* entitled "African Slavery and Other Forms of Social Oppression on the Upper Guinea Coast in the Context of the Atlantic Slave Trade." In this article, Rodney essentially argued that the institution of slavery in Africa was really quite different from, and a more benign form of, what came to be practiced in the Americas. Furthermore, the trans-Atlantic slave trade left deep and lasting scars on societies in Africa.

Paul Lovejoy, professor of history at York University, is writing from a similar perspective as that described for Walter Rodney above. He argues that the trans-Atlantic slave trade significantly transformed African society. It led to an absolute loss of population on the continent and a large increase in the enslaved population that was retained in Africa. The economic advantages of exporting slaves did not offset the social and political costs of participation, there were disastrous demographic impacts, and Africa's relative position in world trade declined. Lovejoy, therefore, supports the "transformation thesis," which holds that the external slave trade dramatically reshaped slavery and society in Africa.

The contrarian view in this issue, presented by John Thornton, professor of history at Boston University, was written in the early 1990s when Walter Rodney and Paul Lovejoy's views, and related structuralist scholarship, were more dominant. He notes that slavery was widespread and indigenous in African society. Most importantly for the time period when he was writing, he argues that African elites had considerable agency (or power) in determining the shape and character of the trans-Atlantic slave trade. He asserts that Europeans worked with existing African slave markets and that African merchants, who were not dominated by Europeans, responded by providing more slaves. African leaders who allowed the slave trade to continue were neither forced to do so against their will, nor did they make irrational decisions. As such, the preexisting institution of slavery in Africa is as much responsible as any external force for the development of the trans-Atlantic slave trade. While Thornton's views are still hotly contested, he did successfully tap into a broader theme in post-structuralist literature on Africa, that is the notion that Africans were not helpless pawns in a world dominated by Europeans, but active and influential participants.

The debate about the impact of trans-Atlantic slavery on Africa, and the role of Africans in this process, was reignited by African American scholar Henry Louis Gates in his 1999 PBS series entitled *The Wonders of the African World*. In the second episode of this series he suggested that contemporary Africans bear a collective guilt for what he referred to as "the black-on-black Holocaust" that occurred during the era of the trans-Atlantic slave trade. The then president of the African Studies Association, Lansiné Kaba, responded to Gates in a November 2000 address that subsequently was published in the April 2001 issue of the *African Studies Review* as "The Atlantic Slave Trade Was Not a 'Black-on-Black Holocaust.'"

YES

Paul E. Lovejoy

The Impact of the Atlantic Slave Trade on Africa: A Review of the Literature

African History and the Atlantic Slave Trade

The significance of the Atlantic slave trade for African history has been the subject of considerable discussion among historians and merits attempts from time to time to review the literature. The present such attempt addresses several, but not all, the key issues that have emerged in recent years. These are, in order of discussion here: What was the volume of the Atlantic slave trade? More specifically, what were the demographic trends of the trade with respect to regional origins, ethnicity, gender and age? Finally, what was the impact of the slave trade on Africa? In brief, what is the state of the debate over the slave trade?

My own position in the debate is clear: the European slave trade across the Atlantic marked a radical break in the history of Africa, most especially because it was a major influence in transforming African society.

> The history of slavery involved the interaction between enslavement, the slave trade, and the domestic use of slaves within Africa. An examination of this interaction demonstrates the emergence of a system of slavery that was basic to the political economy of many parts of the continent. This system expanded until the last decades of the nineteenth century. The process of enslavement increased; the trade grew in response to new and larger markets, and the use of slaves in Africa became more common. Related to the articulation of this system, with its structural links to other parts of the world, was the consolidation within Africa of a political and social structure that relied extensively on slavery.

The transformation thesis identifies slavery as a central feature of African history over the past millennium. The Atlantic trade was only one, although a major, influence on the transformation of society. The Muslim slave trade was also important, and other internal African developments strongly influenced social change as well. According to this interpretation, the task of the historian is to weigh the relative importance of the various factors that incorporated

From *Journal of American History*, vol. 30, 1989, pp. 365–367, 386–393. Copyright © 1989 by Organization of American Historians. Reprinted by permission of Organization of American Historians via the Copyright Clearance Center.

Africa into an "international system of slavery" that included Africa, the Americas, western Europe and the Islamic world.

David Eltis has challenged this interpretation. On the basis of his study of the nineteenth-century Atlantic trade and an analysis of the value of the Atlantic trade between the 1680s and 1860s, Eltis has concluded that neither the scale nor the value of the Atlantic trade was sufficiently large to have had more than a marginal influence on the course of African history. According to Eltis,

> The slave trade for most regions and most periods was not a critically impor-tant influence over the course of African history. At the very least, those who would place the slave trade as central to West African and west-central African history should be able to point to stronger common threads, if not themes, across African regions than have so far come to light.

With respect to slavery, he claims that "whatever the origins or nature of structural changes in African slavery, it is unlikely that external influences could have been very great."

The contribution which Eltis makes is two-fold, it seems to me. First, he brings more precision to an analysis of the volume and direction of the Atlantic trade in the nineteenth century. His study of nutritional trends, age and gender, and mortality are particularly significant. Secondly, he has articulated a model of economic development for the pre-colonial era that must be taken seriously, although I disagree with his conclusions. Did exports determine the extent of economic change, as measured by standard economic indicators? He concludes that an export-led model of economic development has little to offer in inter-preting African history. Climate and human genius, according to Eltis, were far more important than the export sector.

Eltis bases his startling conclusions on an analysis of the relative importance of the Atlantic trade on Africa, as determined on a *per capita* basis. In a study undertaken jointly with Lawrence C. Jennings, it is claimed that the annual average *per capita* trade of those parts of Africa involved in the Atlantic slave trade was significantly less than in other parts of the Atlantic basin and that the African share in world trade declined in relative terms from the 1680s to the 1860s. They conclude that neither the absolute nor the relative value of Atlantic trade was very great; in general, foreign trade had only a weak influence on African economies. According to Eltis,

> . . . on the assumption that the improbably low figure of 15 million people lived in West Africa [in the 1780s] at subsistence levels, then imports from Atlantic trade may be taken at about 9 per cent of West African incomes in the 1780s. With assumptions that are more in accord with reality (i.e. a population of 25 million or more and domestic production in excess of subsistence), then imports decline in importance to well below 5 per cent. For other decades in the century when both slave prices and exports were lower, imports would have been much less significant. For west-central Africa, population densities were much lower but import/income ratios could not have been much greater.

Indeed, "The majority of Africans . . . would have been about as well off, and would have been performing the same tasks in the same socioeconomic environment, if there had been no trading contact" with Europe. Eltis even advances the astonishing conclusion for Asante that ". . . the ratio of the level of exports, either before or after 1807, to any plausible population estimates of Asante suggests that the slave trade can never have been important."

The rise of commodity exports in the nineteenth century had virtually no impact on Africa either. According to Eltis,

> . . . the slave and commodity trades together formed such a small percentage of total African economic activity that either could expand without there being any impact on the growth path of the other. . . . [I]n the mid-nineteenth century neither the slave nor the commodity traders were large enough to have to face the problem of inelastic supplies of the factors of production.

In short, neither the Atlantic slave trade nor its suppression had much influence on African history.

The following review of the recent literature on the Atlantic slave trade provides a context in which to assess the revisionist interpretation of Eltis (and Jennings). I begin with the new studies on the volume of the slave trade, in which a consensus seems to have emerged. I then consider the analytical refinements in the regional and ethnic origins of the exported slave population. The demographic data allow a closer examination of the gender and age profile of the trade, which is the subject of the next section of this article. Finally, I return to an assessment of the arguments of Eltis, particularly with regard to the demographic impact of the trade on Africa. A number of important themes are not considered, including the economic significance of slavery in Africa and the importance of imported commodities on African society and economy. Nonetheless, I believe that I can demonstrate that Eltis' provocative conclusions are seriously flawed. . . .

Impact of the Atlantic Slave Trade on Africa

The discussion of the volume of the trade, the regional and ethnic origins of the exported population, and the sex and age profiles of slaves should indicate that much of Eltis' revisionist interpretation cannot be accepted. Otherwise, these factors would not matter to African history, although they are crucial to the history of slavery in the Americas. While the slight modifications in the volume and direction of the Atlantic slave trade do not affect the argument of Eltis (and Jennings), the issues remain: did the slave trade have a dramatic impact on exporting regions? Did the suppression of the Atlantic trade in the nineteenth century have a significant effect on the course of slavery? My informed opinion is that both the trade and it suppression were major factors in African history, and to show this I will examine, in order, the following issues: (1) the economic impact of the trade; (2) its demographic implications; and (3) the incidence of slavery in Africa. There are certainly other issues, but these will have to suffice.

One of the principal conclusions of Eltis and Jennings seems likely but only modifies my analysis: Africa's share of world trade from the late seventeenth until the mid-nineteenth century was relatively small in comparison with other parts of the Atlantic world, and Africa's share of that trade declined in relative terms during the period of the slave trade. Eltis and Jennings use an estimate of £0.8–£1.1 for *per capita* incomes in western Africa for the 1780s. They calculate that the export trade amounted to £0.1 per person each year. The proportion of exports to total income certainly appears to be very low by comparison with other parts of the Atlantic basin, although the room for error in measuring *per capita* income and the value of the export trade are enormous.

This observation on the value of the export trade can be accepted, but the implications that Eltis and Jennings draw from it cannot. The ratio of the value of the external trade to *per capita* income is not an accurate indicator of the impact of the slave trade on Africa. *Per capita* income in western Africa was certainly very low by the standards of other parts of the Atlantic basin. Africa was very poor. Almost any incremental increase over subsistence would have had a disproportionate impact on the economy. Eltis and Jennings quantify the relative poverty of Africa, but they are wrong to conclude that the lack of prosperity was an accurate gauge of the degree of isolation from the impact of the slave trade.

The simulation model developed by Patrick Manning provides one way to establish that the slave trade had a significant, indeed devastating, impact on Africa. Manning's model is a statistical means of measuring demographic change under conditions of enslavement, slave trade and slave exports. His analysis is based on the demography of the Atlantic slave trade and certain broad assumptions about demographic change that establish the parameters of the historical possibilities. Manning estimates that the population of those areas of West and west-central Africa that provided slaves for export was in the order of 22–25 million in the early eighteenth century. He projects a growth rate for that population during the eighteenth and early nineteenth centuries of 0–5 per cent, which he considers the maximum possibility. His simulation "model suggests that no growth rate of less than one per cent could have counterbalanced the loss of slaves in the late eighteenth-century." He uses a counterfactual argument to make the same point: "With a growth rate of 0.5%, the 1700 populations . . . [of] 22 to 25 million would have led to 1850 populations of from 46 million to 53 million, more than double the actual 1850 population." Manning concludes that "the simulation of demographic impact of the Atlantic slave trade provides support for the hypothesis of African population decline through the agency of the slave trade."

Furthermore, the simulation model suggests that the incidence of slavery increased in Africa. According to Manning, "As an accompaniment to the estimated nine million slaves landed in the New World [between 1700 and 1850] . . ., some twenty-one million persons were captured in Africa, seven million of whom were brought into domestic slavery, and five million of whom suffered death within a year of capture." As the discussion of the sex profile of the export trade makes clear, more women were retained in Africa than men. Not only did the slave population increase, therefore, but the incidence of polygyny increased as well. Indeed, the two phenomena were closely related.

By 1770 the Atlantic trade resulted in a slave population in the Americas of approximately 2,340,000. Manning's simulation suggests that the slave population in West and west-central Africa could not have been much different. It is safe to say that the slave population was at least 10 per cent of the total population of 22–25 million and that the proportion of slaves was rising. Manning concludes that there were 3 million slaves in those parts of Africa that serviced the Atlantic trade at the turn of the nineteenth century, virtually the same number as in the Americas.

The dramatic growth in the African slave population is the transformation that I highlighted initially in 1979 and more fully in 1983. The transformation was the result of a dialectical relationship between slavery in the Americas and the enslavement, trade and use of slaves in Africa. The production of slaves for the Americas also produced slaves for Africa. It is difficult to prove that the Atlantic slave trade *caused* the transformation of slavery in Africa, but it is likely. The simulation model, as well as the thesis that I advanced in *Transformations in Slavery,* consider that enslavement, trade and the use of slaves were interrelated, across the Atlantic and across the Sahara. African, European, and Muslim merchants wanted slaves, and African, European and Muslim slave-owners used slaves. The low value of exports and imports apparently confused Eltis and Jennings so that they did not perceive the importance of this interrelationship, but an examination of any part of Africa that was a supplier of the export trade reveals the dialectic.

Miller's study of Angola provides the most dramatic example of impact of the slave trade on a region in Africa. As the export data make clear, approximately 40 per cent of all slaves in the Americas came from west-central Africa, and Miller estimates that deaths in Africa related to capture and enslavement roughly equalled the number of slaves exported, that is 50,000–60,000 per year in the last half of the eighteenth century. In addition, "fully as many more people [were] seized as slaves but left to reside in other parts of western central Africa." Total population displacement would have been in the order of 100,000–120,000 per year. Admittedly, Miller paints this as a worst-possible scenario, but even if demographic change was less severe it must have been dramatic. No one has argued as much, but it may be that matrilineality and the export trade were interrelated. They certainly reinforced each other.

Miller's analysis confirms the gender and age structure of the trade. In pursuing a discovery made earlier by John Thornton, Miller shows that the sex ratio of the population in those areas most heavily involved in the export trade was strongly skewed towards women and girls. Polygyny was a central institution of wealth and political power, and slaves (females) were most heavily concentrated around the principal courts of the region. Miller refers to the centralization that was associated with the slave trade as the "great transformation," which is solace to the theorist. On the basis of Miller's analysis, it is impossible to conclude that the slave trade had a marginal impact on west-central Africa.

Eltis is on shaky ground in suggesting that the suppression of the slave trade was not a decisive event for Africa. According to his interpretation, the increased incidence of slavery in the nineteenth century was unconnected with the collapse of the Atlantic trade. Instead, increased demand for slaves arose from "rejuvenated Islam" and late in the century from European demand for primary products from Africa. Indeed there was a dramatic increase in slavery as a result of the *jihads* and Muslim commercial expansion in East Africa. Although Eltis does not explicitly argue the point, his proposed revision is one of timing and concentration, not of substance, and he presents no new data. I remain unconvinced. Certainly there was an expansion in production, based on slave labour, late in the nineteenth century, but that development is also part of the transformation thesis.

Eltis disputes the thesis that the slaving frontier continued to move inland during the early nineteenth century and that the number of slaves in Africa increased dramatically in these decades. He bases this conclusion on an analysis of slave prices:

> . . . because the price of all slaves declined, it seems clear that although domestic [African] demand increased, it did not increase sufficiently to offset the decline in trans-Atlantic demand. As a consequence, the number of slaves traded as well as the price of those slaves declined during the century . . .; accordingly, suppression must have meant some reduction in the enslavement of Africans.

Eltis is correct that the price of slaves dropped between the 1790s and the 1820s and continued at a depressed level for most of the continent for the rest of the century. Slaves were cheap, and in real terms prices may have continued to fall in many of the major slave markets, but this does not mean that enslavement decreased in intensity. The cheapness of slaves reflects two factors, the generally low prices of basic commodities in Africa and the glut of the slave market.

Before the suppression of the trans-Atlantic trade, according to Eltis, the demand for slaves was divided into two sectors: one within Africa and the second in the Americas. (In fact, there was a third sector—the external Muslim market.) The collapse of American demand inevitably depressed prices in Africa, He concludes that the African market did not increase sufficiently to offset the loss of American sales; according to Eltis demand and supply declined, although he only provides slave prices as evidence. Prices did not rebound after the decline of the 1790–1820 period, it is true, but the reason was a combination of factors. Indeed Eltis shows that American demand did not decline, in the aggregate, in this period but regained its former heights. Decline only began in the 1850s, well after the period that is crucial to his argument.

Demand is an expression of price, so if prices were generally low, then demand might appear to have been depressed. In fact, the contrary could have been true, if more were known about the price structure of African economies. African demand for slaves was determined by the value of what slaves could produce, and this marginal revenue product was primarily a function of the value of food consumption, housing costs, social requirements, taxation and similar expenditures that were not much affected by international markets. Any qualitative assessment of the eighteenth and nineteenth centuries would judge Africa to have been comparatively poor, as the ratio of exports to *per capita* income reveals. Prices in general were low, and the price structure would have influenced the cost of slaves accordingly.

Eltis and Jennings, in concentrating on export-led economic development, have raised an important consideration: more needs to be known about internal African price structures. Until such information is available, however, it is hard to justify their conclusions, and there is sufficient evidence available to argue the contrary.

Eltis' conclusion that enslavement declined in the early nineteenth century contradicts the research of most Africanist historians who have written on the period. In almost every part of Africa for most of the century, enslavement was rampant. Slaves were generated on a scale previously unknown, as can be attested by the following examples: the wars of the *mfecane* in southern and central Africa, the activities of Arabs, Swahili, Yao, Nyamwezi, Chikunda and others in eastern and south-eastern Africa, and the raiding of Muslim slavers in the southern Sudan and north-central Africa. None of these cases have much, if anything, to do with the suppression of the Atlantic slave trade, and hence could be dismissed by those who favour the Eltis thesis. But what about the phenomenal levels of enslavement during the *jihads,* often in areas that once did or could have fed the Atlantic trade? How are the collapse of the Lunda states and the havoc of enslavement instigated by the Cokwe to be explained? Can the insecurity of Igbo country in the nineteenth century and the enslavement resulting during the Yoruba wars be easily dismissed? The combined impact of these phenomena was to maintain a glutted market and hence a depressed price for slaves almost everywhere. The "transformation thesis" holds that the external slave trade, particularly the trans-Atlantic sector but also the Islamic market, shaped slavery and society in Africa, and that internal factors intensified slavery as the external trade contracted.

The enslavement of people and the growth of the slave population in Africa continued apace for the whole of the nineteenth century, despite local variations. As yet there are few estimates of the scale of the African slave population, but some insights can be gained by a comparison of certain parts of West Africa in *c.* 1900 with the Americas on the eve of emancipation there.

The slave population of the Americas rose from 2,340,000 in *c.* 1770 and peaked at 2,968,000 by the end of the century. The revolt of St Domingue reduced this total considerably; St Domingue had a slave population of 480,000 in 1791. The independence of mainland Spanish America after *c.* 1820, with its slave population of a couple hundred thousand, and the emancipation of 674,000 British slaves in 1834 reduced the total further, but the number of slaves continued to expand in the Spanish Caribbean, the U.S.A. and Brazil, reaching a peak just before the emancipation of U.S.A. slaves in the early 1860s. In 1860, there were almost 4 million slaves in the U.S.A. and another

1.5–1.8 million slaves in Brazil and the Spanish Caribbean, for an estimated total of 5.5–5.8 million slaves. With the freeing of slaves in the U.S.A., the slave population declined considerably to a level well below two million. Puerto Rico had 47,000 slaves in 1867; Cuba 288,000 slaves in 1871, and Brazil 1,511,000 slaves in 1872. With the final emancipation of slaves in Cuba in 1880 and Brazil in 1888, slavery came to an end in the Americas.

We may compare the American figures with those of the Western Sudan that have been assembled by Martin Klein. Various estimates between 1905 and 1913 put the slave population of Haut-Sénégal-Niger at about 702,000, or 18 per cent of the total population of 3,942,000. The slave population of French Guinea was 490,000, or 34.6 per cent of the total population (1,418,000). For the French Sudan as a whole, there were approximately 1,192,000 slaves in a total population of 5,134,000, but these estimates were made *after* the slave exodus that occurred during and immediately after the French conquest. That exodus reached a climax in 1905–06, by which time hundreds of thousands of slaves had fled. Before the exodus, the slave population was probably in the order of 1.5–2 million.

The extent of slavery in the Sokoto Caliphate was comparable. J. S. Hogendorn and I have calculated that the number of slaves in the Caliphate probably represented one-quarter of the total population of 10 million in 1900. Both the percentage of slaves and the scale of the population are intended as conservative estimates. While there is a slight overlap between Klein's figures and our own, these are not significant. Eight of the thirty emirates in the Caliphate came under French rule, but only two are included in Klein's sample, and they were both small emirates. Whether Hogendorn's and my figures are accepted or not, there can be little doubt that the Sokoto Caliphate may well have been the second or third largest slave society in modern history. Only the United States in 1860 (and maybe Brazil as well) had more slaves than the Caliphate did in 1900.

About a decade after the final emancipation of slaves in the Americas, there were at least twice as many slaves in Islamic West Africa as there had been in Brazil and Cuba in 1870 and at least as many as in the U.S.A. at the start of its Civil War. These comparisons are striking evidence that slavery in Africa has to be taken seriously by historians of both Africa and the Americas. As should be obvious, no attempt is made here to estimate the slave populations of other parts of Africa, particularly areas that fed the Atlantic slave trade, but it is known that the percentage of slaves in Asante, the Yoruba states, the Igbo country and elsewhere was high.

Conclusion

The economic costs of the slave trade in African economies and societies were severe, despite Eltis' interpretation to the contrary. First, the low *per capita* income from the trade indicates that the economic advantages of exporting slaves were nowhere near large enough to offset the social and political costs of participation. Secondly, the size of the trade, including enslavement, related deaths, social dislocation and exports, was sufficient to have had a disastrous demographic impact. Thirdly, because the rise of produce exports started at such a low base and at a time when slave exports were becoming less important, western Africa suffered a relative decline in its position in world trade.

There were other heavy costs which Eltis has failed to appreciate. It is possible to calculate the gross barter terms of trade and *per capita* income from the slave trade and compare western Africa with other parts of the world. But it is difficult to assess the full costs of "producing" slaves because of the nature of enslavement. In an economic sense, as Robert Paul Thomas and Richard Bean have demonstrated, slaves were a "free good," like fish, as far as those doing the enslaving were concerned. There were costs associated with "production," but the real cost in human terms included the loss of life from enslavement, subsequent famines and disease. Furthermore, the destruction of property during wars and raids also represented a loss. Manning's simulation model has attempted to account for some of these costs, although it will never be possible to do the kind of analysis that is possible in measuring the volume and direction of the trans-Atlantic trade itself. Miller has come closest to demonstrating the effects of this impact on a particular region, but his analysis, too, is based on a considerable degree of conjecture.

When the indirect costs of enslavement and trading are taken into consideration, the insights of Eltis and Jennings take on a new meaning. Rather than demonstrating that the Atlantic slave trade had virtually no impact on western Africa, it can be concluded that the impact was in fact strongly negative, although profound.

John Thornton

 NO

Slavery and African Social Structure

If Africans were experienced traders and were not somehow dominated by European merchants due to European market control or some superiority in manufacturing or trading techniques, then we can say confidently that Africa's commercial relationship with Europe was not unlike international trade anywhere in the world of the period. But historians have balked at this conclusion because they believe that the slave trade, which was an important branch of Afro-European commerce from the beginning, should not be viewed as a simple commodity exchange. After all, slaves are also a source of labor, and at least to some extent, removal from Africa represented a major loss to Africa. The sale of slaves must therefore have been harmful to Africa, and African decisions to sell must have been forced or involuntary for one or more reasons.

The idea of the slave trade as a harmful commerce is especially supported by the work of historical demographers. Most who have studied the question of the demographic consequences of the trade have reached broad agreement that the trade was demographically damaging from fairly early period, especially when examined from a local or regional (as opposed to a continental) perspective. In addition to the net demographic drain, which began early in some areas (like Angola), the loss of adult males had potentially damaging impacts on sex ratios, dependency rates, and perhaps the sexual division of labor.

In addition to these demographic effects, historians interested in social and political history have followed Walter Rodney in arguing that the slave trade caused social disruption (such as increasing warfare and related military damage), adversely altered judicial systems, or increased inequality. Moreover, Rodney argued that the slave trade increased the numbers of slaves being held in Africa and intensified their exploitation, a position that Paul Lovejoy, its most recent advocate, calls the "transformation thesis." Because of this perception of a widespread negative impact, many scholars have argued that the slave trade, if not other forms of commerce, must have been forced on unwilling African participants, perhaps through the type of commercial inequities that we have already discussed or perhaps through some sort of military pressure (to be discussed in a subsequent chapter).

When Rodney presented his conclusions on the negative impact and hence special status of the slave trade as a branch of trade, it was quickly contested by J. D. Fage, and more recently, the transformation thesis has been attacked by David Eltis. As these scholars see it, slavery was widespread and indigenous in African society, as was, naturally enough, a commerce in slaves. Europeans simply tapped this existing market, and Africans responded to the increased demand over the centuries by providing more slaves. The demographic impact, although important, was local and difficult to disentangle from losses due to internal wars and slave trading on the domestic African market. In any case, the decision makers who allowed the trade to continue, whether merchants or political leaders, did not personally suffer the larger-scale losses and were able to maintain their operations. Consequently, one need not accept that they were forced into participation against their will or made decisions irrationally.

The evidence for the period before 1680 generally supports this second position. Slavery was widespread in Africa, and its growth and development were largely independent of the Atlantic trade, except that insofar as the Atlantic commerce stimulated internal commerce and development it also led to more widespread holding of slaves. The Atlantic slave trade was the outgrowth of this internal slavery. Its demographic impact, however, even in the early stages was significant, but the people adversely affected by this impact were not the ones making the decisions about participation.

In order to understand this position it is critical to correctly comprehend the place of the institution of slavery in Africa and furthermore to understand why the structure of African societies gave slavery a different meaning than it had in Europe or the colonial Americas. The same analysis explains the reasons for slavery's extension (if indeed it was extended) during the period of the Atlantic trade and its correlation with commercial and economic growth.

Thus, as we will see in this chapter and the next, the slave trade (and the Atlantic trade in general) should not be seen as an "impact" brought in from outside and functioning as some sort of autonomous factor in African history. Instead, it grew out of and was rationalized by the African societies who participated in it and had complete control over it until the slaves were loaded onto European ships for transfer to Atlantic societies.

The reason that slavery was widespread in Africa was not, as some have asserted, because Africa was an economically underdeveloped region in which forced labor had not yet been replaced by free labor. Instead, slavery was rooted in deep-seated legal and institutional structures of African societies, and it functioned quite differently from the way it functioned in European societies.

Slavery was widespread in Atlantic Africa because slaves were the only form of private, revenue-producing property recognized in African law. By contrast, in European legal systems, land was the primary form of private, revenue-producing property, and slavery was relatively minor. Indeed, ownership of land was usually a precondition in Europe to making productive use of slaves, at least in agriculture. Because of this legal feature, slavery was in many ways the functional equivalent of the landlord–tenant relationship in Europe and was perhaps as widespread.

Thus, it was the absence of landed private property—or, to be more precise, it was the corporate ownership of land—that made slavery so pervasive an aspect of African society. Anthropologists have noted this feature among modern Africans, or those living in the so-called ethnographic present or traditional societies. Anthropologists have regarded the absence of private or personal ownership of landed property as unusual, because it departs from the European pattern and from the home cultural experience of most anthropological observers, and has therefore seemed to require an explanation. . . .

At first glance, this corporatist social structure seems to allow no one to acquire sources of income beyond what they could produce by their own labor or trade if they were not granted a revenue assignment by the state. Modern commentators on Africa have occasionally noted this, and precolonial African societies have sometimes been characterized as unprogressive because the over-developed role of the state inhibited private initiative by limiting secure wealth. In particular, these commentators believed that the absence of any form of private wealth other than through the state greatly inhibited the growth of capitalism and, ultimately, progress in Africa.

It is precisely here, however, that slavery is so important in Africa, and why it played such a large role there. If Africans did not have private ownership of one factor of production (land), they could still own another, labor (the third factor, capital, was relatively unimportant before the Industrial Revolution). Private ownership of labor therefore provided the African entrepreneur with secure and reproducing wealth. This ownership or control over labor might be developed through the lineage, where junior members were subordinate to the senior members, though this is less visible in older documentation.

Another important institution of dependency was marriage, where wives were generally subordinate to their husbands. Sometimes women might be used on a large scale as a labor force. For example, in Warri, Bonaventura da Firenze noted in 1656 that the ruler had a substantial harem of wives who produced cloth for sale. Similarly, the king of Whydah's wives, reputed to number over a thousand, were employed constantly in making a special cloth that was exported. Such examples give weight to the often-repeated assertion that African wealth was measured in wives, in the sense both that polygamy was indicative of prestige and that such wives were often labor forces.

Of course, the concept of ownership of labor also constituted slavery, and slavery was possibly the most important avenue for private, reproducing wealth available to Africans. Therefore, it is hardly surprising that it should be so widespread and, moreover, be a good indicator of the most dynamic segments of African society, where private initiate was operating most freely.

The significance of African slavery can be understood by comparing it briefly with slavery in Europe. Both societies possessed the institution, and both tended to define slaves in the same way—as subordinate family members, in some ways equivalent to permanent children. This is precisely how slaves are dealt with in *Siete partidas,* following a precedent that goes all the way back to Aristotle, if not before. Modern research clearly reveals that this is also how Africans defined slavery in the late precolonial and early colonial period.

Seventeenth-century African data do not deal with the legal technicalities, though we have little reason to believe that they differed from those uncovered by modern anthropological research. For Kongo, where the remarkable documentation allows glimpses of the underlying ideology, the term for a slave, *nleke*, was the same as for a child, suggesting the family idiom prevailed there.

Where the differences can be found is not in the legal technicalities but in the way slaves were used. In theory, there have been no differences in this respect either, but in practice, African slaves served in a much wider variety of ways than did European or Euro-American slaves. In Europe, if people acquired some wealth that they wished to invest in secure, reproducing form, they were likely to buy land. Of course, land did not produce wealth by itself, but usually the land was let out to tenants in exchange for rents or was worked under the owner's supervision by hired workers. In neither case would such people have to have recourse to slaves to acquire a work force.

From what we know of slave labor in Europe in this period, it would appear that they were employed in work for which no hired worker or tenant could be found or at least was willing to undertake the work under the conditions that the landowner wished. As we shall see, this lay behind most of the employment of slaves in the New World as well. Consequently, slaves typically had difficult, demanding, and degrading work, and they were often mistreated by exploitative masters who were anxious to maximize profits. Even in the case of slaves with apparently good jobs, such as domestic servants, often the institution allowed highly talented or unusual persons to be retained at a lower cost than free people of similar qualifications.

This was not necessarily the case in Africa, however. People wishing to invest wealth in reproducing form could not buy land, for there was no landed property. Hence, their only recourse was to purchase slaves, which as their personal property could be inherited and could generate wealth for them. They would have no trouble in obtaining land to put these slaves into agricultural production, for African law made land available to whoever would cultivate it, free or slave, as long as no previous cultivator was actively using it.

Consequently, African slaves were often treated no differently from peasant cultivators, as indeed they were the functional equivalent of free tenants and hired workers in Europe. This situation, the result of the institutional differences between Europe and Africa, has given rise to the idea that African slaves were well treated, or at least better treated than European slaves. Giacinto Brugiotti da Vetralla described slaves in central Africa as "slaves in name only" by virtue of their relative freedom and the wide variety of employments to which they were put. Likewise, as we shall see, slaves were often employed as administrators, soldiers, and even royal advisors, thus enjoying great freedom of movement and elite lifestyles.

This did not mean, of course, that slaves never received the same sort of difficult, dangerous, or degrading work that slaves in Europe might have done, although in Africa often such work might just as easily have been done by free people doing labor service for the state. In any case, Valentim Fernandes's description of slave labor in Senegambia around 1500, one of the few explicit texts on the nature of slave labor, shows that slaves working in agricultural production worked one day a week for their own account and the rest for their master, a work regime that was identical for slaves serving in Portuguese sugar mills on the island colony of São Tomé in the same period. Slaves employed in mining in Africa may have suffered under conditions similar to those of slaves in European mining operations, though the evidence is less certain.

On the whole, however, African slavery need not have been degrading or the labor performed by slaves done under any more coercion (or involving any more resistance) than that of free laborers or tenants in Europe. Therefore, the idea that African dependence on slave labor led to the development of a reluctant work force or inhibited innovation is probably overdone.

For Europe and the European colonies in America, the distinction between the productivity of slave and free labor may have validity (though even there it is a matter of intense debate); in Africa the distinction is probably less applicable. The exact nature of the labor regime, rather than the legal status of the workers, is more relevant to a description of African economic history, and in this instance, different legal structures led Africans and Europeans to develop the institution of slavery in substantially different ways. Consequently, the conventional wisdom concerning slavery developed from the study of European or colonial American societies with landed private property simply cannot apply in Africa.

African slaves were typically used in two different ways. First of all, slaves became the preeminent form of private investment and the manifestation of private wealth—a secure form of reproducing wealth equivalent to landowning in Europe. Second, slaves were used by state officials as a dependent and loyal group, both for the production of revenue and for performing administrative and military service in the struggle between kinds or executives who wished to centralize their states and other elite parties who sought to control royal absolutism.

The private employment of slaves as heritable, wealth-producing dependents was perhaps the most striking African use. Dapper, in describing private wealth in Kongo, noted that although the households of the nobility were not wealthy in ready cash, nor did they possess much in the way of luxury goods, they were wealthy in slaves. This, he believed, was the main form of wealth in central Africa.

Likewise, slaves represented the way to achieve wealth for ambitious commoners in the Gold Coast states, and the state did attempt to regulate their acquisition. According to de Marees, a commoner who had become wealthy through trade might be able to attain noble status by sponsoring an expensive ceremony in which nobility was conferred upon him. Although the ceremony was ruinously expensive, the noble-to-be was willing to undertake it because it allowed him to acquire slaves, which, as Dapper noted a few years later, would make it possible for him to recover the expenses of the ceremony, for "as soon as he gets some goods he bestows them on slaves, for that is what their wealth consists of."

Recently, several historians have followed the careers of some prominent Gold Coast merchants who rose from relative obscurity to become great economic and political actors on the coast, using documentation from the records of the Dutch, English, and Danish commercial houses. In all these accounts, the acquisition of slaves to carry goods, cultivate lands, protect the household, and assist in trading figures prominently as an essential step.

Indeed, the careers can in some ways be seen as parallel to that of the European commoners who invested first in land and then in titles of nobility, though in Africa, of course, the investment was in slaves and then in nobility.

Slaves as reproducing wealth figured prominently among the Julas and other Moslem commercial groups of the western Sudan and Senegambia. Richard Jobson, the English gold trader who spent considerable time traveling up the Gambia deep into the Sudan in the 1620s, noted that the Julas ("Juliettos") had constructed a chain of villages worked by their slaves, who provided them with provisions and served as carriers on their commercial expeditions. The heads of these villages acquired special rights (in some ways equivalent to those of nobility) from the rulers of the state in which they settled. Philip Curtin's detailed study of the Julas and other Moslem commercial groups in the late seventeenth and early eighteenth centuries emphasizes their extent and organization. Yves Person, focusing on a later period, compared them to the French bourgeoisie rising from common to noble status or seizing power if thwarted: hence he compared a series of "Dyula Revolutions" from the late eighteenth century onward to the French Revolution.

Thus, in Africa the development of commerce and the social mobility based on commerce was intimately linked to the growth of slavery, for slaves in villages performing agricultural work or carrying goods in caravans or working in mines under private supervision were essential to private commercial development.

This last point is significant to consider in transformation thesis. Both Rodney and Lovejoy, advocates of the idea that the development of the Atlantic slave trade extended slavery and resulted in larger numbers of people being enslaved and being worse treated, see this as a direct external input, foreign to African political economy. Yet, the development and extension of slavery, if it did take place (and this point is never proved by either author), might just as well be seen as the result of economic growth in Africa, perhaps stimulated by commercial opportunities from overseas, perhaps by a growing domestic economy. Even the increased incidence of maltreatment (another point that is completely without proof) may indicate only more aggressive use of the labor force by entrepreneurs, just as the European work force faced increased exploitation during the early stages of the Industrial Revolution.

The use of slaves by private people to increase and maintain their wealth was just one of the ways in which slaves were utilized in African societies. Another one, almost of equal importance, was their use by the political elite to increase their power. Slaves employed by the political elite might be used as a form of wealth-generating property, just as they were in private hands, or they might be used to create dependent administrations or armies. In this latter capacity, Africa created many wealthy and powerful slaves.

Most large African states were collections of smaller ones that had been joined through alliance and conquest, and typically the rulers of these smaller constituent states continued to exercise local authority, and the ruler of the large state found his power checked by them. Developing private resources that would answer only to themselves was an important way in which African rulers could overcome such checks and create hierarchical authority centered on their own thrones. Slaves, who could be the private property of a king or his family or might also be the property of the state, were an ideal form of loyal workers, soldiers, and retainers.

The powerful Sudanese empires relied heavily on slave armies and slave administrators to keep a fractious and locally ascendant nobility in check. These nobles were often descendants of the rulers of the constituent smaller states; this was probably the status of the territorial rulers of Mali in al-'Umaris's fourteenth-century description. These constituent states were called *civitas* by Antonio Malafante, Genonese traveler who left a description of the empire of Songhay and its neighbors in 1477, a term that implies both subordination and self-government in Latin. An anonymous description of the "Empire of Great Fulo" written about 1600 states that it dominated the whole Senegal valley and was composed of some twenty smaller units. In accounts of the western provinces of Mali during the late fifteenth and early sixteenth centuries, Portuguese travelers describe local "kings" (heads of constituent states) as virtually sovereign in their local rights and government, yet simultaneously describe Mali as a powerful overlord. These descriptions and later ones of Mali and Kaabu, a state that based its authority on being a province of Mali, all reveal apparent local sovereignty coexisting with the apparently strong rights of the overlord, who at least extracted tribute and obedience and might even intervene in local affairs.

One can observe the same with regard to a somewhat shadowy kingdom of "Kquoja" that dominated Sierra Leone from a capital near Cape Mount in the late sixteenth and early seventeenth centuries. Although Alvares de Almada noted that the Kquoja kings collected regular tribute and taxes from local rulers, historians have generally not seen it as a unitary state.

In some cases, perhaps including both Kaabu and sixteenth-century Mali, the strength of local states did cut in on revenue and authority exercised by their overlords, but slaves often offered a way around this Alvise da Mosto's description of Jolof in the mid-fifteenth century provides a good example. Here, according to da Mosto, the king was beholden to three or four other powerful nobles, each of whom controlled a region (clearly the constituent states), gave him revenue when they chose, and moreover exercised the right to elect him. But the king was able to obtain revenue of his own by distributing slaves in villages to each of his several wives; this income belonged to him. Not only did this give him independent support, but it allowed him to develop a large retinue of dependents who carried out his administrative tasks, numbering some 200 people in all. Unfortunately, the fact that at least one of his subordinates, "Budomel" (title of the ruler of Kajorr [Kayor]), was doing the same thing at the local level may well have ultimately limited his capacity to develop more central power.

Sixteenth- and seventeenth-century evidence from the *Tarikh al-Fettash*, a locally composed source on Songhay, shows quite clearly how the development of an army and administration of slaves helped that empire to become centralized. Tymowski has analyzed this text and showed that rice plantations worked by slaves, as well as villages of slaves settled throughout the country, supported an army of slaves and a bureaucracy of slaves through which the emperors conducted their business, neglecting whatever obligations they may have had to the local nobles.

Slavery probably also aided centralizing monarchs in central Africa as well as West Africa. Kongo seems to have originally been a federation of states, at least as sixteenth- and seventeenth-century tradition and law described it. The original kings of the federation owed their election to the votes of several electors, who were the heads of the member states. But collecting slaves into a central place gave the Kongo kings great power—the capital city of Mbanza Kongo and its surrounding area formed a great agricultural center already in 1491, and probably had ten times the population density of rural areas a century later. The slaves, many of whom occupied estates around the capital, provided Kongo with both the wealth and the demographic resources to centralize. As early as 1526, documents from Kongo show that the provinces (constituent states) were in the hands of royally appointed people (mostly kinsmen), and by the mid-seventeenth century local power and election were regarded more as a curse than a blessing.

Slavery played a role in the centralization of nearby Ndongo as well. Like Kongo, Ndongo rulers may have benefited from the concentration of slaves in their capital—for Kabasa, Ndongo's capital, was also described as a large town in a densely populated area. In addition, the ruler had villages of slaves who paid revenue to him scattered around in his domain. These villages were called *kijiko* (which actually means "slave" in Kimbundu), which a document of 1612 rendered as "populated places whose residents are slaves of the said king." Perhaps more significant in Ndongo, however, was the use that the kings made of slaves as administrators, for the ruler had officials, the *tendala* and the *ngolambole* (judicial and military officials, respectively), who supervised subordinates and collected tax and tribute from his slaves.

We have already seen that African rulers were sometimes limited in the amount of absolute power they could exercise. Some societies had rules of election that allowed officials to choose a weak ruler. In some of the smaller states, the use of slaves may have helped rulers develop more autocratic systems of government. In dealing with the states of the eastern Gold Coast, for example, Dapper noted that they were all quite strongly centralized and, moreover, had an abundance of slaves. Similarly, Alvaro Velho noted that among the smaller states of Sierra Leone, the income that rulers obtained from their slaves was their only steady source of income.

Thus slaves could be found in all parts of Atlantic Africa, performing all sorts of duties. When Europeans came to Africa and offered to buy slaves, it is hardly surprising that they were almost immediately accepted. Not only were slaves found widely in Africa, but the area had a well-developed slave trade, as evidenced by the numbers of slaves in private hands. Anyone who had the wherewithal could obtain slaves from the domestic market, though sometimes it required royal or state permission, as in the Gold Coast. Europeans could tap this market just as any African could.

Moreover, the most likely owners of slaves—wealthy merchants and state officials or rulers—were exactly the people with whom European traders came into contact. Because merchants selling gold, ivory products, mats, copper bracelets, pepper, or any other trade commodity in Africa would also be interested in the buying and selling of slaves, European merchants could readily find sources. This was not so much because Africans were inveterate slave dealers, as it was because the legal basis for wealth in Africa lay in the idea of transferring ownership of people. This legal structure made slavery and slave marketing widespread and created secondary legal mechanisms for securing and regulating the sale of slaves, which Europeans could use as well as Africans.

The significance of African slavery in the development of the slave trade can be clearly seen in the remarkable speed with which the continent began exporting slaves. As soon as the Portuguese had reached the Senegal region and abandoned their early strategy of raiding for commerce 700–1,000 slaves were exported per year, first with caravans bound for the Sahara (after 1448). After Diogo Gomes's diplomatic mission to the West African rulers in 1456, which opened markets north of the Gambia, exports took a dramatic turn upward, reaching as many as 1,200–2,500 slaves per year by the end of the century.

Thus, from 1450 onward, even before their ships actually reached the Senegal River, Portuguese merchants were buying slaves from northward-bound caravans from the post at Arguim, tapping a long-standing trans-Sahara trade. It is not surprising that Avelino Teixeira da Mota has been able to document the diversion of the Saharan slave trade from North Africa to the Atlantic coast in the same period. The reason that such dramatic numbers were reached immediately may indicate nothing more, therefore, than that a preexisting engagement with foreign markets was transferred to Atlantic ones. Most of the early European slave trading with West Africa, even that with such relatively remote regions as Benin and the Niger delta, known in the sixteenth century as the "River of Slaves," was simply an internal trade diverted to the Atlantic. Pacheco Pereira mentioned that the country of "Opuu," probably the Jukun kingdom on the Benue River, was a major source of slaves for the region.

The slave trade of the Benin coast shows another interesting aspect of African slavery and the export slave trade. The Saharan trade was mainly an export trade, but it also involved some internal trade. This is demonstrated by the fact that the Portuguese resold a large number of the Benin coast slaves to the Gold Coast. We know that such slaves were not simply used in the coastal mines (though we can be sure that many were) because the king of Portugal ordered this trade to cease (unsuccessfully, as it turns out) to prevent them from being sold to Moslems. These Moslems had to be northern Jula merchants who also visited the coastal goldfields, and thus these slaves may well have been employed in goldfields located quite far in the interior.

That existing internal use and commerce in slaves lay behind the export trade is even more strongly suggested by the trade of central Africa. Unlike the West African trade, which drew on an ancient slave trade with North Africa and might thus have already been affected by external contacts, the central African region had no such external links. Nevertheless, the king of Portugal regarded Kongo as sufficiently important a potential exporter of slaves that he granted settlers in São Tomé privileges to engage in the slave trade in 1493, just a few years after the development of official trade there. Kongo indeed became an important source of slaves for the Tomistas by 1502. Unfortunately we possess no early statistics for the volume of this trade, but Valentim Fernandes noted that around 1507, in addition to some 2,000 slaves working on sugar plantations, the island held 5,000–6,000 slaves awaiting reexport.

Presumably these slaves were recent imports who had probably arrived within the last year, and certainly half, but probably the majority, originated in central Africa. When the books of the royal factor on the island were inspected by Bernardo da Segura in 1516, they showed annual imports, mostly from Kongo, of nearly 4,500 slaves.

Slaves from central Africa were so numerous that they soon exceeded the capacity of São Tomé and the Mina trade to absorb them, and so they began the long journey to European markets. Although most of the slaves available in the port towns of Lisbon, Balencia, and Seville in the 1470s and 1480s came from western West Africa, Jolof in particular, by 1512 "Manicongos" were arriving in Seville, and Portuguese reports of 1513 mention a whole ship from Kongo making delivery in Europe.

Thus, at some point, probably with twenty years of first contact, central Africa was able to supply exports of slaves equal to the entire exports of West Africa. Clearly this sort of volume could not simply have been the occasional export of odd misfits. Nor have we any reason to believe that the Portuguese were able to either acquire the slaves themselves (except as clients of the Kongo kings) or force the Kongo to obtain the export slaves against their will. Instead, the growth of Kongo's trade had to draw on a well-developed system of slavery, slave marketing, and slave delivery that preexisted any European contact.

We must therefore conclude that the Atlantic slave trade and African participation in it had solid origins in African societies and legal systems. The institution of slavery was widespread in Africa and accepted in all the exporting regions, and the capture, purchase, transport, and sale of slaves was a regular feature of African society. This preexisting social arrangement was thus as much responsible as any external force for the development of the Atlantic slave trade.

POSTSCRIPT

Did the Trans-Atlantic Slave Trade Underdevelop Africa?

Today, John Thornton is not alone in his assertion that African elites had considerable influence on the continent's relationship with Europeans during the slave trading era. David Eltis (see *The Rise of African Slavery in the Americas*, Cambridge University Press, 2000) and Herbert Klein (see *The Atlantic Slave Trade*, Cambridge University Press, 1999) also have arrived at similar conclusions. Nonetheless, John Thornton's views remain quite controversial. While few question his motives or quality of his scholarship, many disagree with his conclusions. It is significant that Thornton ends his analysis before the advent of the eighteenth century at which point important changes in global trade and technology drastically transform the relationship between Africa and Europe. As Patrick Manning notes in a 1993 review of Thorton's book in the *American Historical Review*, "I question whether African institutions of slavery, and especially of enslavement, could have been as extensive in the sixteenth century, when some five thousand slaves were exported annually, as in the eighteenth century, when ten times that many slaves left Africa each year."

Thornton's text, while controversial, has become a departure point for new scholars who have been inspired to put his assertions to the test. One example of this is Walter Hawthorne's book *Planting Rice and Harvesting Slaves: Transformations Along the Guinea-Bissau Coast, 1400–1900* (Heinemann, 2003). Here, Hawthorne examines the Balanta of the Upper Guinea Coast and demonstrates that those living outside of more centralized African states were not mere victims of enslavement. In response to outside pressure, the Balanta developed a new rice production system and often found ways to produce slaves themselves.

A final point worth touching on is Thornton's argument that slavery developed in Africa prior to European arrival because African institutions did not permit private ownership of land, but did permit ownership of labor. It is true that labor has generally been a relatively scarce factor in African farming systems and control of labor certainly would have been a key factor in amassing wealth. Labor control in this context, however, does not necessarily correlate to the type of slavery that evolved alongside capitalism in the Atlantic world. For a good discussion of the latter phenomenon, see Eric Williams' *Capitalism and Slavery* (The University of North Carolina Press, 1994).

For an example of Paul Lovejoy's more recent work on this issue, see his book *Transformations in Slavery: A History of Slavery in Africa* (Cambridge University Press, 2000). While he makes many of the same arguments that he made in his selection for this issue, his argument is bolstered by new evidence on the numbers of slaves traded.

ISSUE 2

Have the Contributions of Africans Been Recognized for Developing New World Agriculture?

YES: Duncan Clinch Heyward, from *Seed from Madagascar* (University of North Carolina Press, 1937)

NO: Judith Carney, from "Agroenvironments and Slave Strategies in the Diffusion of Rice Culture to the Americas," in Karl S. Zimmerer and Thomas J. Bassett, eds., *Political Ecology: An Integrative Approach to Geography and Environment-Development Studies* (Guilford Press, 2003)

ISSUE SUMMARY

YES: Duncan Clinch Heyward, a former Carolina rice planter writing in the middle of the last century, represents the mainstream view that Europeans were primarily responsible for developing South Carolina's remarkable rice plantations in the eighteenth century. In his own accounting of the rise of rice cultivation in the Carolinas, Duncan suggests that the techniques and approaches must have been derived from those observed in China.

NO: Judith Carney, a professor of geography at UCLA, explains that slaves from rice-producing areas in West Africa have only recently been recognized for their intellectual contributions to the development of rice cultivation in the New World. Carney describes how her work, and that of others, challenged the view that slaves were mere field hands, "showing that they contributed agronomic expertise as well as skilled labor to the emergent plantation economy."

$\mathbf{A}$s Judith Carney describes in her selection for this issue, it had long been thought that African slaves contributed little more than labor to the New World's burgeoning plantation economies of the seventeenth, eighteenth and nineteenth centuries. But the pioneering work of Wood (*Black Majority: Negroes in Colonial South Carolina from 1670 through the Stone Rebellion,* Knopf, 1974), Littlefield (*Rice and Slaves: Ethnicity and the Slave Trade in Colonial*

24

South Carolina, Louisiana State University Press, 1981) and Carney (*Black Rice: The African Origins of Rice Cultivation in the Americas,* Harvard University Press, 2001) demonstrated Africans' knowledge of rice production was critical to the success of New World agriculture.

The aforementioned studies also form part of a growing literature on the Atlantic World, a global region centered on the Atlantic basin. Scholars working in this context often focus on the Atlantic Ocean as a conduit for the transmission of people and ideas. Other than the titles just mentioned, other examples of scholarship in this arena include: H. Taylor's *Circling Dixie: Contemporary Southern Culture Through a Transatlantic Lens* (Rutgers University Press, 2001) and Carney and Voeks' 2003 article in *Progress in Human Geography*, entitled "Landscape Legacies of the African Diaspora in Brazil."

In this issue, Judith Carney, a professor of geography at UCLA, explains that slaves from rice-producing areas in West Africa have only recently been recognized for their intellectual contributions to the development of rice cultivation in the New World. Carney describes how her work, and that of others, challenged the view that slaves were mere field hands, "showing that they contributed agronomic expertise as well as skilled labor to the emergent plantation economy."

Carney largely was reacting to an older body of literature that celebrated the contributions of southern planters in establishing successful rice plantations in the Carolinas in the eighteenth century. The selection by Duncan Heyward, a former Carolina rice planter writing in the middle of the last century, is an example of one such tract. According to Heyward, British functionaries identified rice as a suitable crop for the Carolinas and had rice seed sent to the colony. Heyward further suggested that the techniques and approaches for such cultivation must have been observed in China and brought to the Carolinas via European settlers. Those familiar with the Reconstruction and post-Reconstruction periods in U.S. history would not be errant in associating the work of Heyward and others with a larger body of Southern scholarship that tended to glorify the antebellum period. Very interestingly, however, there are a few cases of more contemporary works that highlight the contributions of Southern rice planters. One recent example is Richard Schulze's *Carolina Gold Rice: The Ebb and Flow History of a Low-country Cash Crop* (History Press, 2005). The author is the descendant of a former rice plantation owner and is reviving Carolina Gold rice as an heirloom variety.

YES

Duncan Clinch Heyward

Carolina Gold Rice

Often during my years as a planter, when the rice industry on our South Atlantic coast was rapidly being abandoned, I have sat under a great cypress, growing on my river bank, and, looking across the broad expanse of my rice fields, have thought of their strange and remarkable history. There would come to my mind the great and fundamental changes, racial and social as well as economic, which have taken place in a short space of time. And I have wished that the old tree above me could tell the tragic story of those fields, recounting events of which it had been a silent witness.

If the tree could only have spoken, I know its story would have begun at a time when the swamp, on whose edge it grew, was the favorite hunting ground of the red man. It would then have told of the coming of the white man, who drove the red man far away and took from him his lands. Next it would have told how the black man came, brought from far across the sea, how he felled the trees in the swamps and cleared them of their dense undergrowth, letting the sunshine in; then, how he drained the lowlands and grew crops of golden grain; and finally it would have told of the emancipation of the black man, who, after years of servitude, worked on faithfully as a freedman.

The rest of the story of my rice fields would for me have needed no telling. It would have dealt with the years when the white man was compelled, by conditions beyond his control, to give up planting, and the black man moved away seeking employment elsewhere, leaving fertile lands, the only naturally irrigated ones in this country, to revert to their former state.

The story of our former rice fields begins more than two centuries ago.

Carolina Gold rice, world renowned because of its superior quality as compared with all other varieties of rice throughout the world, was grown from seed brought to the province of Carolina about the year 1685. This rice had been raised in Madagascar, and a brigantine sailing from that distant island happened, in distress, to put into the port of Charles Town. While his vessel was being repaired, its captain, John Thurber, made the acquaintance of some of the leading citizens of that town. Among them was Dr. Henry Woodward, probably its best known citizen, for he had the distinction of being the first English settler in the province. He had accompanied Sandford on his first exploring expedition and had volunteered to remain alone at Port Royal in order that he might study the language of the Indians and familiarize himself with the country, in the interests of the Lords Proprietors.

To Woodward Captain Thurber gave a small quantity of rice—less, we are told, than a bushel—which happened to be on his ship. "The gentleman of the name of Woodward," to quote the earliest account of this occurrence, "himself planted some of it, and gave some to a few of his friends to plant."

Thus it came about that I, on the distaff side a descendant of Dr. Woodward, seem to have been destined to spend the best years of my life in seeking to revive an industry in the pursuit of which four generations of my family had been successful.

Three states bordering on the South Atlantic, North Carolina, South Carolina, and Georgia, are the only states in this country where for upwards of two centuries rice was grown. Nearly all of it, however, was produced in South Carolina and Georgia, partly because of a slightly warmer climate, but mainly because of the numerous tidal rivers which flow through these states and empty into the ocean. Along the Cape Fear River in North Carolina, it must be admitted, the finest quality of rice was grown, and for many years seed raised there was sold to the planters farther south, in order to preserve the quality of their rice.

The principal rivers in South Carolina, along which rice was planted, were the Waccamaw, the PeeDee, the Santee, the Cooper, the Edisto, and the Combahee. There were also many large rice plantations on the Savannah River, which separates South Carolina and Georgia. Farther south in Georgia were the Ogeechee, the Altamaha, and the Satilla rivers, the last near the Florida line. Some of these rivers are long, having their sources in the mountains, while others are much shorter. All of them are affected for a number of miles by the rise and fall of the tide, the result being that the fresh water they contain is backed up in the rivers and then drawn down again as the water in the ocean rises and falls. Great salt-water marshes lie on either side of the rivers as they approach the ocean, while higher up they were originally bordered by dense cypress, gum, and cedar swamps where the water was fresh, though rising and falling with the tide. It was in these fresh-water swamps that rice was successfully grown for the longest period of years.

As early as August 31, 1663, Lord Albemarle, one of the Lords Proprietors, wrote to the Governor of the Barbadoes, advising the planters there to settle in the proposed province of Carolina. Among the inducements offered he suggested the growing of rice. In his letter he said, "The commodyties I meane are wine, oyle, reasons, currents, rice, silk, etc." Of these, rice alone was destined to be successfully produced over a long period of years.

The plans of the Lords Proprietors regarding the growing of rice in the new province took practical shape in 1672, for in that year they had a barrel of rice sent to Charles Town in a vessel named the "William and Ralph"; and one must assume that this rice was intended for seed. By 1690 some headway had been made in the growing of rice, for the leading men of the province petitioned Governor Sothell to arrange with the Lords Proprietors that the people be allowed to "pay their quit rents in the most valuable and merchantable produce of their land," among which they included rice. These products, they reported, were "naturally produced here."

Also during this period the General Assembly of the province had ratified acts to protect those who should perfect labor-saving machinery for the purpose of husking and cleaning rice. A few years later the Assembly protested against an export duty on rice. How different was this attitude of the early rice planters from that of the planters of my day! We wanted an import duty. Though Southerners, we favored a tariff on rice, for we sorely needed protection. However, we never went so far as to claim that ours was an "infant industry."

By the year 1700 there was being produced in the province more rice "than we had ships to transport," according to the Governor and Council. Edward Randolph, collector of customs for the Southern department of North America that year, wrote: "They have now found out the true way of raising and husking rice. There has been above three hundred tons shipped this year to England besides about thirty tons to the Islands." This progress must have caused the Lords Proprietors to be exceedingly optimistic as to the future of rice cultivation in Carolina, for they congratulated themselves upon "what a staple the province of Carolina may be capable of furnishing Europe withall," and added that "the grocers do assure us it's better than any foreign rice by at least 8s the hundred weight."

At any rate, for the praise so soon bestowed by the grocers of London on the quality of the rice exported from the province of Carolina, and for the demand from abroad for this variety of rice, and also for the success which for upwards of two centuries attended the growing of rice in South Carolina and Georgia, we are principally indebted to Captain Thurber. Had it not been for him, the once celebrated Carolina Gold rice probably would never have been planted in America.

Another variety of rice later planted in South Carolina was known as Carolina White rice. This rice made a beautiful sample when prepared for market, and could scarcely be distinguished from the Gold rice, but its tendency to shatter when being harvested, if slightly over-ripe, caused it to be planted only to a limited extent.

It has never been known definitely from what country this Carolina White rice was first imported, but many of our rice planters believed it had been brought from China, where for unnumbered centuries rice has been grown and where there are today numerous varieties. Were I to hazard a guess as to who was responsible for bringing this white rice to the province, I should name Robert Rowand, born in Glasgow in 1738, who, when a boy, came to Charles Town. He later purchased an inland swamp plantation, on Rantowles Creek, about twenty-five miles southwest of Charles Town. He must have succeeded as a planter, for seemingly he was a man of means and traveled extensively. There is every reason to believe that he visited China, and that, while there, he had certain attractive pictures painted, illustrating the way the Chinese planted rice in those days, and showing the implements used in the process.

A few years ago in the town of Summerville, South Carolina, at the home of a friend, the late Mr. S. Lewis Simons, I saw these pictures. (They have since been destroyed by fire.) There were quite a number of them, and I am sure there are no others like them anywhere in this country. In size, they were about eighteen by fourteen inches, exceedingly well executed in bright water colors. They showed in great detail the growing of rice in China, from the preparation of the ground to the gathering and pounding of the grain. The pictures were evidently painted by a Chinese artist. The figures of men and women, the landscape, with its green trees here and there, blue mountains and hills rising out of the level plains intersected by canals, were entirely Oriental. On the front of the cover was written, "Painted in China prior to the Revolutionary War for one of the first South Carolina Rice Planters, Illustrating the Chinese Method of Cultivating Rice." The rice planter referred to was undoubtedly Robert Rowand, and the pictures had come into the possession of Mr. Simons through his wife, a Miss Mayrant, the Mayrant family having been rice planters for several generations, Mrs. Simons was a lineal descendant of Robert Rowand on her maternal side through the Drayton family.

The first of these Chinese pictures shows the plowing and harrowing of the soil of the seed-beds, both processes being done under water, the Chinaman and his black "water buffalo" nearly up to their knees, and the latter looking as if he did not trust his footing and was anxious to turn back. Then follows the sowing of the seed broadcast on the water, the transplanting of the rice by hand in the fields, the cultivating of the growing crop, the harvesting, until finally the rice is carried to the barnyard, where it is threshed and pounded. Anyone at all familiar with the methods used by the early planters in South Carolina cannot fail to be struck by their similarity to the methods shown in the old Chinese pictures, and especially is this true of the implements used. With the exception of sowing the rice in the water and transplanting it, nearly every picture recalled our system of planting. Many of the implements were almost identical with ours. There were the flail-sticks, being used in exactly the same way; the sickle, only a little straighter than ours, with which the rice was cut; the mortar and pestle and hand-fans; the "boards," as the Negroes used to call them, with which, indoors on a floor, the rice was pushed from place to place; and also the baskets in which the rice was carried.

These paintings of Robert Rowand's convinced me that our early methods of rice culture were adopted largely from the Chinese. For if, instead of the Chinese settings of the pictures, if in the place of the men with queues and black slanting eyes, dressed in bright-colored costumes, there could have been substituted the scenery of our rice fields and the Low Country Negroes at work, I could readily have believed the scenes were laid in our Black Border instead of in that far Eastern land.

Judith Carney

Agroenvironments and Slave Strategies in the Diffusion of Rice Culture to the Americas

By the mid-1700s a distinct cultivation system, based on rice, shouldered the American and African Atlantic. One locus of rice cultivation extended inland from West Africas Upper Guinea Coast, another flourished along the coastal plain of South Carolina and Georgia, and a third developed in the corridor between Brazil's Northeast and the eastern Amazon region (Figure 1). This tidal rice cultivation system depended upon enslaved African labor. In West Africa farmers planted rice as a subsistence crop on small holdings, with surpluses occasionally marketed, while in South Carolina, Georgia, and Brazil, cultivation depended on a plantation system and West African slaves to produce a crop destined for international markets.

While rice cultivation continues in West Africa today, its demise in South Carolina and Georgia swiftly followed the abolition of slavery. Brazils experiment in tidal rice cultivation, modeled after that of Carolina, did not withstand its competition in the 19th century. Yet the U.S. South's most lucrative plantation economy continued to inspire nostalgia well into the 20th century when the crop and the princely fortunes it delivered remained no more than a vestige of the coastal landscape. Numerous commentaries documented the lifeways of European American planters, their achievements, and their ingenuity in shaping a profitable landscape from malarial swamps. These accounts have never presented African Americans as having contributed anything but their unskilled labor. The planter-biased rendition of the origins of American rice cultivation prevailed until 1974 when the historian Peter Wood carefully examined the role of slaves in the Carolina plantation system during the colonial period. His scholarship recast the prevalent view of slaves as mere field hands to one that showed that they contributed agronomic expertise as well as skilled labor to the emergent plantation economy. Littlefield built upon Wood's path-breaking thesis by discussing the antiquity of African rice-farming practices and by revealing that more than 40% of South Carolina's slaves during the colonial period originated in West Africa's rice cultivation zone.

While this research has resulted in a revised view of the rice plantation economy as a fusion of both European and African cultures, the agency of African slaves in its evolution is still debated. Current formulations question

Figure 1

Rice cultivation along the Atlantic Basin, 1760–1860

whether planters recruited slaves from West Africa's rice coast to help them develop a crop whose potential they independently discovered, or whether African-born slaves initiated rice planting in South Carolina by teaching planters to grow a preferred food crop. The absence of archival materials that would document a tutorial role for African slaves is not surprising given the paucity of records available in general for the early colonial period, and because racism over time institutionalized white denial of the intellectual capacity of bondsmen. An understanding of the potential role of slaves demands other forms of historical enquiry.

This study is situated in a growing trend in scholarship that integrates detailed ethnographic and ecological investigation, particularly of agroenvironments, with social and environmental history. Such an integration invites the use of multiple and diverse tools, including analysis of archival materials and historical documents (e.g., travelers' narratives, colonial accounts, maps), oral histories, agroecological methods, and ethnographic inquiry. The following discussion of West African rice-farming technology and culture is complemented by extensive field-work conducted on rice systems in Senegambia by the author, by Olga R Linares in Senegal, and by Paul Richards in Sierra Leone. Similarities between today's West African rice culture and that of the antebellum U.S. South do not prove in themselves the case for rice technology transfer by African slaves. Field-based geographical studies, however, can substantiate and elaborate upon often-sparse observations in the archival record; provide theoretical frameworks, inspired by political ecology, for understanding past human–environment relations; and produce a richer portrait of past landscapes.

This [selection] combines geographical and historical perspectives to examine the likely contributions of African-born slaves to the colonial rice economy. The approach identifies and describes the principal West African microenvironments planted to rice in the first section as the basis for examining, in the one following, the systems that emerged in South Carolina during the colonial period. While archival documentation, albeit fragmentary, exists on rice systems in West Africa from the 14th century, the discussion in the first section of these systems and their underlying soil and water management principles is based on modern field studies. Focus then shifts to the history of rice cultivation in South Carolina, especially during the hundred years from 1670 to 1770, which is crucial since it spans the initial settlement by planters and slaves as well as the expansion of tidal (tidewater) rice cultivation into Georgia. In emphasizing the complex nexus that links culture, technology, and the environment, attention is directed to the indigenous knowledge systems formed in West Africa by ethnic groups speaking Mande and West Atlantic languages. Across the Middle Passage of slavery they brought their expertise with them, and then established rice as a favored dietary staple in the Americas. This knowledge system, moreover, enabled enslaved rice growers to negotiate and alter, to some extent, the terms of their bondage. The concluding section raises several questions about the issue of technology development and transfer, suggests a lingering Eurocentric bias in historical reconstructions of the agricultural development of the Americas, and discusses the scholarly implications of this research.

The Agronomic and Technological Basis of West African Rice Systems

Some 4,000 years ago, West Africans domesticated rice along the floodplain and inland delta of the upper and middle Niger River in Mali. The species of rice originally planted in this primary center of domestication, *Oryza glaberrima*, differs from Asian rice, *Orvza sativa*. While both species are currently planted in West Africa, the indigenous African center extends along the coast from Senegal to Côte d'Ivoire and into the Sahelian interior along riverbanks, inland swamps, and lake margins. Within this diverse geographic and climatic setting two secondary centers of *glaberrima* domestication emerged: one, on floodplains of the Gambia River and its tributaries; and another, farther south in the forested Guinea highlands where rainfall reaches 2,000 millimeters/ year. By the end of the 17th century rice had crossed the Atlantic Basin to the United States, appearing first as a rainfed crop in South Carolina before diffusing along river floodplains and into Georgia from the 1750s.

Many similarities characterized rice production on both sides of the Atlantic Basin. In both West Africa and South Carolina the most productive system developed along floodplains. Precipitation in each region follows a marked seasonal pattern, with rains generally occurring during the months from May/ June to September/October. Rice cultivation flourished in South Carolina and Georgia under annual precipitation averages of 1,200–1,400 millimeters, a figure that represents the midrange of a more diverse rainfall pattern influencing West African rice cultivation, where precipitation increases dramatically over short distances from north to south. Accordingly, in the Malian primary center and the Gambian secondary center of rice domestication semi-arid

(900 millimeters/year) conditions prevail, while southward in Guinea-Bissau and Sierra Leone precipitation exceeds 1,500 millimeters per annum.

The topography of the rice-growing region on both sides of the Atlantic presents a similar visual field. Coastlines are irregularly shaped and formed from alluvial deposits that also create estuarine islands. Tidal regimes on the American coast differ somewhat from those of Africa. The steep descent from the piedmont in South Carolina and Georgia delivers freshwater tidal flows to floodplains just 10 miles from the Atlantic coast. But the less pronounced gradient of rivers in West Africa's rice region means that freshwater tides meet marine water much farther upstream from the coast; on the Gambia River, salinity permanently affects the lower 80 kilometers but intrudes seasonally more than 200 kilometers upstream. Rice cultivation is adapted to the annual retreat and advance of the saline corridor. Even coastal estuaries inundated by ocean tides served as a basis for West African rice experimentation. South of the Gambia River, where precipitation exceeds 1,500 millimeters/year, West Africans learned to plant rice in marine estuaries, by enclosing plots and allowing rainfall to flush out accumulated salts. Water saturation is the key to planting such soils, as it prevents oxidization to an acidic condition that would preclude further cultivation. An elaborate network of embankments provides a barrier to seawater intrusion, while dikes, canals, and sluice gates enable field drainage of rainwater used for desalination. . . .

African Rice and American Continuities

By 1860, rice cultivation extended over 100,000 acres along the Eastern Seaboard from North Carolina's Cape Fear River to Florida's St. John's River, and inland for some 35 miles along tidal waterways. The initial stage of the rice plantation economy dated to the first hundred years of South Carolina's settlement (1670–1770) and, especially, the decades prior to the 1739 Stono slave rebellion. Rice cultivation systems analogous to those in West Africa, as well as identical principles and devices for water control and milling, were already evident in this period. Dramatic increases in slave imports during the 18th century facilitated the evolution of the Carolina rice plantation economy. Technology development unfolded in tandem with the appearance of the task labor system that regulated work on coastal rice plantations. As the crop grew in economic importance, agro-environments favored for colonial rice production shifted from uplands to inland swamps and, from the 1730s, to the tidal (tidewater) cultivation system that led Carolina rice to global prominence.

This section presents an overview of the historical and geographical circumstances under which rice became a plantation crop in South Carolina. The technical changes marking the evolution of the colonial rice economy illuminate three issues that bear on comparative studies of technology and culture: first, the need to examine the technical components of production as parts of integrated systems of knowledge and not merely as isolated elements; second, the significance of cultural funds of knowledge for technology transfer; and third, in situations of unequal power relations, the extent to which claims for technological ingenuity can rest on cultural dispossession and appropriation of knowledge.

Slaves accompanied the first settlers to South Carolina in 1670; within 2 years they formed one-fourth of the colony's population; and as early as 1708 they outnumbered whites in the colony. Rice cultivation appears early in the colonial record, with planting already underway in the 1690s. By 1695 South Carolina recorded its first shipment of rice: one and one-quarter barrels to Jamaica. In 1699 exports reached 330 tons, and by the 1720s rice had emerged as the leading trade item. Years later, in 1748, South Carolina governor James Glen drew attention to the significance of rice experimentation during the 1690s for development of the colony's economy.

By the 1740s, documents firmly establish the presence of the upland, inland swamp, and tidal floodplain production systems. But rice cultivation in these areas is implied even earlier in the comments of one plantation manager, John Stewart, who claimed in the 1690s to have successfully sown rice in 22 different locations. One major point distinguished patterns of land use in West African and South Carolinian rice systems. In West Africa, subsistence security shaped the crop's production, thereby favoring cultivation in numerous microenvironments along a landscape gradient. Rice cultivation in colonial Carolina began as a subsistence crop, planted similarly in diverse environments, but as it became a plantation crop emphasis shifted to specific agroenvironments along the landscape continuum—from rainfed, to inland swamp, to tidal production—to maximize yields and returns on capital and labor.

Upland rice production received initial attention because it complemented the early colony's economic emphasis on stock raising and extraction of forest products. Slave labor buttressed this agropastoral system, which involved clearing forests, producing naval stores (pine pitch, tar, and resin), cattle herding, and subsistence farming. Export of salted beef, deerskins, and naval stores in turn generated capital to purchase additional slaves. The number of enslaved Africans imported to the colony dramatically increased from 3,000 in 1703 to nearly 12,000 by 1720, which enabled a shift in rice cultivation to the more productive inland swamp system.

The higher yielding inland swamp system initiated the first attempts at water control in Carolina's rice fields. After clearing swamp forests, slaves developed the network of berms and sluices necessary for converting plots into reservoirs. Like its counterpart in West Africa, the inland swamp system impounded water from rainfall, subterranean springs, high water tables, or creeks to saturate the soil. The objective was to drown unwanted weeds and thereby reduce the labor spent on weeding, as in West Africa. West African principles also guided the cultivation of rice in coastal marshes. Rice was grown in saltwater marshes near the terminus of freshwater streams in soils influenced by the Atlantic Ocean. The conversion of a saline marsh to a rice field depended upon soil desalination, a process not as easily achieved with South Carolina's annual precipitation regime (1,100–1,200 millimeters), which is lower than the average 1,500 millimeters per year that regulate the West African mangrove system. However, by diverting an adjoining freshwater creek or stream, salts could be rinsed from the field. The principle of canalizing water for controlled flooding also extended to other settings, such as in places where subterranean springs flowed near the soil surface. Detailed knowledge of landscape topography and hydrological conditions thus enabled the proliferation of rice growing in diverse inland swamp micro-environments.

During the 18th century rice cultivation in such areas innovated to more elaborate systems of sluices that released reserve water on demand for controlled flooding at critical stages of the cropping cycle. This inland swamp system flourished where the landscape gradient sloped from rain-fed farming to the inner edge of a tidal swamp. Enclosure of a swamp with earthen embankments created a reservoir for storing rainwater, the system's principal source of irrigation. The reservoir fed water, through a sluice gate and canal, by gravity flow to the inland rice field, while a drainage canal and sluice placed at the lower end of the rice field emptied excess water into a nearby stream, creek, or river. Whereas the principle of constructing a reservoir for controlled field flooding is identical to the West African mangrove rice system, the innovative changes that subsequently developed may well provide an instance of what geographer Paul Richards calls "agrarian creolization." The term refers to the convergence of different knowledge systems and their recombination into new hybridized forms, spearheading the process of innovation.

By the mid-18th century the emphasis on rice had shifted from inland swamps to tidal river floodplains, first in South Carolina, and subsequently in Georgia. The swelling number of slaves directly entering South Carolina from West Africa between the 1730s and the 1770s proved crucial in this spatial relocation of the rice economy. Some 35,000 slaves were imported into the colony during the first half of the century and over 58,000 between 1750 and 1775, making South Carolina the largest importer of enslaved Africans on the North American mainland between 1706 and 1775. The share of slaves brought directly from the West African rice coast grew during these crucial decades of tidewater rice development from 12% (1730s) to 54% (1749–1765), and then to 64% (1769–1774) (Richardson, 1991). This pattern is illuminated in a typical handbill from the colonial period, which announces the sale in Charlestown (Charleston) on July 24, 1769 of enslaved men, women, and children from Sierra Leone.

Tidewater cultivation occurred on floodplains along tidal rivers where, similar to its mangrove rice counterpart in West Africa, the diurnal variation in sea level facilitated field flooding and drainage. Preparation of a tidal floodplain for rice cultivation followed principles already outlined for the mangrove rice system. The rice field was embanked at sufficient height to prevent tidal spillover, while the earth removed in the process created adjacent canals. Sluices built into the embankment and field sections operated as valves for flooding and drainage. The next step involved dividing the area into plots (in South Carolina these were termed "quarter sections," of some 10–30 acres), with river water delivered through secondary ditches. This elaborate system of water control enabled the adjustment of land units to labor demands and allowed slaves to directly sow rice along the floodplain. Then the rice was planted directly in the floodplain, as it is in African floodplain cultivation.

Tidewater cultivation required considerable landscape modification and ever-greater numbers of enslaved laborers than rain-fed and inland swamp cultivation. Leland Ferguson, a historical archaeologist, vividly captures the staggering human effort involved in transforming Carolina's tidal swamps to rice fields:

> These fields are surrounded by more than a mile of earthen dikes or "banks" as they were called. Built by slaves, these banks . . . were taller than a person and up to 15 feet wide. By the turn of the eighteenth century, rice banks on the 12½ mile stretch of the East Branch of Cooper River measured more than 55 miles long and contained more than 6.4 million cubic feet of earth. By 1850, aided only by hand-held tools, slaves in the Carolina rice zone had built earthworks "nearly three times the volume of Cheops, the world s largest pyramid."

While such landscape change placed considerable demands on slave labor for construction and maintenance, it reduced the need for manual weeding, one of the most labor-intensive tasks in rice production. The systematic lifting and lowering of water was achieved by sluices, known as "trunks," located in the embankment and secondary dikes; by the late colonial period these devices had evolved into hanging floodgates. With full control of an adjacent tidal river, the rice field could be flooded on demand for irrigation and weeding and to renew the soil annually with alluvial deposits. Because of this increasing reliance on water control technology, in tidal cultivation one slave could manage 5 acres of rice, as opposed to just 2 acres in the inland rice system.

The history of the term "trunk" for sluice gate in Carolina also suggests evidence for technology transfer from the West African rice coast. While the hanging gate technology likely provides another example of agrarian creolization, its name refers to an earlier device. Even when the hanging gate replaced earlier forms, Carolina planters continued to call sluice gates "trunks." In the 1930s planter descendant David Doar stumbled upon the term origin: the earliest sluice gates were formed from hollowed-out cypress trunks. The original Carolina sluice system looked and functioned exactly like its African counterpart. Reference to them as "trunks" throughout the antebellum period suggests that the technological expertise of Africans again proved significant in Carolina rice history.

Tidewater rice cultivation led South Carolina to global economic prominence in the 18th century. It was made possible by the expertise of enslaved Africans in cultivating as well as processing the crop. Their experience with planting a whole range of interconnected environments along a landscape gradient likely permitted the sequence of adaptations that marked the growth of the South Carolina rice industry.

African contributions to Carolina rice history were not limited to cultivation practices. They also extended to the method by which the grain was processed for consumption. Until suitable mechanical mills were developed around the time of the American Revolution, the entire export crop was milled by hand, in the traditional method long used by African women, with a mortar and pestle. Even the fanner baskets used to winnow rice on Carolina and Georgia plantations display a likely African origin, as anthropologist Dale

Rosengarten suggests. She links the coiled-basket-weaving tradition in fanner baskets to the Senegambian rice region, as it did not exist among Native Americans of the Southeast region.

Enslaved Africans thus contributed significantly more than physical labor to colonial rice production. They provided the critical expertise in establishing rice cultivation in South Carolina, even though accounts by planters and their descendants have long claimed for their forebears the ingenuity in developing the system. Planter accounts, however, fail to explain how they learned to transform wetland landscapes by careful observance of tidal dynamics, soils, microenvironments, and water regimes. Such systems of planting cereals in standing water did not exist in England at the time, yet surfaced within two decades of Carolina's settlement. Wetland rice represents a far more complex farming system than the rainfall cultivation practiced by the English. Enslaved Africans from the African rice region were thus the only settlers present in the Carolina colony who possessed this knowledge system.

The delayed recognition of this significant contribution to the history of the Americas stems, in part, from the way that rice has been examined by scholars. By emphasizing rice as a cereal, as a grain consumed and traded internationally, studies have failed to place it within its proper agroecological context for studies of diffusion and technology transfer. An examination of rice as a landscape of microenvironments brings into focus the underlying soil and water management regimes that inform its cultivation as well as its cultural origins. Recovery of the African contribution to American rice history also involves considering consumption as well as production, processing as well as cultivation, and the types of labor and knowledge that mediated the spatial movement of rice from field to kitchen. This requires sensitivity to ecological as well as gendered forms of knowledge in technology transfer.

While this overview of rice beginnings in South Carolina argues that planters reaped the benefits of a rice-farming system perfected by West Africans over millennia, an important question remains. Why would enslaved West Africans transfer a sophisticated rice system to plantation owners when the result spelled endless and often lethal toil in malarial swamps?

The answer is perhaps revealed in the appearance by 1712 of the task labor system that characterized coastal rice plantations. It was distinguished from the more pervasive "gang" form of work typifying plantation slavery. In the gang system, "the laborer was compelled to work the entire day", while "under the task system the slave was assigned a certain amount of work for the day, and after completing the task he could use his time as he pleased." Without underestimating the real toil involved in the two systems, the task system did set normative limits to daily work demands. Such seemingly minor differences between the two systems could deliver tangible improvements in slave nutrition and health, as Johan Bolzius implied in 1751 with his observation: "If the Negroes are Skillful and industrious, they plant something for themselves after the day's work."

The task labor system appeared at the crucial juncture of the evolution of rice as a plantation crop in the Carolina colony and the shift to the more productive, but labor-demanding, inland swamp system. A similar system of limiting demands placed on enslaved labor was already in existence along Africa's Rice Coast. The appearance of the task labor system in Carolina's fledgling rice economy may well represent the outcome of negotiation and struggle between master and slave over knowledge of rice culture and the labor process to implement it. In providing crucial technological acumen, slaves perhaps discovered a mechanism to negotiate improved conditions of bondage. But by the 19th century such gains had eroded, as the frontier for slave escape closed and slavery appeared to be a permanent feature of Southern agriculture. The task labor system became little different than the gang form of slavery.

Conclusion

"What skill they displayed and engineering ability they showed when they laid out these thousands of fields and tens of thousands of banks and ditches in order to suit their purpose and attain their ends! As one views this vast hydraulic work, he is amazed to learn that all of this was accomplished in face of seemingly insuperable difficulties by every-day planters who had as tools only the axe, the spade, and the hoe, in the hands of intractable negro men and women, but lately brought from the jungles of Africa." In 1936, when David Doar, descendant of Carolina planters, echoed the prevailing view that slaves contributed little besides labor to the evolution of the South Carolina rice economy, no historical research suggested otherwise. While recent research challenges such unquestioned assumptions, a bias nonetheless endures against considering West Africans as the originators of rice culture in the Americas.

Even authoritative texts on rice cultivation, such as that of D. H. Grist, express such a bias. In reference to a type of paddy rice cultivation found in British Guiana (now Guyana) and the neighboring former Dutch colony of Surinam, Grist describes the "empoldering" technique as "a method of restricting floods and thus securing adjacent areas from submergence." While this technique is strikingly similar to that employed in mangrove rice production along the West African rice coast, he attributes the system to 18th-century Dutch colonizers. In that era, however, Surinam possessed one of the highest ratios of Africans to Europeans of any New World plantation society (65:1 in Surinam compared to Jamaica's 10:1).

More recent work in Brazilian rice history repeats this perspective. Even though rice was not grown in Portugal during the colonization of the Americas, Pereira attributes its 16th-century introduction in Brazil's eastern Amazon and Northeast to migrants from the Azores and Portugal. There is no discussion of how the African mortar and pestle (a device not used in Portugal) came to be the sole technology for milling rice in Brazil until the mid-18th century, when it was replaced by water mills that successfully removed the hulls without grain breakage. Nor is there any acknowledgment of the possibility that rice culture became established in Brazil, as in South Carolina, because African rice routinely provisioned slave ships, providing the enslaved an opportunity to grow their food staple for subsistence.

Evidence from the American and African Atlantic thus suggests that slaves from West Africa's indigenous rice area established rice culture. A crop initially planted for subsistence became, in 18th-century South Carolina, the first cereal globally traded as a plantation export crop. This complex indigenous knowledge system guided the transformation of Carolina's swamps while serving as a source of technological innovation in rice culture, captured in the notion of agrarian creolization. These achievements in tidal rice diffused southward in the 18th century along rivers in Georgia and Florida, and, from midcentury, overseas to similar environments in Brazils Northeast and eastern Amazon regions. While rice systems of the Americas would eventually bear the imprimatur of both African and European influences, its appearance initially is linked to a knowledge system developed in West Africa and carried across the Middle Passage by slavery's victims.

Thus, as Europeans and Africans faced each other in a new territory under dramatically altered and unequal power relations, the enslaved established a subsistence crop long valued in West Africa. With the abolition of slavery, rice history led to cultural dispossession and appropriation by descendants of slave owners who credited the beginnings of rice farming to European ingenuity and presumed mastery of technology. A careful reading of the archival and historical record—one attuned to agroenvironments, power relations, ecological principles, and social history—reveals a dramatically different narrative.

The ending of this story is not yet settled: this cross-cultural, social–environmental history of transatlantic rice culture also cuts across current political and cultural debates. In the U.S. South, historical preservation of antebellum landscapes is charged with the controversy of memory politics. While many descendants of white planters view preservation of plantation landscapes as a source of pride, many African Americans perceive these as sites of toil, terror, and shame. This discussion of rice technology transfer demonstrates that despite the brutality of bondage, African slaves were active and ingenious shapers of antebellum agroenvironments rather than mere physical laborers. Historical preservation and ecological restoration efforts in the South should acknowledge the rich hybrid nature of these cultural landscapes in a way similar to that currently underway in the reconsideration of southern family histories by black and white descendants of slave owners.

This study also has implications for the hotly debated issue of intellectual property rights over agricultural seeds. Today, cultivars and their germ plasm are increasingly engineered, patented, and privatized. This market logic reduces seeds to their mere biology. As this investigation of rice cultivation on the Atlantic Rim implies, however, seeds cannot be so easily separated from their political and social context. The introduction of African rice in the New World was not simply the movement of seeds from one environment to another, but rather the transfer and transformation of a *rice culture,* with attendant continuities and changes in technology, labor organization, social structures, and cultural meanings.

POSTSCRIPT

Have the Contributions of Africans Been Recognized for Developing New World Agriculture?

Despite the wide acceptance of Carney's scholarship, certain aspects of her work have been critiqued. In a review of Carney's book on this subject, *Black Rice* (summarized in Carney's selection in this issue), in a 2002 issue of the *William and Mary Quarterly*, Philip Morgan raises several questions about her treatment of the slave trade. He disputes her claim that Carolina planters imported a greater percentage of female slaves than did Caribbean planters. He questions whether Carolina planters paid more for female slaves than other New World slave markets (but cannot prove otherwise). He also questions whether South Carolineans were sourcing relatively more slaves from rice-producing areas in West Africa at critical junctures in the development of the rice economy. New scholarship by Max Edelson (see *Plantation Enterprise in Colonial South Carolina*, Harvard University Press, 2006) also suggests that European colonists played a much larger role in the development of a Carolina rice economy than Carney admits.

Another question to ponder, and this is raised by Carney in her selection, is why Africans would have been willing to share their rice-growing expertise with their white oppressors. Carney's answer is that they used this knowledge to bargain for a "task labor system" rather than the more oppressive "gang system," which forced slaves to work the entire day. Under the task system, a slave could use his or her time for their own activities after completing a certain quantity of work. As Carney notes, this negotiated approach was eventually lost in the nineteenth century.

A final issue to consider is the somewhat subjective nature of regions as units of analysis. What the burgeoning scholarship on the Atlantic World demonstrates is that historical transfers of peoples and ideas may bind together the two areas (i.e., the Atlantic sides of the Americas and Africa) that traditionally have been studied separately. Furthermore, it is important to note that Carney was originally trained as an Africanist and undertook most of her scholarship in West Africa. What Carney's scholarship demonstrates is that she was able to use her deep understanding of the African context to shed light on the situation in the Americas. For more reflections on comparative regional studies, see William Moseley's May 2005 article in the *Southeastern Geographer* entitled "Regional Geographies of the U.S. Southeast and Sub-Saharan Africa: The Potential for Comparative Insights."

ISSUE 3

Is European Subjugation of Africans Ultimately Explained by Differences in Land, Plant, and Animal Resources?

YES: Jared Diamond, from "Why Europeans Were the Ones to Colonize Sub-Saharan Africa," in *Guns, Germs, and Steel: The Fates of Human Societies* (W.W. Norton & Company, 1999)

NO: Lucy Jarosz, from "A Human Geographer's Response to *Guns, Germs, and Steel*: The Case of Agrarian Development and Change in Madagascar," *Antipode* (2003)

ISSUE SUMMARY

YES: Jared Diamond, professor of physiology and biogeography at UCLA, argues that Europeans were able to colonize Africa (rather than vice versa) because of the advantages of guns, widespread literacy, and political organization. These advantages stem ultimately from different historical trajectories that are linked to "differences in real estate" (or differences in physical geography).

NO: Lucy Jarosz, associate professor of geography at the University of Washington, is troubled by Diamond's narrow conception of geography and asserts that explaining differences in wealth and power between regions must also take account of social, political, and economic connections. She focuses on the specific case of Madagascar and argues that the intentions of the colonizer are as or more important than their military power for determining the nature of the colonial relationship.

Many in the social sciences at the turn of the last century were heavily influenced by a school of thought known as Social Darwinism. Social Darwinists took the ideas of Charles Darwin and used these concepts to explain perceived differences between human societies and races. One such prominent thinker was the German philosopher Fredrich Ratzel (1844–1904). Ratzel argued that differences in climate largely explained (what he perceived to be) Europeans'

41

advanced state of development relative to that of the various peoples of the tropical regions. Ratzel and others reasoned that the cooler temperatures, changing seasons, and long winters of the temperate regions led to more forethought, energy, and planning, whereas the heat, absence of a harsh winter, and relative abundance of the tropics resulted in contentment, sloth, and a lack of foresight.

This particular perspective came to be known as the geographic factor, environmentalism (different than the contemporary definition of this term) or environmental determinism, and was, not surprisingly, very popular among the colonial powers (e.g., France, England) for explaining or rationalizing their subjugation of African peoples. Many were beginning to doubt environmental determinism by the 1930s, and this blatantly racist perspective eventually fell out of favor. People questioned these ideas because there were too many exceptions. How does one explain the Egyptian pyramids, Mayan temples, or the Great Zimbabwe if people in the tropics are supposed to be less advanced?

Although environmental determinism has long since fallen out of favor, some social scientists are beginning to reassert a milder version of environmental determinism (sometimes referred to as environmental possibilism). Within the discipline of economics, a new subfield known as "new economic geography" has flourished in recent years by explaining lagging development in terms of differences in geography or real estate. Economists writing in this new genre include Jeffrey Sachs and Ricardo Hausmann among others. Europe and North America were twice blessed. They had the most productive economic systems reinforced, and partly caused, by their favorable geographic conditions. In contrast, the tropics and great land-based empires were twice cursed, with weaker economic institutions, and as a rule, poorer geographical endowments" (*The Economist*, 1997).

In this issue, Jared Diamond, trained in physiology, and now a professor of biogeography at UCLA, argues that Europeans were able to colonize Africa because of the advantages of guns, widespread literacy, and political organization. These advantages arose from different historical trajectories that were linked to "differences in real estate". This selection is taken from Diamond's Pulitzer Prize–winning book, *Guns, Germs and Steel*. In the opening chapter of this text, Diamond asserts that he is not an environmental determinist. He further asserts that his theory is anything but racist because he explains varying levels of development in terms of natural endowments and geography rather than mental ability.

Lucy Jarosz, an associate professor of geography at the University of Washington, asserts that explaining differences in wealth and power between regions must also take account of social, political, and economic connections. She focuses on the specific case of Madagascar and argues that the intentions of the colonizer are as or more important than their military power for determining the nature of the colonial relationship. She describes how Madagascar had previously been peopled and colonized by immigrants from South and Southeast Asia, East Africa, and the Arabic Peninsula. These early waves of immigration and colonization led to settled agriculture and international trade, as well as the development of a local elite. According to Jarosz, the colonial experience with the French was quite different because this power reshaped Madagascar's economy for its own benefit.

YES

Jared Diamond

Why Europeans Were the Ones to Colonize Sub-Saharan Africa

Africa's diverse peoples resulted from its diverse geography and its long prehistory. Africa is the only continent to extend from the northern to the southern temperate zone, while also encompassing some of the world's driest deserts, largest tropical rain forests, and highest equatorial mountains. Humans have lived in Africa far longer than anywhere else: our remote ancestors originated there around 7 million years ago, and anatomically modern *Homo sapiens* may have arisen there since then. The long interactions between Africa's many peoples generated its fascinating prehistory, including two of the most dramatic population movements of the past 5,000 years—the Bantu expansion and the Indonesian colonization of Madagascar. All of those past interactions continue to have heavy consequences, because the details of who arrived where before whom are shaping Africa today. . . .

Now let's turn to the remaining question in our puzzle of African prehistory: why Europeans were the ones to colonize sub-Saharan Africa. That it was not the other way around is especially surprising, because Africa was the sole cradle of human evolution for millions of years, as well as perhaps the homeland of anatomically modern *Homo sapiens.* To these advantages of Africa's enormous head start were added those of highly diverse climates and habitats and of the world's highest human diversity. An extraterrestrial visiting Earth 10,000 years ago might have been forgiven for predicting that Europe would end up as a set of vassal states of a sub-Saharan African empire.

The proximate reasons behind the outcome of Africa's collision with Europe are clear. Just as in their encounter with Native Americans, Europeans entering Africa enjoyed the triple advantage of guns and other technology, widespread literacy, and the political organization necessary to sustain expensive programs of exploration and conquest. Those advantages manifested themselves almost as soon as the collisions started: barely four years after Vasco da Gama first reached the East African coast, in 1498, he returned with a fleet bristling with cannons to compel the surrender of East Africa's most important port, Kilwa, which controlled the Zimbabwe gold trade. But why did Europeans develop those three advantages before sub-Saharan Africans could?

As we have discussed, all three arose historically from the development of food production. But food production was delayed in sub-Saharan Africa (compared with Eurasia) by Africa's paucity of domesticable native animal and plant species, its much smaller area suitable for indigenous food production, and its north–south axis, which retarded the spread of food production and inventions. Let's examine how those factors operated.

First, as regards domestic animals, we've already seen that those of sub-Saharan Africa came from Eurasia, with the possible exception of a few from North Africa. As a result, domestic animals did not reach sub-Saharan Africa until thousands of years after they began to be utilized by emerging Eurasian civilizations. That's initially surprising, because we think of Africa as *the* continent of big wild mammals. But . . . that a wild animal, to be domesticated, must be sufficiently docile, submissive to humans, cheap to feed, and immune to diseases and must grow rapidly and breed well in captivity. Eurasia's native cows, sheep, goats, horses, and pigs were among the world's few large wild animal species to pass all those tests. Their African equivalents—such as the African buffalo, zebra, bush pig, rhino, and hippopotamus—have never been domesticated, not even in modern times.

It's true, of course, that some large African animals have occasionally been *tamed*. Hannibal enlisted tamed African elephants in his unsuccessful war against Rome, and ancient Egyptians may have tamed giraffes and other species. But none of those tamed animals was actually domesticated—that is, selectively bred in captivity and genetically modified so as to become more useful to humans. Had Africa's rhinos and hippos been domesticated and ridden, they would not only have fed armies but also have provided an unstoppable cavalry to cut through the ranks of European horsemen. Rhino-mounted Bantu shock troops could have overthrown the Roman Empire. It never happened.

A second factor is a corresponding, though less extreme, disparity between sub-Saharan Africa and Eurasia in domesticable plants. The Sahel, Ethiopia, and West Africa did yield indigenous crops, but many fewer varieties than grew in Eurasia. Because of the limited variety of wild starting material suitable for plant domestication, even Africa's earliest agriculture may have begun several thousand years later than that of the Fertile Crescent.

Thus, as far as plant and animal domestication was concerned, the head start and high diversity lay with Eurasia, not with Africa. A third factor is that Africa's area is only about half that of Eurasia. Furthermore, only about one-third of its area falls within the sub-Saharan zone north of the equator that was occupied by farmers and herders before 1000 B.C. Today, the total population of Africa is less than 700 million, compared with 4 billion for Eurasia. But, all other things being equal, more land and more people mean more competing societies and inventions, hence a faster pace of development.

The remaining factor behind Africa's slower rate of post-Pleistocene development compared with Eurasia's is the different orientation of the main axes of these continents. Like that of the Americas, Africa's major axis is north–south, whereas Eurasia's is east–west. As one moves along a north–south axis, one traverses zones differing greatly in climate, habitat, rainfall, day length, and diseases of crops and livestock. Hence crops and animals domesticated or acquired in one part of Africa had great difficulty in moving to other parts. In contrast, crops and animals moved easily between Eurasian societies thousands of miles apart but at the same latitude and sharing similar climates and day lengths.

The slow passage or complete halt of crops and livestock along Africa's north–south axis had important consequences. For example, the Mediterranean crops that became Egypt's staples require winter rains and seasonal variation in day length for their germination. Those crops were unable to spread south of the Sudan, beyond which they encountered summer rains and little or no seasonal variation in daylight. Egypt's wheat and barley never reached the Mediterranean climate at the Cape of Good Hope until European colonists brought them in 1652, and the Khoisan never developed agriculture. Similarly, the Sahel crops adapted to summer rain and to little or no seasonal variation in day length were brought by the Bantu into southern Africa but could not grow at the Cape itself, thereby halting the advance of Bantu agriculture. Bananas and other tropical Asian crops for which Africa's climate is eminently suitable, and which today are among the most productive staples of tropical African agriculture, were unable to reach Africa by land routes. They apparently did not arrive until the first millennium A.D., long after their domestication in Asia, because they had to wait for large-scale boat traffic across the Indian Ocean.

Africa's north–south axis also seriously impeded the spread of livestock, Equatorial Africa's tsetse flies, carrying trypanosomes to which native African wild mammals are resistant, proved devastating to introduced Eurasian and North African species of livestock. The cows that the Bantu acquired from the tsetse-free Sahel zone failed to survive the Bantu expansion through the equatorial forest. Although horses had already reached Egypt around 1800 B.C. and transformed North African warfare soon thereafter, they did not cross the Sahara to drive the rise of cavalry-mounted West African kingdoms until the first millennium A.D., and they never spread south through the tsetse fly zone. While cattle, sheep, and goats had already reached the northern edge of the Serengeti in the third millennium B.C., it took more than 2,000 years beyond that for livestock to cross the Serengeti and reach southern Africa.

Similarly slow in spreading down Africa's north–south axis was human technology. Pottery, recorded in the Sudan and Sahara around 8000 B.C., did not reach the Cape until around A.D. 1. Although writing developed in Egypt by 3000 B.C. and spread in an alphabetized form to the Nubian kingdom of Meroë, and although alphabetic writing reached Ethiopia (possibly from Arabia), writing did not arise independently in the rest of Africa, where it was instead brought in from the outside by Arabs and Europeans.

In short, Europe's colonization of Africa had nothing to do with differences between European and African peoples themselves, as white racists assume. Rather, it was due to accidents of geography and biogeography—in particular, to the continents' different areas, axes, and suites of wild plant and animal species. That is, the different historical trajectories of Africa and Europe stem ultimately from differences in real estate.

Lucy Jarosz

 NO

A Human Geographer's Response to *Guns, Germs, and Steel:* The Case of Agrarian Development and Change in Madagascar

In his book, *Guns, Germs, and Steel* (1999; hereafter *GGS*), Jared Diamond asks important questions about why wealth and power are distributed so unequally throughout the world and how this pattern originated: "For instance, why weren't Native Americans, Africans, and Aboriginal Australians the ones who decimated, subjugated, or exterminated Europeans and Asians?" (p 15). He identifies the possession of guns, germs, and steel as the critical explanation, tracing their arrival in European imperial hands through a 13,000-year history of agriculture and technology. According to Diamond's argument, Europe's colonization of Africa was due to "accidents of geography and biogeography—in particular, to the continents' different areas, axes, and suites of wild plant and animal species. That is, the different historical trajectories of Africa and Europe stem ultimately from differences in real estate" (p 401).

I appreciate Diamond's emphasis upon the role of geography within the broad sweep of human history, but as a human geographer, I am concerned by the narrow definition of geography that this widely read book puts forward. Geography encompasses the realms of the humanities and the social sciences in its examination and explanation of society-environment relations. Explaining differences in wealth and power among and within world regions and diverse societies through time must take social, economic, and political connections into account, along with their relationship to environmental attributes and ecological change, in an attempt to link global, regional, and local scales of analysis. These explanations must also consider the influence of the human imagination and sociocultural processes in shaping the diversity of agrarian and ecological landscapes.

As an example of the limits to purely environmental explanations of contemporary global disparities, I offer an overview of the political economy of food and agriculture in Madagascar. This island was subject to two distinct forms of colonization, first from East Africa, the Middle East, and Southeast Asia and subsequently from Western Europe. The first wave did not devastate the food-production economy in the way that the second wave did. The reasons for this lie with issues of politics, ideology, and power. I argue that beyond

From *Antipod*, vol. 35, no. 4, 2003, pp. 823–827. Copyright © 2003 by Blackwell Publishing, Ltd. Reprinted by permission.

environment and rates of technological diffusion, human relationships are critical to explaining the dynamics of agrarian development and change, as well as the origins of inequality.

Food and Agriculture in Pre-European Madagascar

Records of Madagascar's aboriginal populations are sparse and based upon archaeological sources and oral history. The Vazimba, the earliest human inhabitants, are believed to be of Indonesian and East African descent and settled the island between the fifth and seventh centuries. Later immigrants and sociocultural influences arrived from South and Southeast Asia, East Africa, and the Arabic peninsula between the 11th and 16th centuries (Kottak 1980). Agricultural practices on the island varied both with regional ecological attributes and with the technologies and sociocultural perspectives of local populations. Shifting cultivation was practiced throughout the island, while in the most densely inhabited area of Madagascar—the central plateau—the Merina and Betsileo people cultivated irrigated rice. Early settlers domesticated livestock in the south, which subsequently diffused to the west. This situation affirms Diamond's thesis about the multiple influences of early immigration and colonization in Africa as well as the importance of settled agriculture to the formation and advancement of sophisticated nation-states. However, the development of agriculture in Madagascar's central plateau did not depend upon exceptional environmental differences. Most of the plateau is made up of poor lateritic clay soils, and only a very small percentage—less than 5% of the total area—is able to support irrigated rice fields. This area's geology is very similar to areas of Zimbabwe, which does not support nearly the population density. This comparison prompted Gourou (1956:346) to remark,

> The geographer would be wrong if he considered the natural environment as independent from man. The natural environment in two ways depends on man: first, man has transformed profoundly the environment . . . ; second, man has interpreted the environment in terms of his techniques. The same natural environment will result in different human landscapes when interpreted (and transformed) by traditional European peasant civilization, by Chinese civilization, and by modern American civilization. The Merina of Madagascar and the Bemba of Rhodesia have created very different human landscapes in similar physical environments. No progress in understanding the human aspects of the landscape is possible if these aspects are simply considered to react to the physical elements of the landscape. Explanation does not progress if the human groups are considered to be compelled by the natural environment to adopt such-and-such techniques.

Food and Agriculture Following European Colonization

When Diego Diaz "discovered" Madagascar in 1500, a Merina monarchy headed a centralized state based upon a caste system of nobles, commoners, and slaves and managed to unite the island under a single rule based upon livestock and rice cultivation. A commercial class was conducting international trade in rice, beef, and slaves. The mixing of various groups of people on the island led to both innovation and conflict. The Merinas' hold on the island was tenuous, as war and slave-raiding among various ethnic groups were commonplace. This led the Merina monarchy to develop political and economic relations with both Britain and France in order to help consolidate its power on the island, and to hold the influence of both imperial powers in tension throughout the 1800s. These changing dynamics of sociopolitical relationships and cultural processes shaped agricultural landscapes and production and triggered imperial interest in the island.

Relationships with Britain and France were used by competing political units on the island and by aspiring dominant groups within the Merina elite to advance their political and economic agendas. Beginning in 1817, British officers helped train the Malagasy army, and a treaty with Britain recognized the Merina claim to control of the whole island. In 1863, the Merina signed trade and diplomatic treaties with both the United States and England concerning Malagasy sovereignty, commerce, and freedom of religion. The French had claimed jurisdiction over all or part of the island since the beginning of the 19th century, and these claims were pressed with growing insistence in response to the development of imperialist competition in Europe. The Merina monarchy aligned itself with Britain, hoping to protect itself from French conquest. This strategy ultimately failed. In 1890, Britain and France signed a treaty exchanging French recognition of British control over Zanzibar for British acceptance of the French claim to Madagascar. In 1896, the French claimed the island as one of its colonies, abolished the Merina monarchy, and ended trade with Britain and the United States, while a system of French monopolies and oligopolies dominated trade and credit.

This brief colonial history of Madagascar illustrates some intriguing parallels and significant discrepancies with Diamond's archetypal European conquest, the overthrow of the Inca Empire at Cajamarca. At the eve of European contact, both societies were highly organized and stratified, practiced intensive agricultural production, and engaged in long-distance trade. Diamond focuses attention on the moment of military conflict to emphasize the importance of guns, swords, horses, and smallpox in Atahuallpa's capture and the eventual conquest of the Inca Empire by Spain. These are the "proximate factors"—the means of conquest—the acquisition which Diamond sees as reflecting the "ultimate factors" of continental size and axes. While the colonial outcome in Madagascar was similar, the definitive factors in this process were not. As in the rest of Africa, germs—in the forms of malaria and dengue fever—delayed and impeded European contact and colonization. And while military power was certainly present, conquest, colonization, and impoverishment were effected by economic power through integration into the global market via taxation, slavery, and forced labor, the establishment of export crops, and resource appropriation and control. This suggests a different set of ultimate factors: the scale and intentions of the societies employing the proximal controls.

Power, Resource Extraction, and Capitalism: From Local to Global Scales

The first wave of Madagascar's colonization established settled forms of agriculture and developed international trade in agricultural products to build and maintain the wealth and power of local, regionally based elites. In the second wave, the goal was to reshape the economy and commerce so as to reorient and extract wealth and profit for French companies and creditors, rather than for the further enrichment of the Malagasy living on the island. Coffee and peas were introduced as export crops, timber was extracted, and environmental disruption and degradation ensued as taxation and forced labor laws spurred waves of regional migration and increased shifting cultivation as a crucial way to address food insecurity. Rice and beef were requisitioned to feed French troops and the slaves on sugar plantations on Mauritius. Famine and chronic food shortages were two key outcomes of the second wave of colonization.

European colonizers were similarly eager to extract and control the Incan empire's labor, land and gold. This was realized through the destruction of the political and economic power of the ruling elite and the subsequent restructuring of the empire's economy to serve the development and commercial interests of the colonizer within the global economy. I suggest that a focus upon the shifting political and economic dimensions of resource control and extraction highlights the primacy of politics and economics in European colonization as vital "ultimate factors." A focus upon the proximal military battles obscures this context and these connections in both the Inca and the Merina examples.

Environmental differences matter in contemporary global inequalities, as Diamond suggests, but so do the processes of colonization. While I agree with Diamond that it is wrong to attribute inequality and processes of colonization to any sort of racial superiority, it is also wrong to ignore the role of racism within the processes of colonization. Malagasy people were treated as animals and slaves in forced labor gangs during European colonization. The image of African people as less than human has consistently permeated racist discourse throughout the colonial and postcolonial periods; it is this aspect of colonization that Diamond challenges. However, the emphasis upon environmental difference in *GGS* lets us off the hook in terms of thinking deeply about geopolitical and economic relationships and the contributions of human ingenuity, imagination, and even cruelty to agricultural development and change. In the case of Africa, European colonization often replaced or appropriated the indigenous systems of agricultural production, resulting in the emergence of food shortages, chronic poverty, and environmental marginalization.

Environmental history and differences alone do not explain why today Madagascar is one of the poorest countries in the world. The importance of geopolitical relationships, the development of capitalism, and dynamics of regional, national, and global food networks within specific environments are critical components of an accurate understanding of inequality and poverty. It is not enough to focus on environmental difference at the millennial scale, since the forms and processes of contemporary disparity are maintained by relationships established in the recent colonial past and reworked and deepened in the postcolonial period. We must not neglect the complex linkages and relationships among European and African societies and environments, as well as the realities of imperialism, power, and racism, when explaining the harsh realities of inequality and poverty that surround us.

POSTSCRIPT

Is European Subjugation of Africans Ultimately Explained by Differences in Land, Plant, and Animal Resources?

A couple of interesting points arise from this issue. The first concerns whether or not the ideas that Diamond and others are espousing may be characterized as environmental determinism. To be fair, Diamond's argument differs from those of early twentieth-century environmental determinists in several respects. First, he does not suggest that climatic conditions directly result in a certain level of social organization and development. Rather, he asserts that settled agriculture and animal husbandry were able to first develop in those places that possessed wild plants and animals that were amenable to domestication. This is important, according to Diamond, because those societies that had densely settled agricultural populations first were more likely to develop: (1) centralized political structures, (2) writing and metallurgy, and (3) immunity to certain communicable diseases after a period of affliction. As such, resource endowments ultimately allow for certain possibilities, but they do not directly determine levels of development. Second, Diamond also attaches considerable importance to the location of a group of people vis à vis other human populations. Those groups that were in contact with other human societies and possessed similar environmental conditions were more likely to benefit from the diffusion of ideas. As such, Europeans were able to benefit from several innovations that diffused from the Middle East and Asia, even though they did make such advances independently.

Some would be more comfortable characterizing Diamond as an environmental possibilist, rather than an environmental determinist. Environmental possibilists argue that the environment presents humans societies with a range of options from which they may pick and choose. Environmental conditions are important because they constitute an initial range of possibilities. However, technology may help groups overcome certain environmental constraints. As such, humans adapt to certain environmental constraints or conditions, but the process of human adaptation is very dynamic. Yet, even allowing for such distinctions or nuances, many remain critical of Diamond (and those who share his views) for his lack of attention to the pernicious effects for Africa of the global capitalist system that slowly emerges from the age of exploration (fifteenth century) forward.

A second point of note concerns the sordid history of environmental determinism. While it is up for debate if Diamond's perspective really constitutes an environmental determinist view, it is worth underscoring that many in the sciences and social sciences in the previous era played a role in and were influenced by colonialism. Theories like environmental determinism helped justify the behavior of colonialists, by supporting the notion that people from the temperate regions (Europe) were superior to people from the tropics. Even though we may think of science as the neutral pursuit of knowledge, we should also recognize that science may be influenced by culture and politics.

For other examples of readings that partially explain varying levels of development in terms of differences in geography, see Jeffrey Sach's 1997 article in the *Economist* entitled "Nature, Nurture and Growth" or Ricardo Hausmann's 2001 article in *Foreign Policy* entitled "Prisoners of Geography." For a text that questions this view, see *Late Victorian Holocausts* by historian Mike Davis (Verso Press, 2002).

ISSUE 4

Did Colonialism Distort Contemporary African Development?

YES: Marcus Colchester, from "Slave and Enclave: Towards a Political Ecology of Equatorial Africa," *The Ecologist* (September/October 1993)

NO: Robin M. Grier, from "Colonial Legacies and Economic Growth," *Public Choice* (March 1999)

ISSUE SUMMARY

YES: Marcus Colchester, director of the Forest Peoples Programme of the World Rainforest Movement, argues that rural communities in equatorial Africa are today on the point of collapse because they have been weakened by centuries of outside intervention. In Gabon, the Congo, and the Central African Republic, an enduring colonial legacy of the French are lands and forests controlled by state institutions that operate as patron-client networks to enrich indigenous elite and outside commercial interests.

NO: Robin M. Grier, assistant professor of economics at the University of Oklahoma, contends that African colonies that were held for longer periods of time tend to have performed better, on average, after independence.

The degree to which the colonial experience has impacted contemporary patterns of development in Africa is a major issue of discussion. Prior to 1880 roughly 90 percent of sub-Saharan Africa was still ruled by Africans. Of course slavery had had a profound impact on the continent, but the European presence in Africa was limited largely to coastal enclaves before this time. At the famous Berlin Conference of 1884–1885 (at which Africans were not represented), the European powers established ground rules to divide up the continent. Two decades later the only uncolonized states were Ethiopia and Liberia. The principal colonial powers in Africa were Great Britain and France, followed by Portugal, Belgium, Germany, and Spain. Italy would also control some African countries in the late colonial period.

What were the objectives of European colonial endeavors in Africa? Of course the colonizers themselves suggested, or rationalized, that they were agents of progress who had a civilizing influence on the African people. The reality, widely accepted by scholars today, is that African lands and peoples were colonized to provide key raw materials for the European powers. While accepting resource extraction as the principal goal of colonialism, some scholars assert that the experience had some positive benefits, namely the development of infrastructure (roads, railroads, etc.) and educational and medical systems that benefit the African peoples today. Others suggest that the influence of colonialism has been overblown, and that African leaders merely use the colonial experience as a scapegoat for their own mismanagement of African affairs.

Those who suggest that colonialism has had an enduring negative influence on Africa point out that the infrastructure, as well as the educational systems left behind, nonsensical national borders, and the political legacy of colonial governance, all serve to distort, rather than to facilitate, contemporary economic and political development. For example, the roads and railways built during the colonial era often extend from the capital or port city to interior regions rich in resources, rather than connecting a country in a fashion that would promote national unity. Educational systems emphasized rote learning as they were developed to train low-level civil servants, rather than managers and directors. Enduring and nonsensical national borders have compromised the economic viability of many African nations (there are a large number of landlocked countries in Africa) and aggravated ethnic tensions (because they often do not respect ethnic boundaries). Finally, colonial governance was anything but democratic.

In the following selections, Marcus Colchester and Robin M. Grier present contrasting views on the enduring legacy of colonialism in Africa. Colchester examines contemporary patterns of resource extraction in equatorial Africa and draws a link between these and colonial practices. In Gabon, the Congo, and the Central African Republic, an enduring colonial legacy of the French are lands and forests controlled by state institutions that operate as patron-client networks to enrich indigenous elite and outside commercial interests. In many ways, Colchester is suggesting that colonial patterns of resource extraction never really ended; we simply have gone from overt colonial control to neocolonial regimes of extraction in the postindependence era. In contrast, Grier argues that on average, African colonies that were held for longer periods of time tend to perform better after independence. Furthermore, she asserts that the level of education at the time of independence helps explain the development gap between former British and French colonies in Africa.

Marcus Colchester

Slave and Enclave: Towards a Political Ecology of Equatorial Africa

The three countries of Equatorial Africa—Gabon, the Congo and the Central African Republic (CAR)—are among the most urbanized in Africa, largely as a result of the resettling of rural communities in colonial times. Of a total population of five million, only some 40 per cent live in rural areas, comprising about one hundred, linguistically closely-related peoples who are described in Western anthropology as the "Western Bantu", as well as some 120,000 "pygmies". Those remaining in the forests are reliant on self-provisioning economies, based on shifting cultivation, treecropping, hunting and fishing.

Some 47 million hectares of closed tropical forests in the three countries, combined with those of neighbouring Angola, Cameroon, Zaire and Equatorial Guinea, make up the second largest area of closed tropical forests in the world after Amazonia. These forests are some of the most diverse in Africa, and contain an abundance of wildlife, including forest elephants, lowland gorillas, various kinds of chimpanzees, forest antelopes and a wide variety of birds.

The social and political structures of Equatorial Africa have been markedly transformed by the European slave trade, the French colonial era and by the subsequent interventions of commercial interests and the new African states. Despite the current political liberalization taking place in Gabon, the Congo and the Central African Republic after three decades of single party politics, the forests and the peoples who rely on them are still being sidelined.

The Slave Trade

Long before Bantu society came into contact with colonial Europeans, its egalitarian traditions—a reflection of mobile, decentralized settlements which included an unease towards the accretion of power—had been progressively overlain during several centuries by more hierarchical forms of social organization, resulting from warfare and competition for land. This process had gradually reduced the accountability of leaders to their people with disastrous social and, later, ecological consequences. The European slave trade, however, is the most obvious example of this phenomenon, during which several millions of

Africans died and millions more were transported overseas. The Portuguese began the trade in slaves on the coasts of Equatorial Africa around 1580, but it only became vigorous after about 1640. The European slavers themselves, however, were minimally engaged in raiding, never going far inland. Capture was carried out by Africans which not only intensified raiding and war between local African communities but also transformed previous systems of bondage and servile working conditions into those of absolute slavery.

This meant that slaving had a profound impact not only on those communities whose members were captured but also on those engaged in the trade. To gain control of the trading network, dispersed and differentiated social groups merged their numbers and identities to increase their power and domain. These groups were dominated by "trading firms" often comprising a chief and his sons. The increasing importance of inheritable wealth, capital accumulation and the corresponding need to resist redistributive customs led many matrilineal societies of the middle Congo to become patrilineal. Trading firms swelled their numbers by recruiting male and female slaves as labour and as wives to produce pliable heirs devoid of inheritance rights through the maternal line.

Colonial Repression and Resistance

Direct colonial rule of Equatorial Africa by the French from the 1880s onwards further exacerbated the tendency towards more hierarchical forms of social organization. As the French government was unable and unwilling to administer directly the vast area of more than 700,000 square kilometres, it allocated 80 per cent of the region to some 40 companies.

Within these vast concessions—the area controlled by the Compagnie Française du Haut Congo encompassed 3.6 million hectares—the companies had almost sovereign control including the right to their own police force and legislation, slavery, violence, killing and inhuman punishment were widely documented. Their express aim was to extract the natural resources—chiefly wild rubber, timber, ivory, and later coffee, cocoa and palm oil—as cheaply and as quickly as possible.

Labour shortages, rather than shortages of land, were the main constraint of these enclave economies. To extract labour for the concession areas, plantations, road-building, portage and, in the 1920s and 1930s, for building the Congo-Ocean railroad, "man hunts" became fundamental to the colonial economy. The military was used to support concessionaires who had insufficient labour. In the rubber regions of Ubangi (now the Central African Republic), for example, villagers who did not manage to flee from the troops sent in to ensure their "participation" were tied together and brought naked to the forests to tap the rubber vines. They lived in the open and ate whatever they could find. A French missionary who witnessed the scene wrote: "The population was reduced to the darkest misery . . . never had they lived through such times, not even in the worst days of the Arab [slaving] invasions."

The colonial authorities also introduced various taxes and levies to oblige local peoples to enter the cash economy; in practice, this meant to work for the concessionaires. Along the coasts, logging rapidly replaced the trade in non-timber products, becoming the foundation for the political economy of the region. The extraction was carried out with axes and handsaws, the huge logs being dragged by hand to the rivers and floated out to waiting trading ships. By the 1930s, an estimated third to one half of men from the interior villages of what is now Gabon had been brought down to the logging camps on the coast, where they worked for minimal wages and in appalling conditions for months at a time. Disease was rife, alcoholism rampant and thousands died. Meanwhile, the workload of the women and children who remained in the villages increased correspondingly and their health too was undermined by the numerous diseases—influenza, yellow fever, sleeping sickness and venereal infections—which returning labourers brought back.

The conscience of the colonial authorities was obviously pricked by the all too evident degradation and exploitation of the local people. As Governor General Reste noted in 1937:

> "The logging camps are great devourers of men . . . Everything has been subordinated to the exploitation of the forest. The forests have sterilized Gabon, smacking down the men and taking off with the women. This is the image of Gabon: a land without roads, without social programmes, without economic organization, the exploitation of forests having sapped all the living force from the country . . . There is not a single indigenous teacher, doctor or vet, agricultural officer or public works agent."

Those making the profits—some two billion francs between 1927 and 1938—were a few French companies in whose hands the logging concessions were concentrated. By 1939, of the one million hectares of Gabon under concessions, 66 per cent was controlled by just seven companies with only some 84 others controlling the rest. These companies were to play a key role in the transition to Independence.

Resistance, however, was widespread throughout French Equatorial Africa; villages flared up against demands to yield labour and forest products to the concessionaires and taxation to the French administration. The result was a protracted and brutal war in which the colonial regime sought to bring the whole interior of the colony under its control to facilitate its commercial exploitation. The taking of hostages, including women and children, pillage, arbitrary imprisonment, executions and massacres, the torching of settlements and the sacking of whole communities were commonplace. By the 1930s, when the last areas of resistance were being quashed in what is now the west of the Central African Republic, the French were using planes to spot villagers hiding out in the forests before sending in the army to bring them out.

Regroupement des Villages

Resettlement of dispersed and shifting African communities into larger, permanent villages on roads and portage trails became a central plank of French administrative policy throughout its colony. One of the main aims of this *regroupement des villages* was to control the local people—to oblige them to render tax and labour and to prevent further rebellions.

Regroupement had devastating impacts on the local peoples. One missionary reported to André Gide that the local people:

> "prefer anything, even death to portage . . . Dispersion of the tribes has been going on for more than a year. Villages are breaking up, families are scattering, everyone abandons his tribes, village, family and plot to live in the bush like wild animals to escape being recruited. No more cultivation, no more food . . . "

In the early days of colonial rule, it was carried out with little if any consideration of customary land rights, causing conflicts over land between different social groups. Traditional institutions, residence patterns and ties with the land were overturned while overcrowding in the new villages led to declining standards of nutrition and exposed people to epidemics. Sleeping sickness increased throughout the region in the first half of the 20th century, causing a massive decline in population.

Even after Independence in 1960, Gabon and the Congo pursued the policy right into the 1970s. As a regional *préfèt* noted in Gabon in 1963:

> "We have had enough of these isolated hamlets, which, being so numerous and of eccentric location, lost in the vastness of the Gabonese forest, have never allowed the Gabonese government to have control of their populations or permanent contact with them and have thereby prevented an improvement of their standard of living."

Convinced that "no family head can cut himself off from the duty to modernize", the post-colonial government continued to tear villages away from their crops without any compensation, overturning residence patterns that reflected local ways of life and throwing into disarray, at least temporarily, traditional systems for allocating rights to land. In some respects, *regroupement* under the independent administration was more onerous than in the colonial era: houses in the new settlements had to be laid out in regular rows with defined sizes of houseplots and pathways.

The Indigenous Elite

The striking continuity between the colonial and independence policies was assured by an élite of French-educated Africans. Under French law, most Africans were subject to the *indigenat*, a set of laws which ascribed an inferior status to local people: "persons under the *indigenat* were subject to penalties and taxation without the legal protection afforded 'citizens'". However, a small number of Frenchified indigenous people were considered as *évolué* and thus accorded "citizen" status, becoming a local "élite attuned to the French presence and subservient to its interests".

Cooption of the indigenous leadership extended down to the community level through a hierarchy of *chefs du canton* and *chefs du village*, chosen to act as intermediaries between the villagers and the authorities. Dependent on the colonial administration for their positions and often resented and even secretly ridiculed by the villagers themselves, these leaders became ready tools in the colonialists' hands and assisted with the unjust exploitation in the concessions. Favoured ethnic groups emerged, considered to be more "evolved" and less "backward"; groups which had been intermediaries in pre-colonial trade now became an important support base for the administration. This structure and practice still persist; local leaders and chiefs, and favoured ethnic groups, continue to owe their primary allegiance to the urban élites and to the administration, not to the villagers or to the remoter, more traditional, rural communities.

Independence: *Plus Ça Change . . .*

After Independence from France in 1960, French Equatorial Africa was divided into the three countries of Gabon, the Congo and the Central African Republic, a division based on the previous colonial administrative divisions. The crucial concern of the departing colonial power was to ensure that the new "independent" governments supported French interests; President de Gaulle warned African states that "France would intervene if it considered its interests in jeopardy." In both Gabon and the Congo, France's principal aim was to guarantee that French logging companies were assured continued access to the forests. Maintaining access to strategic minerals, notably manganese and uranium, the latter being of critical importance to France's civil and military nuclear programme, was also central to French policy. In the Central African Republic, France's main preoccupation was to protect its cotton, coffee and diamond interests.

Gabon

French interests were decisive in selecting the future leadership in Gabon after Independence; French logging interests poured funds into the successful election campaign of Leon Mba, an *évolué* from the coastal region. After Mba's accession to power, the press was suppressed, political demonstrations banned, freedom of expression curtailed, other political parties gradually excluded from power and the Constitution changed along French lines to vest power in the Presidency, a post that Mba assumed himself. However, when Mba dissolved the National Assembly in January 1964 to institute one-party rule, an army coup sought to oust him from power and restore parliamentary democracy.

The extent to which Mba's dictatorial regime was synonymous with "French interests" then became blatantly apparent. Within twenty-four hours of the coup, French paratroops flew in to restore Mba to power. After a few days of fighting, the coup was over and the opposition imprisoned, despite widespread protests and riots. The French government was unperturbed by international condemnation of the intervention; the paratroops still remain in the Camp de Gaulle on the outskirts of Gabon's capital, Libreville, to this day, where they share a hilltop with the presidential palace, an unforgettable symbol of the coincidence of interests between the French and the ruling indigenous élite.

With the establishment of a one-party state, abuse of power and office became the norm. Wealth became more concentrated in the hands of the ruling élite, and the network of patronage became further removed from the concerns of ordinary citizens. The Presidency passed smoothly from Mba to Omar Bongo, "the choice of a powerful group of Frenchmen whose influence in Gabon continued after independence." Bongo and his cronies have since amassed substantial fortunes, having "transformed Gabon into their private preserve, handsomely enriching themselves in the process". They have transferred *billions* of French francs annually to Swiss and French banks. Opponents of the regime have been arbitrarily imprisoned and tortured, among other human rights violations.

Central African Republic

Post-Independence politics in the Central African Republic were not dissimilar. After the independent-minded first President Barthelemy Boganda died in an aeroplane accident, his successor, David Dacko, received strong French support. But Dacko's repressive policies and lack of effective economic reforms made him unpopular locally; he was widely perceived as a "French puppet caring only about cultivating French interests."

When Jean-Bedel Bokassa replaced Dacko on New Year's Day 1966, it seemed that the country, which had been virtually bankrupted by Dacko's regime, might be given a chance to recover. However, Bokassa's capricious and violent rule became synonymous with the worst excesses of African dictatorship—"the systematic perversion of the state into a predatory instrument of its ruler". Massive corruption was the norm, and Bokassa himself appeared to make no distinction between the revenues to the state treasury and his personal income.

France only withdrew its support for the regime in 1979, when it was revealed that Bokassa visited prisons personally to torture and kill those who had stood up to his whims. As in Gabon, French paratroops were sent in and Dacko restored to power, to be replaced on his death in 1981 by army strongman General Andre Kolingba, the current President.

Congo

Independence in the Congo pursued a different course. Initially, the post-Independence regime was modelled in the neo-colonial mould—servile to French political and economic interests. However, "it was swiftly corroded by venality and became an embarrassment not only to its internal supporters but also to its French sponsors". After a street uprising in 1963, the regime was overthrown and a Marxist-Leninist government assumed power. The French did not intervene.

French influence within the Congo remained strong, however, and, despite the Congolese government's rhetoric to the contrary, the role of foreign capital was scarcely diminished. Although the state created marketing monopolies for agriculture and forestry, and nationalized some other sectors—including the petroleum distribution network—the timber concessions, some of the oil palm plantations and many other import-export concerns remained in foreign hands. Foreign oil companies, too, were assured a satisfactory cut.

Logging Enclave Perpetuated

In all three countries of Equatorial Africa, logging has intensified since Independence. Mechanized logging extended the area of extraction during the 1970s and 1980s, up to the remote forests of the northern Congo and the south of the CAR; the rate of extraction increased some six-fold between 1950 and 1970. The industry has remained an enclave of foreign companies who enjoy the patronage of the governing élites. In the Congo, foreign companies, or joint operations dominated by foreign capital, produce the vast bulk of the timber—nearly 80 per cent of the sawlogs, 90 per cent of the sawn wood and 92 per cent of the plywood. In common with both the Gabon and the CAR, the Congolese government "largely lacks adequate technical and economic competence to control and rationally manage its forests".

During the 1970s, logging in the Congo was widely used as a fraudulent mechanism for capital flight, through false declarations of the quantity and type of timber being exported and through transfer pricing. The government attempted to curb this by creating a state monopoly to market timber, but the inefficient and ineffective agency ran at a loss due to collusion between loggers and officials.

A leaked report, prepared for the World Bank, reveals that the logging industry in the Congo is still swindling the government of millions of dollars. Unpaid taxes, stamp duty, transport and stumpage (duty payable on each tree cut) fees are estimated to exceed US$12 million on declared production alone, while huge quantities of timber are slipping across the border illegally into neighbouring Cameroon and Central African Republic. According to the report, "almost all the companies in the forestry sector are 'outside the law'" and "forestry administration is nonexistent". As a result, "the forest is left to the mercy of the loggers who do what they like without being accountable to anyone".

Companies are taking maximum advantage of this lack of supervision. For example, the French company, Forestière Nord Congo, has exclusive rights over 10 years to log some 187,000 hectares in the north of the country. Its contract obliges the company to process 60 per cent of the logs on site and to establish a major sawmill and wood-processing works constructed out of new, imported materials. In exchange, Forestière Nord Congo has received generous benefits—substantially reduced import duties and a five-year tax holiday on wood production, including company taxes, property tax and stumpage fees. Yet, in complete violation of the agreement, the company bought a non-functioning second-hand mill, has not processed any timber, has exported sawlogs for six years through its tax loophole, and has not paid even the tax it should have rendered. In total, Forestière Nord Congo has cost the Congo some US$2.9 million in lost revenue.

Elsewhere, the Société Congolais Bois de Ouesso (whose board includes the Congolese President himself) received foreign "aid" in the late 1980s and early 1990s to install a highly-sophisticated saw mill and veneer producing works. With technical advice from the Finnish company, Jaako Poyry Oy, the World Bank backed the project with some US$12 million. But costs soon rocketed from an estimated US$39 million to US$63 million. Further loans were incurred from several African banks, but the mill was never completed; today only a small sawmill is working. The World Bank report notes "the situation is catastrophic and no further activity within the present arrangement is possible". The company's failure is attributed "quite simply to the overvaluation of the project which has allowed some vultures to enrich themselves immeasurably at the Congo's expense."

In the Central African Republic, where concessions have been granted in 48 per cent of the "exploitable" forests, the accountability of the logging industry is more lax. Illegal cross-border logging into the forests of north Congo was observed by FAO [Food and Agriculture Organization] technicians in the mid-1970s, and smuggling of timber down the Oubangi and Congo rivers to the Congolese capital, Brazzaville, on the Zairean border was normal. Today it is common knowledge in Bangui, the capital of the Central African Republic, that nearly all the forest concessions are being illegally logged, the regulations are flouted and much of the timber is clandestinely leaving the country via new road connections with Cameroon. CAR President Kolingba himself is alleged to be closely linked to businessman M. Kamash who owns SCADS, the company which processes timber illegally slipped across the border from north Congo. In common with all the concessionaires in the country, "SCAD carries out no management and employs no foresters—they are just timber merchants who mine the forests".

Since the Gabonese forestry service is funded from the central government budget rather than through stumpage fees and other tariffs on logging itself, there are few incentives for foresters to impose the many rules and regulations to control logging, while the loggers themselves make sure the foresters are provided with suitable incentives not to apply them.

Rural Stagnation

For the rural communities of Equatorial Africa, the long history of exploitative, extractive and enclavistic development has meant marginalization and poverty. Despite the statistically high per capita incomes of Gabon and the Congo relative to other Sub-Saharan countries, the rural people are poor and getting poorer.

The explicit aim of most government efforts concerning agriculture has been to replace itinerant, family-based, labour-intensive agriculture with fixed, capital-intensive, mechanized agriculture serviced by wage labour. Heavily-subsidized agribusiness schemes to promote large-scale farming—cattle ranches, sugar plantations, battery farms of poultry, rice schemes, rubber and oil palm estates, and banana plantations—have undercut small farmers, destroying the last elements of a cohesive rural society.

A century of neglect and disruption of small-holder agriculture has had inevitable consequences. In the Central African Republic, only one per cent of the country is farmed. In Gabon, agriculture accounts for only eight per cent of the GDP [gross domestic product], occupies only 0.5 per cent of the land area and supplies only 10–15 per cent of the country's food needs, the remaining 85 per cent being imported; even traditional peasant crops such as taro, yams, mangoes, avocados and vegetables are imported from neighbouring states, particularly Cameroon.

In the Congo, agriculture yields only 5.9 per cent of GDP. Since Independence, there has been a massive migration to the cities. By 1990, 52 per cent of the total population, and 85 per cent of men aged between 25 and 29 years, lived in two cities alone, Brazzaville and Pointe Noire, although the Congo barely has any industrial base. As in colonial times, the lack of young men in the countryside means that 70 per cent of Congolese farms are managed by women. Education, preferentially given to young men, exacerbates this trend, resulting in the towns being considered the domain of men and the countryside that of women.

The marginalization of smallholder agriculture has also transformed local political institutions. Increasing mobility has weakened community ties and diminished customs which favour the redistribution of wealth and land. Echoing the political shifts which took place during the European slave trade, matrilineal groups have become more patrilineal and marriages with women classified as "slaves" (that is, without lineage and therefore without kin to make demands on agnatic inheritance) have been favoured. These internal trends have been reinforced by imposed national laws which favour cognatic succession, all tendencies which have further weakened the status and security of women.

Robin M. Grier

 NO

Colonial Legacies and Economic Growth

Introduction

Development theorists have long hypothesized whether the identity of the colonial power mattered for subsequent growth and development. Many authors . . . once concluded that the colonial experience was insignificantly different under the major colonial powers. Recent research though has shown that colonialism did significantly affect development patterns. . . . In this [selection], I examine whether the duration of colonization has a significant effect on later development and growth and whether human or physical capital in place at the time of independence can help to explain why British colonies perform significantly better than French ones.

In the first empirical application of the [selection], I pool data from 63 former colonies and find that the length of colonization is positively and significantly correlated with economic growth over the 1961–1990 period. While the direction of causality is not conclusive, I find no evidence to support exploitation theory. Given that a country was colonized, since it would be impossible to test the counterfactual hypothesis, the longer it was held by the mother country, the better it did economically in the post-colonial era.

In the second empirical application, I reduce my sample to 24 countries in Africa. . . . I find that the length of colonization is still positively and significantly related to economic growth and that former British colonies still outperform their French counterparts. . . . I find that the newly independent British colonies were significantly more educated than the French ones. . . . I find that the inclusion of education at independence can explain the development gap between the former British and French colonies and the positive relationship between length of colonization and growth. . . .

Data and Variables

My empirical work addresses two questions. First, does the length of the colonization period matter for subsequent growth and development? Second, can education levels at the time of independence explain why British ex-colonies perform significantly better than their French counterparts?

From *Public Choice*, March 1999, pp. 317–318, 321–326, 328. Copyright © 1999 by Springer Science and Business Media. Reprinted by permission.

In the first empirical application of the [selection], I perform a cross national study of 63 ex-colonial states and test to see whether the length of colonization is correlated with subsequent growth rates. . . . In the second empirical application, I reduce the sample to British and French Africa and test whether the duration of colonization matters for later development and whether human or physical capital levels at the time of independence can help to explain why British ex-colonies perform better on average than French ones. . . .

Econometric Results

Does the Identity of the Colonizing Power Matter for Economic Growth?

Five year averages are calculated on data from 63 countries for the years 1961–1990, resulting in 6 observations for each country and a sample size of 378 data points. . . .

Because of the vast differences in the length of colonization for different ex-colonial states, I add a variable called TIME to determine the effect of the duration of colonialism on subsequent growth, where TIME is the year of independence less the year of arrival. The most common argument against colonialism is that it exploited the native population, causing dependency and instability in the colonial states. The results . . . show that TIME is positively and significantly related to subsequent economic growth. I do not claim that longer colonization causes higher economic growth, but my findings do reject a crude form of the exploitation theory. While it is possible that countries in my sample might have had higher growth rates if they had not been subjected to colonialism, the results do show that colonies that were held for longer periods of time than other colonies have had more economic success in the post-colonial era. . . .

Does Colonialism Matter for African Development?

. . . I found that former French colonies perform significantly worse on average than British ones. It is possible that an African effect is exaggerating the development gap between the two. Because all of the French colonies were African (except Haiti, whose population is primarily African), and Africa has been characterized by poverty and underdevelopment in the last century, it may be that an African effect is biasing the earlier results. Limiting the sample to Africa also gets rid of the high-performing British outliers, like the United States and Canada, and helps to better distinguish the differences between French and British non-settlement colonies. . . .

French ex-colonies perform 1.38 percentage points worse on average than their British counterparts. That is, even when the sample is limited to Africa, the former French colonies still lag significantly behind the British ones. . . .

The results also show TIME to be positively and significantly related to economic growth, which implies that the length of colonization is positively related to growth and development. The next section, which examines the institutional legacies of colonialism, tries to determine why TIME is significantly related to growth and why the French ex-colonies perform worse than British ones, even when the sample is restricted to Africa.

The Colonial Legacy

To determine why ex-British colonies perform better than French ones, I look at the level of human and physical capital the colonizing power left at independence. . . . [E]ducation is an important component of growth and development. The British and French had contrasting philosophies of education, which translated into very different types of colonial education. The largest difference between colonial education policies is that the British made a conscious effort to avoid alienating the native culture, by teaching in the vernacular languages and training teachers from the indigenous tribes. While most of the teachers in French Africa were imported from France, the Advisory Committee on Native Education in the British Tropical African Dependencies recommended that, "Teachers for village schools should, when possible, be selected from pupils belonging to the tribe and district who are familiar with its language, tradition, and customs. . . ."

Students in British Africa were, for the most part, taught in their native language and in their tribal villages, which significantly eased the learning process. In contrast, in the French system, most students were boarded and only able to go home for the summertime vacation. Students were required to speak French, and all vernacular languages were forbidden. . . .

Conclusion

The literature on colonialism and underdevelopment is mostly theoretical and anecdotal, and has, for the most part, failed to take advantage of the more formal empirical work being done in new growth theory. This essay has tried to close that gap by presenting some empirical tests of oft-debated questions in the literature.

I find that the identity of the colonizing power has a significant and permanent effect on subsequent growth and development, which would deny the validity of a crude exploitation hypothesis. Colonies that were held for longer periods of time than other countries tend to perform better, on average, after independence. This finding holds up even when the sample is reduced to British and French Africa.

I also find that the level of education at the time of independence can help to explain much of the development gap between the former British and French colonies in Africa. Even correcting for the length of colonization, which has a positive influence on education levels and subsequent growth, I find support for a separate British effect on education. That is, the data imply that the British were more successful in educating their dependents than were the French.

POSTSCRIPT

Did Colonialism Distort Contemporary African Development?

Colchester describes a long process wherein relatively egalitarian and decentralized rural Bantu settlements in equatorial Africa were slowly transformed into more hierarchical forms of social organization. This process began with warfare and competition among Africans, was exacerbated by the slave trade and French colonial rule (for an excellent discussion of contemporary academic debates regarding the involvement of Africans in the trans-Atlantic slave trade, see Lassina Kaba's 2000 article in the *African Studies Review*, entitled "The Atlantic Slave Trade Was Not a 'Black-on-Black' Holocaust"), and continues today as the indigenous elite are more responsive to outside commercial interests than their own people. The limited accountability of leaders to their own people has led to exploitative logging with disastrous social and ecological consequences. As such, colonialism is not solely responsible for the lack of accountability among some African leaders in equatorial Africa today, but Colchester would argue that it definitely facilitated such behavior and created a set of relationships between French and African elites that persist today.

The process by which African elites were co-opted is worth highlighting. Colchester describes a Frenchified indigenous elite who were considered "advanced" enough to be granted French-citizen status. Through a process of acculturation, this elite came to share in and promote the interests of the French in their colonies. This approach, adopted by the French in their African colonies, is often referred to as the *policy of assimilation*. The policy of assimilation held out the carrot to all Africans (in French colonies) of potentially becoming French citizens. Although seemingly egalitarian on the one hand, it was a terribly ethnocentric policy on the other because it asserted that Africans only became civilized by adopting French culture. In many ways, the French policy of assimilation was an effective strategy for developing the group of "dependent elites" conceptualized by Andre Gunder Frank in his dependency theory.

The French policy of assimilation may be contrasted with the British policy of indirect rule. In nonsettler colonies such as Ghana and Nigeria, the policy of indirect rule meant that the British administered a country via its traditional leaders (up to a certain level in the colonial hierarchy). This difference in policy approaches is often used to explain why the British invested more heavily in education (because they relied on more Africans to run the colonial civil service). This is also a difference highlighted by Grier in her article for this issue. Grier further notes that the British encouraged instruction, at least at the lower grade levels, in local languages, whereas the French insisted that local people be educated in French (an approach consistent with their policy of assimilation).

Of course the French and the British were not the only colonial powers in Africa, but their approaches receive the most attention among academics because they had the largest number of colonies. For further information on the legacy of British and French colonialism, see a book chapter by the well-known Africanist Crawford Young, entitled "The Heritage of Colonialism," in John W. Harbeson and Donald Rothchild, eds., *Africa in World Politics: The African State System in Flux* (Westview Press, 2000). The Belgians and Portuguese have a reputation for having been particularly brutal colonial powers. See Adam Hochschild, *King Leopold's Ghost: A Story of Greed, Terror, and Heroism in Colonial Africa* (Houghton Mifflin, 1998) for a gripping account of conditions in the Belgian Congo, or Allen Isaacman, *Cotton Is the Mother of Poverty: Peasants, Work, and Rural Struggle in Colonial Mozambique, 1931–1961* (Heinemann, 1996), regarding the situation under the Portuguese in Mozambique.

Internet References . . .

World Bank Group for Sub-Saharan Africa

World Bank Group for Sub-Saharan Africa includes annual reports, publications, speeches, and other sources of information about issues including rural development, education, and the incorporation of indigenous knowledge into development.

```
http://web.worldbank.org/WBSITE/EXTERNAL/COUNTRIES/
     AFRICAEXT/0,,menuPK:258649~pagePK:158889
        ~piPK:146815~theSitePK:258644,00.html
```

United Nations Development Programme

The United Nations Development Programme provides information on UN development work in Africa. A wide range of topics is covered, including poverty and globalization.

```
http://www.undp.org/dpa/publications/
            regions.html#Africa
```

Economic Commission for Africa

The United Nations' Economic Commission for Africa provides information on the regional integration of African economies, including information on regional economic organizations. The organization is attempting to reform and integrate African economies to improve the quality of life on the continent.

```
http://www.uneca.org/
```

United States Agency for International Development (USAID) in Africa

USAID in Africa details African development from the perspective of USAID, the bilateral development assistance arm of the U.S. government. Information is available by country, topic, or date and ranges from short articles and press releases to full publications.

```
http://www.usaid.gov/locations/sub-saharan_africa/
```

Development

*W*hat constitutes "development" in the African context very much *remains an open question. Since the majority of African nations gained independence in the 1960s, how best to pursue this process has been an oft-debated question. The role of the state, the commercial sector, international financial institutions, and nonprofit organizations in development is highly contested. Controversies also have raged over the extent to which Africa's progress on the development front has been influenced by its position in the global economic system, its relationship to major economic powers, and its resource endowments.*

- Have Free-Market Policies Worked for Africa?
- Are Abundant Mineral and Energy Resources a Catalyst for African Development?
- Is Increasing Chinese Investment Good for African Development?

ISSUE 5

Have Free-Market Policies Worked for Africa?

YES: Gerald Scott, from "Who Has Failed Africa? IMF Measures or the African Leadership?" *Journal of Asian and African Studies* (August 1998)

NO: Thandika Mkandawire, from "The Global Economic Context," in B. Wisner, C. Toulmin, and R. Chitiga, eds., *Towards a New Map of Africa* (Earthscan, 2005)

ISSUE SUMMARY

YES: Gerald Scott, an economist at Florida Atlantic University, argues that structural adjustment programs are the most promising option for promoting economic growth in Africa. He disputes the evidence used to suggest that these programs have a deleterious effect on economic growth in Africa.

NO: Thandika Mkandawire, director of the UN Research Institute for Social Development, counters that, even though African governments have reshaped domestic policies to make their economies more open, growth has faltered. Mkandawire assesses structural adjustment from a developmental perspective, judging its effects on economic development and the eradication of poverty. He suggests that structural adjustment policies designed to integrate Africa into the global economy have failed because "they have completely sidestepped the developmental needs of the continent and the strategic questions on the form of integration appropriate to addressing these needs."

Both the World Bank and the International Monetary Fund or IMF (along with the World Trade Organization) are sometimes referred to as Bretton Woods institutions because they (or their predecessors) were established during a conference of the major economic powers at Bretton Woods, New Hampshire, in 1944 (as the end of World War II was in sight). The World Bank, or International Bank for Reconstruction and Development (IBRD), was established to rebuild Europe and Japan in the aftermath of the war and the IMF was created to provide loans to help countries resolve short-term balance of payment problems. The IMF and the World Bank have persisted as major multilateral economic development institutions that are particularly influential in Africa. These institutions are more influential in Africa because much of the debt incurred by national governments is public rather than private (i.e., loans from bilateral or multilateral development agencies rather than loans from commercial banks). In Africa, the IMF tends to focus on lending to resolve short-term problems (e.g., controlling inflation) whereas the World Bank has a slightly longer, "developmental" view.

Following the Third World "debt crisis" of the 1970s, the World Bank and the IMF initiated a form of policy-based lending known as structural adjustment. Prior to this time, much of the lending of the World Bank, in particular, had been project or program based. So, for example, in the 1960s the World Bank funded a number of infrastructure projects in Africa (such as dams), slowly transitioning to more programmatic funding related to basic needs in the 1970s (such as rural health care projects). The policy-based lending that began in the 1980s was somewhat different (than traditional project or program-based lending) in that loans were held out as a carrot for countries that agreed to undertake a series of policy reforms. The basic aim of structural adjustment reform was to balance state budgets and, as either a cause or effect of the first, promote economic growth. According to the World Bank, the basic way to achieve such an end was to cut government expenditures and raise revenues, but not in a way that would encumber economic growth.

Policy reforms under the structural adjustment rubric in Africa include the privatization of inefficient state-run enterprises (which, if they are inefficient enough, may be a drain on the state treasury); a reduction of staffing and programming in state agencies in order to cut costs; the devaluation of national currencies in situations where they are deemed overvalued; and a redoubling of efforts in the export sector to foster the generation of foreign exchange. Overvalued currencies are seen as problematic because they may make a country's exports artificially expensive (and may reduce export potential) and its imports artificially inexpensive (and thereby encourage the overconsumption of imported products).

As evidenced by the readings in this issue, the effectiveness and appropriateness of structural adjustment in the African context is hugely controversial. In this issue, Gerald Scott, an economist at Florida State University, argues that structural adjustment programs are the most promising option for promoting economic growth in Africa. He disputes the evidence used to suggest that structural adjustment programs have a deleterious effect on economic growth in Africa. Furthermore, he suggests that economic malaise in Africa is a result of corruption and mismanagement. In contrast, Thandika Mkandawire, director of the UN Research Institute for Social Development, finds little evidence to suggest that structural adjustment policies have been successful. After over 20 years of adjustment, he suggests that it is now widely accepted that these policies have failed to promote development. He argues that African countries now need to "bring development back in" by introducing "more explicit, more subtle and more daring policies to stimulate growth, trade, and export diversification than hitherto."

YES

Gerald Scott

Who Has Failed Africa? IMF Measures or the African Leadership?

Introduction

Many writers have suggested that International Monetary Fund (IMF) Structural Adjustment Programs in Africa have not only damaged growth prospects for many countries, but have further worsened an already badly skewed income distribution. Some of these writers have claimed that IMF programs have ignored the domestic social and political objectives, economic priorities, and circumstances of members, in spite of commitments to do so. In a recent article, an African critic submitted that IMF measures have failed Africa. He claimed that "after adopting various structural adjustment programs, many [African] countries are actually worse off." Not unlike many, he seems to be suggesting that IMF programs have been somewhat responsible for the severe decline in economic conditions. Some critics of IMF programs have pointed out that the fact that economic conditions have deteriorated is not conclusive proof that conditions would be better without IMF programs. They do however stress that the developments associated with IMF programs have been extremely unsatisfactory. At the same time, this association does not necessarily imply that IMF programs cause economic decline in the region.

The main purpose of this [selection] is to argue that of all the feasible alternatives for solving Africa's current economic problems, IMF Programs are the most promising. The [selection] will not contend that the panacea for the seemingly unsurmountable problems rest with the IMF. However, it will argue that IMF programs are better poised to help Africa reach its economic goals, or improve economic performance. . . .

Why Has Sub-Saharan Africa (SSA) Performed So Poorly?

The problems of slow growth, high inflation, and chronic balance of payments problems continue to plague SSA well into the 1990s. In general these problems can be traced to international or domestic factors. During the last two decades a number of adverse events in the international economy have contributed to the economic decline in the region. These include oil crises, global recessions,

From *Journal of Asian and African Studies*, August 1998, pp. 265–274. Copyright © 1998 by Brill Academic Publishers. Reprinted by permission.

deteriorating terms of trade, protectionism in the developed countries markets, rising real interest rates, and the lack of symmetry in adjustment to payments problems. In addition a number of adverse developments in the domestic economy have inhibited productive capacity and thwarted the attempts to initiate and sustain economic growth.

No doubt, many countries lack appreciable amounts of essential resources and adequate infrastructure for sustained growth. It is also true that growth and development in many nations have been set back by droughts, civil wars, and political disturbances. It may even be true that colonial economic structures still account for many inflexibilities that inhibit economic growth. However, many countries could significantly improve economic performance and reduce poverty significantly if they managed their economies more efficiently, controlled population growth, and abandoned those policies that are so obviously anti-developmental.

The major setback has been gross mismanagement, which has largely resulted from corruption, rather than from incompetence and absence of skilled administrators. In many nations, national resources for investment, growth and welfare have been consistently diverted into private hands and used largely for conspicuous consumption. Poor public sector management has resulted in large government budget deficits, which contribute to inflation, which in turn encourage undesirable import growth and serious balance of payments deficits. Quite simply African leaders, administrators, businesses, and political insiders have been engaged in corruption on a massive scale. The result has been almost complete destruction of the economic potential in many nations.

For the purpose of solving Africa's serious economic problems, there is need for the political will to attack the fundamental causes. If the present disquieting trends are not urgently tackled with the appropriate policies, then an even more somber future looms on the horizon for many Africans. Any package of measures should include policies designed to revitalize, expand, and transform the productive sectors into viable and self-sustaining entities. In the absence of corruption public resources can be allocated efficiently to facilitate growth in the productive sectors. The microeconomic efficiency that results from efficient resource allocation, coupled with appropriate macroeconomic stabilization policies, would greatly enhance the prospects for economic growth and prosperity.

Assessing IMF Programs

Studies aimed at evaluating IMF programs in Africa conclude that the results are mixed, ranging from disappointing to marginally good. Inasmuch as it is difficult to assess the overall effect of IMF programs some studies have shown that they have been somewhat successful in terms of a number of key economic indicators. One main reason for the contention that IMF programs have been harmful is that many countries with programs have performed as badly as those without IMF programs. One must be cautious in examining the performance of key economic indicators following IMF programs because of the dynamics of the setting in which they are implemented. But let us suppose for the sake of argument that IMF programs actually result in deteriorating economic conditions immediately following the program. For example, suppose economic growth declines as a result of the program. Even though economic growth is perhaps the most important objective of national development policy, it is still reasonable to consider a program successful if it laid down the basis for future realization of economic growth, within some reasonable time period. In other words if it established the economic structure that promotes and facilitates long term growth, then it can still be regarded as successful. In addition it is possible that even though conditions did not improve, the program may have prevented economic conditions from deteriorating even more. It is not possible to subject IMF programs to controlled experiments. However, it seems more reasonable to argue that without IMF programs, in many countries, conditions would have been much worse, than one would argue that IMF programs cause conditions to worsen.

It has somewhat been fashionable, especially amongst those with very limited knowledge of the various economic rational behind IMF recommendations, to reject those recommendations without presenting a feasible alternative. Many object to the IMF and some regard it not only as a representation of western economic interest, but as too uncompromising and arrogant in its relationship with nations in crisis. The indications are that IMF is usually anxious to intervene even before conditions deteriorate into a crisis. But like any prudent banker it has to be concerned about repayment prospect, which is essential for its very own survival and continuous provision of its service to other deserving members.

Why IMF Programs May Be the Answer for Africa

IMF programs in the 1990s should have a major attraction for Africans genuinely concerned with the welfare of the people for a number of reasons. First, the programs are no doubt based on sound theory, always a useful guideline for policy-formulation.

The peculiar social, political and economic circumstances of African nations and the inability or refusal of the IMF to take them into account in the design and implementing of programs have been cited as reasons why IMF programs have "failed" in Africa, or are doomed to fail. On the contrary, these particular African circumstances are in fact another good reason why IMF programs may be the right answer to the problem. Because of the nature of African economic circumstances, particularly problems in economic administration, the conspicuous absence of commitment on the part of politicians and administrators to the development and welfare of the nations, the absence of institutional capacity and the weak civic consciousness, the best policy is to embrace IMF programs. IMF programs encourage the dismantling of controls and simplification of the bureaucratic process; emphasize the strengthening of institutional capacity; require public accountability and responsibility; emphasize efficiency and economic discipline; encourage private sector participation in the economy; foster coordination in economic decisions and promote macroeconomic stability; and emphasize measures designed to expand aggregate supply.

The optimal policy intervention for dealing with an inefficiency or distortion is to seek the source of the problem. IMF programs are attractive because they are designed to attack the problems at their source. In African nations there are many problems that are outside the control of the officials and administrators. However corruption is not one such problem and it need not be so pervasive and economically destructive. Although it is very important not to under-emphasize the importance of many other problems of development, corruption is an obstacle that can largely be controlled, if the top leadership is committed to that objective. It is not the same problem as say drought or poor resource endowment, or an absence of a skilled workforce, that is largely outside the control of officials.

One major attraction of IMF programs is that they tend to remove all opportunities for corruption, i.e., they seek the source of the problem. For example, the suggestion that controls should be dismantled is in recognition that the reliance on physical controls for resource allocation is inferior to the market mechanism, especially in the absence of an efficient administrative machinery for the effective administration of controls. But perhaps the more relevant point is that a proliferation of controls usually lays the foundation for corruption, which has continued to destroy economic life in the region.

In reality it is not the IMF who has failed Africa, but the African leadership. The politicians and public sector officials have conspired with private businessmen and firms to adopt and implement policies that benefit themselves at the expense of national development and welfare. The inability or unwillingness of Africans to demand more accountability and responsibility from both politicians and public servants ensures that violations of the public trust are not treated as illegal, immoral, unethical or non-nationalistic actions. If the IMF has failed Africa, it has done so by failing to vigorously condemn or expose corruption or even assign it the prominent place it deserves in the design of programs.

Many who oppose IMF programs have argued that they impose severe economic harm on the deprived peoples of Africa. Whom are these deprived peoples and what is the evidence? The majority of them are rural inhabitants who have virtually been untouched by modernity. They are largely farmers, have limited participation in the modern economy, consume limited manufactured goods and have very limited access to basic social services provided by governments. In the urban areas there are Africans of diverse economic circumstances ranging from those in abject poverty and squalor, to those of enormous wealth. The urban population is usually more politically powerful and its views have been the barometer used to measure or assess the political climate. On balance IMF programs will tend to harm the urban poor given the structure of their consumption basket and their production pattern. On the other hand the rural population could benefit immensely from IMF programs for similar reasons, and the efficiency gain to the nation would more than compensate for the loss experienced by the urban population. No convincing evidence has been advanced to support the claim of impoverishment of the majority of rural African peoples.

Even though the urban poor could face the most severe hardship as a result of IMF programs, such adverse consequences could be mitigated even within the context of those same programs that supposedly impose such hardships. There is some empirical evidence that IMF reforms will improve the distribution of income and help the poor. There is also evidence that appropriate exchange rates and price incentives improve economic performance, and that private enterprises perform better than state enterprises.

What Africans need is a set of institutions that would enable them to effectively demand the very modest conditions the people deserve and subject all officials to full responsibility and accountability. Given the levels of ignorance, ethnic loyalties, poverty, disillusionment and despair, absence of strong nationalistic and patriotic attitudes, I shudder to imagine the difficulties associated with establishing such institutions. Notwithstanding, the task is possible if the leadership is committed to doing so. Based on the current structure of African institutions, and the record of policy makers, IMF programs are more likely to be effective than other possible alternatives.

Let us examine some of the recommendations and issues in IMF programs and discuss their effects on national welfare.

Devaluation

A devaluation increases the prices of traded (relative to nontraded) goods and will induce changes in production and consumption. First, as imports become more expensive less will be demanded, thereby curbing excessive import demand which is a major source of balance of payments deficits. At the same time production of import substitutes will be encouraged. Secondly, exports will become expensive so that less will be consumed locally and more will be produced. Exports will also be cheaper in foreign countries, so that more will be demanded. Foreign firms that split production into several stages will find the country attractive for their investments, and tourism will also receive a boost. The devaluation will therefore stimulate the export and import substitution sectors. The political concern usually is that the urban consumers whose purchasing power has already been eroded by inflation partly from excessive government spending, will have to pay more for basic manufactured goods, the bulk of which are imported. Not surprisingly, there is usually an anti-devaluation sentiment in the main urban areas. It is very important to emphasize that the devaluation by itself will not correct the problem of macroeconomic instability. It must be accompanied by sound fiscal management that complements rather than counteracts the effects of the devaluation. For example, if the government continues to maintain significant fiscal deficits after devaluation, then the devaluation would soon be reversed as the exchange rate becomes overvalued again. An overvalued exchange rate is subversive to long-term growth and balance of payments adjustment.

The African rural population consumes imported manufactured goods only in limited amounts, but could potentially benefit from devaluation because it will increase the price of agricultural exports. A program that prescribes a devaluation so that exchange rates are competitive, should ensure that the producers of exports are not unreasonably exploited by middlemen (including government) to the extent that they have no incentive to expand production.

A legitimate concern is that devaluation will raise the price of essential inputs and stifle the supply response as the cost of production rises. In the first place, as long as cost of production lags behind prices, producers will find it profitable to expand production. In any case the appropriate supply response could be encouraged by an appropriate production subsidy. This of course involves an additional strain on the budget, and the IMF insists on fiscal restraint as we will see shortly. Fiscal reform involves maximizing tax revenue and ensuring that it is used to maximize macroeconomic performance. This means that those who have been avoiding their tax burden, especially the self employed, must be made to meet their tax obligations, and that frivolous and wasteful expenditures must be avoided.

Government Budget Deficit

When IMF programs recommend reductions in government expenditures, the concern is not only with the adverse effects of budget deficits on inflation and the balance of payments, but also with bogus budgetary appropriations that benefit private individuals and deprive the nation of developmental resources. As a result of the pervasiveness of corruption, many governments typically appropriate funds for the salaries of nonexistent civil servants or for goods and services that are not received. Similarly it is common for governments not only to pay highly inflated prices for goods and services, some of which are totally inessential, but also for governments to receive far less than market value for goods bought by some individuals or firms. IMF prescriptions on the budget can be viewed as perhaps a subtle way of telling African leaders that from their past record they cannot be trusted to appropriate the nation's resources in the national interest. This appears paternalistic, but should be acceptable to all concerned with the welfare of the mass of African peoples.

Government budget deficits as a percentage of GDP [gross domestic product] increased sharply after independence in many countries, as the states intervened ostensibly to correct the perceived flaws of a market economy. The evidence indicates that throughout the region the states have failed to perform the role of a prudent entrepreneur, and government investments have resulted largely in considerable inefficiency. Public enterprises have been inefficiently operated, as they have largely been used as a way of providing patronage to political insiders.

Government budget deficits financed largely through money creation, have contributed to serious inflation and balance of payments problem. These deficits have not been consistent with other macroeconomic objectives of the government. The control of the deficit usually requires reducing expenditure, including the elimination of subsidies to consumption, and increasing taxes. In many African nations it is common for the government to subsidize the consumption of essential food items, gasoline, electricity, public transportation etc. The major beneficiaries are the urban population and mostly political insiders who for example obtain goods at subsidized prices and resell at black market rates. The typical rural inhabitant, because of the structure of the consumption basket does not benefit much from government subsidies.

Market Prices

IMF programs attempt to promote a strong link between work effort and reward. This involves appropriate prices of goods and services, and factors of production. Prices not only provide information to producers but serve as an incentive that facilitate efficient resource allocation. The major problem in African countries has been inadequate production. Production has been constrained by a large number of factors including inappropriate prices. In many African countries the tax system has turned the terms of trade against agriculture and has resulted in very slow or negative growth rates in this sector. Overvalued exchange rates are an implicit tax on exporters since exporters receive the official rate.

The imposition of market prices for agricultural commodities typically results in higher food prices. Rural farmers benefit as producers, but as consumers they lose. However as long as they can respond sufficiently as producers, their gains will be more than enough to compensate for their losses and the nation as a whole will benefit. The challenge of reforming prices is to ensure adequate production response, which may require other complementary policies.

The continuous proliferation of price controls will only continue to stifle production, worsen shortages, and reduce incentive for investment.

Privatization

African governments have argued that they have an obligation to provide goods and services usually provided by private enterprises in developed countries, because too often the market fails to do so. Thus they are compelled to invest in capital formation that will increase output, improve efficiency in resource allocation, and make the distribution of income more equitable. Those are desirable objectives and any government that achieves them deserves widespread commendation. Unfortunately the record of the public enterprises which are usually set up to pursue these objectives, have been very disappointing. These public enterprises have been very inefficiently administered, and have been widely used by politicians as opportunities for patronage to their supporters.

In recommending privatization of certain public enterprises, IMF programs attempt to deal with two problems. The first is micro inefficiency in the productive sector, and the second is government budget deficits that result partly from the need to subsidize inefficiently run enterprises. Private enterprises that continuously make losses go out of business, but government enterprises with similar balance sheets receive political relief. By turning over certain enterprises to private institutions, the pressure on the budget eases, and there is a greater chance of increasing efficiency in production. . . .

Conclusion

African economic problems over the last two decades, can be traced mainly to a host of international and domestic factors. Many of the international factors and some of the domestic factors such as lack of suitable resource endowment, are outside the control of the governments and administrators. However, a significant part of the problems can be traced to corruption and other forms of inefficiencies. Instead of blaming the IMF for the dismal performance in Africa, we should focus on the African leaderships and their policies. The level of their commitment and the policies they have adopted and implemented increasingly seem to confirm only their deplorable lack of compassion for fellow Africans and a callous detachment from the people's welfare. The status quo must change to prevent further erosion of the economic base on the continent.

The best foreign assistance is one that has a lasting effect; it is one that would empower Africans to fully participate in the growth process, and provide them with the irrevocable ability to effectively demand the modest living conditions that they have been unjustly deprived of by their leaders for so long.

The Global Economic Context

Africa illustrates, perhaps better than elsewhere, that globalization is very much a policy-driven process. While in other parts of the world it may be credible to view globalization as driven by technology and the "invisible hand" of the market, in Africa most of the features of globalization and the forces associated with it have been shaped by Bretton Woods Institutions (BWIs) and Africa's adhesion to a number of conventions such as the World Trade Organization (WTO) which have insisted on opening up markets. African governments have voluntarily, or under duress, reshaped domestic policies to make their economies more open. The issue therefore is not whether Africa is being globalized but under what conditions the process is taking place and why, despite such relatively high levels of integration into the world economy, growth has faltered.

The word that often comes to mind whenever globalization and Africa are mentioned together is "marginalization." The threat of marginalization has hung over Africa's head like the sword of Damocles and has been used in minatory fashion to prod Africans to adopt appropriate policies. In most writing globalization is portrayed as a train which African nations must choose to board or be left behind. As Stanley Fischer, the Deputy Director of the IMF, and associates put it, "globalization is proceeding apace and sub-Saharan Africa (SSA) must decide whether to open up and compete, or lag behind." *The Economist*, commenting on the fact that per capita income gap between the USA and Africa has widened, states that "it would be odd to blame globalization for holding Africa back. Africa has been left out of the global economy, partly because its governments used to prefer it that way."

Globalization, from the developmental perspective, will be judged by its effects on economic development and the eradication of poverty. Indeed, in developing countries the litmus test for any international order remains whether it facilitates economic development which entails both economic growth and structural transformation. I shall argue that in the case of Africa this promise has yet to be realized. The policies designed to "integrate" Africa into the global economy have thus far failed because they have completely sidestepped the developmental needs of the continent and the strategic questions on the form of integration appropriate to addressing these needs. They consequently have not led to higher rates of growth and, their labeling notwithstanding, have not induced structural transformation. Indeed the combined effect of internal political disarray, the weakening of domestic capacities, deflationary policies and slow world economic growth have placed African economies on a "low equilibrium growth path" against which the anaemic Gross Domestic Product (GDP) growth rates of 3–4 per cent appear as "successful" performance. I will illustrate this point by looking at two channels through which the benefits of globalization are suppose to be transmitted to developing countries: trade and investment.

The [section] is divided into three sections. The first section deals with what globalization and the accompanying adjustment policies promised, what has been delivered and what has happened to African economies during the era of globalization. The second deals critically with some of the explanations for Africa's failure. And the last part advances an alternative explanation of the failure with respect to both trade and access to foreign finance.

The Promise of Globalization and Achievements

The Promise of Trade

Expanded opportunities for trade and the gains deriving from trade are probably the most enticing arguments for embracing globalization. The Structural Adjustment Programmme's (SAP's) promise was that through liberalization African economies would become more competitive. As one World Bank economist, Alexander Yeats, asserts, "If Africa is to reverse its unfavourable export trends, it must quickly adopt trade and structural adjustment policies that enhance its international competitiveness and allow African exporters to capitalize on opportunities in foreign markets." Trade liberalization would not only increase the 'traditional exports' of individual countries but would also enable them to diversify their exports to include manufactured goods assigned to them by the law of comparative advantage as spelled out and enforced by "market forces." Not only would trade offer outlets for goods from economies with limited markets but, perhaps more critically, it would also permit the importation of goods that make up an important part of investment goods (especially plant and equipment) in which technology is usually embodied.

By the end of the 1990s, and after far-reaching reforms in trade policy, little had changed. The few gains registered tended to be of a one-off character, often reflecting switches from domestic to foreign markets without much increase in overall output. Indeed some increases in exports of manufactured goods even occurred as the manufacturing sector contracted. . . .

Furthermore recent changes in Africa's exports indicate that no general increase had occurred in the number of industries in which most of the African countries have a "revealed" comparative advantage. Indeed, after decades of reforms, the most striking trend, on that has given credence to the notion of "marginalization of Africa", is the decline in the African share of global non-oil exports which is now less than one-half what it was in the early 1980s representing "a staggering annual income loss of US$68,000 million—or 21 per cent of regional CDP."

The Promise of Additional Resources

A persuasive promise made by BWIs was that adhesion to its policies would not only raise domestic investment through increased domestic saving but would relax the savings and foreign exchange constraints by allowing countries to attain higher levels of investment than would be supported by domestic savings and their own foreign exchange earnings. One central feature of adjustment policies had been financial liberalization. . . . The major thesis has been that "financial repression" (which includes control of interest rates and credit rationing by the state) has discouraged saving and led to inefficient allocation of the "loanable funds." The suggested solution then is that liberalization of markets would lead to positive real interest rates which would encourage savings. The "loanable funds" thus generated would then be efficiently distributed among projects with the highest returns through the mediation of competitive financial institutions. Significantly, in this view saving precedes investment and growth. After years of adjustment there is little discernible change in the levels of savings and investment.

Perhaps even more attractive was the promise that financial liberalization would lead to increased capital inflows and stem capital flight. Indeed, most African governments' acceptance of IMF policies has been based on precisely the claimed "catalytic effect" of agreements with IMF on the inflow of foreign capital. Governments were willing to enter the Faustain bargain of reduced national sovereignty in return for increased financial flows. Even when governments were sceptical of the developmental validity of BWIs policies, the belief that the stamp of approval of these institutions would attract foreign capital tended to dilute the scepticism.

To the surprise of the advocates of these policies and to the chagrin of African policy-makers, the response of private capital to Africa's diligent adoption of SAPs has, in the words of World Bank, "been disappointing." The market "sentiments" do not appear to have been sufficiently persuaded that the policies imposed by the BWIs have improved the attractiveness to investors. The much-touted catalytic effect of IMF conditionality has yet to assert itself. The scepticism of private investors about the BWIs stamp of approval is understandable in light of the history of non-graduation by any African country. Indeed, there is the distinct danger that, since economies under BWIs' intensive care never seem to recover, IMF presence may merely signal trouble. The BWIs seem to be unaware of the extent to which their comings and goings are a source of uncertainty among businessmen and evidence of a malaise. This said, there is, nevertheless, a trickle of foreign investment into Africa but this has not been enough to increase Africa's share in global FDI flows. The rise in foreign direct investment in the latter part of the 1990s is cited as evidence that globalization and SAPs are working (Pigato, 2000). This celebration is premature. There are a number of significant features of the financial flows to Africa that should be cause for concern over their developmental impact and sustainability.

First, there is the high country concentration of investment with much of the investment going to South Africa. Secondly, there is the sectoral concentration on mining. Little of this has gone into the manufacturing industry. As for investment in mining, it is not drawn to African countries by macro-economic policy changes, as is often suggested, but by the prospects of better world prices, changes in attitudes towards national ownership and sector-specific incentives. Third, there is the problem of the type of investment. The unintended consequence of the policies has been the attraction of the least desirable form of foreign capital. Most of the new investment has taken the form of the highly speculative portfolio investment attracted by "pull factors" that have been of a transitory nature—extremely high real domestic interest rates on Treasury Bills caused by the need to finance the budget deficit—and temporary booms in export prices which attract large export pre-financing loans. It has also been driven by acquisitions facilitated by the increased pace of privatization to buy up existing plants that are being sold usually under 'fire sales' conditions. Such investments now account for approximately 14 per cent of Foreign Direct Investment (FDI) flows into Africa. Little has been driven by plans to set up new productive enterprises. Some of the new investment is for expansion of existing capacities, especially in industries enjoying natural monopolies (e.g., beverages, cement, furniture). Such expansion may have been stimulated by the spurt of growth that caused much euphoria and that is now fading away. It is widely recognized that direct investment is preferable to portfolio investment, and foreign investment in green field projects is preferable to acquisitions. The predominance of these types of capital inflows should be cause for concern. However, in their desperate efforts to attract foreign investment, African governments have simply ceased dealing with these risks or suggesting that they may have a preference for one type of foreign investment over others.

Finally, such investment is likely to taper off within a short span of time, as already seems to the case in a number of African countries. Thus, for Ghana, hailed as a "success story" by the BWIs, FDI which peaked in the mid-1980s at over US$200 million annually due mainly to privatization was rapidly reversed to produce a negative outflow. It should be noted, in passing, that rates of return of direct investments have generally been much higher in Africa than anywhere in other developing regions. This, however, has not made Africa a favourite among investors, largely because of considerations of the intangible "risk factor," nurtured by the large dose of ignorance about individual African countries. There is considerable evidence to show that Africa is systematically rated as more risky than is warranted by the underlying economic characteristics.

Capital Flight

Not only is Africa still severely rationed in financial markets, but during much of the globalization there is evidence that Africa is probably a net exporter of capital. Paul Collier and associates have suggested that in 1990, 40 per cent of privately held wealth was invested outside Africa and that in relation to the workforce, capital flight from Africa has been much higher than in other developing country groups. In a recent more systematic attempt to measure the extent of capital flight, James Boyce and Léonce Ndikumana show that for the period 1970–96 capital flight from sub-Saharan Africa was US$193 billion, and with imputed interests the amount goes up to US$285 billion. These figures should be compared with the combined debt of these countries which stood at US$178 billion in 1996. . . .

So far financial liberalization has not done much to turn the tide. In a World Bank Study of the effects of financial liberalization in nine African countries, Devajaran et al conclude that the effects of liberalization on capital flight are "very small. . . ."

All this indicates that financial liberalization in itself may not be the panacea for reducing capital flight. Effective policy measures to reduce capital flight in the African context may need much deeper and more fundamental changes in the economic and political systems. One policy implication of both the reluctance of foreign capital to come to Africa and the huge amounts of wealth held outside Africa has been the calls for policies intended not so much to attract foreign capital but Africa's own private capital. While this is a valid option, the political economy of such attraction and the specific direct policy measures called for are rarely spelled out.

The Failed Promise of Growth

A comparison between Africa's economic performance during the period over which globalization is often said to have taken hold—the last two decades of the 20th century—and earlier periods shows clearly that thus far globalization has not produced rates of growth higher than those of the 1960s and 1970s. Per income growth was negative over the two decades, a serious indictment to those who have steered policies over the decades. This slower rate of growth is not peculiar to Africa as is suggested by some of the "Afro-pessimist" literature. During the period of globalization economic growth rates have fallen across the board for all groups of countries. The poorest group went from a per capita GDP growth rate of 1.9 per cent annually in 1960–80, to a decline of 0.5 per cent per year (1980–2000). For the middle group (which includes mostly poor countries), there was a sharp decline from an annual per capita growth rate of 3.6 per cent to just less than 1 per cent. Over a 20-year period, this represents the difference between doubling income per person, versus increasing it by just 21 per cent. The other groups also showed substantial declines in growth rates. The global decline in growth is largely due to deflationary bias in orthodox stabilization programmes imposed by International Financial Institutions (IFIs).

Explaining the Poor Performance: Has Africa Adjusted?

The poor performance of Africa with respect to the channels through which the positive effects of globalization would be gained (i.e., increased access to markets and finance) is now widely accepted. There are, however, disagreements over the cause of the failure. The BWIs have adhered to two explanations.

The first one is simply that African countries have rather incomprehensibly persisted with their doomed "dirigiste" ways and refused to swallow the bitter but necessary pills of adjustment. Inadequate implementation of reforms and recidivism are some of the most common themes running through the literature on African economic policy. In the 1994 report the World Bank's view was that adjustment was 'incomplete' not because of any faults in the design of the programmes but because of lack of implementation.

The second explanation was that insufficient time had elapsed to reap the gains of adjustment and, therefore, of globalization. Coming from the BWIs, this is a strange position. It was these very institutions that, in dismissing the structuralist argument on the inelasticity of the response of developing countries to economic stimuli, claimed that liberalization would elicit immediate and substantial responses and bring about "accelerated development" (the promise of the Berg Report). Indeed, in the early years, the World Bank was so certain about the response to its policies that it measured economic success by simply looking at the policy stance and assuming that this axiomatically led to growth.

Today, there is recognition that the axiomatic mapping of policies into performance was naïve and misleading. There are admissions, albeit grudging, to having underestimated the external constraints on policy and the vulnerability of African economies to them. Equally the responsiveness of the economies and the private sector has been overestimated, while the wrong sequence of policies eroded state capacities and responsibilities ("policy ownership"). However it is still insisted that the passage of time will do its job and the posture recommended to African countries has been to sit tight and wait for the outpouring of gains. There is no recognition that the accumulated effects of past policy errors may have made the implementation of "market friendly" policies in their pristine form more difficult.

By the second half of the 1990s neither of these arguments carried any weight. African countries have made far more adjustments than any other global region. Indeed the BWIs themselves began to point proudly to the success of their programmes, suggesting that enough time had transpired and a large number of African countries had perservered in their adjustment to begin to reap the fruits of the adjustment process. IMF officials talked about a "turning point" and that the positive per capita growth rates of 1995–97 (4.1 per cent) "reflected better policies in many African countries rather than favourable exogenous developments."

President of the World Bank James Wolfensohn, for example, reported in his 1997 address to the Board of Governors that there was progress in sub-Saharan Africa, "with new leadership and better economic policies." Michel Camdessus, the then Managing Director of the International Monetary Fund, at the 1996 annual meeting of the World Bank and the IMF, said, "Africa, for which so many seem to have lost hope, appears to be stirring and on the move." The two vice presidents for Africa at the World Bank, Callisto Madavo and Jean-Louis Sarbib, wrote an article, appropriately titled "Africa on the

Move: Attracting Private Capital to a Changing Continent," which gave reasons for this new "cautious optimism." The then Deputy Managing Director of the International Monetary Fund, Alassane Quattara, would say the following about the good performance: "A key underlying contribution has come from progress made in macroeconomic stabilization and the intro-duction of sweeping structural reforms." The major World Bank report on Africa of 2000 stated "many countries have made major gains in macroeco-nomic stabilization, particularly since 1994" and there had been a turn around because of "ongoing structural adjustment throughout the region which has opened markets and has a major impact on productivity, exports, and invest-ment." Even the Economic Commission for Africa (ECA), a strident critic of SAP in the past, joined the chorus.

And so by the end of the millennium, African countries had been largely adjusted. There can be no doubt that there has been a sea-change in the African policy landscape. Africa is very heavily involved in "globalization" and is very much part of the global order and much of the policy-making during the last two decades has been designed deliberately to increase Africa's participation in the global economy. In any case, more devaluations, lowering of tariffs and privatization of marketing were imposed in Africa than any-where else. By the mid-1980s, with the exception of the franc zone countries, most SSA countries had adopted flexible exchange rate policies and there had been major real exchange rate depressions. Major reforms in marketing, including the abolition of marketing boards, had been introduced. Arguments that African countries had refused or been slow to adjust or that enough time had not transpired became less credible, especially in light to the celebratory and self-congratulatory remarks by the BWIs themselves.

However, by 1997 the growth rates had begun to falter. By 1999, in its report on global prospects and the developing countries, the World Bank made a downward revision of the 1999 growth rate "despite continued improvements in political and economic fundamentals." The report blamed the poor performance on terms of trade and the Asian crisis. In a sense we had been there before. "Success stories" have been told many times before and countries have fretted and strutted on this "success" stage only to be heard of no more. . . .

Rather than abandon the deflationary policies, supporters of adjustment have simply reframed the question to read: "Why is it that when the recom-mended policies are put into place (often under the guidance of—and pressure from—the International Monetary Fund and the World Bank) the hoped for results do not materialize quickly." The answer was: lack of "good Governance" and of "good Institutions." These assertions conceal a clear loss of certainty and a growing sense of intellectual disarray. This is apparent in the World Bank study, *Can Africa Claim the 21st Century?* Unlike earlier approaches, the report speaks in a much more subdued and less optimistic tone, based more on faith than analysis. There is an admission, albeit grudging, that policies of the past have not worked. The new agenda is much more eclectic and more a reflection of confusion and loss of faith than the discovery of a coherent, comprehensive policy framework. The additional set of reforms is nebulous, eclectic and largely of a more political and institutional character—good governance, participation of and consultation with civil society, democracy etc. Increasingly the World Bank's new solutions suggest that there is little to be done by way of reform on the economic front. . . .

Trade, Low Growth and Absence of Structural Change

The slow growth discussed above has also had an impact on the growth of exports and diversification by weakening the investment-export nexus crucial to the process. Here again, the orthodox view has been that increased trade or openness measured in various ways is a determinant of growth. Consequently, the major policies with respect to trade have involved trade liberalization and adjustments in exchange rates largely through devaluation.

The failure on the trade front is linked to the failure in the structural transformation of African economies so that they could produce new sets of commodities in a competitive and flexible way. Globalization in Africa has been associated with industrial stagnation and even de-industrialization. African economies were the quintessential 'late latecomers' in the process of industrialization. I have argued elsewhere that although the writing on African economies is based on the assumption that Africa had pursued import substitution for too long, the phase of import substitution was in fact extremely short—in most countries it was less than a decade. SAPs have called for policies that have prematurely exposed African industries to global competition and thus induced widespread processes of de-industrialization. African economies have somehow been out of sync with developments in other parts of the world. When most economies embarked on import substitution industrialization, financed by either borrowing or debt default, much of Africa was under colonial rule, which permitted neither protection of domestic markets nor running of deficits. And even later when much of industrialization was financed through Eurodollar loans, Africans were generally reluctant borrowers so that eventually much of their borrowing in the 1980s was not for industrialization but to finance balance-of-payments problems.

Every case of successful penetration of international markets has been preceded by a phase when import substitution industrialization was pursued. Such a phase is necessary not simply for the "infant industry" arguments that have been stated ad infinitum, but also because they provide an institutional capacity for handling an entirely new set of economic activities. The phase is also necessary for sorting out some of the coordinating failures that need to be addressed before venturing into global markets. A "revisionist" view argues three main points. First, that substantial growth was achieved during the phase of import substitution industrialization; second, that even successful "export oriented economies" had to pass through this phase and maintain many features of the import substitution (IS) phase; and finally that important social gains were made.

The IS phase did lead to the initial phases of industrialization. Significantly, UNIDO notes that African countries were increasingly gaining comparative advantage in labour intensive branches, as indicated by revealed comparative advantage (RCA) but then notes:

> It is particularly alarming to note that the rank correlation of industrial branches by productivity growth over 1980–95 and RCA value in 1995 is very low. Productivity has fallen in furniture, leather, footwear, clothing, textiles, and food manufacturing. An export oriented development strategy cannot directly stimulate Total Factor Productivity (TFP). Policy must focus on increasing technological progress within the export industries—many of which have seen very rapid progress in the application of the most modern technologies (informatics, biotechnological, etc) to their production and distribution system.

Given the conviction that import substitution in Africa was bad and had gone on for too long, there was no attempt to see how existing industries could be the basis for new initiative for export. The policy was simply to discard existing capacity on the wrong assumption that it was the specific micro-economic policies used to encourage the establishment of these industries that accounted for failure at the macro-level. The task should have been to extend and not reverse such gains by dismantling existing industrial capacity. The rates of growth of manufacturing value added (MVA) have fallen continuously from the levels in the 1970s. UNIDO estimated that MVA in sub-Saharan Africa was actually contracting at an annual average rate of 1.0 percent during 1990–97. UNIDO shows that for Africa as a whole in ten industrial branches in 38 countries labour productivity declined to an index value of 93 in 1995 (1990 = 100). Increases in productivity were registered only in tobacco, beverages and structural clay products. In many cases, an increase in productivity has been caused by a fall in employment growth (UNIDO).

The decline in total factor productivity of the economy as a whole is attributed to de-industrialization which it defines as "synonymous with productivity growth deceleration." Output per head in sub-Saharan manufacturing fell from US$7924 in 1990 to US$6762 in 1996. The structural consequence is that the share of manufacturing in GDP has fallen in two-thirds of the countries. The number of countries falling below the median has increased from 19 during 1985–90 to 31 during the 1991–98 period. While admitting such poor performance in manufacturing industry during the era of structural adjustment, supporters of SAP argue that such decline in industrialization is a temporary and welcome process of weeding out inefficient industrialization and also that insufficient time for adjustment has passed to ensure benefits from globalization through the establishment of new industries. Considering that this argument has been repeatedly deployed since 1985, Africa may have to wait for a long time before the gains from globalization materialize.

Students of historical structural changes of economies inform us that structural change is both cause and effect of economic growth. As Moshe Syrquin observes, a significant share of the measured rate of aggregate total factor productivity is owing to resource shifts from sectors with low productivity to sectors with high productivity. We have learnt from the "new trade theories" and studies on technological development how countries run the risk of being "locked" in a permanently slow-growth trajectory if they follow the dictates of static comparative advantage.

To move away from such a path, governments have introduced policies that generate externalities for a wide range of other industries and thus place the economy on more growth-inducing engagement with the rest of the world. For years, UNCTAD economists have pointed to the importance of growth for trade expansion. They have argued that it is the absence of growth, or more specifically an investment-export nexus that accounts for the failure of many countries to expand and diversify their export base. Rapid resource reallocation may not be feasible without high rates of growth and investment. The principle means for effecting export diversification is investment. Many empirical tests of "causation" have been conducted and suggest that there are good theoretical and empirical grounds for taking the reverse causation seriously as the dynamics of high growth lead to even greater human and physical investment and greater knowledge formation; which, by Verdoon's Law, leads to more productivity and therefore greater competitiveness.

Experience of successful export drives clearly shows a strong relationship between rates of structural change and rates of growth in value added in manufacturing the rates of growth of exports. Lessons from countries that have embraced trade liberalization and achieved some degree of success suggest clearly that liberalization should be in conjunction with policies that ensure that relative prices will be favourable to export industries (and not just to non-tradables) and that interest rates will support investment and economic restructuring. Successful export promotion strategies have required a deliberate design of an investment–export nexus. Diversification of exports that is developmental needs to go beyond the multiplication of primary commodities and include industrial products. This requires not merely the redirection of existing industrial output to the external but the expansion of such output and investment in new activities. There is a need to design a system of incentives that favours investments that open up new possibilities or introduce new technologies to the country. In this respect infrastructure and human resource development are important preconditions for the success of pro-export policies.

The instruments used to promote investment have included not only public investment but also the provision of subsidized inputs by public enterprises, direct subsidies through tax incentives including exemptions from duties, industrial policy which, in turn, has meant selective allocation of credit and encouragement of investment by cheapening imported investment goods (often by manipulation of exchange rates in favour of the import of plant and equipment and export sector). While "diversification" has always featured in virtually all adjustment programmes, there has been no clear spelling out how this was to be achieved. In most cases, the need for diversification was overshadowed by the short-term pressures to exploit static "revealed" comparative advantage and reduce public spending. The failure to stimulate new economic activities (especially industrial ones) has meant not only sluggish growth in exports but also failure to diversify.

Under SAP all these instruments have been off limits. Evidence that more successful cases have had some kind of "industrial policy" has been dismissed on the grounds that African countries had neither the type of government nor the political acumen to prevent "capture" of these policies by rent-seekers and patron-client networks. Governments have been left with no instrument for stimulating investment and industrial development directly or for creating an environment for robust demand and profitability in which investment, or complementary public inputs such as infrastructure, research and development, education and training, could thrive. It is this passivity that has led to failure for structural transformation and the establishment of an investment-export nexus that would have led to increase and diversification of exports. . . .

Concluding Remarks

The African policy landscape has changed radically during the last two decades. Liberalization of trade, privatization and reliance on markets have replaced the widespread state controls associated with import substitution. One would expect by now to see some signs of the "accelerated development" promised by the Berg report in 1981. That adjustment has failed as a prerequisite for development, let alone as a "strategy for accelerated development," is now widely accepted. These failures can, in turn, be traced to the displacement of developmental strategic thinking by "an obsession" with stabilization—a point underscored by low levels of investment and institutional sclerosis. The key "fundamentals" that policy has sought to establish relate to these financial concerns rather than to development. The singular concentration on "opening" up the economy has undermined post-independence efforts to create, albeit lamely, internally coherent and articulated economies and an industrial structure that would be the basis for eventual diversification of Africa's export base. The excessive emphasis on servicing the external sector has diverted scarce resources and political capacities away from managing the more fundamental basis for economic development. Even the issue of "poverty" has received little attention, except perhaps when it has seemed politically expedient to be seen to be doing something to mitigate the negative effect of adjustment. SAP, owing to its deflationary bias, has placed African economies on such a low-growth trajectory, which has then conditioned the levels and types of Africa's participation in the global economy.

Over the last two decades, Africans have been faced with not merely a set of pragmatic measures but a full-blown ideological position about the role of the state, about nationalism and about equity, against which many neo-liberals, including Elliot Berg, had ranted for years. It is this ideological character of the proposals that has made them impervious to empirical evidence including those generated by the World Bank itself and it is this that has made policy dialogue virtually impossible. The insistence of "true believers" on the basic and commonsense message they carry has made dialogue impossible. The assumption that those on the other side are merely driven by self-interest and ignorance that might be remediable by "capacity building" has merely complicated matters further. Things have not been made easier by the supplicant position of

African governments and their obvious failures to manage their national affairs well. These policies were presented as finite processes which would permit countries to restore growth. With this time perspective in mind, countries were persuaded to put aside long-term strategic considerations while they sorted out some short-term problems. The finite process had lasted two decades.

There are obvious gains to participation in increased exchange with the rest of the world. The bone of contention is: what specific measures should individual countries adopt in order to reap the benefits of increases exchange with other nations? With perhaps a few cases, developing countries have always sought to gain from international trade. Attempts to diversify the export base have been a key aspect of policy since independence. Import substitution was not a strategy for autarky as is often alleged but a phase in eventual export diversification. However, for years the integration of developing countries into a highly unequal economic order was considered problematic, characterized as it is by unfavourable terms of trade for primary commodities, control of major markets by gigantic conglomerates, protectionism in the markets in the developed countries together with "dumping" of highly subsidized agricultural products, volatile commodity and financial markets, asymmetries in access to technology etc. From this perspective gains from trade could only be captured by strategizing and dynamizing a country's linking up with the rest of world.

It is ironic that while analysis in the "pre-globalization" period took the impact of external factors on economic growth seriously, the era of globalization has tended to concentrate almost exclusively on internal determinants of economic performance. Today, Africa's dependence on external factors and the interference in the internal affairs of African countries by external factors are most transparent and most humiliating and yet such dependence remains untheorized. Theories that sought to relate Africa's economies to external factors have been discredited, abandoned or, at best, placed on the defensive. The focus now is almost entirely on internal determinants of economic performance—economic policies, governance, rent-seeking and ethnic diversity.

While the attention on internal affairs may have served as a useful corrective to the excessive focus on the external, it also provides a partial view of African economies and can be partly blamed for the pursuit of policies that were blind to Africa's extreme dependence and vulnerability to external conjuncture—a fact that the BWIs have learnt as exogenous factors scuttled their adjustment programmes. Indeed, unwilling to discard its essentially deflationary policies and faced with poor performance among many countries which have been "strong adjusters," the World Bank's explanations have become increasingly more structuralist-deterministic and eclectic. . . .

It is now admitted that many mistakes have been made during the past two decades. When errors are admitted, the consequences of such errors are never spelled out. . . . Policy failures, especially those as comprehensive as those of SAP's can continue to have effects on the performance of the economy long after policy failures are abandoned. It may well be that the accretions of errors that are often perfunctorily admitted have created *maladjusted* economies not capable of gaining much from globalization. Both the measures of "success" used for African economies and the projections for the future suggest that essentially the BWIs have put Africa's development on hold. This clearly suggests the extreme urgency of Africans themselves assuming the task of "bringing development back in" in their respective countries and collectively. To benefit from interacting with the rest of the world, African policy-makers will have to recognize the enormous task of correcting the maladjustment of their economies. They will have to introduce more explicit, more subtle and more daring policies to stimulate growth, trade and export diversification than hitherto.

POSTSCRIPT

Have Free-Market Policies Worked for Africa?

The debate presented here may have as much to do with the authors' conceptualization of "development" as it does with the effectiveness of structural adjustment policies (which are premised on a certain vision of development) in Africa. Although both of the authors are economists, development is a vague term that has been articulated in vastly different manners.

The type of development that structural adjustment policies are designed to facilitate (and the type of development advocated by Scott in this issue) is export-led, laissez-faire economic growth. The belief (under this conceptualization of development) is that if you get the general policy environment "right," and minimize interference of the state, then capitalist factors will make efficient and rational decisions that lead to the generation of wealth, which will eventually trickle down to all members of society. Furthermore, as individual nation states exist in a global economic system, it makes sense for them to specialize in the production of goods that they can create relatively cheaply and to trade for those that others can produce more efficiently. Proponents of this view often point to the Asian Tigers (e.g., Taiwan, Singapore, South Korea) as examples of countries that successfully pursued export-led economic growth.

Other than questioning the effectiveness of structural adjustment along the narrow lines of whether or not it promotes economic growth, critics of these policies and, more broadly, development conceptualized as export-led, laissez-faire economic growth, generally raise at least three issues. First, they assert that laissez-faire economic growth often does not help the majority of the population but, rather, may serve to concentrate wealth in the hands of a few powerful individuals or entities. This is particularly problematic in the African context where large economic operators may face little to no competition. Konadu-Agyemang (in an article in a 2000 issue of the *Professional Geographer* entitled "The Best of Times and the Worst of Times"), for example, highlighted the very uneven pattern of development promoted by structural adjustment policies in Ghana, one of the World Bank's success stories. Second, critics assert that it is often problematic for African nations to engage in free trade with the rest of the world because they are relegated to the production of primary commodities for which prices are low and declining. Furthermore, use of the Asian Tigers as examples of successful export-led growth is disingenuous (see, e.g., an article by Carmody in a 1998 issue of the *Review of African Political Economy* entitled "Constructing Alternatives to Structural Adjustment in Africa"). This, according to the critics, is because these states actively protected infant industries, and provided subsidies to promote the development of their export sectors (at least during the early years of developing this aspect of their economies), rather than pursuing a minimalistic role for the government in the economy. Finally, many of the critics would argue that an entirely different vision of development needs to be emphasized, a vision that prioritizes the fulfillment of basic human needs (e.g., adequate food, clean water, health care) and the development of human capital (via improved education). This is the perspective taken by, for example, Macleans Geo-Jaja and Garth Mangum in a 2001 article in the *Journal of Black Studies* entitled "Structural Adjustment as an Inadvertent Enemy of Human Development."

The other point worth noting is that Mkandawire is writing six or seven years after Scott, and thus has had more time to observe the effectiveness, or noneffectiveness of structural adjustment policies. In the time period between the writing of the two selections, a new hybrid approach was developed known as "structural adjustment with a human face" that is cognizant of the role of sound social services (and the development of human capital) in long-tem economic development. Cynics view this change as superficial (and an approach that only was developed by the World Bank and IMF under pressure from its critics), while others see it as a real, positive development. Despite this change, Mkandawire still sees SAPs as a failure because they do not account for the inherently unfair global economic context.

ISSUE 6

Are Abundant Mineral and Energy Resources a Catalyst for African Development?

YES: Oliver Maponga and Philip Maxwell, from "The Fall and Rise of African Mining," *Minerals and Energy* (2001)

NO: Sunday Dare, from "A Continent in Crisis: Africa and Globalization," *Dollars and Sense* (July/August 2001)

ISSUE SUMMARY

YES: Oliver Maponga, Economic Affairs Officer in the Southern Africa Office of the United Nations Economic Commission for Africa, and Philip Maxwell, professor at the Western Australian School of Mines at Curtin University of Technology, describe a resurgence in the African mining industry in the 1990s after several lackluster decades. They assert that mineral and energy mining can make a positive contribution to economic development in Africa.

NO: Sunday Dare, a Nigerian journalist, describes how "much sorrow has flowed" from Africa's resource blessing. While Dare blames African leaders for corruption and resource mismanagement, he also implicates transnational corporations (TNCs) as key contributors to this problem. He states that TNCs have acted as economic predators that support repressive African leaders in order to garner uninterrupted access to resources. The result, Dare suggests, is that Africa's "raw materials are still being depleted without general development."

$\mathbf{T}$he authors in this issue are basically wrangling over the validity of the "resource curse thesis" in contemporary Africa. This thesis posits that countries with great natural resource wealth have a tendency to grow more slowly than resource-poor countries. There are at least two types of problems (that potentially inhibit economic growth) frequently linked to resource abundance in African countries. First, is the notion that resource abundance may lead to a simplification or concentration of national economies, with increasing dependence on a single export mineral or fuel. The idea is that decision makers will tend to gravitate toward the easy money and shirk investments in other aspects of the economy. Nigeria is a potential example of this problem as productivity in a number of sectors (most notably food production and manufacturing) declined with the rise to prominence of the petroleum industry in the 1970s.

The second issue often linked to resource wealth is civil conflict. This problem may manifest itself in a couple of different ways. Rival groups may fight for control of key resources and then finance their military aggression through proceeds from the sale of these resources (such as diamond trading by rebel groups in Sierra Leone). Or, corrupt governments may sequester the proceeds from resource extraction to line their own pockets and to bankroll the suppression of opposition groups—a tactic that often leads to future opposition and unrest.

In their selection, Oliver Maponga and Philip Maxwell impugn the resource curse thesis in contemporary Africa. While acknowledging several lackluster decades in the mineral and energy sector, they describe a resurgence in the African mining industry in the 1990s. They maintain that mineral and energy extraction can make a positive contribution to economic development in Africa, ending their article on the optimistic assertion that "resource development will be seen as a blessing rather than a curse by the year 2010."

Sunday Dare counters that the resource curse thesis is alive and well in Africa. Dare blames African leaders for corruption and resource mismanagement, but he also implicates transnational corporations (TNCs) by asserting that TNCs have acted as economic predators that support repressive African leaders in order to gain access to resources.

In addition to the issues already raised, there are a few other points introduced by the authors in these texts that deserve some foregrounding. In the 1960s, when many African nations gained independence, there was a great deal of concern that transnational or multinational corporations acted as neo-imperialistic forces on the African continent. Dependency theorists suggested that major industries (including mines) either needed to be run by the government or indigenous entrepreneurs, or strictly regulated, in order to ensure that profits remained within a country's borders. This thinking led to a wave of nationalizations (or government takeovers) of foreign-owned enterprises in the 1960s and 1970s. Since the early 1980s these nationalized industries have gradually been re-privatized as part of the World Bank and International Monetary Fund's structural adjustment programs. The rationale for these privatizations is that governments are incapable of efficiently running enterprises and that foreign ownership needs to be permitted in order to encourage outside investment and technology transfer. Both of these policies, nationalization on the one hand and privatization on the other, are highly contested in the literature and, not surprisingly, appraised quite differently by the authors of the following selections.

YES

Oliver Maponga and
Philip Maxwell

The Fall and Rise of African Mining

Introduction

Africa has twenty per cent of the earth's landmass and, in 2000, was home to about 800 million people. There is a highly prospective geology in much of the continent and minerals play an important role in the economic activities of many of its more than fifty sovereign nations. One reflection of this is the observation by [Graham] Davis that, in 1991, there were sixteen mineral dependent economies in Africa. They included Algeria, Angola, Botswana, Cameroon, Congo, Gabon, Guinea, Libya, Mauritania, Namibia, Niger, Nigeria, South Africa, Togo, Zaire (now the Democratic Republic of Congo) and Zambia.

Yet in a relative sense, the continent's minerals industry is still in its infancy. It has not achieved its full potential despite a long history of mining. This is in apparent contrast with the situation in Australia, Canada, the United States and Latin American nations such as Chile, where mineral discovery and exploitation has been an important source of subsequent economic development. Over the past decade there has been considerable debate about the role of natural resources in the economic development process. Authors such as Auty, Sachs and Warner and Gelb have argued that natural resources have been an economic curse for many nations. A contrary view appears in Davis.

One can classify almost every African nation as a developing economy. According to the African Development Bank, 39 African countries had GNP [gross national product] per capita levels of less than USD 1000 in 1998. The most affluent were Libya (USD 6160), Gabon (USD 4170), South Africa (USD 3310) and Botswana (USD 3070)—each major mineral producers. This compared with GNP per capita levels of USD 30600 in the United States, USD 20050 in Australia and USD 19320 in Canada in 1999.

Despite the resource curse argument, further expansion of the resources sector remains a major hope for the growth and development of many African nations. This is because of its potentially strong contribution to Gross Domestic Product [GDP] and to export income, as well as its role in generating forward and backward linkages to other parts of these economies.

There was widespread nationalisation of minerals in Africa early in the post-independence era after 1960. In response to this foreign mineral investors showed little interest in mineral exploration or investment in most African nations during the 1970s and 1980s. This led to a loss of earlier mineral

From *Minerals and Energy*, 2001, pp. 9–10, 17–25. Copyright © 2001 by Taylor & Francis. Reprinted by permission via Rightslink.

competitiveness in countries such as Zambia, Zaire, Guinea, Nigeria and Tanzania. South Africa and Botswana stood almost alone as the continent's world-class hard rock mineral producers during this time. The continent's oil and gas also struggled, particularly after 1980 when oil prices began a long period of nominal and real price decline.

Since the early 1990s the situation in Africa and elsewhere has been changing. The demise of the Soviet Union and communism, and the continuing push of global capitalism has been an important part of this story. Over the past decade, there has been a major revision of mineral policy throughout the continent to encourage foreign investment in exploration and new mineral projects. In this new area, African nations have been attracting more mineral exploration spending. This has also led to a series of new mineral projects, which are likely to boost the economic fortunes of several nations, particularly if political decision makers choose to invest taxes and royalty payments wisely. . . .

The Performance of African Economies— 1970 to 1990

An important . . . issue . . . is whether the stagnation of the resources sector in Africa adversely affected the relative performance of its mineral dependent economies. In addressing this issue it is useful initially to compare GDP growth rates in African economies with those elsewhere. . . . African economic growth between 1970 and 1979 lagged behind that in Asia and South America. Yet it was higher than in OECD [Organization for Economic Cooperation and Development] member nations. During the 1980s, the situation changed, with African economic growth comparable to that in South America, but lagging considerably behind Asia and the OECD.

When one moves to consider the performance of mineral and non-mineral economies in Africa, the results seem consistent with those put forward by Sachs and Warner. Between 1975 and 1990, the real GDP at factor cost in Africa's mineral dependent economies grew at 0.9 per cent per annum less than in the non-mineral economies. Economic growth rates in the five African fuel-exporting nations were remarkably similar to those in the eleven hard rock mineral exporting economies.

It is useful also to consider the performance of some of the related quality of life indicators used by authors such as Davis. He considered movements in indicators such as life expectancy, infant mortality, daily calorie supply, primary school enrollment and the adult literacy rate. Focusing on the fortunes of 22 mineral economies and 57 never-minerals economies in developing nations between 1970 and 1991, Davis found more favourable movement in these measures in the mineral dependent economies.

. . . Between 1975 and 1990, the average life expectancy in Africa's mineral dependent economies increased by about 4.8 years. The fuel exporting economies experienced an increase of 6.1 years while other mineral economies rose by 3.4 years. The corresponding change in non-mineral dependent economies was 3.3 years.

Daily calorie supply, which had been at similar levels in 1975 in mineral and non-mineral economies, increased by about 100 calories more in non-mineral economies than in mineral economies. Daily calorie intakes rose 260 calories in fuel exporting nations but fell by more than fifty calories in non-fuel mineral economies. Infant mortality rates began at somewhat higher levels in the non-mineral economies than in the mineral economies in 1975. They fell by somewhat more in the non-mineral economies over the next fifteen years but still remained at higher levels in those nations.

So the findings from this analysis of quality of life variables between 1975 and 1990 are mixed. A longer time period of analysis would seem necessary to reach more definitive conclusions.

The Past Decade—Is a Renaissance Underway?

The combination of a poor investment climate, political instability and the lack of supportive infrastructure including poor geological information contributed to the decline in the minerals industry in Africa generally up until 1990. In this environment it is hardly surprising that mineral economies did not perform well. But the economic geography of the world minerals industry has been changing in recent years. A reversal of the disinvestment trend between the 1960s and the 1980s has taken place since 1990 in many developing nations. Prospective nations in Latin America, Africa and Asia have received increased exploration spending. Inflows of foreign direct investment [FDI] have also been rising. An important early indicator of a broader change has been an increase in gold production from African nations outside of South Africa. The discussion of this section considers the extent of change and some of the reasons for it. It concludes by reflecting on whether the new operating environment has had any noticeable effect on the economic welfare of mineral dependent nations.

(a) Exploration Spending and Foreign Direct Investment in Mineral Development

The Metal Economics Group, which collects key mining data from large resource sector companies, reported a significant increase in the share of exploration spending in Africa during most of the 1990s. There was an apparent increase in the region's share of exploration spending from around six per cent in 1993 to more than thirteen per cent in 1998. It fell to 11.5 percent in 1999. Exploration spending in Africa increased from USD 165 million in 1993 to USD 670 million in 1997. Between 1997 and 1999 there was a decline in mineral exploration activity throughout the world. The fall in estimated mineral exploration spending in Africa to USD 323 million in 1999 reflects this. By the late 1990s Africa had overtaken the Asia-Pacific region as the second most favoured investment destination in the developing world after Latin America. . . .

Foreign direct investment (FDI) inflows to Africa increased generally during the 1990s, compared with the 1970s and 1980s. UNCTAD [United Nations Conference on Trade and Development] estimated that FDI inflows rose from USD 2 billion in 1990 to USD 10 billion in 1998. Despite the increase in the 1990s, investments by transnational corporations into Africa represented only 1.2 percent of global FDI flows and five percent of total foreign direct investment into developing nations. Although these data refer to direct investment in all industries, the authors of the UNCTAD report acknowledge that investment in natural resources in Africa has been the main focus of foreign direct investment.

The major presence of Canadian and Australian exploration and mining companies in Africa in the 1990s reflects this change. For Canadian-based resource companies, the growth of junior exploration companies, coupled with the success of Canadian stock exchanges, provided major stimulus for overseas investment. Campbell notes that Canadian companies responded aggressively to new liberalised operating environments in Africa in the 1990s. By 1996 there were over 170 Canadian-registered companies operating on the African continent. In the early 1990s hardly any Canadian companies had operations there. Campbell attributes the overseas involvement of Canadian mining companies particularly to competitive advantages as well as to the availability of risk capital from the Vancouver Stock Exchange.

Australian-based resource companies also became active in exploration and mine development in Africa during the 1990s. In 1985, Bridge Oil was apparently the only Australian resources company with interests in Africa. By 1992 fifteen Australian companies had African interests and this had increased to seventy-five by 1997. They operated in thirty African nations. . . . Australian companies had 134 projects in thirty African nations in 1999. This compared with 88 projects in 1995. Data collected by the Minerals Council of Australia also show increased offshore exploration spending by Australian mining companies, with Africa as one of the major destinations.

One reflection of the revival of Africa as a major mineral producer is the recent growth of the gold industry outside of South Africa. Despite declining prices, the gold sector has been the largest beneficiary of the new investment boom. Output increased from 40 tonnes in 1990 to more than 140 tonnes in 1998. Successful exploration has led to significant new gold mines coming on stream in Ghana, Mali, Tanzania, Guinea and Burkina Faso.

Tanzania's first mine in more than thirty years, Golden Pride, opened in 1998. The opening of Mali's Sadiola gold mine in 1997 propelled the country to one of the top twenty gold producers in the world. Mali now ranks as Africa's fourth largest gold producer behind South Africa, Ghana and Zimbabwe. Ghana's experience since 1988 illustrates the renaissance of the region's minerals industry more than any other country. Ghana's gold output increased from 12 tonnes in 1988 to over 70 tonnes in 1998. Australian companies opened two new gold mines at Damang (Ranger Minerals) and Obotan (Resolute) in the late 1990s.

Despite these positive developments . . . between 1989 and 1998 . . . Africa lost market share for ten of the eleven minerals reported. One might explain this apparently perverse trend by arguing that the new exploration and investment is taking several years to exert its full impact. Other forces may, however, be important. Before turning to this later issue we consider further some of the positive influences.

(b) Positive Influences on the Competitiveness of African Mining

Several factors have played a role in facilitating a re-emergence of African minerals and energy. They include:

- the modernisation of mining regimes through new legislation, formal mineral policy statements and observation of international agreements;
- availability of investment insurance;
- greater political stability in several prospective nations;
- a movement of privatisation of state mining companies; and
- changed conditions in home countries which have led to international expansion.

Otto reports that "Between 1985 and 1995 over 90 nations introduced, or commenced working on, new or major revisions to mining sector legislation." African nations were well represented in this group. This has created a more favourable environment for private sector investment. Campbell recognises the importance of these reforms to inflows of Canadian investment in Africa in the mid-1990s.

During the 1990s, fiscal regimes continued to evolve as competition for shrinking investment budgets increases. Countries like Botswana, one of the continent's most stable and attractive economies, introduced a new Mines and Minerals Act in 1999. This abolished free equity for government and simplified licensing systems. The Government of Namibia enacted a new Diamond Act in 1999, while Nigeria introduced its Mining and Minerals Decree No. 34. Recent changes to fiscal regimes in Benin, Burkina Faso, Central African Republic and Cote d'Ivoire have resulted in increased investor activity. Because of these changes the highly prospective Birimian greenstone belts in West and Central Africa have become major attractions for Canadian and South African mining companies.

The efforts of the World Bank to regenerate the African minerals industry are also playing a facilitating role. This occurs particularly through the activities of three of its associated organisations, the International Development Association (IDA), the Multilateral Investment Guarantee Agency (MIGA) and the International Finance Corporation (IFC).

Through its technical assistance program, the International Development Association currently makes credit available to countries wishing to reform their minerals sector. The International Finance Corporation (IFC) provides equity finance for projects in the developing world and helps mobilise private loans for private investors in the developing world. The Multilateral Investment Guarantee Agency provides investment risk guarantees to lower the risk profile of mining projects for foreign investors. Forty-two African nations were signatories to the MIGA convention by 1999. MIGA provides insurance against transfer restrictions, expropriation (direct and creeping), war and civil disturbance and against breach of contract by governments and helps mobilise insurance. The organisation also provides a mechanism for the settlement of investment disputes. Between the commencement of its guarantee scheme in Africa in 1991 and 1999, MIGA had issued 61 guarantees. Two examples of the work of IFC and MIGA relate to loans to finance the Sadiola gold mine in Mali and the Mozal Aluminium Smelter in Mozambique.

Institutions in Britain, France, Belgium, the United States and Canada have also been active in supporting investment risk protection measures to encourage movement of their companies into Africa. Two examples of these institutions are OPIC (for U.S. companies) and the Export Development Corporation (for Canadian companies).

Despite some notable exceptions, Africa was more politically stable in the 1990s, compared with the previous 30 years. The changes in political climate in countries such as Mozambique, Angola and the Democratic Republic of Congo, together with the post-apartheid government in South Africa, created a more favourable investment climate in the minerals sector. This had a particularly favourable impact for the major South African mining companies. They followed a program of greater diversification into the rest of the continent to replace aging and costly mines at home. Relative political stability in Mozambique and Angola led to legal mining resuming in these nations. Two diamond properties in the Luo and the Catoca in the kimberlite areas of Angola came into production in 1996. The aluminium smelter in Mozambique became a viable project after the UN supervised elections in the mid-1990s. Successes of foreign mining companies in Ghana, Tanzania and Mali and Mauritania have also enhanced the region's image.

Whereas privatisation of state-owned enterprises in most developed countries began in the mid-1980s, the process started much later in developing nations. Gathering momentum after 1990, it has been an important influence in attracting foreign direct investment. There have been several different privatisation approaches. They have included change in ownership status, complete divestiture or partial divestiture. Seventy percent of total FDI inflows into Africa in 1999 were in Angola, Egypt, Nigeria, South Africa and Morocco where major privatisations had occurred. UNCTAD reports that South Africa received USD 1.4 billion of foreign direct investment between 1990 and 1998. Ghana attracted USD 769 million, Nigeria, USD 500 million, Zambia USD 420 million, and Côte d'Ivoire USD 373 million.

Changing policy and legislative frameworks in the developed mining nations have also influenced the move of foreign mining companies into Africa. Factors such as more demanding environmental legislation and native title issues at home have been particularly important in encouraging European, North American and Australian resource companies to consider moving offshore. The activities of junior exploration companies have played a key role in promoting this change. Willing to take more risks, they have often been thwarted at home because mining and exploration tenements are more difficult to obtain.

(c) Mining Sector Reform and Economic Performance

Despite the above changes, the impact of reform in mineral rich African nations did not translate into economic or quality of life gains during most of the

1990s. . . . [B]etween 1990 and 1998, GDP at factor cost in Africa's mineral dependent economies grew at an average rate of 1.7 percent per annum. It compares with a growth rate of 3.1 percent in non-mineral economies. Furthermore, . . . a reduction in life expectancy in the mineral economies from 1990 to 1998 [occurred], as opposed to an increase in the non-mineral economies. Daily calorie supply increased at a faster rate in non-mineral economies and infant mortality rates declined more quickly than in their mineral dependent counterparts. . . . [F]uel exporting mineral economies fared considerably better than the non-fuel exporting mineral economies.

It is tempting to appeal directly to the resource curse thesis to provide an explanation for these trends. It would seem premature, however, to do so for at least two reasons. Firstly, the reform and renaissance of the African minerals sector is a process from which tangible benefits may take perhaps five or ten years more to flow into expected economic gains. Without consistent and continuing investment, a minerals industry loses its competitive strength. Rebuilding this in a consistent manner will take perhaps two decades, since it requires investment in infrastructure and human capital as well as exploration and mine development. The new policy and regulatory frameworks are establishing a good foundation for this to take place but the process is far from complete. Secondly, the poor performance of quality of life indicators in the non-fuel mineral economies appears to reflect the impact of the HIV/AIDS epidemic in Southern Africa.

An associated line of empirical investigation is to review the most recent rates of economic growth—say between 1996 and 1998—in African nations. In the 16 mineral dependent economies, real GDP at factor cost grew from an estimated USD 348.5 billion to USD 365.3 billion during this time—a growth rate of 2.3 percent per annum. In the 37 non-mineral economies estimated GDP at factor cost grew from USD 143.5 billion to USD 155 billion. This was an annual growth rate of 4.1 percent per annum. It is clear that a minerals-driven recovery is not yet under way.

(d) Mineral Endowment, Labour Productivity, Comparative and Competitive Advantage

. . . Africa's mineral endowment is substantial. The continent's favourable geology and the relative lack of recent mineral exploitation means that there are many high quality and potentially profitable deposits available, other things being equal. Recent mineral sector reforms and other legislative changes have apparently "levelled the playing field" for potential African mineral producers.

Despite this, developed nations such as the United States, Canada and Australia retained their percentage shares of world mineral production during the 1990s. This followed an increase between 1980 and 1990, despite a significant decline in ore grade at operating mines. By utilising new mineral processing technologies, adopting modern mining methods and operating more efficiently in other ways (particularly through outsourcing), resource companies in these nations improved their fortunes. In recent papers on the U.S. copper industry,

Aydin and Tilton and Tilton and Landsberg find that labour productivity tripled between 1975 and 1985. Between 1985 and 1995 this enabled the US industry to recover the share of world copper output lost in the preceding ten years. New technology and innovation appeared either as important or more important than mineral endowment in shaping comparative advantage in the copper industry. Australia's re-emergence in the 1980s as a major world gold producer and its holding of this position in the 1990s seem consistent with these findings.

It is useful to reflect on a model such as the Porter "diamond" in assessing the current position of the African mineral industry. The four attributes in this model that determine competitive advantage are

- factor conditions. As well as mineral endowment, these include the quality of human and knowledge resources, the availability of capital and the quality of infrastructure.
- home demand conditions and the potential for their growth,
- the presence of and development of related and supporting industries, and
- firm strategy, structure and rivalry.

"Chance" events such as major technological or input cost discontinuities, surges in world demand, shifts in world financial markets or exchange rates, political decisions by foreign governments or wars may also affect these main determinants.

The role of government policy stance is also important. As well as establishing a suitable mineral policy framework its activities in other areas such as education, taxation, environmental protection, road, rail and telecommunications have an important complementary role. These will enhance factor conditions, encourage the growth of domestic demand and promote the growth of supporting industries. If applied over an extended period of a decade or two it will set the stage for movement through the factor-driven stage of national competitive development towards the investment-driven and innovation-driven stages. It is during these stages that nations move towards the "developed economy" status. Nations such as Canada, Australia and the United States have reached the innovation-driven stages with their mineral industries and this has facilitated the broader development of the rest of their economy.

Porter notes that "to progress, the developing nations face the daunting task of upgrading all four parts of the national "diamond" sufficiently to reach the threshold necessary to compete in advanced industries." Yet successes of Japan, Korea, Taiwan and Hong Kong in the second half of the twentieth century provide important case studies of this taking place. The recent strong economic performance of China and India is also encouraging. From a mineral and energy sector perspective, the emergence of nations such as Saudi Arabia, Chile and the United Arab Emirates suggests promise. The development experiences of countries such as South Africa, Brazil and Mexico are also worthy of mention.

An important conclusion from this discussion is that new mine development (or the expansion of existing mines) requires more than a favourable mineral endowment and the delineation of viable deposits with recent mineral exploration activity. As well as a favourable policy environment, technology and management issues are an important part of mineral sector development. Strong supporting infrastructure and a capable human capital base both are necessary to reap major benefits and to retain competitiveness over longer periods of time. Political stability is essential. For new mineral development to provide a platform for economic growth and development in African nations with major mineral endowments, as it has in Canada, Australia and the United States, the process will take perhaps a generation or more. It has recently taken each of the High Performing Asian Economies (Japan, China and the Asian Tigers) two or three decades to build their human and physical capital bases to a point where they have been able to compete favourably with the developed nations.

Concluding Remarks

With high geological prospectivity in many nations a safer and more attractive investment climate, Africa has recently shown the capacity to capture a greater share of the investment budgets of global mining companies. If this is to continue further, African nations must continue to change images of a continent of civil unrest, starvation, deadly diseases and economic disorder.

The [selection] has shown that in general, FDI in Africa has increased in recent years due to improved regulatory frameworks, permitting profit repatriation, tax incentives provision and trade liberalisation. Progress on modernisation is uneven on the continent but countries have generally embraced the importance of private-sector led investment growth and realised that governments have to play a regulatory role. Sustaining a long-term renaissance will depend on many factors including the pace of reform, political stability, economic growth and developments in other investment destinations such as Asia and Latin America.

Ethnic disturbances and military coups remain major challenges to political stability. Political stability is also related to good governance, low levels of corruption and transparency. Weak institutional capacity remains a major constraint in many African countries.

The success of many current projects will be critical in ensuring a sustained flow of investors to Africa. Good macro-economic performance is a key for continued inflow of foreign investment and also for local investors. The change in the policy and regulatory environment, deregulation and privatization programs are each important areas in reversing investment trends towards Africa. Programs supported by the United Nations and the World Bank to improve the operating environment in the region also appear to have an important place in this process.

Although the recent signs appear promising, it remains too early to appraise whether the "renaissance" of the African minerals sector will provide the impetus for the large number of mineral dependent nations to move forward significantly in their development. Given the difficult experiences of many African nations in their immediate post-colonial histories, an optimistic hope is that resource development will be seen as a blessing rather than a curse by the year 2010. Perhaps by that stage, economists will be writing of an African economic miracle under way.

References

African Development Bank (2000). *African Development Report 2000.*

Auty, R. (1986). "Multinational Resource Corporations, Nationalization and Diminished Viability: Caribbean Plantations, Mines and Oilfields in the Seventies," in C. Dixon et al. (Eds), *Multinational Corporations and the Third World,* Croom Helm, London, pp. 160–187.

Auty, R. (1993). "Determinants of state mining enterprise resilience in Latin America," *Natural Resources Forum,* pp. 3–11.

Aydin, H., and J. Tilton (2000). "Mineral Endowment, Labor Productivity, and Comparative Advantage in Mining," *Resource and Energy Economics,* Vol. 22, pp. 281–293.

Blainey, G. (1993). *The Rush that Never Ended: A History of Australian Mining,* Fourth edition, Melbourne: Melbourne University Press.

British Geological Survey (2000). *World Mineral Statistics.* Keyworth: Nottingham.

Campbell, B. (1998). "Liberalisation, Deregulation, State Promoted Investment—Canadian Mining Interests in Africa," *Journal of Mineral Policy, Business and Environment,* Vol. 13, No. 4. pp. 14–34.

Crowson, P. (1998). *Minerals Handbook 1998/99,* Mining Journal Books, London.

Davis, G. (1995). "Learning to Love the Dutch Disease: Evidence from the Mineral Economies," *World Development,* Vol. 23, No. 10, pp. 1765–99.

Ericsson, M. (1991). "African Mining: Light at the End of the Tunnel," *Review of African Political Economy,* Vol. 51, pp. 96–107.

Gelb, A.H. (1988). *Oil Windfalls: Blessing or Curse?* Oxford University Press, New York.

Minmet Australia (2001). . . .

Minerals Council of Australia (various years): *Mineral Industry Survey,* Canberra. . . .

Norrie, K. and D. Owram (1996). *A History of the Canadian Economy,* 2nd edition, Toronto: Harcourt Brace Jovanovich.

O'Brien, J. (1994). *Undoing a Myth: Chile's debt to Copper and Mining,* Ottawa: International Council on Metals and the Environment.

O'Neill, D. (1992). "Australian Miners in Africa: An Australian Perspective," *Mining Review,* Vol. 16, No. 4, pp. 34–40.

Otto, J.M. (1997). "A National Mineral Policy as a Regulatory Tool," *Resources Policy,* Vol. 23, Nos. 1/2, pp. 1–7.

Otto, J.M. (1998). "Global Changes in Mining Laws, Agreements and Tax Systems," *Resources Policy,* Vol. 23, No. 4, pp. 79–86.

Porter, M. (1990). *The Competitive Advantage of Nations,* Macmillan, Basingstoke.

Premoli, C. (1998). "Mineral Exploration in Africa: The Long View," in S. Vearcombe and S.E. Ho (Eds.), *Africa: Geology and Mineral Exploration, AIG Bulletin,* No. 25, pp. 35–46.

Radetzki, M. (1985). *State Mineral Enterprises: An Investigation into Their Impact on International Mineral Markets,* Resources for the Future, Washington, DC.

Radetzki, M. (1990). *A Guide to Primary Commodities in the World Economy,* Basil Blackwell, Oxford.

Sachs, J. and A. Warner (1995). "Natural Resource Abundance and Economic Growth," Development Discussion Paper No. 517a, Harvard Institute for International Development, Cambridge, USA.

Sinclair, W.A. (1976). *The Process of Economic Development in Australia,* Melbourne: Longman Cheshire.

Slater, C.L. (1996). "The Investment Climate for Gold Mining: Comparing Australia with the USA," *Natural Resources Forum,* Vol. 20, No. 1, pp. 37–48.

South African Chamber of Mines (1998). . . .

Tilton, J. (1989). "The New View of Minerals and Economic Growth," *The Economic Record,* Vol. 65, No. 190, pp. 265–278.

Tilton, J., and H. Landsberg (1999). Innovation, Productivity Growth and the Survival of the U.S. Copper Industry, in R.D. Simpson (Ed.), *Productivity in Natural Resource Industries: Improvement through Innovation,* Resources for the Future, Washington, DC.

UNCTAD (1999). *Foreign Direct Investment in Africa: Performance and Potential,* UNCTAD/ITE/IIT/Misc. 15, United Nations, Geneva.

UNCTAD (2000). *The World Investment Report 2000: Cross-border Mergers and Acquisitions and Development,* United Nations, Geneva.

United States Geological Survey (2000). *Mineral Industry Surveys.* . . .

World Bank (1992). *Strategy for African Mining,* Technical Paper No. 181, Mining Unit and Energy Division, Washington, DC.

A Continent in Crisis: Africa and Globalization

From the oil fields of the Niger Delta in Nigeria, to the diamond and copper fields of Sierra Leone, Angola, and Liberia, to the rich mineral deposits of the Great Lakes region, to the mountain ranges, plains and tourist havens of the East African countries, the continent of Africa is undoubtedly blessed.

From these blessings, however, much sorrow has flowed. During the colonial era, most Africans did not benefit from the continent's resources. African economies were geared toward cultivating raw materials for export, and roads, health care, and other infrastructure were available only in areas where those materials were produced. The end of colonialism unleashed struggles for political control, social emancipation, and access to resources—struggles that, in turn, have degenerated into conflicts and internecine wars. Retarded in their development, unbridled in their lust for power, steeped in official corruption, chaotic in their political engineering, many African states are now sprinting toward total collapse.

Much of the blame for Africa's spiral of violence belongs to generations of opportunistic and venal African leaders, who have done little to develop their societies and emancipate their peoples. But the expansion of corporate dominance has accentuated the steady descent into near economic strangulation and political chaos. Many transnational corporations (TNCs) have acted as economic predators in Africa, gobbling up national resources, distorting national economic policies, exploiting and changing labor relations, committing environmental despoliation, violating sovereignties, and manipulating governments and the media. In order to ensure uninterrupted access to resources, TNCs have also supported repressive African leaders, warlords, and guerrilla fighters, thus serving as catalysts for lethal conflict and impeding prospects for development and peace.

TNCs and the African State

In the post-colonial period, many African leaders have exerted dictatorial control over their societies. Through their undemocratic policies, they have spread dissatisfaction among the people, which has manifested over time in nationalistic feelings and even popular rebellions. These political tensions, in turn, have generated fierce conflicts over resource control.

From *Dollars & Sense*, July/August 2001. Reprinted by permission of Dollars & Sense, a progressive economics magazine. www.dollarsandsense.org.

In response to these conflicts, many African governments have embraced collaboration with TNCs and other foreign investors. Lacking the technological capacity to harness massive reserves of oil, gold, diamonds, and cobalt, these leaders grant licenses to foreign corporations to operate in their domain, and then appropriate the resulting revenue to maintain themselves in power. For example, both the late General Sani Abacha of Nigeria and the late Mobutu Sese Seko of Zaire looted hundreds of millions of dollars in government funds derived from corporate revenue, stashed the money in private foreign accounts, and used it for political patronage and to silence political opponents.

In turn, these authoritarian governments have stifled economic growth. Frequent changes in leadership through *coups d'etat* have made it impracticable to implement development plans. Each new government comes in with a new set of policies that often undermines earlier progress by previous governments. Also, many African leaders have used revenue to reward political pals with bogus contracts for white-elephant projects that contribute nothing to development. In the late 1990s, for example, President Daniel Arap Moi of Kenya built an airport—which handles almost no traffic—in his own hometown of Eldoret. And of course, money used as handouts to members of the ruling elite and to fight political opposition is money *not* spent on development.

After decades of economic mismanagement and political gangsterism, most African societies are in terrible shape. African unemployment rates are at crisis levels, with over 65% of college graduates out of jobs. Because manufacturing is at a low ebb, unskilled workers suffer a similar fate. Wages are also low. According to the *United Nations Development Report*, the average unskilled worker earns about 55 cents daily, while the average white-collar employee brings home a monthly check of between $50 and $120. Many African societies are characterized by minimal opportunities for education and self-development, collapsed infrastructure, and a debilitating debt burden.

These conditions have made the continent even more susceptible to international financial control. Typically, TNCs seek out societies with low production costs, poor working conditions, and abundant and easily exploitable resources, where profits can be maximized and repatriated without legal constraints. The icing, of course, is a political leadership that is weak, corrupt, and ready to cut deals. TNCs make huge investments in countries that meet those criteria, and many African countries fit the bill.

Economic Exploitation in Africa

The sheer growth of TNCs in recent decades has had profound consequences for Africa. The average growth rate of TNCs is three times that of the most advanced industrial countries. Of the 100 biggest economies in the world, more than half are corporations. TNCs hold enormous power to transform the world political economy, and Africa's vast resources, cheap labor, huge population, and expanding markets are crucial to their plans.

The globalization optimists maintain that global capital has served as a dynamic engine of growth, opening the window for diverse opportunities in terms of goods and services, creating employment, and boosting government revenues. This has been true in a few cases. In South Africa and Nigeria, for example, gold mining and oil companies respectively have brought new technology, attracted subsidiary industries, and made it possible for indigenous personnel to acquire skills.

However, any such benefits are far outweighed by activities that deplete local resources, stifle local or indigenous industry, and subvert the fragile democratic process. Africa is still confined to the role it played in the industrial revolution(s) that preceded globalization. Its raw materials are still being depleted without generating development.

In addition, the continent's increasing dependence on imported capital and consumer goods and services has left various sectors of the domestic economy comatose. African markets are specially targeted as dumping grounds for new and second-hand goods. Because of stiff competition from these products, infant manufacturing established earlier in Africa has quickly withered away. For example, imports of used clothing from the United States are threatening to destroy Kenya's domestic textile industry.

Finally, as soon as the TNCs have African economies firmly in their grip, they deploy funds and patronage to manipulate the media and influence government policies. Governments, in turn, grant them *carte blanche* to sidestep labor and environmental laws.

Other global institutions have contributed to the deregulation of African economies. The Generalized Agreement on Tariffs and Trade, the World Trade Organization, and the International Monetary Fund (IMF) all promote increased liberalization of international trade. The IMF's structural adjustment programs (SAPs) require African states to freeze wages, devalue currency, remove public subsidies, and impose other austerity measures, which have brought about even greater unemployment and under-utilization of productive capacity. These policies have caused considerable turmoil in Africa. In the early 1980s, Uganda was rocked by weeks of demonstrations, as industrial workers and students took to the streets to denounce President Milton Obote's IMF-imposed economic program. In 1990, Matthew Kerokou of the Benin Republic in West Africa was swept out of power in a wave of anti-SAP riots.

Corporations and Lethal Conflict

At the advent of the new millennium, Africa is hurting badly. Most parts of the continent are embroiled in independence wars, ethnic conflicts, violent wars for political and resource control, and cross-border conflicts. In a recent study of armed conflicts around the world, the University of Maryland's Center for International Development and Conflict Management found that 33 countries were at high risk for instability. Of these, 20 were in Africa.

In their quest to unravel the forces generating conflict in Africa, human-rights groups are closely scrutinizing TNCs. TNCs are not always responsible for the genesis of the crisis. But some of the deadliest conflicts that litter Africa's political landscape, at least in the last decade, can definitely be traced to the expansion and domination of TNCs.

This is especially true in extractive states where resources with global appeal, value, and markets are found. While the state's interest in generating revenue from these resources coincides with that of the TNCs, the latter's interest in maximizing profits conflicts with the welfare of the citizens. Thus, the state is caught between protecting a vital source of revenue, and defending the rights and privileges of its citizens. Too often, the state, in order to ensure an ongoing flow of revenue, sides with the TNCs against the citizens.

For example, the oil-producing Niger Delta region is perpetually at war with the government and oil corporations. For decades, successive Nigerian governments have been beholden to the TNCs that possess the technology, technical expertise, and capital to exploit the country's oil. The exploitation has resulted in serious environmental damage, developmental neglect, human-rights abuses, economic oppression, and inequitable resource allocation. These abuses, and the need for redress, are at the heart of the conflict. In recent months, calls for secession by the oil-yielding region have grown louder. As other parts of the country caught up in oil politics fight to defend their interests, the drums of war continue to beat. . . .

TNCs have played a major role in the Nigerian conflict. They gave their unalloyed support to the brutal military regimes of Generals Ibrahim Babangida and Sani Abacha. Under Abacha, Ken Saro-Wiwa and eight other activists were hanged for crusading against the government and the oil companies. Officials at Royal Dutch Shell, which dominates the lucrative Nigerian oil industry, admitted in a press statement that the company could have stopped the hangings if it had so desired. Shell executives also confessed publicly to purchasing arms for the Nigerian State Police, who have attacked community residents and picketers. Also, in 1998, oil giant Chevron used its own helicopter to carry Nigerian soldiers, who stormed Parambe, an oil-yielding community, and killed several protesters.

In Angola, meanwhile, the global trade in diamonds—widely known as "blood diamonds" or "conflict diamonds" because of their lethal consequences—has helped to perpetuate more than 20 years of civil war. With revenue from the illegal mining and sale of rough diamonds, the UNITA [Portuguese acronym for the National Union for the Total Independence of Angola] rebels, led by Jonas Savimbi, have been able to purchase and stockpile ammunition to prolong the war. Though fully aware of this, a number of corporations—such as American Mineral Fields (AMF), Oryx, and the world's leading diamond company, De Beers—continue to do business in the war-torn territory, where more than half a million citizens have been killed.

Also, Jean-Raymond Boulle, AMF's principal shareholder, is known to have invested millions of dollars in support of corrupt African governments and rebel leaders in order to secure juicy mineral contracts. The late Congolese leader Laurent Kabila used Boulle's jet and funds to prosecute his war against Mobutu of Zaire. When Kabila came to power in 1997, AMF secured exploration rights to 600 million pounds of cobalt and three billion pounds of copper, among other deals.

Similarly, the Foday Sankoh-led Revolutionary United Front (RUF) in Sierra Leone derives most of the funds it has used to unleash terror and mayhem on the country's people from the international trade in conflict diamonds. The RUF continues to fight a war that has claimed more than 80,000 lives, with no end in sight. According to the U.S. State Department, revenue from rough and uncut diamonds mined in conflict areas forms a large percentage of the commodity's over $50 billion in annual sales.

The conflicts that grip Africa can also be traced to a steady flow of arms. To safeguard their economic interests, Western corporations are procuring weapons and providing arms training in areas of conflict. Embattled African leaders, anxious to defend their own interests and protect their hold on power, readily grant contracts to private security armies run by TNCs. Since the early 1990s, the growth of the corporate private security sector in Africa has been phenomenal. TNCs have become direct parties to conflicts by recruiting or hiring private security companies to help protect their installations, operations and staff. In the process, they have connived with governments and some-times with rebels, whichever is most expedient, thereby instigating further conflict and perpetuating civil war.

For example, in 1995, Executive Outcome (EO), a private security company, arrived in Sierra Leone. The Sierra Leonean government paid EO almost $40 million in cash, along with mining concessions, to assist in its campaign against the RUF. The peace it secured did not last; rather, the country was plunged into deeper crisis. EO was also in Angola, training the national army and helping to recapture lucrative mineral fields. In 1993, the Angolan state oil company, Sonangol, contracted with EO to provide security for its installations against UNITA attacks. The Angolan government also signed a three-year, $40 million contract with EO to supply military hardware and training.

In addition, J. & S. Franklin, a British supplier of military equipment, won a contract to train the Sierra Leonean military using the notorious U.S.-based Gurkha Security Guards. The Guards have carried out a series of military attacks in various mining areas to protect the activities of TNCs. J. & S. Franklin has also won supply contracts with several other African governments engaged in conflicts.

Clearly, where minerals abound, TNCs find the lure irresistible. They accrue substantial profits from diamonds, which are sold in wedding rings, bracelets, and necklaces all over Europe and the United Stares. TNCs also profit enormously from cobalt, a vital raw material for the manufacture of jet fighters. The unbridled lust for excessive gain has deadened the senses of corporate giants like De Beers, Royal Dutch Shell, Chevron, AMF, and others to the damaging impact of their activities.

Out of the Labyrinth

Because of the twin problems of rogue leadership and the exploitative tendencies of TNCs, Africa is caught between a rock and a hard place. As the history of conflicts in Africa shows, the extraction of mineral resources creates and rein-forces government corruption, which easily begets repressive societies. As would be expected, poverty, unemployment, and insecurity spread, while social services decay. This leaves the citizens more prone to take up arms and fight in oil, diamond, and copper wars, as the conflicts in Sierra Leone, Angola, Nigeria, Sudan, Liberia, and the Great Lakes region all attest.

How can Africa wrench itself from itself and curb the rampaging TNCs? In response to corporations' bad behavior, and their brazen disregard for the political stability and economic viability of the states in which they operate, international human-rights organizations have tried to establish mechanisms of accountability.

The key, however, is action by Africans on their own behalf. Their options for ending the circle of violence and economic exploitation are few but practicable. Africa needs a new generation of leaders to define and pursue a dynamic political and economic agenda. The African states must renegotiate their terms of trade in the international marketplace. Diverse groups must achieve a sense of national pride and internal cohesiveness, in order to create an atmosphere conducive to implementing development programs. As long as the resources have not yet been depleted, there is still hope of rising again for a continent that has tarried for too long in the labyrinth.

POSTSCRIPT

Are Abundant Mineral and Energy Resources a Catalyst for African Development?

The issue of resource abundance and economic growth in Africa has received renewed attention in recent years due to at least three developments: increased interest by the United States in African energy resources leading up to and after the 2003 Iraq War, particularly brutal civil conflicts in Sierra Leone and Angola financed by the sale of mineral resources, and growing investments by South African entrepreneurs in the mining sectors of other African countries since the end of apartheid.

First, with escalating concerns about dependence on oil from the Middle East, the United States increasingly has become interested in oil exploration and oil field development in a number of African countries. In a January 13, 2003, *Los Angeles Times* article entitled "U.S. Quest for Oil in Africa Worries Analysts, Activists," Warren Vieth reports that "the Bush administration's search for more secure sources of oil is leading it to the doorsteps of some of the world's most troubled and repressive regimes: the petroleum-rich countries of West Africa." While the Bush administration states that it is committed to improving conditions in Africa, the concern among Africanist scholars and policy analysts is that production will be put ahead of balanced reform and development. The history of U.S. interaction with other oil-rich African nations does not portend well for good governance and broad-based development.

Second, in the last several years the links between brutal civil conflicts and the diamond trade in Sierra Leone and Angola have become increasingly clear. This recognition led to the appellation of diamonds from these countries as blood, or conflict, diamonds. See a recent book by Greg Campbell entitled *Blood Diamonds: Tracing the Deadly Path of the World's Most Precious Stones* (Westview Press, 2002).

Finally, the mining sector in Africa has been transformed in recent years by the infusion (some would say invasion) of South African capital and expertise. This is related to the fact that South Africans were often prohibited from investing in other parts of the continent prior to the end of apartheid in 1994. Given the history of antagonism between South Africa and the frontline states, many countries are leery of a growing South African presence in their economies. Despite these concerns, some are grateful to have a new eager investor. See a February 17, 2002, *New York Times* article by Rachel Swarns entitled "Awe and Unease as South Africa Stretches Out."

ISSUE 7

Is Increasing Chinese Investment Good for African Development?

YES: Ali Zafar, from "The Growing Relationship Between China and Sub-Saharan Africa: Macroeconomic, Trade, Investment and Aid Links, *World Bank Research Observer* (Spring 2007)

NO: Padraig R. Carmody and Francis Y. Owusu, from "Competing Hegemons? Chinese versus American Geo-Economic Strategies in Africa," *Political Geography* (2007)

ISSUE SUMMARY

YES: Ali Zafar, a macroeconomist with the World Bank, acknowledges the downside of increasing Chinese economic interests in Africa, but foresees more potential winners than losers. Among the big winners of increasing Chinese trade are oil exporters (Angola, Gabon, and Sudan) and resource-rich countries (Mauritania, South Africa, Mozambique, and Zambia). Chinese foreign direct investment is also increasing rapidly in those countries where it has trade interests.

NO: Padraig R. Carmody of Trinity College Dublin and Francis Y. Owusu of Iowa State University are less sanguine about Chinese involvement in Africa. Even though they also perceive potential benefits from increasing trade with China, they describe how increasing resource flows are strengthening authoritarian states and fuelling conflict.

Chinese trade with Africa has grown by leaps and bounds over the past several years. The value of Chinese trade with Africa rose from $10.6 billion in 2000, to $40 billion in 2005, to $55.5 billion in 2006. It is predicted to surpass $70 billion by the end of 2007, and the Chinese Ministry of Commerce has projected that it is likely to reach $100 billion by 2010.

Although increasing trade with China appears to be one of the major reasons why average economic growth rates are increasing in Sub-Saharan Africa (in fact, average economic growth rates for Sub-Saharan Africa doubled between 2000 and 2005), a number of concepts from the development literature suggest that African countries need to carefully negotiate this situation if they wish to secure lasting development gains.

Dependency theory might be deployed to portray some aspects of China's relationship with Africa. Dependency theorists, like Andre Gunder Frank, wrote about Europe's relationship with its colonies. For Frank, the primary role of the colonies was to provide raw materials to the metropole. Economies were often changed through taxation policies, infrastructure installed, and elites trained for the sole purpose of guaranteeing the smooth export of unprocessed resources. As such, many former colonies were "underdeveloped" as their economies were reshaped to provide such raw materials. The problem is that this type of colonial relationship (which often persists in the form of neocolonialism) produces a situation of dependency in which cheap unprocessed materials are exported or exchanged for relatively expensive manufactured goods.

Another such idea is that of the "resource curse" phenomenon or "Dutch Disease." While the resource curse idea has several facets, the aspect most relevant to this issue is the notion that the extraction of particularly lucrative resources may lead to the simplification, or concentration, of national economies, with increasing dependence on a single export mineral or fuel. "Dutch Disease" is a slight variation on this same theme and specifically refers to the decline of the manufacturing sector in the face of particularly profitable resource extraction opportunities. This term was first used by the *Economist* magazine in 1977 to describe the decline of the manufacturing sector in the Netherlands after the discovery of natural gas in the 1960s. Although simple trade models suggest that a country should specialize in the export of goods for which it has a comparative advantage, such as oil for an oil-rich country, the reality is often more complicated. If the natural resource begins to run out, or there is a downturn in prices for the good, it will be much more difficult for a country to begin or renew an industrial sector because they will face stiff (if not crushing) competition from other countries that have been investing in this area all along.

In this issue, Ali Zafar, a macroeconomist with the World Bank, acknowledges the downside of increasing Chinese economic interests in Africa, but foresees more potential winners than losers. Among the big winners of increasing Chinese trade are oil exporters (Angola, Gabon, and Sudan) and resource-rich countries (Mauritania, South Africa, Mozambique, and Zambia). Chinese demand for African resources has led to an upswing in prices and a boost in real GDP for Sub-Saharan Africa. Chinese foreign direct investment is also increasing rapidly in those countries where it has trade interests. Zafar suggests that China presents an opportunity for Africa to reduce its marginalization in the global economy.

Padraig Carmody of Dublin City University and Francis Owusu of Iowa State University are less positive about Chinese involvement in Africa. They describe how African trade flows are reorienting from the "Global North" to the "Global East." They further explore the political and economic impacts of increased geo-economic competition between the East and the West in Africa. While they perceive potential benefits from increasing trade with China, they describe how increasing resource flows are strengthening authoritarian states and fuelling conflict.

YES

Ali Zafar

The Growing Relationship Between China and Sub-Saharan Africa: Macroeconomic, Trade, Investment, and Aid Links

This article surveys the main trade, investment, and aid links between China and Sub-Saharan Africa and assesses the principal dynamics of the relationship. It also examines the indirect macroeconomic effects of China's policies on Africa, particularly in relation to global output, savings, and commodity prices. Using trade and commodity price data, the article seeks to understand the nature of the Sino-African trade relationship and focuses on two important sectors—oil and textiles. It concludes by briefly examining the potential positive and negative effects of Chinese trade and investment in Africa.

China's Africa Policy and the Beijing Consensus

. . . The signs of China's economic expansion are becoming increasingly manifest in Sub-Saharan Africa. Over the last decade, China has built a network of trade, aid, and investment links with close to 50 African countries, and there has been a rush to buy up concessions to Africa's natural resources. Chinese companies are mining oil in Angola and Sudan, building roads in Ethiopia, working with the electricity sector in Kenya, building infrastructure and developing the tourism industry in Sierra Leone, and servicing mobile phone networks in Kenya and Nigeria. Throughout Sub-Saharan Africa, Chinese companies are building vital infrastructure, including dams, ports, and roads, and helping to renovate government offices and other buildings. China's foreign policy is being increasingly driven by its domestic development strategy and the need for resources. However, the interest is not confined solely to natural resources, as Chinese firms have ventured into the light manufacturing and services sectors and entered into agroprocessing, apparel, and telecommunications. Meanwhile, Africa is increasingly awash with low-cost Chinese motorcycles, electronic goods, and T-shirts, benefiting the consumers in the continent.

Over the last several years, China has intensified diplomatic links with Africa. Under the auspices of the China–Africa Cooperation Forum of 2000, comprising 46 of 53 African countries, bilateral trade and economic cooperation

From *The World Bank Research Observer*, Spring 2007. Copyright © 2007 by Oxford University Press Journals. Reprinted by permission via Rightslink.

have entered a new realm. In a symbolic gesture that carries much hidden weight, the Chinese foreign minister has maintained a policy of making his first official overseas trip each year to Africa. In January 2006, the Chinese government issued its official Africa policy, calling itself the world's largest developing country and seeking the establishment of a new strategic partnership with Africa marked by an intensification of dialogue on the political front combined with closer economic cooperation (China Ministry of Foreign Affairs 2006). In November 2006, a very high-level China–Africa summit, with the participation of more than 40 African heads of state, was held in Beijing to cement trade and investment relations between the world's fastest growing economy and the world's poorest continent. . . .

As a rising power, China is altering some of the prevailing practices and parameters in development assistance. One analyst, Joshua Cooper Ramo, has termed the Chinese approach the "Beijing Consensus," with the development of new attitudes toward politics, development, and the global balance of power (Ramo 2004). China's distinctive approach involves a combination of aggressive diplomacy and the cultivation of friendly ties with a "no-strings attached" financial and technical assistance package. The only real prerequisite for Chinese assistance is support for Beijing's one-China policy (in relation to Taiwan, China). China's pledge of noninterference in countries' internal affairs and lack of lending conditions on governance or fiscal management have elicited positive reactions from several governments.

However, China's lack of attention to governance, democracy, and human rights issues in Africa, as testified by its support of pariah regimes in Sudan and Zimbabwe and its delinking of aid from political reform, has raised concerns that the flow of Chinese aid may cause African governments to delay reforms that promote openness and accountability. Given the propensity for corruption in the management of natural resources, China's lack of attention to matters of resource transparency and mechanisms of oversight among its African partners has been a cause for concern. Moreover, the tendency of Chinese companies to import labor from China, coupled with allegations of poor labor practices and unfair competition against local enterprises, has generated an anti-Chinese backlash in several African countries, notably South Africa and Zambia. Finally, the disregard for environmental impact assessments risks derailing the progress that has been made on that front over the last two decades. In sum, there are fears that this neglect of governance and proper standards may be detrimental to many countries' overall development efforts. . . .

To systematically examine these issues, this article analyses the channels of transmission between China and Sub-Saharan Africa—global macroeconomics, trade flows, and foreign direct investment and aid. Jenkins and Edwards (2005) identify several direct impact channels: growth of African exports to China (complementarity effect), increased competition from China in third-country markets (competitive effect), increased competition of China in African country markets (competitive effect), and effects of foreign direct investment (competitive or complementarity effects). Besides the direct impacts, China can exert an indirect impact by pushing up prices of primary commodities, even if the country does not export directly to China. Increased Chinese demand will affect global demand, which will also influence Sub-Saharan economies. . . .

Global Macroeconomics

China, through the effects of its financial and trade policies on the international macroeconomic environment, exerts an indirect effect on economic management in Africa. As a global price-setter, its actions have major repercussions on world interest rates, output, and inflation. The Chinese have directly contributed to macroeconomic management in Sub-Saharan Africa by helping create the large commodity booms that have resulted in the inflows of capital into the continent. . . .

A second potential channel of Chinese influence on Africa is through China's effects on global prices, interest rates, and commodity prices. First, China has helped to maintain low interest rates and bond yields through its financing of the U.S. deficit. There is some empirical evidence that high commodity prices are influenced by low real interest rates. Second, by contrast, supply-side factors in China are creating downward price pressures in a number of industrial sectors globally, including light manufactures like textiles and clothing, and high technology products.

Commodity Prices and Terms of Trade

One of the key variables through which China has affected the rest of the world economy is the impact on commodity prices and the resulting terms of trade effects. China has become a key driver of price dynamics in the metals market. It is the world's largest consumer of steel, copper, coal, platinum, and cement, and it is responsible for much of the rise in *The Economist's* commodity-price index in recent years. Offsetting its downward impact on prices of global manufactures, rising prices for steel, soybeans, copper, oil, and platinum due to China's large appetite are affecting countries' terms of trade. Countries like Argentina, Australia, and Canada are seeing significant gains from commodity exports to China. Among the five basic food, energy, and industrial commodities—grain, meat, oil, coal, and steel—consumption in China has eclipsed that of the United States in all but oil. . . .

The impact of China's growing demand has been particularly strong in Sub-Saharan Africa, where more than three-quarters of export revenues come from commodities. In 2004, real GDP in Sub-Saharan Africa accelerated to 5.1 percent, the highest in almost a decade, underpinned by the strength of the global economy and, even more, by oil and commodity prices. In 2005, economic growth reached 5.2 percent, with metal prices jumping more than 15 percent. The surge in prices due to China has generated rents for resource-rich countries as well as windfalls for companies in the extractive industries. While commodity markets are notoriously volatile, characterized by frequent boom–bust cycles, the rise of China and other large emerging markets may have led to a fundamental change in long-term price trends, and the world

Figure 1

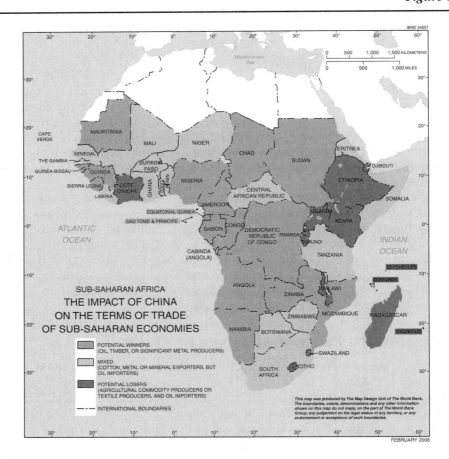

may be entering a period of sustained high prices, particularly of metals. While metal prices are expected to retreat over the medium term as new capacity comes online, they will most likely not fall to earlier levels, in part because of the increase in production costs due to higher energy prices.

To assess China's impact on terms of trade in Sub-Saharan Africa, a quantitative analysis was conducted for 2000–2005. . . . The goal was to calculate the relative contribution of China to the growth in global demand and consumption growth for African export commodities from 2000 to 2005, and then, based on an analysis of the commodity composition of exports and imports, assess China's overall impact on the terms of trade for each country, measured as the ratio of export prices to import prices. Countries were classified as winners, mixed winners–losers, and losers based on a qualitative assessment of the general effect of China on their terms of trade (figure 1). China's effect on oil and metal prices was considered a positive shock, while its downward effect on the prices of global manufactures, especially textiles and apparel, was considered a negative shock. The analysis seeks to isolate the effect of China from the effects of other countries on these economies. A measurement of the development and potential poverty-reducing impact is beyond the scope of the study.

- *Winners.* Oil exporters and resource-rich countries, like Angola, Gabon, and Sudan, and base metal exporters, such as Mauritania (iron ore), Mozambique (aluminum), South Africa (platinum), and Zambia (copper) have been positively affected by the surge in international prices for oil, wood, and metals, due partly to increased China's import demand. From 2000 to 2005, international oil prices increased 89 percent, and China accounted for 18 percent of the growth in world demand for oil. Partly because of China's demand, world production capacity has been at its peak, and oil prices are unlikely to return to $20 a barrel. Similarly, aluminum prices went up by more than 20 percent, and copper prices have more than doubled between 2000 and 2005, and China is responsible for a significant increase in world consumption for both. Angola's terms of trade index rose from 86 in 2002 to 109 in 2005, and Zambia registered a parallel gain from 93 to 114. Finally, while gold prices increased by close to 60 percent in the last 5 years, Chinese demand plays a small but rising role for Africa's gold producers of Ghana, Mali, South Africa, and Tanzania.
- *Mixed.* For some resource-rich but oil-importing countries like Botswana and the Central African Republic, the effects of China have been ambiguous, since the upward pressure on metal prices has been partially offset by the higher oil import bill, with the impact on the smaller economies particularly strong. Since these countries do not export aluminum, copper, steel, or zinc, the China effect on their metal exports has been more modest. Cotton exporters (Benin, Burkina, and Mali) are benefiting from the slight turnaround in international cotton prices since 2004 due to increases in China's import demand, but suffer because of the higher cost of oil imports. China has long been the world's largest cotton producer and consumer, but in recent years its soaring economy and global textile demand have driven its cotton imports far beyond that of any other market's.
- *Losers.* Oil-importing countries that are also textile exporters, like Madagascar and Mauritius, will suffer from negative terms of trade shocks resulting from the added costs of oil imports and the competition of China's textile imports, resulting in job losses and shrinkage in domestic manufacturing. Due to increased Chinese competition in third-country markets, these countries will lose world market share. Moreover, countries that are both coffee producers (Burundi, Ethiopia, Rwanda, and Uganda) and exporters of other agricultural commodities (Côte d'Ivoire, Kenya, Malawi, Tanzania, and Zimbabwe) as well as oil importers will be hurt, because agricultural prices have not increased over the last several years. China currently accounts for less than 1 percent of global coffee and cocoa consumption, and excess supply in world markets has already caused price collapses over the last few years. Moreover, these African countries do not have a strong comparative advantage in the production of any of China's main agricultural imports—wheat, corn, beef, and soybeans. As a result, these countries will most likely face a worsening of their trade balances. . . .

Trade

. . . The stylized facts reveal an interesting story about changing trade patterns. First, there has been a dramatic increase in direct trade between China and Sub-Saharan Africa in the last few years, especially since 2001, resulting in trebling of trade volumes from close to $10 billion in 2002 to more than $40 billion in 2005 and more than $50 billion in 2006 (figure 2). Second, over the last 3 years, the relationship has been evolving in the direction of growing Chinese trade deficits with Sub-Saharan Africa. Third, China tends to import mineral fuels and metals from Africa and export cheap consumer and capital goods, and there is little trade in intermediate goods. Fourth, China's imports are concentrated among a small number of natural resource economies lacking product diversification in their export structure. More than 75 percent of China's trade takes place with four countries—South Africa, Sudan, Angola, and Nigeria (figure 3). Noncommodity exports from Africa to China are not significant, accounting for less than 10 percent of African exports and include textiles and apparel, processed food, and small manufactures. These exports tend to be technologically simple and are either finished consumer goods or intermediate inputs in the case of textiles. Finally, the dispersion of China's trade with Africa shows that resource endowments trump geographic proximity as an explanatory variable for trade flows. . . .

One striking pattern is the redirection of Sub-Saharan African trade away from its traditional Western markets toward the rising Asian economies. While Europe and the United States represented more than two-thirds of African

Figure 2

China's Trade with Sub-Saharan Africa, 1990–2006

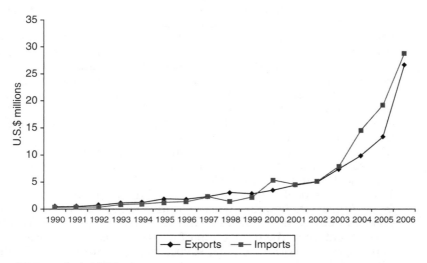

Source: UN Comtrade data 2006.

Figure 3

China's Trade with the Top 12 Sub-Saharan African Countries in 2004

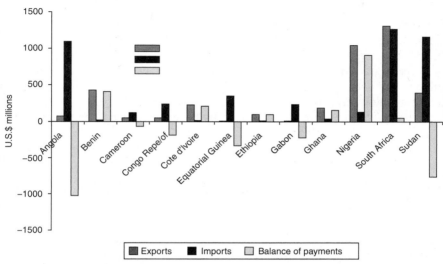

Source: UN Comtrade data 2005.

exports in 2003/2004, Asia's share has been rising progressively, while Europe's has been stagnating or even declining. China has become Sub-Saharan Africa's third largest trade partner after the United States and France, and it has increased its share of the African market from 5.8 percent in 2002 to more than 10 percent in 2004.

Trade flows between Sub-Saharan Africa and China closely follow what would be expected from comparative advantage and the predictions of the Heckscher–Ohlin model, with China exporting labor-intensive manufactures and high-technology products and Africa exporting raw materials and mineral fuels. While during the 1980s and 1990s, China exported mostly clothing, footwear, and light manufactured goods, during the first 5 years of the twenty-first century, there has been a shift toward higher technology exports, like electronic goods and machinery, which account for close to 50 percent of China's exports. One important factor is the absence of agricultural exports from Sub-Saharan Africa to China (excluding raw cotton), explained largely by the strong comparative advantages in agriculture of commodity-producing exporters like Argentina, Canada, and Chile. . . .

The Quest for Oil

China's growing demand to fuel large economic expansion amid an increasing shortage of raw materials and the needs of growing large- and small-scale industry have led it to intensify its search for oil, notably in the Middle East, Russia, and Africa. While historically China has met most of its energy needs by burning coal, a combination of environmental and financial reasons has led it to diversify. China's quest for oil is becoming an integral part of its foreign policy. As part of a global effort to gain energy security, China is spending billions of dollars on the promising African oil market, which has long been dominated by U.S. and European petroleum interests. . . .

The major beneficiaries of the Chinese boom have been Angola and Sudan. Angola, currently Africa's second largest oil producer after Nigeria, is China's top supplier, providing more than 400,000 barrels per day, or close to 15 percent of China's oil imports, comparable to U.S. oil imports from Angola. Plagued by decades of war, burdened by reconstruction costs, and castigated by international development institutions for lack of transparency in oil revenue management, the Angolans have welcomed China's interest. In return for concessions and oil contracts, the Chinese are providing financial incentives. A $2 billion line of credit (1.5 percent interest over 17 years) by the EximBank of China has helped finance vital infrastructure in this post-conflict economy, and an additional $2 billion loan was granted in 2006. In Angola, Chinese workers are constructing office buildings, housing developments of up to 5,000 units, sections of railway damaged and neglected during the country's quarter-century civil war. A fiberoptic network stretching more than 100 miles, and hospitals, schools, and hundreds of miles of roads. However, projects financed by Chinese money are obliged to contract only 30 percent of the work to domestic firms.

Sudan, Africa's largest country, accounts for 5 percent of China's oil imports. The Government of China has its largest overseas oil project there and has built a $700 million oil refinery. The stale-owned China National Petroleum Corporation (CNPC) has invested more than $15 billion in Sudanese oil and helped the government capture more than $2 billion in oil windfalls in 2004. Half of China's overseas oil comes from Sudan, and 10,000 Chinese workers have been deployed to build a 900-mile pipeline linking the Heglig oilfield in Kordofan Province with Port Sudan on the Red Sea. This has given the poor country a possible transit corridor to the greater shipping lanes of the Middle East and made Sudan one of the fastest growing economies in Africa. In 2005, China purchased half of Sudan's oil exports.

In January 2006, the state-owned Chinese energy company CNOOC Ltd announced the purchase of a 45 percent stake in an offshore Nigerian oilfield for $2.3 billion. Moreover, the Chinese have committed to build a rail system connecting Lagos with Abuja, the capital of Nigeria, and to install telephone services in rural areas of Nigeria using Chinese government loans of more than $200 million. Thus, in all these countries, and to a lesser extent in Gabon and the Republic of Congo, China has created lucrative partnerships. . . .

The impact of Chinese investment in the African oil sector has been mixed. Most importantly, the Chinese have contributed to financing infrastructure in several poor, war-torn post-conflict countries. This focus on providing the infra-structural foundations for economic development in low-income economies is important for helping these countries emerge from poverty. However, China has not been actively involved in the public financial management of the windfall gains and has not linked its loans to these countries to social expenditure. The employment impact in this highly capital-intensive industry has been minimal, partly due to the large inflow of Chinese labor. There is a risk that this new relationship between developing countries will be one of resource extraction and that human capital development may be neglected. Finally, the concern among many Western policymakers is that China will undermine efforts by bilateral donors and international financial institutions to regulate revenue management and reduce corruption.

Chinese Investment in Sub-Saharan Africa

In parallel with the surge in trade, Chinese investment and aid on the continent have also increased dramatically, driven in part by market consider-ations. From $20 million a year in the early 1990s, Chinese foreign direct investment (FDI) in Africa jumped to close to $100 million in 2000 to close to $400 million by 2005 and reached more than $1 billion in 2006, a growth rate higher than Chinese FDI to any other part of the world.

Historically, of the Chinese-owned investment projects in Africa from 1979 to 2000, in value terms manufacturing (especially spinning and weaving textiles and agroprocessing) accounted for 64 percent, while resource-based industries (oil, timber, and mining) accounted for 28 percent (World Bank 2004). However, the volume and share of Chinese FDI in resource extraction in the mining and petroleum sectors has surged in the last few years in parallel with the country's resource needs. Another growing sector for Chinese investment is construction and infrastructure, where Chinese firms have developed a reputation for low-cost and reasonable-quality roads. The country location of Chinese FDI in Sub-Saharan Africa is highly diversified, with South Africa, Zambia, and Sudan being important destinations. Chinese enterprises currently number more than 700, operate in 50 countries and employ close to 80,000 Chinese workers. In contrast, African FDI in China is small, with the exception of several prominent South African companies in the services and mining sectors, including SAB Miller, which operates China's largest brewery, and Sasol, the energy giant, which is expanding its activities in China's coal mining sector. . . .

China is rapidly becoming an important aid donor to Africa, and its role is beginning to overshadow that of many traditional Western donors, although precise figures on the magnitude and terms of the Chinese loans are not easily available. Aid is being used principally to facilitate trade and improve access to natural resources. In a recent Sino-African summit in 2006, Chinese President Hu Jiantao promised to double Chinese aid by 2009 and to provide $5 billion in preferential loans and export credits to Sub-Saharan Africa over 2006–2009. He also pledged to set up a $5 billion China–Africa development fund. In a recent tour of eight African countries, President Hu promised billions in no-interest loans, prompting concerns among Western aid donors that China's lending may be generating new debt in many econo-mies that have recently been granted debt relief from official creditors. However, the initial evidence suggests that some of China's lending is in grant form. Moreover, in 2004, China cancelled close to $1.2 billion in debt for 31 African countries, and new debt relief has been promised. China is upscaling humanitarian and health assistance by sending medical workers and agricultural experts to a range of post-conflict countries, from Rwanda to Sierra Leone, and has pledged to increase aid to Africa for HIV/AIDS and malaria prevention and treatment. Finally, more than 10,000 African students will visit China in 2006 and 2007 for professional training.

Conclusions

. . . For Sub-Saharan Africa, China's economic boom has been a mixed blessing. On the positive side, China has helped accelerate economic growth in Africa by contributing to a strong commodity boom due to the upward swing in the prices of oil and metals exported by many African economies. Second, it has deepened trade and investment on a continent that has been marginalized from flows of international trade and global capital, and China is investing significantly in Africa's transport and education infrastructure. Third, it has given many Africans access to low-cost consumer goods. Fourth, China's low-transactions–cost way of doing business and its noninterference in countries' internal affairs—eschewing political conditionalities on loans provided that countries adhere to its one-China policy—has won it some support in the developing world. Fifth. China's ascent has created more competition in the aid market and increased countries' bargaining power with donors. China may contribute to the continent's economic development and act as a force for change in Africa.

On the minus side are several important challenges and risks. First, there is some concern that Chinese investment in Africa will be based on capital-intensive natural resource extraction and will not contribute to local employment generation and the continent's long-term economic development. Second, China's influence on global energy demand and on oil markets will lead to increased energy prices for net oil importers in Africa and a worsening of their terms of trade. Third, the supply shock to world manufacturing, particularly in textiles, and the growing imports of cheap Chinese goods in Africa, coupled with increasing competition between Chinese and African textiles in third-country markets, threaten to hinder economic diversification in Africa and contribute to deindustrialization. In this context, a growing backlash against Chinese investment in the continent, amid allegations of improper labor and human rights standards, may gather momentum. Fourth, important issues like corruption and governance, which had moved to the forefront of the development agenda, may slide back down again. There may be some slippage in the progress that has been made in the development agenda with regard to transparency and civil society participation.

Padraig R. Carmody and
Francis Y. Owusu

 NO

Competing Hegemons? Chinese versus American Geo-Economic Strategies in Africa

When elephants fight, the grass gets trampled (African proverb).

Introduction

. . . From tourism in Sierra Leone, to bike factories in Ghana and oil refineries in Sudan, Chinese investment in Africa is rising. Since 2000, Chinese trade with Africa has more than tripled. Whereas China only accounted for 7% of African imports in 2003, imports from Africa grew an astounding 87% in 2004 alone. More than 60% of African timber exports are now destined for East Asia, and 25% of China's oil supplies now come from the Gulf of Guinea. China launched Nigeria's first space satellite, and by the end of 2005, China overtook Britain as Africa's third largest trading partner. . . .

This paper investigates the implications of Chinese and American investment and trade strategies for Africa. It begins by exploring recent Chinese interest and involvement on the continent. It then moves to describe the Chinese geo-economic strategy for the continent, and the advantages it brings to resource competition with the US. The economic and political impacts of Chinese investment and trade with Africa are then explored. The paper then examines the impacts of increased American oil investment on the continent and stepped up security assistance, with which this is associated. It concludes by examining progressive alternatives requiring more robust international cooperation.

Resource Colonialist and "Anti-Imperialist"? Chinese Interests and Involvement in Africa

China's desire to become a global economic powerhouse and a counterweight to U.S. hegemony in the international system is now clear. The expansion of the Chinese economy currently accounts for 25% of all global economic growth and by some estimates, at purchasing power parity, the Chinese economy will be as big as the US in 2015. This phenomenal economic growth has increased the country's demand for resources, especially oil. In 2003, China surpassed Japan as the world's second largest oil consumer, and it now accounts

From *Political Geography*, June 2007. Copyright © 2007 by Elsevier Science Ltd. Reprinted by permission.

for 40% of total global growth in oil demand. China's demand for oil increases by 1% for every percentage increase in its gross domestic product, versus 0.4% for the Organization for Economic Cooperation and Development (OECD) countries, whose economies are heavily biased towards services. The search for resources to fuel the country's phenomenal economic growth and the need to find markets for its products requires a global geopolitical strategy and the formation of new alliances. . . .

China's demand for industrial resources is huge, but Africa has the potential to substantially meet this demand, as it is three times larger than China and rich in resources. The annual rate of growth for Chinese consumption of copper is 17%, 15% for zinc and 20% for nickel. China is now the world's largest consumer of copper, the price of which rose from $1319 per tonne in 2001 to $8800 in 2006. It is no wonder that Chinese companies have invested $170m in the copper industry in Zambia; re-opening the Chambishi mine which closed in 1988 and employing 2000 people. While the neoliberal policies promoted by the Western-controlled international financial institutions (IFIs) compounded the continent's economic problems (see Mkandawire, 2005), Chinese investment is partially, and unevenly, reversing their deflationary bias. This comes with a harsh labor regime, however. For example, workers in the Chinese-owned Collum mine in Zambia never get a day off.

China's Geo-Economic Strategy for Africa

"States" are comprised of sets of practices and social relations, rather than unified actors. Nonetheless, developmental state's policies, such as China, are marked by coherence, given the over-riding goal of economic growth and structural transformation. Unlike different branches of the United States government involved in relief, energy procurement or defense, which view Africa largely as a site of humanitarian intervention, resource extraction, and security threat, respectively, the Chinese state appears to "look" at Africa as a strategic-economic space. This geopolitical code reflects the challenges of economic transformation for China, versus international system maintenance for the U.S.

While more focused empirical studies of sectors, firms, countries and regimes are needed in order to shed light on the complexity, specificity and experimental nature of Chinese involvement on the continent, the following emergent elements of China's geo-economic strategy in Africa can be identified: (1) to ensure access to critical natural resources, particularly oil and natural gas, to maintain the country's economic growth, (2) to recycle its massive foreign exchange (forex) reserves into profitable investments overseas, (3) associated with both of these; to facilitate the development of Chinese multinational corporations, (4) to find markets for the products of Chinese industry, (5) to develop African agriculture to provide non-food agriculturals to supply Chinese industry and consumers, and also food products for China's burgeoning cities, and (6) to source knowledge workers in Africa to support Chinese economic transformation. Different African countries have different resource geographies, from oil to beaches, and macro-economic stability, and they consequently play different roles in the emerging division of labor with China. Nonetheless there is a coherence between the different elements of economic engagement; not driven by a coherent plan, but by structural imperatives. Export-oriented industrialization in China has generated a forex reserve, some of which must be recycled overseas, for example. . . .

Current Chinese aid is concentrated in the productive sectors of physical infrastructure, industry and agriculture. When President Zeming visited Nigeria he concluded deals on Chinese assistance in developing the country's light weapons industry, oil refinery construction, power plants, and possible Chinese rehabilitation of the rail system in deals totalling up to US $7bn. China is also involved in rail, road and fibre optic cable construction in Angola. In many ways, therefore, China's aid and investment in Africa is reminiscent of earlier colonial investments to ensure access to raw materials. . . .

A Benevolent Hegemon? Chinese "Soft Power" in Africa

According to the China's Liang Guixan (2005) Minister Counsellor, the "Chinese model" of development that is currently on offer is based on "sophisticated technology appropriate to African countries' low cost and expertise in poverty alleviation and SMME [small, micro- and medium-sized enterprise] development". It has eschewed outright privatisation and other elements of the "Washington Consensus" (Stiglitz, 1998 cited in Adésínà, 2006).

The Chinese . . . African Human Resources Development Fund pays for 10,000 Africans annually to train in Beijing. However, in addition to being an act of goodwill, these knowledge workers are expected to contribute to China's economic transformation.

Chinese and African leaders at a 2003 trade summit agreed to build political and economic ties to counter western dominance and improve the position of poor countries. This is seen to be a way of deflecting U.S. "hegemonism." Moreover, China's own experience of dependence makes it possible for them to make reference to things like structural imbalances in trade relations. This represents a revival of the philosophy of Third Worldism, with China playing the lead roie; but this time with the material resources to back it up.

A Chinese official in Africa argued that "economic rights" are the main priority of developing nations and take precedence over personal, individual rights as conceptualised in the West. Indeed, the view among some senior Chinese officials is that "multi-party politics fuels social turmoil, ethnic conflicts and civil wars". China also sees the human rights discourse as a tool of Western neo-imperialism. This is a particularly attractive philosophy for incumbent African political élites, and is helped by its plausibility. . . .

Because of state involvement, Chinese companies are better positioned to make short-term losses for long-term gains. For instance, the representative of China's state-owned construction company in Ethiopia revealed that he was instructed to bid low on tenders, without regard to profit, and China's largest telecoms manufacturer gifted equipment to Telkom Kenya. However, China is merely "following a very traditional path established by Europe,

Japan and the United Stales: offering poor countries comprehensive and exploitative trade deals combined with aid". Chinese companies have other competitive advantages too in that they are often willing to pay bribes and under-the-counter signing bonuses. While this was standard practice in the past, Western companies are now more open to reputational risk and are under pressure to sign up to the Extractive Industries Transparency Initiative, promoted by Tony Blair, and the "Publish What You Pay" campaign supported by George Soros. Corruption scandals involving Western oil companies in Africa nonetheless continue too.

Free Trade Imperialism or South–South Cooperation? The Economic Impacts of China

In some policy circles in the U.S., the rise of China and a new questioning of "free" trade are linked. A study for the US Army War College on Chinese influence in Latin America argues that "in previous decades, dependence on Western capital was a key vehicle for forcing Latin American nations to accept neoliberal economic policies and free trade, limiting the degree to which they could buy social peace with state institutions and government largesse". However, China is now seen to be creating a "neoimperialistic dynamic in the hemisphere" and by displacing domestic manufacturers through imports possibly deepening class disparities and corruption. This represents a shift towards "realist," structuralist, and away from normative neoclassical economics in some US policy circles. In relation to Latin America, Chinese officials have told their counterparts to let manufacturing industry die and concentrate on primary commodity exports. The ability to introduce counter-vailing anti-dumping measures is circumscribed by many countries' desire to grant China "market economy" status under World Trade Organization (WTO) agreements, in order to maintain their access to the Chinese market. However, Latin American countries have also been successful in negotiating voluntary export restraints with China, enabling them to enjoy a continuing trade surplus—again showing China's long-term concern with resource supply, rather than short-term market expansion. The same sorts of competitive displacement pressures are at play in Africa as in Latin America, although with per capita incomes 90% lower, the results are even more devastating there.

Creating industrial employment is central to improved security prospects in Africa, and to democracy promotion. The development of an autonomous civil society, with its own material base in the labor movement and private sector in the "West" have historically held the state accountable, although the exact meaning and content of African "democracy" is context specific and subject to negotiation.

Africa has recently been hit with a Chinese "Textile tsunami". The number of companies registered in Botswana doubled over the last few years; many of them were Chinese (import) trading companies. Out of every 100 t-shirts imported to South Africa, 80 are from China. This has resulted in a "double whammy" as African industry is undermined by Chinese import competition, while the phasing out of the Multi-Fibre Agreement in 2005, meant the value of preferences under the US African Growth and Opportunity Act (AGOA) were undermined for the continent. Textile and clothing exports account for 99.14% of Lesotho's export earnings, however, more than 10 clothing factories closed there in 2005, throwing 10,000 people out of work. South Africa's clothing exports to the US fell from $26m in the first quarter of 2004 to $12m for the first quarter of 2005, with 30,000 people losing their jobs. In the Muslim Kano and Kaduna areas of Nigeria, imports have devastated the local textile and consumer goods industries. The Nigerian textile and clothing workers union estimates 350,000 direct job losses as a result of Chinese import competition and 1.5 million indirectly over the last 5 years. While African trade unionists estimate that 250,000 jobs in the textile and clothing industries have been lost due to Chinese import penetration, roughly the same number as created by AGOA.

The reorientation of trade from manufactures to oil is evidenced by the fact that Angola and Chad surpassed Lesotho in 2004 as exporters to the U.S. The increased emphasis on oil and mineral extraction is resulting in a relative technological downgrading of Africa's economies.

The imposition of temporary restrictions on Chinese textiles entering the US and EU markets is currently providing some respite, as Chinese textile manufacturers are again investing in Africa, in the short-term, as a way around this. For example, all the textile factories which had closed in Lesotho have now been reopened. However under the WTO, the ability to use "safeguard actions" to provide relief from import surges will largely expire in 2008, and completely end in 2013.

The Chinese have noted that "the fundamental reason for the increase in Chinese textile and clothing imports [into Africa] is the high demand for Chinese goods" (Guixan, 2005). However critics of Chinese policy in Africa argue that it represents a new neo-colonialism, disguised as South–South cooperation. As Moletsi Mbeki, argues, "we sell them raw materials and they sell us manufactured goods with a predictable result—an unfavourable trade balance against South Africa". . . .

China's WTO entry has thereby served to lock in global market access for its export-oriented industrialization. Thus, while there may be some potential for "pro-poor" employment growth in South Africa, in the export-oriented fruit and vegetable subsectors in particular, the growth of China may further exacerbate income inequality there, reinforcing the previous capital intensive growth path. As Neva Seidman Makgetla, an economist for the Congress of South African Trade Unions, argues, "There's no question that for upper classes it's a boon . . . the problem is any lower-class South African's would rather have a job". Only 13% of "black" South Africans are currently employed in the formal sector of the economy compared to 34% in 1970, although there was some employment growth in 2005/6, mostly in agriculture. . . .

The Impacts of Chinese Involvement on African State Restructuring

. . . Sixty percent of Sudanese oil goes to China, and the oil refinery in Sudan was the first one the Chinese built outside China. Debt service payments for it have priority over all others, such as to the World Bank and the IMF. Chinese companies have also built three small-arms factories in Khartoum and sold weapons to the regime. Supplying the Sudanese government with jet fighters allows it to protect the oil fields in the South, where the Chinese have substantial interests. Indeed, during the (North–South) civil war, government troops used the CNPC facility to launch attacks and dislodge southerners in the vicinity of the new oil fields.

A Chinese official at the Ministry of Trade also noted in relation to human rights in Sudan that "we import from every source we can get oil from" or in the words of the deputy foreign minister "business is business". China's new African policy specifically states that it will increase its assistance to African nations with "no political strings attached". Such a position has led to assertions that China has no values, only interests.

In an era of globalized capital markets there are costs to such an approach, however. While the absence of a formal, independent civil society and free press in China frees companies from reputational risk domestically, the flotation of the CNPC on the New York Stock exchange had to be withdrawn and refashioned because of negative publicity over what the proceeds might be used to do in Sudan. After this débacle, China refused to veto Sudan being sent to the International Criminal Court over its actions in Darfur. . . .

The Chinese are also rekindling relations with other highly corrupt former leftist regimes, such as Angola. In Angola, the IMF estimates $1 to 5 billion dollars of oil revenue goes missing every year, while half of Angolan children continue to be malnourished (O'Connor, 2004). Yet China's Eximbank provided the country a $2bn line of credit to rebuild its infrastructure as part of an oil deal. China's state-owned oil companies and British Petroleum have a joint venture in the country and Angola is now China's largest supplier of oil. . . .

The Chinese also pay little attention to the environmental impacts of their investments. As explained by an African diplomat "they just come and do it. We don't start to hold meetings about environmental impact assessments and human rights and bad governance and good governance". Western corporations are also substantial polluters, however, with Shell recently fined $1.5bn for pollution of the Niger delta. Thus, Chinese practices in Africa represent "business as usual," rather than a radical break with the past. . . .

Conclusion

. . . America is a somewhat more normative power than China, with a developed civil society exerting pressure for conformity with (civil and political) human rights norms. Nonetheless, it operates on the basis of *realpolitik*. Increasingly close cooperation between Khartoum and Western intelligence agencies in the "war-on-terror" may be blocking war crimes prosecutions in Darfur, for example.

There is already evidence of U.S. interest in cooperating with China in relation to Africa, with Jendayi Frazer recently visiting China. However, if China wishes to promote peace in Africa, it will have to curb its own arms industry and it might also sign up to a code of conduct along the lines of

NEPAD and the EU. Enhanced international cooperation will be needed to deliver on the promises of improved governance and economic transformation of NEPAD. . . .

While the revival of economic growth which this has brought to the continent is potentially progressive in its impacts, to date it has largely been confined to enclaves, and upper classes/state élites. Also, while the international community has played a vital role in ending wars in Liberia, Sierra Leone and the Democratic Republic of Congo, among others, oil investment has fuelled local conflict and made many states less accountable to their populations.

A key challenge is to shift African states from authoritarian/patrimonial to developmental mode. Perhaps this is not seen to be in the interests of either the US or China, as these states would then keep their own resources, rather than placing them on the international market. Given the general underdevelopment of the continent, Africa is the only region of the world where net oil output is predicted by the U.S. government to grow substantially faster than consumption—by 91 compared to 35%, respectively, from 2001 to 2025. However, there is a price to be paid by the international community for the current set up. For the moment it is a price they are willing to (let other people) pay.

POSTSCRIPT

Is Increasing Chinese Investment Good for African Development?

$\mathbf{A}$s is demonstrated in the selections for this issue, increasing trade between China and Africa is viewed in very different lights depending on the commentator. The United States has tended to view the situation with increasing alarm as it views African oil resources in particular as crucial given the uncertainty of supplies from the Middle East and its precarious relationship with Venezuela. Others in the human rights community are concerned about China's support for undemocratic regimes (such as those in Zimbabwe and Sudan) in countries where it wishes to maintain or expand access to certain types of resources. In China's defense, it contends that it provides substantial levels of direct foreign investment in those countries where it trades. In the absence of such investment, vital infrastructure might not be maintained or expanded.

African commentators are also clearly split on the issue. Although the oil-rich countries in particular have benefited from increased export revenues and Chinese investment, those countries that possessed a small- or medium-sized manufacturing sector have been very hard hit. Even though West African markets used to be replete with cheap plastic consumer goods manufactured in Abidjan or Lagos, it is rare to now find anything of this sort that is not made in China. The textile industries in Zimbabwe and South Africa have been similarly devastated by inexpensive Chinese exports.

One aspect of Chinese investment that was not discussed in either of the selections is the involvement of ethnic Chinese in the manufacturing sectors of some African nations. In a 2003 article in *African Affairs*, entitled "Close Encounters: Chinese Business Networks as Industrial Catalysts in Sub-Saharan Africa," Deborah Brautigam argues that Chinese nationals have been a catalyst for industrial development in Mauritius. In contrast, their involvement in the Nigerian industrial sector has been more problematic. In her book *Disabling Globalization* (UC Berkeley Press, 2002), Gillian Hart also documents the problematic nature of mainland Chinese and Taiwanese investment in South Africa.

If there is a middle road to be taken, it would be for those African countries that are benefiting from trade with China (or with any other global power for that matter) to strategically reinvest the proceeds from this trade in the development of human capital (via increased education expenditures) and in other sectors of the economy that show promise. Although the article does not explicitly deal with the Africa-China relationship, H. J. Bruton makes an argument along these lines in his 1998 piece in the *Journal of Economic Literature* entitled "A Reconsideration of Import Substitution."

For other perspectives on this issue, see Domingos Muekalia's 2004 article in the *African Security Review* entitled "Africa and China's Strategic Partnership" or Chris Alden's 2005 article in *Survival* under the title "China in Africa."

Internet References . . .

AFROL News—Agriculture

AFROL News of the Heifer Project International provides information on agriculture from across Africa, including general agricultural trends for the continent and country-specific news.

```
http://www.afrol.com/categories/
        agriculture_nutrition
```

African Conservation Foundation

The African Conservation Foundation website allows one to search its databases of African environmental topics by country, organization, type of information, and environmental category.

```
http://www.africanwebsites.net/
```

African Data Dissemination Service

The US Government's African Data Dissemination Service offers a warning system for possible famine or flood conditions. It also allows one to download data, both map based and tabular, regarding crop use, hydrology, rainfall, and elevation (as well as several other datasets).

```
http://earlywarning.usgs.gov/adds/
```

United Nations Environment Programme: Regional Office for Africa

The United Nations Environment Programme: ROA provides information on UN environmental initiatives in Africa, both in restoring the natural environment and harnessing the environment for human use in an environmentally friendly way.

```
http://www.unep.org/ROA/
```

Food and Agriculture Organization of the United Nations

The Food and Agriculture Organization of the United Nations website contains news articles and other information about agriculture, food, and environmental issues. Contains information with both African and international emphases.

```
http://www.fao.org/
```

Agriculture, Food, and the Environment

*A*s a region equally known for the abundance and destruction of its resources, questions regarding environmental management, agriculture, and food production have loomed large in debates concerning Africa. Resource scarcity is often posited as one cause of mounting civil strife. Real and imagined crises also have fueled discussions over how to prevent famine and augment food production without undermining the integrity of the ecosystem. Debates also rage of the cause, extent, and existence of various forms of environmental degradation.

- Does the Conflict in the Darfur Region of Sudan Have Environmental Causes?

- Is Food Production in Africa Capable of Keeping Up with Population Growth?

- Does African Agriculture Need a Green Revolution?

- Is Sub-Saharan Africa Experiencing a Deforestation Crisis?

ISSUE 8

Does the Conflict in the Darfur Region of Sudan Have Environmental Causes?

YES: UN Environment Programme, from "Conflict and the Environment," *Sudan: Post-Conflict Environmental Assessment* (June 2007)

NO: Lydia Polgreen, from "A Godsend for Darfur, or a Curse?" *New York Times* (July 22, 2007)

ISSUE SUMMARY

YES: The UN Environment Programme argues that there is a strong link between land degradation, desertification, and conflict in Darfur, Sudan. It suggests that declining rainfall in Darfur, ecological collapse, and population growth have triggered social disintegration and the conditions for conflict that are then sustained by political, tribal, or ethnic differences.

NO: Lydia Polgreen, reporter for the *New York Times*, questions whether environmental degradation is at the root of the Darfur Crisis. Making such a causal link leads to the faulty conclusion that the conflict may be resolved by improving environmental conditions. An alternative explanation for the conflict lies in the land-use patterns promoted by the government of Sudan and the development policies of the World Bank and the IMF.

Sudan has been wracked by conflict since before it gained independence from the British in 1956. For most of the past 60 years, the tension has been between a largely Arab and Muslim North and a predominantly African, Christian, and animist South. These differences and tensions were fanned by the British who employed a practice of divide and rule, administering the North and South separately during the colonial occupation and prohibiting the movement of people between the two regions from 1924. The first Sudanese civil war arose out of this North-South tension, in which the South feared dominance by the North following independence. The conflict lasted from 1955 until 1972, ending with a peace brokered and held for 10 years under the Addis Ababa agreement. The peace agreement granted the South considerable autonomy.

Hostilities broke out again in 1983 when the Sudanese government attempted to impose a more tightly consolidated federal government. The Sudan People's Liberation Army (SPLA) was the key rebel force in the South. This second civil war lasted for another 20 years and was often fanned by support to the different sides from other countries. Peace talks made substantial progress in 2003 and 2004, and a peace agreement was signed in early 2005. This agreement granted autonomy to the South for six years, after which time there would be a referendum concerning independence. The North and the South also agreed to split oil revenues equally. The North-South agreement appears to be in a very precarious situation as the SPLA recently withdrew from the national government in protest over the slow implementation of the 2005 peace agreement.

Fighting in Darfur has occurred intermittently over the past 30 years. These tensions escalated in 2003 to a full-scale conflict. Much of the tension has been between pastoralists and agriculturalists. Rebel groups have accused the central government of neglecting Darfur economically. While atrocities have occurred on both sides, much of the blame has fallen on Arab militias known as the Janjaweed, who are armed groups appointed by the central government. Over two million people have been displaced and from 200,000 to 500,000 have died. A peace agreement, brokered by the African Union, was reached in May 2006, but it was not signed by all of the groups involved in the conflict. Hostilities have continued.

Recent pronouncements by the UN Secretary General, Ban Ki-moon, and publications produced by his organization, suggest that land degradation and desertification are significant contributors to the conflict in Darfur. This chain of causality is sometimes referred to as environmental security, a term coined by political scientist Tad Homer-Dixon (1994). These ideas were popularized in a controversial 1994 article in the *Atlantic Monthly*, entitled "the Coming Anarchy" that was penned by the journalist Robert Kaplan. Homer-Dixon and like-minded analysts assert that future political conflicts will increasingly be driven by tension over scarce resources. They further argue that resource scarcity is largely driven by population pressure.

In this issue, the UN Environment Programme asserts that there is a strong link between land degradation, desertification, and conflict in the Darfur region of Sudan. It is suggested that declining rainfall in Darfur, ecological collapse, and population growth have triggered social disintegration and the conditions for conflict that are then sustained by political, tribal, or ethnic differences. Their report notes that "there is substantial evidence of a strong link between the recent occurrence of local conflict and environmental degradation of rangeland and rain-fed agricultural land in the drier parts of Sudan."

In contrast, Lydia Polgreen questions whether environmental degradation is at the root of the Darfur Crisis. Making such a causal link leads to the faulty conclusion that the conflict may be resolved by improving environmental conditions or the discovery of new resources. She specifically describes how the recent detection of underground water resources in Sudan have led some to suggest that this could bring an end to the conflict. She cites scholars who question the causal weight assigned to environmental factors. An alternative explanation for the conflict lies in the land-use patterns promoted by the government and the development policies of the World Bank and the IMF.

Conflict and the Environment

Introduction and Assessment Activities

Introduction

Sudan has been wracked by civil war and regional strife for most of the past fifty years, and at the time of finalizing this report, in June 2007, a major conflict rages on in Darfur. At the same time, Sudan suffers from a number of severe environmental problems, both within and outside current and historical conflict-affected areas. UNEP's assessment has found that the connections between conflict and environment in Sudan are both complex and pervasive: while many of the conflicts have been initiated partly by tension over the use of shared natural resources, those same resources have often been damaged by conflict. . . .

This selection provides an overview of the role of natural resources in the instigation and continuation of historical and current conflicts, listing the major resources of concern and focusing specifically on conflicts involving rangelands and rain-fed agricultural land . . .

Overview of Conflicts in Sudan

A Complex Mosaic

Conflicts have directly affected over 60 percent of the country for the last 50 years, and hence greatly influenced its development. Understanding Sudan's complex mosaic of conflicts is an essential first step in establishing the linkages between conflict and environment in the region. . . .

The history and current status of each of the major conflict areas is briefly described below. The geographical extent of the various conflicts as interpreted by UNEP is shown in Figure 1.

Darfur

Fighting in Darfur has occurred intermittently for at least thirty years. Until 2003, it was mostly confined to a series of partly connected tribal and local conflicts. In early 2003, these hostilities escalated into a full-scale military

Figure 1

Conflicts in Sudan: 1957–2006

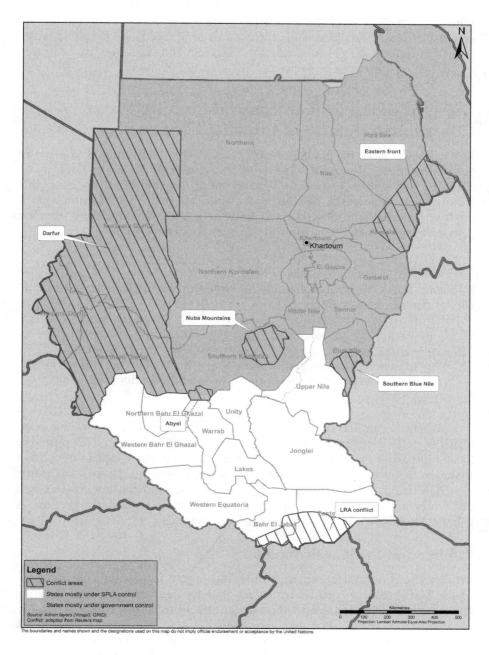

confrontation in all three Darfur states, which also frequently spills into neighbouring Chad and the Central African Republic.

The ongoing Darfur conflict is characterized by a 'scorched earth' campaign carried out by militias over large areas, resulting in a significant number of civilian deaths, the widespread destruction of villages and forests, and the displacement of victims into camps for protection, food and water. Over two million people are currently displaced, and casualties are estimated by a range of sources to be between 200,000 and 500,000. . . .

Analysis of the Role of Natural Resources as a Contributing Cause of Conflict in Sudan

It is acknowledged that there are many factors that contribute to conflict in Sudan that have little or no link to the environment or natural resources. These include political, religious, ethnic, tribal and clan divisions, economic factors, land tenure deficiencies and historical feuds. In addition, where environment and natural resource management issues are important, they are generally **contributing** factors only, not the sole cause for tension. . . .

Four Natural Resources Closely Linked to Conflict in Sudan

In Sudan, four categories of natural resources are particularly linked to conflict as contributing causes:

1. oil and gas reserves;
2. Nile waters;
3. hardwood timber; and
4. rangeland and rain-fed agricultural land (and associated water points).

Potential conflicts over oil, Nile waters and hardwood timber are national-scale issues. Tensions over rangeland and rain-fed agricultural land are primarily local, but have the potential to escalate and exacerbate other sources of conflict to the extent of becoming national-scale issues, as is presently the case in Darfur.

The linkages between these resources/land uses and conflict are discussed below; the fourth category is examined in more detail in a separate section, as it has strong ties to the ongoing conflict in Darfur. . . .

Timber and the War Economy

While there is no indication that timber has been a major contributing cause of the instigation of conflict in Sudan, there is clear evidence that revenue from hardwood timber sales helped sustain the north-south civil war. Timber became part of the war economy, and there are now signs that this process is being repeated with charcoal in Darfur. Overall however, the timber-conflict linkage in Sudan is considered to be mainly an environmental impact issue (rather than a conflict catalyst). . . .

Local Conflicts over Rangeland and Rain-Fed Agricultural Land

Local clashes over rangeland and rain-fed agricultural land have occurred throughout Sudan's recorded history. In the absence of demographic and environmental change, such conflicts would generally be considered a social, political or economic issue and not warrant an assessment purely on environmental grounds. However, environmental issues like desertification, land degradation and climate change are becoming major factors in these conflicts. This topic is addressed in more detail in the following section.

Environmental Linkages to Local Conflicts over Rangeland and Rain-Fed Agricultural Land

Introduction and Limits to the Observed Linkages

It is important to note that while environmental problems affect rangeland and rain-fed agricultural land across virtually all of Sudan, they are clearly and strongly linked to conflict in a minority of cases and regions only. These linkages do exist, but their significance and geographic scale should not be exaggerated.

That said, there is substantial evidence of a strong link between the recent occurrence of local conflict and environmental degradation of rangeland and rain-fed agricultural land in the drier parts of Sudan.

The Actors of Conflict at the Local Level: Three Major Competing and Conflicting Groups

The rural ethnic and livelihood structures of Sudan are so complex and area-specific that any summary of the issue of resource competition on a national scale is by definition a gross simplification. For instance, traditional pastoralist and agricultural societies in Sudan are not always clearly separated: in many areas, societies (families, clans and even whole tribes) practice a mixture of crop-growing and animal-rearing. Nonetheless, there are some relatively clear boundaries—defined as much by livelihoods as by any other factor—between different tribes, clans and ethnic groups.

For the purposes of this discussion, UNEP has classified the hundreds of distinct rural social units present in the current and historical conflict regions into three major groups, based on livelihood strategies:

1. predominantly sedentary crop-rearing societies/tribes;
2. predominantly nomadic (transhumant) livestock-rearing societies/tribes; and
3. owners of and workers on mechanized agricultural schemes.

All three groups depend on rainfall for their livelihood. The other major rural group is comprised of farmers using river and groundwater for irrigation.

To date, however, irrigated agriculture has not been a major factor in local conflicts in Sudan.

Most of the recorded local conflicts are within and between the first two groups: pastoralists and agriculturalists fighting over access to land and water. The third group, the mechanized farming lobby, is generally not directly involved in conflict, but has played a very strong role in precipitating it in some states, through uncontrolled land take from the other two groups. In the Nuba mountains and in Blue Nile state, combatants reported that the expansion of mechanized agricultural schemes onto their land had precipitated the fighting, which had then escalated and coalesced with the major north-south political conflict.

The Historical Background: A Tradition of Local Conflict and Resolution

Violent conflict resulting partly from competition over agricultural and grazing land is a worldwide and age-old phenomenon. In Sudan—and particularly in Darfur and Kordofan—there is an extensive history of local clashes associated with this issue. A 2003 study on the causes of conflict in Darfur from 1930 to 2000, for example, indicates that competition for pastoral land and water has been a driving force behind the majority of local confrontations for the last 70 years.

Until 1970, there is also a well-documented history of local resolution for such conflicts, through established mediation and dispute resolution mechanisms. Since then, however, legal reforms have essentially destroyed many of these traditional structures and processes, and failed to provide a viable substitute. In addition, the last thirty years have seen an influx of small arms into the region, with the unfortunate result that local conflicts today are both much more violent and more difficult to contain and mediate.

Theories of Natural Resource Scarcity and Application to Local Conflict in Sudan

Academic research and the discourse on the role of natural resource scarcity as a driver of conflict have developed significantly over the last decade. In light of the ongoing Darfur crisis, Sudan is a prime example of the importance, complexity and political sensitivity of this topic. The following analysis borrows heavily from the language and concepts used by leading researchers in this field.

As a basis for discussion, the environmentally significant factors that contribute to conflict related to rangeland and rain-fed agricultural land have been divided into four groups:

- supply: factors affecting the available resources;
- demand: factors affecting the demand for resources;
- land use: changes affecting the way remaining resources are shared; and
- institutional and development factors.

While all the purely environmental factors are 'supply' issues, they have to be put into the context of 'demand' and 'institution-specific' factors.

Supply—An Unreliable and Dwindling Resource

The noted environmental issues affecting agriculture in Sudan all result in a dwindling supply of natural resources:

- **Desertification, soil erosion and soil exhaustion** (depletion of nutrients and compaction) lower agricultural productivity and, in the worst cases, take land out of use for the long term. This has been well documented but poorly quantified in Sudan;
- **Deforestation**, particularly in the drylands, has resulted in a near permanent loss of resources including seasonal forage for pastoralists and natural fertilizer/soil recovery services for farmers. Deforestation rates in the areas studied by UNEP average 1.87 percent per annum;
- **Historical climate change** has reduced productivity in some areas due to a decline in rainfall. A major and long-term drop in precipitation (30 percent over 80 years) has been recorded in Northern Darfur, for example. The implications of such a decline on dry rangeland quality are obvious and
- **Forecast climate change** is expected to further reduce productivity due to declining rainfall and increased variability, particularly in the Sahel belt. A drop in productivity of up to 70 percent is forecast for the most vulnerable areas.

Ever Increasing Demands on Resources

The demand for natural resources in Sudan is uniformly increasing, due to the following factors:

- **Human population growth** is the underlying driver of increased demand for natural resources. Sudan has an overall growth rate of over 2.6 percent per annum, masking much higher localized rates. In central Darfur, for example, government statistics indicate a regional population (linear) growth rate of 12 percent per annum, from 3 persons/km^2 in 1956 to 18 persons/km^2 in 2003. These growth rates are indicative of large-scale in-migration, in this case mainly from the north and possibly due to environmental factors such as desertification; and
- **Livestock population and growth rates**; government officials and academics have tracked the population increase of livestock since the 1960s. In northern and central Sudan alone, it is estimated to have increased by over 400 percent between 1961 and 2004.

Land Use Changes—A Dwindling Share of Resources for Pastoralists

The horizontal expansion of agriculture into areas that were previously either rangeland or forest has been a well recognized trend for the last four decades.

The northwards expansion of rain-fed agriculture into marginal areas histori-cally only used for grazing has been particularly damaging. Examples from the recent UNEP-ICRAF study of land use changes illustrate a major reduction in rangeland areas due to expanding agriculture. . . .

- In the Um Chelluta region of Southern Darfur, rain-fed agricultural land increased by 138 percent between 1973 and 2000, while rangeland and closed woodland decreased by 56 and 32 percent respectively.

In addition to the loss of grazing land, agricultural expansion has also blocked livestock migratory routes between many of the widely separated dry and wet season pastures, and between the herds and daily watering points. A further complication is that sedentary farmers are increasingly raising their own livestock, and are hence less willing to give grazing rights to nomads in transit. . . .

The Net Result—Disappearing Livelihoods for Dryland Pastoralist Societies

The clear trend that emerges when these various elements are pieced together is that of a **significant long-term increase in livestock density on rangelands that are reducing in total area, accessibility and quality.** In environmental terms, the observed net result is overgrazing and land degradation. In social terms, the reported consequence for pastoralist societies is an effectively permanent loss of livelihoods and entrenched poverty.

Pastoralist societies in Sudan have always been relatively vulnerable to losing their livelihoods due to erratic rainfall, but the above-noted combina-tion of factors has propelled many pastoralists into a negative spiral of pov-erty, displacement, and in the worst cases, conflict. Their coping strategies, which have been well documented, include:

- Abandoning pastoralism as a livelihood in favour of sedentary agriculture, or displacement to cities;
- Increasing or varying the extent of annual herd movements where pos-sible, with a general trend towards a permanently more southerly migration;
- Maximizing herd sizes as an insurance measure (assisted by the provision of water points and veterinary services);
- Changing herd composition, replacing camels by small animals, mainly sheep, in response to the curtailment of long-distance migration;
- Competing directly with other grazers for preferred areas of higher productivity (**entailing a conflict risk**);
- Moving and grazing livestock on cropland without consent (**entailing a conflict risk**); and
- Reducing competition by forcing other pastoralists and agricultural-ists off previously shared land (**as a last resort—the proactive conflict scenario**).

Variations of all of these strategies can be observed throughout Sudan, particularly in the drier regions.

Conclusions on the Role of Environmental Issues in Conflicts over Rangeland and Rain-Fed Agricultural Land

Pastoralist societies have been at the centre of local conflicts in Sudan throughout recorded history. The most significant problems have occurred and continue to occur in the drier central regions, which are also the regions with the largest livestock populations, and under the most severe environmental stress.

As there are many factors in play—most of which are not related to the environment—land degradation does not appear to be the dominant causative factor in local conflicts. It is, however, a very important element, which is growing in significance and is a critical issue for the long-term resolution of the Darfur crisis. The key cause for concern is the **historical, ongoing and forecast shrinkage and degradation of remaining rangelands in the northern part of the Sahel belt.**

Lydia Polgreen

 NO

A Godsend for Darfur, or a Curse?

The announcement by researchers at Boston University last week that a vast underground lake the size of Lake Erie had been discovered beneath the barren soil of northern Darfur, a blood-soaked but otherwise parched land racked by war for the past four years, was greeted by rapturous hopes. Could this, at last, bring deliverance from a cataclysmic conflict that has killed at least 200,000 people and pushed more than 2.5 million from their homes?

That hope is built upon an argument, advanced by a United Nations report released last month and an opinion article in The Washington Post by Ban Ki-moon, the United Nations secretary general, that environmental degradation and the symptoms of a warming planet are at the root of the Darfur crisis.

"There is a very strong link between land degradation, desertification and conflict in Darfur," said the United Nations Environmental Program report, which noted that rainfall in northern Darfur has decreased by a third over the last 80 years. "Exponential population growth and related environmental stress have created the conditions for conflicts to be triggered and sustained by political, tribal or ethnic differences," the report said, adding that Darfur "can be considered a tragic example of the social breakdown that can result from ecological collapse."

The idea that more water—unearthed through a thousand wells sunk into the underground lake—could neatly defuse the crisis is seductive. Messy African conflicts, from Congo to Liberia, from northern Uganda to Angola, have a way of defying all efforts to solve them. Instead, they seem to become hopelessly more complex as they drag on, year after agonizing year. A scientific explanation for the problem (environmental degradation) along with a tidy technological solution (irrigation) gratifies the modern humanitarian impulse.

But the history of Sudan, a grim chronicle of civil war, famine, coups and despotism, gives ample reason to be skeptical.

"Like all resources water can be used for good or ill," said Alex de Waal, a scholar who has studied the impact of climate variation in Sudan and who witnessed the 1984–85 famine that is often cited as the beginning of the ecological crisis gripping Darfur. "It can be a blessing or also a curse. If the government acts true to form and tries to create some sort of oasis in the desert and control who settles there, that would simply be an extension of the crisis, not a solution."

The droughts that gripped Sudan in the 1980s, and the migrations and other social changes they forced, have doubtlessly played a role in the conflict by increasing competition for water and land between farmers, who tend to be non-Arab, and herders, many of whom are Arabs. But an environmental catastrophe cannot become a violent cataclysm without a powerful human hand to guide it in that direction.

"These wider environmental factors don't have impact in and of themselves" in terms of fomenting conflict, Mr. de Waal said. "The question is how they are managed."

In fact, while different regions and social groups suffer severely, Sudan as a whole has riches to spare, in oil, fertile soil, and even water. Indeed, history suggests that this newly discovered lake is just as likely to become a source of conflict as a solution to the bloodshed.

Successive Sudanese governments and their colonial precursors have adopted agricultural policies that have almost inevitably led to conflict. They have favored large mechanized farms and complex irrigation schemes, controlled by the government and its allies, over the small, rain-fed farms that are the backbone of the rural economy in much of Sudan.

In eastern Sudan, where a rebellion has been brewing for years, the Beja people have nursed grievances since Britain and Egypt ruled Sudan jointly during the first half of the 20th century. Under their rule, irrigation programs for commercial farming deprived the Beja of their prime grazing land.

Post-colonial governments, which in the early years had the blessing of the World Bank and the International Monetary Fund, took vast tracts of land in the name of agricultural development, turning farmers who worked their own land into wage laborers for the state and its allies.

Some Sudanese have even been pushed off their land entirely. In the early 1990s the Nuba people were forced into "peace villages," where they provided a steady supply of cheap, captive labor to mechanized farms. In other areas, including parts of Darfur, intensive mechanized farming by the government and investors who were heedless to the need to protect the fertility of the land left large tracts barren.

A vast new agricultural scheme in a largely uninhabited swath of northern Darfur is more likely to fit into this destructive pattern than not, said John Prendergast, a founder of the Enough Project, an initiative of the Center for American Progress and the International Crisis Group to abolish genocide and mass atrocities.

"Climate change and the lack of rain are much less important than the land-use patterns promoted by the government of Sudan and the development policies of World Bank and I.M.F., which were focused on intensive agricultural expansion that really mined the soils and left a lot of land unusable," said Mr. Prendergast, who has been studying Sudan for 20 years. "That was probably the principal impetus for a lot of intra-Darfur migration in the decades leading up to the conflict in Darfur."

During those years, the government exploited tensions over water and land to achieve its own aims, putting down a rebellion among the non-Arab tribes, who rose up because they wanted a greater share of Sudan's wealth and power. It armed tribal militias to fight the rebels, and these militias unleashed a tide of violence that ultimately would become, according to the Bush administration and many others, the 21st century's first genocide.

A report released last year by the Coalition for International Justice on the role that oil and mechanized farming have played in human rights abuses in Sudan concluded: "The predominant root of conflict in Sudan is the instability that results from the systemic abuse of the rural (and recently urbanized) poor at the hands of the economic and political elites of central Sudan."

In this analysis, the heart of the Darfur conflict, as in all conflicts in Sudan, is the battle for control of resources and riches, but not between farmers and herders, northerners and southerners, Christians and Muslims, or Arabs and non-Arabs.

It is a conflict between those at the center of the country, the elites who have controlled Sudan and its wealth for the past century and a half, and the desperately poor people who beg for scraps from the periphery.

Until that equation changes, many analysts argue, nothing else will.

POSTSCRIPT

Does the Conflict in the Darfur Region of Sudan Have Environmental Causes?

The environmental security framework has been much debated in the academic literature. Critics abound, such as Betsy Hartmann [see her 2001 chapter, entitled "Will the Circle Be Unbroken? A Critique of the Project on Environment, Population and Security," in Peluso and Watts's *Violent Environments* (Cornell University Press, 2001)]. These critics see resource scarcity as largely driven by powerful interests, rather than population growth. In fact, it is often the battle to control natural resources, and local people around them, that is the real reason for oppression and strife.

This critique of environmental security bears some resemblance to certain aspects of the "resource curse thesis." While this thesis contains a broader set of ideas about patterns of development, one dimension of this idea is that resource wealth (not scarcity) may lead to civil conflict. In such instances, rival groups may fight to control valuable resources in order to finance their aggression (such was the case with diamond trading and rebel groups in Sierra Leone). In a similar arguement, corrupt government may use the proceeds from resource extraction for their own benefit and to pay for the suppression of opposition groups.

In terms of further sources on the environmental conditions and the ongoing conflict in Sudan, there are several good texts by Alex de Waal, including his classic text on the drought and famine of the mid-1980s entitled *Famine That Kills: Darfur, Sudan* (Oxford, 2004). He also has a more recent co-edited volume on the current conflict that features the contributions of several Sudanean scholars. See *Darfur: A Short History of a Long War* by Julie Flint and Alex de Waal (Zed Books, 2006). Also recommended is Mahmood Mamdani's recent essay "The Politics of Naming: Genocide, Civil War, Insurgency" (*London Review of Books*, March 2007).

ISSUE 9

Is Food Production in Africa Capable of Keeping Up with Population Growth?

YES: Michael Mortimore and Mary Tiffen, from "Population and Environment in Time Perspective: The Machakos Story," *People and Environment in Africa* (John Wiley & Sons, 1995)

NO: John Murton, from "Population Growth and Poverty in Machakos District, Kenya," *The Geographical Journal* (March 1999)

ISSUE SUMMARY

YES: Michael Mortimore, a geographer, and Mary Tiffen, a historian and socio-economist, both with Drylands Research, investigate population and food production trajectories in Machakos, Kenya. They determine that increasing population density has a positive influence on environmental management and crop production. Furthermore, they found that food production kept up with population growth from 1930 to 1987.

NO: John Murton, with the Foreign and Commonwealth Office of the British government, uses household-level data to show that the changes in Machakos described by Mortimore and Tiffen "have been accompanied by a polarization of land holdings, differential trends in agricultural productivity, and a decline in food self-sufficiency." As such, he argues that the "Machakos experience" of population growth and positive environmental transformation is neither homogenous nor fully unproblematic.

There is a long-standing debate about the ability of agriculture to keep up with population growth in Africa. Those who are concerned that population growth will outstrip agricultural production are often referred to as neo-Malthusians. This perspective is designated as such in deference to the eighteenth-century British clergyman, Thomas Malthus, who posited such a scenario as inevitable in his famous 1798 tract, *Essay on the Principle of Population*. The neo-Malthusians generally have dominated contemporary debates concerning global population growth and food supplies and are led by such figures as Paul Ehrlich (*The Population Bomb*, Simon and Schuster, 1968) and Lester Brown (see numerous World Watch Institute publications). The major contrarian perspective in African studies is the Boserupian view point, named after Ester Boserup (*The Conditions of Agricultural Change*, Aldine Publishing, 1965). She established that increasing population densities may induce farmers to intensify their efforts and thereby produce food at a rate that keeps pace with population increase.

A third perspective, often referred to as the technocratic or cornucopian view, is somewhat akin to the Boserupian population thesis. This view, most commonly associated with the late Julian Simon (*The Great Breakthrough and Its Cause*, University of Michigan Press, 2000), asserts that human ingenuity will resolve resource constraints created by population growth if the free market is allowed to operate and appropriate price signals are transmitted to producers. The major difference between the Boserupian and technocratic viewpoints is that the former tends to emphasize indigenous methods of adaptation whereas the latter stresses the importance of market-led change.

To some extent, both of the perspectives in this issue are sympathetic to the Boserupian view, but they arrive at different conclusions in the final analysis. The case presented by Michael Mortimore, a geographer, and Mary Tiffen, a historian and socio-economist, about the situation in Machakos, Kenya, is probably the most well-referenced piece of analysis supporting the Boserupian thesis in African studies. Mortimore and Tiffen assert that increasing population density has had a positive influence on environmental management and crop production. Furthermore, they find that food production kept up with population growth from 1930 to 1987. The study shows that farmers were able to reverse land degradation, enhance their livestock, invest in their farms, and increase productivity despite increasing population density.

John Murton, with the British Foreign and Commonwealth, agrees with the findings of Mortimore and Tiffen in the aggregate, but then uses household survey data to demonstrate that there is a difference between the trends for wealthier households with access to nonfarm income and poorer households without access to such revenues. It is households with nonfarm income that are able to invest in the inputs needed for increasing agricultural productivity. For those households unable to make such investments, yields are declining. As such, Murton is essentially saying that increasing labor alone will only go so far in the agricultural intensification process, after which point capital expenditure on inputs is critical.

YES

Michael Mortimore and
Mary Tiffen

Population and Environment in Time Perspective: The Machakos Story

Introduction: Linkages Between Population Growth and the Environment

The linkages between population growth and environmental degradation are controversial. The view, widely held, that rapid population growth is incompatible with sustainable management of the environment is influenced, knowingly or not, by the neo-Malthusian belief that resources are limited. According to literature prepared for the United Nations Conference on Environment and Development (the Rio Earth Summit), 'the number of people an area can support without compromising its ability to do so in the future is known as its population carrying capacity.'

In agricultural terms, each agro-ecological zone is believed to have a carrying capacity which must not be exceeded if environmental equilibrium is to be maintained. In the words of Mustapha Tolba, formerly head of the United Nations Environment Programme, 'when that number is exceeded, the whole piece of land will quickly degenerate from overgrazing or overuse by human beings. Therefore, population pressure is definitely one of the major causes of desertification and the degradation of the land'. According to such a view, degradation threatens to diminish food production, and thereby the human carrying capacity, in a cumulative downward spiral.

More sophisticated estimations of population supporting capacities take account of technological alternatives to the low-input systems that are found in much of the tropical world. A recent study shows that if technology is varied (or levels of inputs increased), the limits rise accordingly. The critical constraint, for practical purposes, is access to technology. However, poverty inhibits investment, and the poor are said to be incapable of conserving their environment: rather, 'poverty forces them to exploit their limited stocks just to survive, leading to overcropping, overgrazing, and overcutting at unsustainable rates. A vicious circle of human need, environmental damage and more poverty ensues.'

A negative view of the effects of population pressure on the environment, which has been underwritten by several UN organizations, the Rio Earth Summit, and influential writers carries great weight in the environmental debate. Nevertheless it is not supported by some well-documented situations in Africa.

One of these, Machakos district of Kenya, is the subject of a recent study of resource management by African smallholders. The study covered the period 1930–90, which is long enough to control for rainfall variability, and for changes in the political economy. Profiles of change were constructed for all the major environmental and social variables. The linkages in what the World Bank has called the 'population, agriculture and environment nexus' were systematically investigated. The study shows positive, not negative influences of increasing population density on both environmental conservation and productivity.

Characteristics of Machakos District, Kenya

Machakos lies in south-east Kenya. Its northernmost point is about 50 km from the capital, Nairobi, from which it stretches some 300 km southwards. Since at least the eighteenth century it has been inhabited by agropastoralists known as the Akamba, who also populated the neighbouring Kitui district. Men looked after the livestock and cleared new land, while women cultivated a small plot for food crops. . . .

Setting the Scene for an Ecological Disaster

When British rule was imposed on Kenya, the Akamba people were confined in the Ukamba Reserve by the colonial government's Scheduled Areas (White Highlands) policy. . . . It was bounded by European settlers' farms and ranches on the north and west. To the east and south were uninhabited Crown lands, on which the government allowed only grazing, by permit. Thus encircled, the Akamba grew in numbers, and in livestock, while clearing extra land for shifting cultivation of maize and other crops, and chopping down trees for fuel burning and construction of their homes. Despite their protests, the government refused to relax its policy of containment.

During the period 1930–90, the population of Machakos district grew from 238 000 to 1 393 000, and an annual rate of increase of over 3% was maintained from the 1950s until after 1989. After 1962, the Akamba were allowed to settle on the semi-arid former Crown lands, and also took over some of the Europeans' farms in government schemes. Thus the land available to them effectively doubled. However, the growth of the population reduced the amount of land available to less than a hectare per person by 1989.

This conjunction of rapid population growth with unreliable rainfall, frequent moisture stress, low soil fertility and high erodibility, suggests the likelihood, on the premises outlined above, of population-induced degradation on a grand scale. This was indeed the diagnosis offered in assessments of the reserve in the 1930s. A disastrous series of droughts (in 1929, 1933, 1934, 1935 and 1939) caused major crop failures, losses of livestock, pest outbreaks, the deterioration of vegetal cover and accelerated erosion. In 1937, Colin Maher, the government's soil conservation officer, wrote despairingly:

> The Machakos Reserve is an appalling example of a large area of land which has been subjected to uncoordinated and practically uncontrolled

development by natives whose multiplication and the increase of whose stock has been permitted, free from the checks of war and largely from those of disease, under benevolent British rule.

Every phase of misuse of land is vividly and poignantly displayed in this Reserve, the inhabitants of which are rapidly drifting to a state of hopeless and miserable poverty and their land to a parching desert of rocks, stones and sand.

No less than eight official visits, reports and recommendations were commissioned between 1929 and 1939, strongly reflecting an official consensus view centred on overstocking, inappropriate cultivation, and deforestation in a reserve thought already to be overpopulated in relation to its carrying capacity. Did events bear out this gloomy prognosis? . . .

A Farming Revolution

Change in Machakos was multi-faceted. Technical innovation was not restricted to soil and water conservation. . . . An inventory of production technologies in Machakos identified 76 that were either introduced from outside the district or whose use was significantly extended during the period of the study. They included 35 field and horticultural crops, 5 tillage technologies and 6 methods of soil fertility management. The technical options available to farmers were thereby extended, adding flexibility to the farming system. Such flexibility is a great advantage in a risky environment.

Making Money From Farming

In the 1930s, capital was mostly locked up in livestock, and occasional sales provided needed cash. From cultivating maize, beans and pigeon peas for subsistence, farmers have since moved into marketing crops. The most successful of these, until its price fell in the 1980s, was coffee. Some Akamba learned to grow it while employed on European coffee farms, but in 1938 the government expressly forbade 'native' coffee growing in order to protect the European producers' interests. After the overturning of this ban in 1954, strict rules were enforced in the growing, processing and marketing of coffee. African producers successfully achieved high grades. Coffee was an attractive component of rehabilitation programmes, since it was profitable and had to be grown on terraces. Coffee output increased spectacularly in the 'boom' of the later 1970s. It generated investment funds, and supported improved living standards, in the sub-humid zone. This had spill-over effects in the drier areas, through the demand of coffee-growing farmers for agricultural labour, for food and livestock products in which they might no longer be self-sufficient, and for a whole range of consumer goods, housing improvements and services. By 1982–83 over 40% of rural incomes in Machakos district were being generated by non-farm businesses and wages.

In contrast to coffee, cotton, which is recommended for the drier areas, was not a success in the long term. Its price was only rarely high enough to compensate for its tendency to compete with the food crops for labour and capital, and the profit margins were reduced by marketing inefficiencies.

Three attempts to promote cotton—in the 1930s, 1960s and 1978–84—ran into the sand. Output limped along, and in 1991 the closed ginnery at Makueni offered silent testimony of failure.

Both coffee and cotton were sold to monopsonist parastatal marketing boards and required government support in extension and supervision, and in supervising officially sponsored co-operatives for input provision, processing and grading. By contrast, expanded growing of a great variety of perennial and annual fruit and vegetables was closely linked with the growth of Kenya's canning industry, the Nairobi and Mombasa retail markets, and exports of fresh vegetables by air. Itinerant Asian buyers, firms operating contract-buying and enterprising Akamba, as individual traders or in formal co-operatives or informal groups, have all played a role. A generally high value per hectare facilitated the skillful exploitation of wet micro-environments, even in the driest areas, and the development of technologies such as micro-irrigation and the cultivation of bananas in pits. Fruit production is attractive to women farmers, as trees do not compete with food crops (for which they often have the main responsibility).

Akamba farmers have adapted rather well to the opportunities provided by the market. No amount of promotion can succeed without incentives. But given these, innovation in both production and marketing aspects is commonplace. Meanwhile, livestock sales, on which they depended for market income in the 1930s, have steadily declined.

Achieving Food Sufficiency

The staple food of the Akamba is white maize. The shortness of the two growing seasons, and the high probability of drought, call for varieties that either resist drought or escape it by maturing quickly. In the 1960s, the government's local research station began a search for drought-escaping varieties that culminated in the release of Katumani Composite B (KCB) maize in 1968.

The new maize was promoted by the extension service, and it was steadily, if unspectacularly, adopted by the farmers. Various surveys suggest that from two-thirds to three-quarters use it, but it is not known how much of the maize area is planted to it, nor what proportion of output it contributes. Of 40 farmers interviewed in five locations in 1990, only a third said they used it exclusively, and another third used it together with local and hybrid varieties.

This was no 'green revolution.' The ambivalent response has, however, an explanation. Given the unpredictable rainfall, farmers need to keep their options open. Their local varieties, though slower to mature, are more resistant to drought, and hybrids do better in wetter sites. KCB is liked because, in combination with other varieties, it strengthens this flexibility rather than undermines it. Some farmers cross-pollinate it with their local varieties, further enhancing their adaptive choice.

With and without KCB, food crop production per person kept up with population growth from 1930 to 1987 although imported foods remained necessary after a series of bad seasons. The district's dependence on imported food in the period 1974–85 was less than in 1942–62 (8 kg per person annually compared with 17), notwithstanding major droughts in both periods. Food output per person in 1984 (after three seasonal droughts) was slightly higher than in 1960–61 (after two seasons with drought, and one with floods).

Faster Tillage

In view of the reputation then enjoyed by the Akamba for resistance to change, it is surprising that the ox-plough, introduced to the district as early as 1910, had spread to about 600 (or 3%) of the district's households by the 1930s. Farmers trained their own cattle, and ploughs were cheap (about equivalent to the price of a cow in 1940); furthermore the technology was being tested and developed on nearby European farms where some Akamba worked. Ownership greatly increased the area a farmer could cultivate, and enabled him to sell maize or cotton. Its adoption called for the cessation of shifting cultivation, and facilitated the adoption of row planting and better weeding, in place of broadcasting seed.

After the Second World War, ex-soldiers who had seen ploughs in India returned with the capital to buy their own. Proceeds from trade and employment outside the district were also invested in ploughs. The government made ox-ploughs the basis of a new farming system imposed on a supervised settlement at Makueni location. The government, and traders, provided some credit. Coffee (after 1954), horticulture and cotton (in some years) generated investment funds. Adoption accelerated in the 1960s and was more or less complete by the 1980s. Surveys found 62% or more of farmers owning a plough, the remainder being too poor, or having fields too small and steep for its use.

The plough proved to be both a durable and a flexible technology. The first ones in use were adapted to opening new land, with teams of six or eight oxen. Farmers later selected a lighter, two-oxen instrument suitable for work on small, terraced, permanent fields. The Victory mouldboard plough, though much criticized on technical grounds, is used everywhere, and for several operations—primary ploughing, seed-bed preparation and inter-row weeding— and attempts to promote its replacement by a more expensive tool-bar have failed. It saves labour, and is also used by women. The 'oxenization' of Akamba agriculture was, in a measure, a triumph of capitalization in a capital-poor, risk-prone and low productive farming system.

Fertilizing the Soil

Shifting cultivation used to rely on long fallows for replenishing the soil. In the 1930s, there was very little systematic manuring. But the fertility of arable land, as measured by yields, was low. The Agricultural Department favoured farmyard manure over inorganic fertilizers. It also, unsuccessfully, promoted composting. It was not until the 1950s that manuring became widespread, in the northern sub-humid areas. By this time, arable fields were fixed, and cultivated every year. The silent spread of this practice can be judged from the fact that by the 1980s, 9 out of 10 farmers were doing it, in both wetter and drier areas. Now, most arable land is cultivated twice a year—in both rainy seasons— and composting is being adopted by small farmers with few livestock.

By contrast, the use made of inorganic fertilizers is minimal, the bulk of it on coffee. Manure is made in the *boma* (stall or pen) and supplemented with trash and waste. The amount applied depends on how many livestock there are, and how much labour and transport are available when needed. Every farmer knows that, under present technical and economic conditions, sustaining output depends on the use made of boma manure. Few can afford inorganic fertilizers in quantity.

Feeding the Livestock

At the beginning of our period (the 1930s), Akamba women cultivated food crops at home, while their men used to take the livestock away to common grazing lands for several months of the year. However, common grazing land vanished as it was transformed into new farms. After about 1960 settlement on Crown lands could no longer be restrained, and thousands of families moved into them. Each household must now keep its animals within the bounds of the family farm, or obtain permission to use another family's land, often in return for some rent or service. More than 60% of the cattle, sheep and goats are stall-fed or tethered for a part or all of the year. When in the boma, cut fodder and residues are brought to them, which requires additional labour. Fodder grass is grown on terrace banks. These changes are most advanced in the sub-humid zone. A third of the livestock are grazed all the time, mostly in the dry semi-arid zone. The effort required to maintain livestock is making grade or crossbred cattle popular (estimated to number about 9% of the total in 1983 and to have grown rapidly since), whose milk yields and value are superior to those of the native zebu, though their increased health risks call for frequent dipping.

Farming the Trees

From the 1920s, the Forest Department believed that reafforestation was necessary to arrest environmental desiccation, and supply the growing need for domestic fuel and construction timber. For several decades the department struggled, under-resourced, to reserve and replant hilltop forests. In 1984, however, estimates of household fuel requirements put the need for new plantations at 226 000 ha (15 times the area of gazetted forest reserves!). The destruction of surviving natural woodland seemed an imminent possibility.

But sites photographed in 1937 and 1991 showed little sign of woodland degradation. A fuel shortage has failed to develop on the expected scale and the district does not import wood or charcoal in significant quantities. Indeed it exports some. Part of the explanation for this expert miscalculation lay in ignoring the use made of dead wood, farm trash, branch wood from farm trees, and hedge cuttings, for domestic fires. The other part lay in failing to appreciate a major area of innovative practice: the planting, protection and systematic harvesting of trees. Forest policy in the 1980s was shifting towards farm forestry promotion, but in this it was following, not driving, farmers.

Tree densities on farmland in one location, Mbiuni, averaged over 34 per ha (14 when bananas are excluded) by 1982. Furthermore, the smaller the farm, the greater the density. The range of trees planted includes both exotic and indigenous, both fruit and timber species. Akamba women generally manage fruit trees, while the men look after the timber trees. Owners of grazing land manage the regeneration of woody vegetation, which is used for timber, fuel, browse, honey production, edible and medicinal products.

Producing More With Less

These were some of the features of a revolution in farming wrought in unpromising circumstances. What was the driving force behind these changes?

The growth of population had two important outcomes: the subdivision of a man's landholdings among all his sons, according to Akamba custom, and the increasing scarcity of land as former communal grazing and Crown land became new private farms.

As holdings shrank in size, the arable proportion rose, leaving less and less land for grazing while the cultivated area per person stagnated. [T]he percentage of arable land increased from the older settled areas to the new, and from the wetter to the drier areas.

These changes created the imperative for intensification. By intensification we mean the application of increasing amounts of labour and capital per ha to raise crop yields. Crop–livestock integration is intrinsic to this process in dryland farming systems in Africa. It was driven by the needs for draft energy on the farm, for fodder (the stalks of maize and haulms of beans, for example), for manure and milk.

Two changes—to intensive livestock feeding systems, and to permanent manured fields, often under plough cultivation—were pivotal in this transformation, whose outcome was an increasingly efficient system of nutrient cycling through plants, animals and soil. The changes could not have occurred without security of title. Akamba custom had already recognized individuals rights in land, including the right of sale, in the older settled areas by the 1930s. Security has been reinforced by statutory registration of title, a slow legal process which began in Machakos in 1968 and has still not covered all areas.

Equally important were sources of investment capital. This was not only required for terraces and ploughs. To clear and cultivate new land, build hedges or plant trees requires labour which often has to be hired, as well as tools and expertise. The off-farm incomes earned by Akamba men inside and outside the district have contributed for decades to agricultural investment. Such incomes are often high in households with small farms, and there is little evidence that investment per ha falls where farmers are poorly resourced in land.

The outcome of this process of intensification was an increase in the value of output per square kilometre (at constant prices) from 1930 to 1987. This was calculated by taking output data for the only three available years before 1974 (1930, 1957 and 1961), selecting two later years which were climatically average (1977 and 1987), and converting all the values into maize equivalent at 1957 prices. The year 1957 was an unusually good one and 1961, as already noted, unusually bad, hence the upward trend was interrupted. The trend continued despite the additions of large areas of the more arid types of land in 1962. Output per capita closely reflected this curve.

We conclude that, contrary to the expectations expressed in the 1930s, the Akamba of Machakos have put land degradation into reverse, conserved and improved their trees, invested in their farms, and sustained an improvement in overall productivity. . . .

No Miracle in Machakos?

What happened in Machakos did not contravene the laws of nature, as the Malthusian paradigm would express them, but rather grew logically from a conjunction of increasing population density, market growth and a generally supportive economic environment. The technological changes we have described, in conservation and production, cannot be adequately understood as exogenous, as mere accidents that gave breathing space on a remorseless progression towards irreversible environmental degradation and poverty. Rather, as argued long ago by Ester Boserup and more recently by Julian Simon, they were mothered by necessity. Technological change was an endogenous process, in which multiple sources and channels were employed, involving selection and adaptation by farmers.

Increasing population density is found, then, to have positive effects. The increasing scarcity (value) of land promoted investment, both in conservation and in yield-enhancing improvements. The integration of crop and livestock production improved the efficiency of nutrient cycling, and thereby the sustainability of the farming system.

The Machakos experience offers an alternative to the Malthusian models of the relations between population growth and environmental degradation. Elsewhere in Africa, there are more documented cases of positive associations, though it would be foolish to ignore the differences.

Successful intensification under rising densities has certain preconditions. These are peace and security, for trade and investment, and a marketing and tenure system in which economic benefits are shared by many, rather than monopolized by a few. Degradation may occur, as it did in Machakos, when a change from a long fallowing system is first needed, but when population densities or other conditions are not conducive. Normally, as population grows, so do the opportunities for specialization and trade. To the stick of necessity the market adds the carrot of incentives and resources for investment in new technologies.

In the past, development planners tried to transform farming systems that were seen as inefficient and technically conservative. In fact, they are changing themselves, as studying them in time perspective shows, and there is scope for supporting positive change with appropriate policies. The guiding principle must be to go with the grain of historical change. This means encouraging investment, by encouraging trade and by improving farm-gate prices (for example, by improving roads and by avoiding heavy taxation of agricultural products). There is also a need to protect investment when crises (e.g. famines) threaten to force households to sell their assets. Increasing the technical options available to local resource users in a risky environment is one of the most productive avenues to pursue, by encouraging endogenous experimentation; by increasing information through general education as well as agricultural extension, and by creating new avenues for technological development and transfer.

John Murton

Population Growth and Poverty in Machakos District, Kenya

The influential book *More People Less Erosion* investigated population growth and environmental change in Machakos, Kenya. Tiffen *et al.* argued that population growth need not lead to environmental degradation, since if smallholder farmers were allowed to operate freely within competitive markets, responding profitably to new agricultural opportunities, they would logically manage their resources in a sustainable way, with a resultant benefit to society and the economy. Although environmental improvements in Machakos seem beyond dispute, Rocheleau argues that the aggregate District level data used by Tiffen *et al.* mask social and economic differentiation as a result of these changes, and that many farmers in Machakos are experiencing declining welfare amidst the improving environment.

The current paper seeks to address this debate by examining the results of a household-level village study in the old Machakos District of Kenya. The new research found that agricultural intensification has not been a homogeneous experience. Rising living standards have been experienced largely by those families who have access to non-farm (and usually urban-derived) income. This income facilitates security in agricultural crises such as drought, and enables a virtuous cycle of on-farm investment, leading to higher agricultural yields, rising incomes and higher standards of living. In contrast, families without access to such income were found to be experiencing a cycle of declining soil fertility and declining yields per head. These divergent experiences of vicious cycles and virtuous spirals were found side by side within neighbouring households in the study area. In the past it was easy for farmers to obtain non-farm income and so make social and economic progress. However, the combination of population increase, slow economic growth, and structural changes in the Kenyan economy mean that poor families are now enjoying less social mobility than they did previously.

This paper highlights how differential access to non-farm income has driven a polarization of land holdings within the village, with the result that, for poorer families at least, environmental sustainability is no longer proving to be a guarantee of livelihood sustainability under conditions of rapidly rising population.

From *The Geographical Journal*, March 1999, pp. 37–45. Copyright © 1999 by Blackwell Publishing, Ltd. Reprinted by permission. www.blackwell-synergy.com

The Study and Study Site

In common with other recent work studying environmental transformation, and work in Kenya investigating agricultural change and differentiation, change in Machakos was studied by means of a longitudinal data set. The results of research into agricultural practices and land holdings conducted in Machakos in 1965 by Frederick Owako were compared to new data from the same area today. Both sets of research were conducted in Ndueni village of Mbooni location, in what is now Makueni District; Makueni District having been created when the old Machakos District was carved in two in 1993.

Owako's research formed part of a PhD thesis entitled "The Machakos Problem," and investigated the ability of local agriculture to cater for the growing number of people in the District. His work compared the state of agriculture in study villages in Mbooni, Iveti, Masii, Kangundo and Nzaui locations. He found uneven distributions of land and livestock in each of the villages, with more skewed distributions in the most densely populated areas. Owako believed that agriculture would not be able to continue to support the growing population of Machakos District, and that a landless class would evolve which supported itself through non-agricultural activities and professions.

The current research sought to investigate temporal processes of change, and was carried out between January and May 1996, involving a survey of households from Ndueni village, followed by rapid rural appraisal work conducted in Iveti, Masii and Kangundo, and archival research in Nairobi. For the purposes of comparison, fieldwork in Ndueni followed the door-to-door sampling procedure adopted by Owako, but utilized improved methods of field measurement and crop and income recording. In this way the current survey was able to conduct questionnaires in 180 households in Ndueni, with only three households refusing to answer the questionnaire. After the questionnaire a stratified sample of 56 households was revisited for more in-depth interviews regarding the results of the first phase of the study. In addition to the data collected by Owako on land and livestock holdings, the present research also elicited information on agricultural and non-farm income, as well as investigating the agricultural labour market.

The study was conducted in Ndueni village, Mbooni location, 35 kilometres from Machakos town (population 80 000) along a dirt road which is often muddy, and occasionally impassable during the rainy seasons. Nairobi is a further 60 kilometres from Machakos, and is the destination of many of the cash crops from the village. Whilst the dominant crops are mixes of maize and beans, export crops such as French beans grown in Mbooni are purchased by export companies and flown out of Nairobi International Airport. Other horticultural produce is trucked down to Nairobi and Mombasa by local traders. Coffee from the area is processed at the Kenya Planters Cooperative Union in Nairobi, as well as at independent millers in adjacent Thika District.

The study village, Ndueni, lies on the side of a highland massif which rises out of the Makueni lowlands. The bottom of the village lies near the valley floor at 1400 metres, whilst the upper parts of Ndueni reach a height of just over 1850 metres. Most of the village is thus quite cool and temperate, and similar to other high-potential areas of Machakos such as Kangundo and Iveti. Rainfall is moderate but unpredictable, with an average of 1250 millimetres a year in a bimodal pattern. The area is of a fairly high agricultural potential, lying between agro-ecological zones 2 and 3, and supporting coffee and rain-fed horticulture. Despite this the most widely-grown crops are the maize, beans and peas which form the basis of most people's diets. The area also has many zero grazed dairy cows, and sends milk down to the nearby lowlands on a daily basis.

Change in Ndueni

Much of the change seen in Ndueni mirrors the development of the wider area described by Tiffen *et al.* Because of its high agricultural potential, Mbooni (of which Ndueni is a part) was the first area of Machakos or Makueni to be settled by the people of the Akamba tribe, who make up over 95 per cent of the population of the two districts. However, as land grew more scarce in Mbooni, farmers began to move to other hill areas, and thereafter down on to the less well-watered lowlands of Machakos and Makueni.

Just as in the rest of Machakos and Makueni, Ndueni village has been experiencing rapid population growth. Ndueni was first settled by six families from nearby villages in around 1840, and 161 of the 180 households in the village's survey were traced to these original pioneers. This rapid population growth has forced a decrease in the average size of landholdings in Ndueni, as the original holdings carved out by pioneers have been subdivided amongst their descendants. This decline has driven the adoption of more intensive agricultural practices as families seek to maintain agricultural livelihoods.

Crop Patterns

Table 1 shows changes in cropping patterns since Owako's survey in 1965. The main points to note are an increase in the area planted to cash crops such as

Table 1

Cropping patterns in Ndueni

Crop	% Area 1965	% Area 1996
Maize, beans, peas	63	63
Grazing and waste land[1]	18	9
Coffee	4	13
Vegetables	4	4
Root crops	2	3
Millet, sorghum	2	negligible
Tobacco	2	none recorded
Tree lots	none recorded	3
Housing	none recorded	3
Others	5	2

Note: [1] Over 4% of the village is covered by expanses of exposed granite which are of little use for either grazing or cultivation, although are used as water collectors for downhill crops.

coffee, and an increase in tree cover (including a big rise in the number of fruit trees, often interplanted with food crops). Other changes seen include a big decrease in the amount of grazing land as it is given over to food and cash crops, and a virtual disappearance of traditional grains such as millet and sorghum.

These aggregate changes appear similar to those described by Tiffen *et al.* However, the household-level data collected in the current survey show how only 57 per cent of farmers have been able to afford the capital necessary for investment in cash crops. In contrast, the abandoning of sorghum and millet has not necessitated capital expenditure, and has been carried out by almost everyone in the village. Whilst the adoption of crops such as coffee has increased the diversity and the sum of many farmers' income, the move away from traditional grains has led to a reduction in the income diversity of poorer farmers, and increased dependence on only maize and bean cultivation on the smallest farms.

Livestock

Traditionally, it was thought that cattle were kept by the Akamba for the status they conferred, and only more lately for their meat. Stock were grazed in the open and looked after by young men and boys. The period since 1965, however, has seen an almost complete transition towards the zero grazing of cattle. This has allowed the stocking density of cattle per hectare to rise at the same time as land devoted to grazing has fallen. Despite this, cattle numbers have not grown as fast as human populations and there are thus fewer cattle per household. Zero grazing has been accompanied by a widespread transition from traditional breeds to exotic dairy cattle and half breeds, as farmers seek to maximize revenue from the sales of milk, which made up 34 per cent of agricultural income in the village.

These changes are much as described by Tiffen *et al.*, but the current household-level survey shows such changes to have been accompanied by a switching of gender roles, as those aspects of livestock care traditionally associated with women such as foddering and milking have become ever more important as male roles (herding and guarding) have declined. Women have guarded their roles carefully, with the result that livestock are now almost entirely under the care of women, who consequently often control the money from dairy sales.

Terracing

Unlike much of more lowland Machakos, terracing in Mbooni was almost complete by the time of Owako's survey in 1965. As early as 1955 the Divisional Officer for Mbooni was able to report that

> Bench terracing has proceeded at an ever greater pace during the year, and I believe it should be possible within only two years to ensure that all cultivation takes place on benches only.

KNA DC/MKS/3/1

The current survey is thus in many ways a study of changes occurring after the environmental transformation described by Tiffen *et al.* (1994). Despite this, terracing has continued to affect the relationship between society and its environment beyond the initial purpose of erosion control. For instance, terracing (together with the decreases in livestock holdings per family) now acts as a brake upon mechanization, and has led to a wide-scale abandonment of previously common technology such as ploughing, and a reversion to more labour intensive technologies such as hoeing. In 1965 over 25 per cent of farmers in the study area owned ploughs; in 1996 the figure was less than two per cent.

The trends outlined above show how, whilst *More People, Less Erosion* was able to overturn many received wisdoms regarding the relations between environmental degradation and population growth, household-level data have been able to reveal a more nuanced picture of change. Erosion control and agricultural intensification have not occurred simply as a result of societal processes, subsequently to exist in isolation from that society; but rather have reacted back in a dialectical way upon consequent economic and societal decisions. Such a process has been charted in sociology by Giddens and industrial geography by Massey, being only more recently applied to development studies by Leach *et al.* Landscape change is a fundamentally political process, and no assessment of environmental transformation is complete without a consideration of the accompanying economic and social change. The rest of the paper uses household-level data to describe more of the social and economic impacts of agricultural intensification.

Findings from Household-level Data Analysis

A significant polarization of wealth has occurred in the village in recent years, largely as a result of farmers' differential ability to tap into sources of urban capital.

In 1965 the poorest fifth of households owned eight per cent of the land whereas by 1996 the figure was three per cent and so the amount of land owned by poor families had decreased. In 1965 the richest quintile of farmers owned 40 per cent of the land, but the figure is now over 55 per cent, and so the amount of land owned by the rich has increased. In absolute terms this means that whilst average landholdings amongst the most landed 20 per cent are currently over 3.4 hectares, those with the smallest 20 per cent of holdings now own an average of only 0.2 hectares of land.

More uneven than the current distribution of land is the very unequal distribution of non-farm income in the village. Whereas the 20 per cent of families earning the most non-farm income controlled 67 per cent of the non-farm income of the village, earning an average of over $102 a month (US$1 = 58 Kenyan Shillings), over 30 per cent of the households in the village earn no non-farm income at all, except for the small amounts they can gain from occasional agricultural wage labour.

It is this differential access to non-farm income that has driven unfavourable changes in the distribution of land holdings and agricultural incomes. This is because land is very expensive in Ndueni and only people with non-farm income can afford to buy it. Irrigated land and land planted to coffee in the village is sold for prices in excess of $3400 per hectare, whilst other plots can expect to fetch around $1700 per hectare. By comparison, casual agricultural labour rates hover at around $0.90 a day when work is available. There is no tradition of rural money lending in Machakos in the same way as exists in parts of West Africa, and thus it is only people with access to income from non-farm employment, and more particularly, the soft loans and credit circles associated with formal sector work, that can afford to buy significant portions of land in the village.

For example, J- M- is one of the biggest landowners in the village, but has so far inherited nothing but an education from his father. He has purchased all his land from the proceeds of loans from his job as a Store Manager at the Ministry of Water in Machakos. Similarly, N- M- is a local entrepreneur who buys vegetables at the local market and then transports them down to Mombasa for sale. The profits from this trade have funded the acquisition of over 90 per cent of Nzasi's 16 hectares of land—the largest holding in the village. Thus whilst Owako thought that those taking up urban professions would be the rural poor, it appears that it is those households who have secured significant non-farm incomes who have been able to accumulate the most land in the countryside.

High earners are, therefore, climbing up the village land-holding scale from whatever position they started at because they have access to loans and credit to help them buy land. Indeed a limited reversal in the village wealth hierarchy has occurred over the last 50 years, as in the early colonial period it tended to be the sons of the poorest farmers (who had no cattle to provide a livelihood) who were the first to be sent to schools, and who then proceeded to buy land with the income from their urban jobs. For instance M- M-'s father was poor and had very little land or livestock. The clan (a form of extended family) sent M- to school, after which he secured a job driving road graders for the colonial administration. His wages enabled him to buy a lot of land before he retired.

In the past, farmers who made distress sales of land to people like M- were able, if things got too difficult in Mbooni, to migrate down to the lowlands where they could settle new land of lower agricultural potential. In this sense, many of the very poorest people from Ndueni are no longer there any more, but have been spun out of the upland system. However, such migration to escape poverty is no longer feasible for the poorest families in Mbooni, owing to the rising costs of migration and the closure of the land settlement frontier. Such people are now forced to remain in the uplands farming micro-scale holdings often less than 0.2 of a hectare.

The Productivity of Agriculture

According to the Boserup hypothesis, the decline in farm sizes occurring as a result of population growth and also, amongst the poorest families in Ndueni, owing to distress sales of land to richer farmers, should be offset by an increase in the productivity of agriculture per hectare, thereby preventing food availability decline. However, just as non-farm income has allowed farmers to invest in the quantity of land that they own, it is also becoming an increasingly necessary part of investment in the productivity of the land, with those farmers unable to purchase manure or artificial fertilizers struggling to maintain (let alone improve) the productivity of land per hectare with additional labour inputs alone. Average maize yields in Ndueni have fallen from 14.8 bags (90 kilograms per bag) per hectare in 1948 (DC/MKS/18/5) to only 12.3 bags per hectare in 1996. This decline has occurred despite the adoption of improved seed varieties and farming techniques such as planting before the rain, suggesting an inherent fall in the fertility of the soil.

Land in many parts of Mbooni has been cultivated for over 200 years. In the last 30 or so of these years, many fields have been continuously cultivated without breaks for fallow. Using the spatial analogue soil survey technique adopted by Tiffen *et al.*, a soil survey in the village showed that concentrations of soil nutrients in fields which had never received applications of manure or fertilizer were less than in non-cultivated areas or sites where such productivity investments regularly took place. Thus for poorer farmers in the village without access to livestock or non-farm income 'More People' may have meant 'Less Erosion', but it did not guarantee 'More Productivity'. The families which were found to be most able to invest in the maintenance and improvement of soil productivity were those earning significant quantities of non-farm income, with the result that those families who were most prosperous off the farm, were also likely to be the most prosperous on the farm. This can be demonstrated by looking at the maize yields achieved by farmers in Ndueni, whereby a significant positive correlation ($r = 0.155$, significant $r = 0.123$ at 0.05 uncertainty) exists between non-farm income and maize yields.

More significant is the inverse relationship between maize yields and area planted ($r = -0.284$, significant $r = 0.231$ at 0.001 uncertainty), a relationship observed elsewhere by Sen and Hill. This inverse pattern reflects the more careful and labour intensive cultivation practices of farmers with microholdings, and has presumably existed in Mbooni ever since land shortages began. However, the trend is bucked by the higher yields obtained by the farmers planting the very largest amounts of maize and using more capital inputs. The five largest planters in the village achieved average yields of over 20 bags a hectare—raising the figure for the richest quintile, and creating a reverse 'J' distribution. What this suggests is that whilst Sen's theory is correct for the majority of smallholders, there now exists a small group of very commercial farmers who through their capitalization of production have managed to raise yields above those obtained by most of their more labour intensive peers. This breakdown of the inverse relationship between yields and area as a result of new technology and capital inputs has already been noted by Rahman in Bangladesh, and Lipton and Longhurst in India.

Social and Economic Trends

As a result of shrinking holdings of land due to the population growth and economic polarization described earlier, and, as a result of the static or declining productivity of agriculture on many poorer farms with no non-farm income, over 90 per cent of families are unable to feed themselves throughout the year from the food they harvest from the fields. Fortunately around 60 per cent of households in the village can afford to plant some cash crops, and so can make up a varying proportion of this subsistence gap by selling commodities such as coffee or tomatoes. However, over 40 per cent of farmers are, for between two and ten months of the year, dependent on selling their labour to buy food. For the majority who are unable to find permanent jobs in the towns, this results in participation in rural labour markets. These labour markets exist to supply the labour required for cash crops such as coffee and French beans grown by the richer farmers. However, when agricultural wage labour is unavailable locally, poor people in Mbooni go hungry.

A recent welfare survey in Makueni by a Danish International Development Agency (DANIDA) group found that malnutrition in the district was highest in Mbooni, despite the abundant greenery and horticultural exports. Food availability in Mbooni obviously does not equate easily with food entitlements. In contrast, the dryer but more sparsely populated lowlands enjoyed greater food security. This is counter-intuitive, even to people in other parts of Machakos and Makueni. Thus when a local councillor, T- M-, made a request for food aid for Mbooni at a District council meeting he was told 'You councillor, you just keep quiet!'. T- complained about people from other areas:

> Once they see all these trees (in Ndueni) they think that we are quite alright here—but trees are never eaten. At times the experts come and they go to (the local) market and they find a lot of sukumawiki (a local vegetable), cabbages and somebody goes away thinking that everybody has (food), while others living in the same area, unless they reach deeper into their pockets cannot even afford sukumawiki for a day.

Whilst these processes do show differentiation, only more recently has such differentiation been accompanied by class formation and diminishing social mobility. Before the late 1970s it was still relatively easy for members of even the poorest families to obtain an education and subsequently secure employment. Indeed, some of the richest people in the village today are old men from what were very poor families, who were sent to school by their clans, and who then accumulated land from the proceeds of their jobs, just as in the case of M- M- described earlier. However, as a result of recent economic reforms raising the costs of education and the concomitant decline of the clan as an institution of welfare support, poorer families are increasingly unable to afford an education for their children at the same time as educational requirements for jobs have been increasing. Consequently children from poor families are finding it more difficult to escape from poverty by working in the towns in the way that their forebears did in the past, and an undeniable element of structure is building up in society.

The Growing Importance of Capital in Agricultural Innovation and Environmental Conservation

The non-farm economy of Mbooni is largely focused around remittances from migrant labour in Machakos town and Nairobi. In a similar way, many of the other examples of high population density and sustainable intensive cultivation in Africa are to be found near major urban centres such as Kano. Without the widespread availability of such urban capital agricultural intensification may take an involutionary path of diminishing returns to effort. It is in this context that Haugerud acknowledges how the economic sustainability of rural Embu has only been maintained by becoming an 'outpost' of the wider Nairobi and Kenyan economy.

Agricultural intensification and conservation technology in Mbooni appear to have come in two waves, with 'second phase' technologies being increasingly dependent upon inputs of (urban derived) capital. Whilst almost everyone has adopted those first phase intensification practices that required no monetary inputs and only labour (such as terracing and mulching), second phase agricultural practices which require capital availability (such as manuring or the use of inorganic fertilizer) have been adopted only by those that can afford them. Families without access to such capital are, therefore, experiencing a detrimental and involutionary cycle of declining yields, declining soil fertility and diminishing returns to labour, as first phase conservation and productivity gains are overtaken by population growth. As one poorer respondent noted 'in the past there was a desire for more people, but now there is a fear'.

Thus Boserupian intensification on richer farms, and a form of Geertzian involution on poorer farms are seen to be proceeding side by side within the same village. At a village level, if the demands of population growth increase faster than the supply of capital to meet those demands through investments in productivity and new cash crops, then the village will tend further down the involutionary path of declining yields and returns to labour.

In such a situation, the importance of non-farm income becomes twofold. Richer farms use non-farm income to make productive investments in agriculture, and so 'straddle' the urban and rural economies. Poorer households, on the other hand, are forced to use non-farm income to make up shortfalls in food needs, after which they often have very little investible surplus to put into agricultural production. Only greater access to land or non-farm income will enable escape from this trap. By contrast, continued population growth is increasing land hunger still further, and consequently inflating the numbers of people looking for non-farm employment in a slowing Kenyan economy. More people chasing a static number of jobs will only serve to push down the value of wages in real terms, and further reduce the ability of local farmers to 'straddle' the rural and urban economies.

Conclusions—Wealth Comes From the City

Having studied in the area of the ODI project 'More People Less Erosion', this research can agree with many of the findings of the ODI project regarding the environmental effects of agricultural intensification and can also agree that it has come about as a result of people's profitable responses to market opportunities. However as a result of its focus on household-level processes, the new study is able to show that there has been a polarization of landholdings in the study village, driven largely by differential access to urban wages and capital. The application of such capital to production on the land, has resulted in those who earn the most off the land earning the most on the land as well. Recent changes have accelerated this process, and made it more difficult for the poorest farmers to enjoy upward social mobility.

Whilst these findings cannot be unproblematically extrapolated to other areas undergoing agricultural intensification, this study is not alone in observing increasing differentiation in such an area. A recent study in the Kabale region of Uganda by Lindblade *et al.* also noted a polarization of wealth, as did Haugerud in Embu, Kenya. In Rwanda, André and Platteau graphically chart the role of extreme land hunger and differentiation in fuelling the recent genocide. However, what is clear in Machakos at least, is that increasing inequality has not arisen, by and large, as a result of exploitation of the poorest farmers by a local bourgeoisie within rural labour markets; as has been shown to be the case in areas of India. Rather, such agricultural labour (generated by richer farmers growing new labour-intensive crops such as coffee and French beans) creates a lifeline to poorer households in the area, enabling them to cling onto their stake in the rural economy.

Polarization, appears to have been driven by the application of, and differential access to, the 'investible surplus' from non-farm income. Whilst this is largely a function of non-farm income, it cannot be divorced entirely from the existing distribution of landholdings within the village. Farmers with the most land are likely to spend less of their income making up subsistence shortfalls, and thus will be able to utilize a greater proportion of their non-farm income to buy land and invest upon it. Obtaining non-farm income in this way helps smaller farmers to hold their economic ground in the face of increased pressures stemming from population growth. In contrast, those who fail to tap into new income streams are deriving diminishing returns from ever smaller pieces of land, lacking as they do the capital to intensify productively.

For many poorer families then, the environmental sustainability charted by Tiffen *et al.* has not been accompanied by a similar economic sustainability, with the implication that ecological and economic sustainability ought to be decoupled in the manner suggested by Mortimore and Munasinghe. Furthermore, the wealth and investment capital of many of the richer families in Ndueni has come from the city, with the implication that proponents of rural development ought to be looking to create not more rural 'Machakoses' but more urban 'Nairobies'. In the absence of greatly increased capital availability for investment in agricultural productivity, population growth will continue to drive many households in Ndueni along an involutionary spiral of poverty amidst green and terraced fields.

POSTSCRIPT

Is Food Production in Africa Capable of Keeping Up with Population Growth?

An interesting aspect of Mortimore and Tiffen's Machakos story was this rural community's ability to positively engage with the market. This is also a key point that Murton makes, as it is those households with nonfarm incomes who are most successful at agricultural intensification. This stands in contrast to a large amount of Africanist scholarship, which sees interaction with the global market as extremely problematic. Boserup herself, whose theory was described in the introduction, and whose ideas drove both of these studies, saw the market as a potential stumbling block. Her concern was that employment opportunities elsewhere would draw off enough labor that the intensification process would be derailed. This concern is not entirely unfounded in the African context where labor (often more than land) is frequently the key constraint to agricultural production. Both Mortimore and Tiffen, as well as Murton, suggest that nonfarm income seems to more than compensate for any loss of labor in Machakos. What is crucial, however, is that households are willing to continually invest in this area. In other African contexts, labor constraints and lack of investment have been much more pronounced. See, for example, Jeffrey Alwang and P.B. Siegal's article in the August 1999 issue of *World Development* entitled "Labor Shortages on Small Landholdings in Malawi: Implications for Policy Reforms."

Murton is not alone in his criticism of Mortimore and Tiffen's analysis of the Machakos situation (but his study is an ideal match for this issue as it occurred in the same locale). Diane Rocheleau was actually the first scholar to articulate (in published form) the concern that Mortimore and Tiffen did not address properly the problem of economic differentiation over time (i.e., a growing gap between the rich and poor). For an excellent, and concise, articulation of this concern, see Rocheleau's September 1995 piece in the journal *Environment* entitled "More on Machakos." The same issue of the journal also carries a response to Rocheleau by Tiffen and Mortimore. Many other scholars have also sought to critically examine the relationship between population growth and agricultural change in African situations. For example, Thomas Conelly and Miriam Chaiken, in a 2000 article in *Human Ecology* entitled "Intensive Farming, Agro-Diversity, and Food Security Under Conditions of Extreme Population Pressure in Western Kenya," study an area in Western Kenya with similarly high population densities. Despite the wide variety of sophisticated practices that maintain a high level of agro-diversity, they conclude that intense population pressure has led to smaller land holdings, poorer diet quality, and declining food security.

Two final points about Machakos case are worth considering. First, free hold tenure (or private property that may be bought and sold) now prevails in Machakos. This is not the case in many areas of Africa where only use, or usufruct, rights to land are allocated to community members (and, therefore, land may not be bought and sold). Some would view the lack of private property as a problem (because they believe this inhibits investment in land) while others would see the tradition of usufruct rights as beneficial because it may slow down the transfer of land from rich to poor households. Because there are local land and labor markets in Machakos, scholars should also consider how power differences between households might influence these economic transactions.

The second point to consider is that both authors in this issue agree that food production, on average, was able to keep up with population growth in this area. This is analogous to what is happening on the global scale over the same time frame, that is, global food production is keeping up with global population growth. The problem is that not all households are able to keep up and some may not even have the resources to buy available food on the market. This insight has important policy implications as it means that simply developing technologies to produce more food will not solve the problem for everyone (as these technologies, or the food produced, may be inaccessible to poor households). As such, finding ways for poor households to access food (through their own production or purchase) may be as or more important than simply producing more food.

For further reading on this topic, see a volume edited by Turner, Hyden and Kates (*Population Growth and Agricultural Change in Africa*, University Press of Florida, 1993) that includes case studies from around the continent; or an article by Lamdin *et al.* in the December 2001 issue of *Global Environmental Change* entitled "The Causes of Land-Use and Land-Cover Change: Moving Beyond the Myths." For a more Malthusian perspective, see a book by Cleaver and Schreiber entitled *Reversing the Spiral: The Population, Agriculture, and Environment Nexus in Sub-Saharan Africa* (World Bank, 1994).

ISSUE 10

Does African Agriculture Need a Green Revolution?

YES: Kofi A. Annan, from Remarks on the Launch of the Alliance for a Green Revolution in Africa at the World Economic Forum, in Cape Town, South Africa (June 14, 2007)

NO: Carol B. Thompson, from "Africa: Green Revolution or Rainbow Revolution?" *Foreign Policy in Focus* (July 17, 2007)

ISSUE SUMMARY

YES: Kofi Annan, former UN Secretary General, deplores the fact that Sub-Saharan Africa is the only region where per capita food production has declined. Annan is now leading a new organization that answers the call of many African leaders to build on the achievements and lessons learned from the Green Revolution in Asia and Latin America that began several decades earlier. He is spearheading an African Green Revolution that aims to increase African food production.

NO: Carol Thompson, professor of political economy at Northern Arizona University, suggests that increasing yields of a few targeted crops will not solve Africa's food problems. Rather, she argues that sustaining Africa's food crop diversity and indigenous ecological knowledge is the key to reducing hunger. She further eschews food security built on global market dependence in favor of food sovereignty.

Humans have long sought to increase agricultural output through the use of improved seed. Initially this was done by repeatedly (over generations) saving seeds from plants with the most desirable characteristics. African farmers have been found to maintain and utilize an amazing number of crop varieties. Even when fields are not intercropped (i.e., several different crops planted in the same field), African farmers will often plant different varieties of the same crop in accordance with soil and moisture conditions that may vary throughout the field. Preserving the rich genetic diversity among crops at the local level in Africa has been a concern of some environmentalists.

Formal plant breeding emerged at the end of the eighteenth century. Here, crops were systematically cross-fertilized in hopes of obtaining plants with a desirable mix of characteristics. A significant advance was the development of a technique known as hybridization in the early twentieth century. Hybridization involves cross-breeding two inbreds from desirable parentage, a technique that produces highly productive plants. In the 1960s, a concerted effort, known as the Green Revolution, was undertaken to boost food crop production in the developing world. The Green Revolution, involving highly productive hybridized crops in conjunction with pesticides and inorganic fertilizers, largely benefited Asia and South America because it devoted most of its attention to food crops prevalent in these regions, mainly rice, wheat, and maize to a lesser extent. Africa was bypassed by the Green Revolution for the most part, with a few significant exceptions such as maize in Zimbabwe. Although the Green Revolution of the 1960s and 1970s did boost food production, it has been criticized for not really resolving the hunger issues it was designed to address, tending to favor wealthier farmers and spawning a host of new environmental problems related to chemically intensive agriculture.

Now, some 40 years after the first Green Revolution, a group of policy leaders is calling for a new Green Revolution in Africa. The views of Kofi Annan, the former UN Secretary General, are presented in this issue, and he is also supported by the likes of Jeffrey Sachs, a prominent adviser to the UN and director of the Earth Institute at Columbia University. According to Annan, there is nothing more important than addressing poverty at its core, by increasing the ability of African farmers to improve their productivity, food security, and incomes. For Annan and others, Africa's basic problem is that it does not produce enough food to feed itself. As such, increasing agricultural yields is the best way to address hunger on the continent. Annan's organization, Alliance for a Green Revolution in Africa, is in the process of launching several programs, including those to develop improved seeds, to improve agricultural expertise, to improve the health of soils, to better manage water resources, and to improve crop storage, transport, and marketing.

Carol Thompson, a professor of political economy at Northern Arizona University, is concerned about the environmental sustainability and human health implications of a new Green Revolution in Africa. This concern extends to previous Green Revolution approaches that emphasized a few crops (and thereby limited crop biodiversity), the growing reliance on external sources for improved seeds, and the limited recognition of local technologies and approaches. She argues for an approach known as food sovereignty, which seeks to develop food security through local technologies and solutions rather than by reliance on the global market.

One question in this debate is whether food insecurity in Africa is a question of underproduction or maldistribution. Until quite recently, there was a consensus among specialists that hunger was more often the result of conflict, mismanagement, or poor distribution than underproduction. This former consensus was catalyzed, in large part, by the pioneering work of the Nobel laureate economist, Amartya Sen, who showed how national markets could be replete with grain, yet poor households might still not have the means to access this food.

YES

Kofi A. Annan

Remarks on the Launch of the Alliance for a Green Revolution in Africa at the World Economic Forum

Three years ago, as Secretary-General of the United Nations, I addressed the Africa's Green Revolution Seminar in Addis Ababa—a gathering of African leaders committed to achieving a goal that has eluded us for too long—lifting tens of millions of our children, parents, brothers and sisters out of poverty and hunger into a world of opportunity and hope.

Today, I have the high honour of accepting the position of Chairman of the Alliance for a Green Revolution in Africa. I am humbled, and yet excited.

I do this alongside all of you—our farmers, scientists, entrepreneurs, and elected leaders. And I accept this challenge with gratitude to the Rockefeller Foundation, the Bill & Melinda Gates Foundation, and all others who support our African campaign.

I do this because, for me, there is nothing more important. We must address poverty at its core. In Africa, this means enabling small-scale farmers to grow and sell Africa's food. Our goal is to dramatically increase the productivity, food security, incomes and livelihoods of small-scale farmers, many of whom are women.

All of us yearn for practical solutions to address the major cause of our continental poverty—an agricultural sector that has languished, but is now poised to be so much more productive and dynamic. We know that the path to prosperity in Africa begins at the fields of African farmers who, unlike farmers almost anywhere else, do not produce enough food to nourish our families, communities, or the populations of our growing African cities.

The facts are well known. Sub-Saharan Africa is the only region in the world where per capita food production has steadily declined. One-third of the continent's population is chronically undernourished. Most of our farmers lack access to productive crop varieties, adequate water resources and soil nutrients. In fact, our soils are the most depleted in the world. Good roads are scarce. Universities, and the research and talent they produce, are poorly staffed and underfunded.

We face many challenges. But, through this Alliance, we have reason for hope. But hope must be more than a dream—it requires the mobilisation of knowledge, capacity and resources to end the human misery that ravages our continent.

Many of our leaders have spoken about what is involved in launching a uniquely African Green Revolution—a revolution that looks to improved agricultural production as the basis of a larger effort to take Africa confidently into a new era of sustainable development; a revolution that improves the lives of farmers and delivers greater opportunity, enterprise and prosperity.

Such a vitalisation of African agriculture involves an ambitious agenda, and AGRA has such an agenda. Eager for results, AGRA has begun implementing its first programmes:

> In 2006, we began working with our partners to develop new seeds for small-scale farmers that are more productive and resilient varieties of Africa's major food crops. Also in 2006, we launched educational programmes to accelerate the development of African agricultural expertise, and to monitor and evaluate our work.

Over the next four years, we will systematically build on these programmes, adding initiatives to address other key aspects of the agricultural value chain.

> In 2007, we will launch a programme to improve the health of Africa's soils, now the most depleted in the world.
> In 2008, we will launch a water management initiative to help Africa's small-scale farmers get the most "crop for each drop".
> By 2009, we will address the key challenges facing off-farm systems and markets, such as improvements in market information systems, crop storage, processing, and transport.

Along with all of this work, AGRA will strongly advocate for policies that support small-scale farmers; those that promote rural development, environmental sustainability, and trade favourable to poor farmers in Africa.

Only with advocacy and policy change at national, regional, and global levels will small-scale farmers succeed in dramatically increasing yields, ending poverty and hunger, and lifting the economies of Africa.

Beyond this five-year time frame, the work of AGRA will continue to be informed by African farmers in the field, women's associations, and partners and leaders from all sectors of agriculture. We expect to see dramatic improvements in the livelihoods of small-holder farmers within 10 to 20 years.

We know that success depends on partnerships, and our approach is inclusive: all who share our goals are invited to this table. We are listening to others and learning about the approaches that are already improving food production in Africa. We launched our programmes only after extensive discussions with farmers in the field, as well as with our partner African institutions and experts who are carrying out this work.

In the coming months, AGRA will build upon and expand these partnerships. We will meet with farmer's unions, women's associations, networks of agro-dealers and civil society organisations. We will listen carefully to their needs and priorities, and learn from their perspectives and experience.

Many African heads of state have already committed to reaching the African Union's goal of reaching a 6 percent annual increase in farm production by 2015 and cutting food insecurity in half. AGRA fully endorses these goals, and will do all we can to help countries reach them.

While ambitious, ours is a practical campaign. We are focused on developing locally-driven and adapted solutions that address the full range of reforms required to ensure dramatically increased productivity on Africa's small-scale farms. Our farmers want better seeds, soils, and prices for what they sell. They want access to water, markets, and credit. They need to see national policies put in place that accelerate rural economic growth, investment, and job creation.

And, though we know this is a journey, that doesn't stop us from being in a hurry. We aim to make a concrete difference in our lifetimes. With respect to seeds, AGRA is already in the fields, working with African farmers and African agricultural scientists to breed new varieties of maize, cassava, rice, beans, sorghum and other major crops that will offer better resistance to disease and pests.

Our goal is to produce 100 new crop varieties in five years. And to ensure farmers have access to these seeds, we will also move to create a wider network of local seed distributors and agro-dealers to better serve remote rural areas.

Building on the Africa Fertiliser Summit held in Nigeria last year, we will launch a soil health initiative to improve soil management practices. We absolutely must improve the quality and health of our farm lands. We owe it to ourselves and future generations to enhance Africa's natural resource base and ensure sustainable production.

Water management is a cornerstone of our plans. A crucial challenge ahead will be to improve water use, especially where water is scarce. We will do this by working with farmers who are eager to develop low-cost, small-scale water management and irrigation techniques.

None of this will be possible without market improvements to increase access to credit for small-scale farmers. The ability of these farmers to sell their surplus crops is critical to any gains in African food production. So, we will work with existing and new organisations on this continent to make this uniquely African Green Revolution a lasting force for economic and social progress.

AGRA is answering the call of many African leaders to build on the achievements and lessons learned from the Green Revolution in Asia and Latin America that began more than a generation ago. That campaign—initiated by the Rockefeller Foundation—saved hundreds of millions of lives and more than doubled cereal production. There is much to be learned from these tremendous successes, as well as from their shortcomings.

That said, ours is a Revolution of the 21st century, one that we Africans will own, whose destiny we will shape, and which responds to the specific environmental challenges facing our continent. We will offer a wide range of innovative solutions. African nations and farmers will choose those that are best suited for our African cultures, climates, and economies.

We will move forward by empowering farmers and engaging rural communities to improve agriculture production in ways that reduce social and economic inequity. Our success in this regard will necessarily be linked with policies that support Africa's women farmers. Women do the lion's share of Africa's farming. It is they who grow, process, and prepare the continent's food. It is they who gather water and wood. Yet, women lack adequate access to credit, technology, training, and agricultural services.

We will be vigilant in protecting the environment that gives us our water, air, and land. We will conserve and make use of the natural biodiversity of Africa's crops and learn from the knowledge of our farmers.

The world remains captive to the old idea that we face a choice between economic growth and conservation. This is a false choice. Our fight against poverty is directly linked to the health of the earth itself. Let me be especially clear on this point: we will revitalise agriculture for Africa's small-scale farmers while protecting and enhancing the quality of our environment.

No doubt, ours is an ambitious agenda. And some would say that, in Africa, we are awash in ambitious agendas yet nothing changes. But I am convinced that the effort I am embracing today is moving us beyond a general commitment to help Africa's poor, towards specific solutions backed by the resources, talent and partnerships needed to produce tangible results.

You will be able to measure our progress by weighing the harvests as they come in from the field, by testing the soils on the farms, and by looking at the improvement in the livelihoods of farmers across Africa.

I have spent decades listening to people talk about Africa's problems, making promises to help. It's an experience that has left me thirsty for concrete action. AGRA is about taking action now, today, in a clear and meaningful way.

The final point I wish to make is this: no country or region of significant size has been able to lift itself out of poverty without raising productivity in its agricultural sector. This is our challenge. It is a long-term effort, but one that—with our partners—is within reach.

We in Africa know that, in the words of the Nigerian Chinua Achebe, it is always "morning yet on creation day." We now have an opportunity to create a new day, and with it, a new morning, for Africa.

I close today with the plea that I offered in Addis Ababa three years ago—let us all do our part to help Africa's small-scale farmers end chronic poverty. Let us generate a uniquely African Green Revolution—a revolution that will help the continent in its quest for prosperity and peace.

Carol B. Thompson

Africa: Green Revolution or Rainbow Evolution?

Kofi Annan has just agreed to head the Alliance for a Green Revolution in Africa, funded by the Bill and Melinda Gates Foundation and the Rockefeller Foundation.

The goals of these foundations are ambitious. "Our initial estimate is that over ten years, the program for Africa's seed systems (PASS) should produce 400 improved crop varieties resulting in a 50 percent increase in the land area planted with improved varieties across 20 African countries," reads the initiative's press release. "We have also initially estimated that this level of performance will contribute to eliminating hunger for 30–40 million people and sustainably move 15–20 million people out of poverty."

But can Africa afford this proposed "green revolution" in terms of human health and environmental sustainability? The foundation goals require resources that the continent does not have while derogating the incredible wealth it does possess. Although scientists, agriculturalists and African governments all agree that the continent has not remotely reached its agricultural potential, their advocated policies for food sovereignty drastically diverge from the high-tech, high-cost approach promoted by Gates and Rockefeller.

In 2002, while UN secretary general, Kofi Annan asked, "How can a green revolution be achieved in Africa?" After more than a year of study, the appointed expert panel of scientists (from Brazil, China, Mexico, South Africa and elsewhere) replied that a green revolution would not provide food security because of the diverse types of farming systems across the continent. There is "no single magic technological bullet . . . for radically improving African agriculture," the expert panel reported in its strategic recommendations. "African agriculture is more likely to experience numerous 'rainbow evolutions' that differ in nature and extent among the many systems, rather than one Green Revolution as in Asia." Now Annan has agreed to head the kind of project his advisors told him would not work.

Behind the Green Revolution

The green revolution of the 1970s promoted increased yields, based on a model of industrial agriculture defined as a monoculture of one or two crops,

From *Foreign Policy In Focus Brief*, July 17, 2007. Copyright © 2007 by The Institute for Policy Studies. Reprinted by permission.

which requires massive amounts of both fertilizer and pesticide as well as the purchase of seed. Although this approach to food production might feed more people in the short term, it also quickly destroys the earth through extensive soil degradation and water pollution from pesticides and fertilizers. It ruined small-scale farmers in Asia and Latin America, who could not afford to purchase the fertilizers, pesticides, and water necessary for the hybrid seed or apply these inputs in the exact proportions and at the exact times. To pay their debts, the farmers had to sell their land.

Increasing yields to provide food for the hungry remains the central justification for a green revolution. But as the expert panel above analyzed in great detail, increased yields of one or two strains of one or two crops ("monoculture within monoculture," as stated by a Tanzanian botanist) will not solve Africa's food problems. Africa's diverse ecological systems, and even more diverse farming systems, require multiple initiatives, from intercropping on to permaculture, from respecting and using traditional ecological knowledge to training and equipping more African geneticists. The UN Food and Agriculture Organization, for example, now promotes farmers' breeding seeds (*in situ*) as a better conservation measure than collecting seed for refrigeration in a few large seed banks (*ex situ*). The very best food seed breeders in Africa, the "keepers of seed," are women who often farm less than one hectare of land.

The key to ending hunger is sustaining Africa's food biodiversity, not reducing it to industrial monoculture. Currently, food for African consumption comes from about 2,000 different plants, while the U.S. food base derives mainly from 12 plants. Any further narrowing of the food base makes us all vulnerable because it increases crop susceptibility to pathogens, reduces the variety of nutrients needed for human health, and minimizes the parent genetic material available for future breeding.

Seeds are a key element in the equation. One figure not often quoted among the depressing statistics from the continent is that African farmers still retain control over this major farming input: of the seed used for food crops, 80% is saved seed. Farmers do not have to buy seed every season, with cash they do not have. They possess a greater wealth—their indigenous seeds, freely shared and developed over centuries. The proposed green revolution would shift the food base away from this treasure of seed. Instead, African farmers would have to purchase seed each season, thus putting cash into the hands of the corporations providing the seed. Is there a way of developing new varieties without further enriching Monsanto or DuPont by removing genetic wealth from African farmers?

Corporate development of new seed varieties, as promoted by the foundations, raises other questions. Will the new varieties be patented or protected by farmers' rights? Who will own and control the seed? One major reason for the decline of the World Trade Organization (WTO) is the global South's resistance to patenting life forms. In 1999, the African Union, representing all African governments, asked that its unanimous resolution rejecting any patenting on life be put on the agenda at the Seattle WTO meeting. The United States refused the request.

Another source of African wealth derives from indigenous ecological knowledge, reflecting centuries of adaptation to the different ecological zones, which values interspersing different plants to enrich the soil and deter pests from food crops. Shade trees, often cut down to open the land for monoculture farming, are not necessarily in the way of a plowing tractor. African farmers have the knowledge to use these trees as wind breaks, medicine, habitats for biodiverse insect communities, and food for all.

This wealth of knowledge raises another question whether the African continent needs newly manufactured varieties of food crops, or is the problem the lack of scientific recognition and market valuing of what African farmers have cultivated for centuries? Does the color green in this Green Revolution favor crops known and owned by the global North?

Sorghum is one example of a crop lost to markets in the global North but not to Africa. On the continent, it is planted in more hectares than all other food crops combined. As nutritious as maize for carbohydrates, vitamin B6, and food energy, sorghum is more nutritious in protein, ash, pantothenic acid, calcium, copper, iron, phosphorus, isoleucine, and leucine. One of the most versatile foods in the world, sorghum can be boiled like rice, cracked like oats for porridge, baked like wheat into flatbreads, popped like popcorn for snacks, or brewed for nutritious beer.

Although indigenous knowledge designed these diverse and rich uses of sorghum, most contemporary scientists have ignored its genetic wealth. "Sorghum is a relatively undeveloped crop with a truly remarkable array of grain types, plant types, and adaptability," concludes the National Research Council in the United States. "Most of its genetic wealth is so far untapped and even unsorted. Indeed, sorghum probably has more undeveloped genetic potential than any other major food crop in the world."

Engaging African scientists to discover the potential genetic wealth of sorghum would assist African food security. In a first glimpse of foundation expenditures, however, we see funds directed to the Wambugu Consortium (founded by Pioneer Hi-Breed, part of DuPont) for experiments in genetically modified sorghum. By adding a gene, rather than mining the genetic wealth already there, the consortium can patent and sell the "new" variety at a premium price for DuPont.

Toward Sustainability

Given the well-documented destruction of the previous green revolution, what if we decided that Africa's lack of use of fertilizer is a sign of *sustainable* development not of backwardness? Africa's use of chemical fertilizers is extremely low: nine kilograms per hectare in Sub-Sahara Africa, compared to 135 kilograms per hectare in East and Southeast Asia, 100 kilograms in South Asia, and an average of 206 kilograms in industrialized countries. Originating from excess nitrogen production left over after World War II, the massive use of chemical fertilizers defined industrial agriculture in the 20th century. Surely for the 21st century, yields can be increased without such a high cost of African environmental degradation.

The African continent also uses different terminology from that of the green revolution. Instead of food security, African voices articulate the goal of *food sovereignty.* Food sovereignty expresses resistance to the notion that food security can be provided by reliance on global markets, where price and supply vagaries can be as capricious as African weather. Experiencing political manipulation of global markets by the more powerful, African governments seek to control decisions about food sources, considering such choices as vital to national sovereignty.

African governments work to defend local, small-scale farmers from highly subsidized farmers in the United States or Europe. In most of Africa—with South Africa a notable exception—the majority of the population still lives in rural areas and still derives their incomes from farming. Dislocation of farmers to consolidate land for high-tech, green revolution farming is as serious a threat as chemical pollution of the environment.

Should the green wealth of ecological and farming knowledge among local small-scale farmers be destroyed for the cash wealth of much fewer large-scale farmers buying all their inputs from foreign corporations?

Each African government will answer the above questions about a green revolution differently. The diversity of policies matches the diversity of the continent. Yet they all reject patenting of life forms and strive to attain food sovereignty. High-tech answers to Africa's food crises are no answers at all if they pollute the environment with fertilizers and pesticides, destroy small-scale farming, and transform the genetic wealth of the continent into cash profits for a few corporations.

POSTSCRIPT

Does African Agriculture Need a Green Revolution?

The new Green Revolution for Africa, pushed by Kofi Annan and others, is both similar and different to the Green Revolution of the 1960s and 1970s. It is similar to the extent that it views hunger as largely caused by an underproduction of food, that it emphasizes improved seed varieties and seed packages as a major thrust of the initiative, and that it has the support of some very large donors (the Rockefeller Foundation was/is a key player in both efforts). It is, however, also different in some respects. The more recent effort is not limiting itself to hybrid seeds as its leading technology, but also appears to be open to experimenting with genetically modified (GM) seeds. The key advance of GM seeds, over hybridization, is that plant breeders are now able to insert genes from other (unrelated) species to affect desirable characteristics in a food crop. Even though GM seeds are purported to have several advantages (e.g., higher yields, lower need for traditional pesticides), they also evoke a host of other concerns. These include unknown human health effects, the escape of genes from GM plants into other crops and plants, the need to continually invent and introduce new GM seeds in response to insect populations that become resistant to old GM seeds, and concern about undue reliance on the companies who develop such seeds. More information on Annan's group, Alliance for a Green Revolution in Africa, may be found at http://www.agra-alliance.org/.

Carol Thompson's emphasis on "food sovereignty" also deserves further explanation. At the Forum for Food Sovereignty in Sélingué, Mali, 27 February 2007, about 500 delegates from more than 80 countries adopted the Declaration of Nyéléni, which says "Food sovereignty is the right of peoples to healthy and culturally appropriate food produced through ecologically sound and sustainable methods, and their right to define their own food and agriculture systems." Food sovereignty is distinct from two closely related terms, *food security* and *food self-sufficiency*. Food security refers to access to enough food at all times for a healthy life (irrespective of the source of the food), whereas food self-sufficiency emphasizes the production of sufficient quantities of food within the borders of a country to feed its population. Food self-sufficiency was an explicit goal of many African nations in the 1970s and 1980s, whereas food security was the dominant parlance of the 1990s. Although food sovereignty is similar to food self-sufficiency in that it tends to emphasize local (or national) production of food, it differs with its stress on ecological sustainability and local participation. Food sovereignty is also quite different from food security in terms of how it views the market. Food security analysts often see the market as an acceptable means for acquiring additional food stuffs, whereas food sovereignty proponents typically view the market with great suspicion. They not only view the global market place as unfair to African producers, but as controlled by large corporate interests. For more information on food sovereignty, see, for example, a 2006 article by Hans Holmén in *The European Journal of Development Research* entitled "Myths about Agriculture, Obstacles to Solving the African Food Crisis," or the official website of the 2007 World Forum on Food Sovereignty in Mali (http://www.nyeleni2007.org/?lang=en).

ISSUE 11

Is Sub-Saharan Africa Experiencing a Deforestation Crisis?

YES: Kevin M. Cleaver and Götz A. Schreiber, from *Reversing the Spiral: The Population, Agriculture, and Environment Nexus in Sub-Saharan Africa* (The World Bank, 1994)

NO: Thomas J. Bassett and Koli Bi Zuéli, from "Environmental Discourses and the Ivorian Savanna," *Annals of the Association of American Geographers* (March 2000)

ISSUE SUMMARY

YES: World Bank economists Kevin M. Cleaver and Götz A. Schreiber argue that Africa is engaged in a downward spiral of population growth, poor agricultural performance, and environmental degradation.

NO: Academic geographers Thomas J. Bassett and Koli Bi Zuéli counter that it is dominant perceptions of environmental change, rather than concrete evidence, that lie behind the widely held belief that Africa is engaged in an "environmental crisis of staggering proportions."

$\mathbf{I}$t has long been assumed that Africa is experiencing high levels of deforestation and that drastic measures must be undertaken to curb this disturbing trend. While this characterization still pervades much of the literature on environmental change in Africa, this view has been challenged in recent years by a series of books and articles questioning the degree and nature of deforestation in Africa.

One may gain perspective on debates concerning the nature and extent of environmental degradation in Africa by considering a number of broader, theoretical viewpoints. Contemporary scholars who believe that population growth is the main cause of environmental degradation in Africa are often described as neo-Malthusians. The neo-Malthusian label stems from the work of the original Malthusian, Thomas Malthus, and his 1798 treatise entitled *Essay on the Principle of Population*, as well as the subsequent and related work of neo-Malthusians such as Paul Ehrlich and his book entitled *The Population Bomb* (Simon and Schuster, 1968). Malthus suggested that human population will tend to expand until it has outstripped the capacity of the land to support it. Neo-Malthusians have updated this idea by accounting for improvements in agricultural productivity and family planning technologies, while still maintaining that high rates of population growth lie behind most forms of environmental degradation. During the colonial era in Africa, many European administrators, foresters, and academics adopted Malthusian-leaning viewpoints, portraying Africa as a scene of environmental destruction driven by excessive population expansion and poor management practices. Since independence, the neo-Malthusian perspective has tended to flourish following natural disasters (such as the Sahelian droughts of 1968–1972 and 1984–1985) and during periods of heightened international attention to environmental issues (such as that surrounding the 1992 United Nations Conference on Environment and Development in Rio de Janeiro).

There have been a number of scholarly traditions countering the neo-Malthusian perspective. In Africa, cultural ecologists (an interdisciplinary field examining human-environment interactions in developing-country settings) have conducted field studies demonstrating that many traditional natural resource management practices are ecologically sound. Another closely related line of scholarship was developed in the wake of the pioneering work of Ester Boserup, who, in her 1965 book, *The Conditions of Agricultural Growth* (G. Allen and Unwin), argues that population increase leads to sustainable increases in agricultural production via a process of intensification over the medium to long term. In Africa, scholars such as Michael Mortimore have documented agricultural intensification in northern Nigeria and the highlands of East Africa.

More recently, scholars working in the tradition of political ecology have focused on the effect of broad-scale political and economic processes on local-level ecological dynamics (both real and perceived). Political ecologists have often drawn on Marxist-inspired discourse theory to highlight the role of political and economic power, rather than "neutral" empirical observation, in shaping our understanding and diagnosis of environmental problems.

In this issue, Kevin M. Cleaver and Götz A. Schreiber present deforestation as a major problem in sub-Saharan Africa and in West Africa in particular. While acknowledging that data on forest resources and rates of extraction are imperfect, the authors argue that this information is reliable enough to describe the scale and trend of the problem. Cleaver and Schreiber suggest that the causes of deforestation include a number of activities driven by population growth and international demand, especially forest conversion to farmland, road construction in environmentally fragile areas, timber extraction, and commercial fuelwood harvesting.

Thomas J. Bassett and Koli Bi Zuéli contend that there is only shaky evidence to support the perception of Africa as physically disintegrating due to the destructive practices of its inhabitants. They are particularly critical of National Environmental Action Plans (NEAPs) that the World Bank has sponsored in a number of African countries. NEAPs that misdiagnose the nature and causes of environmental change may, in fact, lead to policy prescriptions that acerbate, rather than assuage, real environmental problems.

189

YES

Kevin M. Cleaver and
Götz A. Schreiber

Reversing the Spiral: The Population, Agriculture, and Environment Nexus in Sub-Saharan Africa

Introduction

Over the past thirty years, most of Sub-Saharan Africa (SSA) has experienced very rapid population growth, sluggish agricultural growth, and severe environmental degradation. Increasing concern over these vexing problems and the apparent failure of past efforts to reverse these trends led the authors to take a fresh look at the available research findings and operational experience. The objective was not to compile and address all of the agricultural, environmental, and demographic issues facing Africa or simply to juxtapose these three sets of problems. It was to gain a better understanding of the underlying causes and to test the hypothesis that these three phenomena are interlinked in a strongly synergistic and mutually reinforcing manner.

The need to survive—individually and as a species—affects human fertility decisions. It also determines people's interactions with their environment, because they derive their livelihood and ensure their survival from the natural resources available and accessible to them. Rural livelihood systems in SSA are essentially agricultural, and agriculture is the main link between people and their environment. Through agricultural activities people seek to husband the available soil, water, and biological resources so as to "harvest" a livelihood for themselves. Such harvesting should be limited to the yield sustainable from the available stock of resources in perpetuity so as to ensure human survival over successive generations. Improvements in technology can increase the sustainable yields or reduce the resource stock required. Population growth should thus be matched or surpassed by productivity increases so as to safeguard the dynamic equilibrium between the stock of resources and the human population depending on it for survival. Over the past thirty years, this has not been the case in most of Sub-Saharan Africa.

This study's findings confirm the hypothesis of strong synergies and causality chains linking rapid population growth, degradation of the environmental resource base, and poor agricultural production performance. Traditional African crop and livestock production methods, traditional methods of obtaining woodfuels and building materials, traditional land tenure systems and land use arrangements, and traditional gender roles in rural production and household maintenance systems were well suited to survival needs on a fragile environmental resource endowment when population densities were low and populations growing slowly. But the persistence of these traditional arrangements and practices, under severe stress from rapid population growth in the past thirty to forty years, is causing severe degradation of natural resources which, in turn, contributes further to agricultural stagnation.

Rapid population growth is the principal factor that has triggered and continues to stimulate the downward spiral in environmental resource degradation, contributing to agricultural stagnation and, in turn, impeding the onset of the demographic transition. The traditional land use, agricultural production, wood harvesting, and gender-specific labor allocation practices have not evolved and adapted rapidly enough on most of the continent to the dramatically intensifying pressure of more people on finite stocks of natural resources.

Many other factors also have a detrimental impact on agriculture and the environment. These include civil wars, poor rural infrastructure, lack of private investment in agricultural marketing and processing, and ineffective agricultural support services. Inappropriate price, exchange rate, and fiscal policies pursued by many governments have reduced the profitability and increased the risk of market-oriented agriculture, prevented significant gains in agricultural productivity, and contributed to the persistence of rural poverty.

A necessary condition for overcoming the problems of agricultural stagnation and environmental degradation will be, therefore, appropriate policy improvements along the lines suggested in the 1989 World Bank report on Sub-Saharan Africa's longer-term development prospects (World Bank 1989d). These policy changes will be instrumental in making intensive and market-oriented agriculture profitable—thus facilitating the economic growth in rural areas necessary to create an economic surplus usable for environmental resource conservation and to provide the economic basis for the demographic transition to lower population fertility rates. That this can occur has been demonstrated in a few places in Africa that pursued good economic and agricultural policy, invested in agriculture and natural resource conservation, and provided complementary supporting services to the rural population. This study provides evidence for both the causes of the problem and its solution.

The Three Basic Concerns

Population Growth

Sub-Saharan Africa lags behind other regions in its demographic transition. The total fertility rate (TFR)—the total number of children the average woman has in a lifetime—for SSA as a whole has remained at about 6.5 for the past twenty-five years, while it has declined to about 4 in all developing countries taken together. As life expectancy in Sub-Saharan Africa has risen from an average of forty-three years in 1965 to fifty-one years at present, population growth has accelerated from an average of 2.7 percent per annum for 1965–1980 to about 3.0 percent per year at present. Recent surveys appear to signal, however, that several countries—notably, Botswana, Kenya, and Zimbabwe—are at a critical demographic turning point. This study discusses the factors that have contributed to the beginning of the demographic transition in these countries.

Agricultural Performance

Agricultural production in Sub-Saharan Africa increased at about 2.0 percent per annum between 1965 and 1980 and at about 1.8 percent annually during the 1980s. Average per capita food production has declined in many countries, per capita calorie consumption has stagnated at very low levels, and roughly 100 million people in Sub-Saharan Africa are food insecure. Food imports increased by about 185 percent between 1974 and 1990, food aid by 295 percent. But the food gap (requirements minus production)—filled by food imports, or by many people going with less than what they need—has been widening. The average African consumes only about 87 percent of the calories needed for a healthy and productive life. But as with population growth, a few African countries are doing much better, with agricultural growth rates in the 3.0 to 4.5 percent per annum range in recent years (Nigeria, Botswana, Kenya, Tanzania, Burkina Faso, and Benin). The policies of these countries help show the way forward.

Environmental Degradation

Sub-Saharan Africa's forest cover, estimated at 679 million ha in 1980, has been diminishing at a rate of about 2.9 million ha per annum, and the rate of deforestation has been increasing. As much as half of SSA's farmland is affected by soil degradation and erosion, and up to 80 percent of its pasture and range areas show signs of degradation. Degraded soils lose their fertility and water absorption and retention capacity, with adverse effects on vegetative growth. Deforestation has significant negative effects on local and regional rainfall and hydrological systems. The widespread destruction of vegetative cover has been a major factor in prolonging the period of below long-term average rainfall in the Sahel in the 1970s and 1980s. It also is a major cause of the rapid increase in the accumulation of carbon dioxide (CO_2) and nitrous oxide (N_2O), two greenhouse gases, in the atmosphere. Massive biomass burning in Sub-Saharan Africa (savanna burning and slash-and-burn farming) contributes vast quantities of CO_2 and other trace gases to the global atmosphere. Acid deposition is higher in the Congo Basin and in Côte d'Ivoire than in the Amazon or in the eastern United States and is largely caused by direct emissions from biomass burning and by subsequent photochemical reactions in the resulting smoke and gas plumes. Tropical forests are considerably more sensitive than temperate forests to foliar damage from acid rain. Soil fertility is reduced through progressive acidification. Acid deposition also poses a serious risk to amphibians and insects that have aquatic life cycle stages; the risk extends further to plants that depend on such insects for pollination.

Unlike the situation of population growth and agriculture, there are few environmental success stories in Africa, although there remain large parts of Central Africa that are little touched. In looking closely, however, places can be found, such as Machakos District in Kenya, where environmental improvements have occurred along with rapidly expanding population. Good agricultural and economic policy, and investment in social services and infrastructure, are found to be the critical ingredients to such success (English and others 1993; Tiffen and others 1994). These positive experiences form the empirical basis for an action program to overcome the downward spiral elsewhere. . . .

Agricultural Stagnation and Environmental Degradation

The Deteriorating Natural Resource Base and Ecological Environment

Much of Sub-Saharan Africa's natural resource base and ecological environment is deteriorating. If present trends continue, this deterioration will accelerate. The most pressing problem is the high rate of loss of vegetative cover—mainly the result of deforestation and the conversion of savanna to cropland—which in turn leads to loss of soil fertility and soil erosion. Global and regional climatic changes and deviations from longer-term average conditions are also causal factors—but human impact on the environment in Sub-Saharan Africa may itself be an important element contributing to these climatic changes.

Deforestation

In much of Sub-Saharan Africa, deforestation is a major problem—with significant local, national, and global consequences. Forests provide a multitude of products and serve many functions, including essential environmental ones. With deforestation, these are lost. Forests and woodlands are cleared for farming and logged for fuelwood, logs, and pulp wood. Data on forest resources and rates of extraction and clearing are imperfect, as are data on most of Africa's environmental resources, but information is continually improving and reliable enough to suggest the scale of the problem. In 1980, there were about 646 million hectares of forests and woodlands in Sub-Saharan Africa. A 1980 FAO/UNEP [Food and Agriculture Organization/United Nations Environment Programme] study estimated that 3.7 million hectares of tropical Africa's forests and open woodlands were being cleared each year by farmers and loggers (Lanly 1982). More recent estimates suggest that close to 2.9 million hectares were lost each year during the 1980s, mainly through conversion to farm land, but the rate of deforestation may be accelerating as the aggregate area still under forests continues to shrink. Reforestation during the 1980s amounted to 133,000 hectares per year, only about 5 percent of the area lost each year to deforestation.

Aggregate data obviously obscure important differences among regions and countries. Deforestation has been particularly rapid in West Africa, with East Africa and southern Africa also suffering substantial losses in forest cover. Large tracts of tropical forest still remain, especially in Zaire, Gabon, Congo, the Central African Republic, and Cameroon. It would take many years for Central Africa's forests to be completely destroyed, but the process has started. In most of East Africa and southern Africa, as well as in the West African coastal countries, the process is far advanced. . . .

Managing the Natural Resource Base

Forests

About 30 percent of Sub-Saharan Africa's land area is classified as forests or woodlands. But only about 28 percent of this area is closed forest—compared with about two-thirds in Latin America and in Asia. About 34 percent is shrub-land and 38 percent is savanna woodland; both are multiple-use resource systems, utilized for meeting local requirements for fuelwood and other tree and forest products as well as for farming and forage.

. . . The most important causes of deforestation are conversion to farm-land, infrastructure development in environmentally delicate areas, timber extraction, and commercial fuelwood harvesting. Growing and migrating human populations as well as international demand for tropical timber drive these processes. Timber exports from Sub-Saharan Africa amount to about US$700 million per year at present. Cropland is expanding at a rate of 1 million ha annually—to a large extent at the expense of forest areas and woodlands. A number of agricultural development projects supported by external aid donors, including the World Bank, have facilitated the conversion of forest and rangelands into cropland.

The most important areas for action to stop the degradation of Sub-Saharan Africa's forest resources lie outside the immediate purview of forestry sector policy. They are: (a) reducing population growth, and (b) intensifying agricultural production at a rate which exceeds population growth, in order to encourage sedentary agriculture and livestock raising and to discourage further invasion of the remaining forests. Rapidly growing numbers of people, barely surviving in land-extensive agricultural systems, have no option than to continue to invade and destroy forests. This points again to the complex mutual dependency of agricultural and nonagricultural activities.

For the forests that remain, improved management for multiple uses will be vital. These uses range from the provision of critical environmental services to the supply of timber and nontimber products, and from tourism and recreational uses to mineral extraction. It is unrealistic to expect that all forests can be conserved in their present state. For almost all of Africa's forests the issue is not whether to use them or not to use them—but how to use them. If people (and governments) feel that there is little benefit from forests, they will continue to be mined for urgently needed export revenue or converted into agricultural land.

To address these problems effectively, there is no alternative to planning, orchestrated by governments. This can be done within Tropical Forestry Actions Plans (TFAPs), National Environmental Action Plans (NEAPs), or simply forestry master plans. Each will involve some form of land use and natural resource planning. Land use plans for forest areas should identify conservation areas, parks, areas designated for sustainable logging, mining areas, farming and grazing areas, and areas designated for infrastructure development. . . .

National Environmental Action Plans

The development of national environmental resource management strategies must be a national affair. The main instrument for this process is the National Environmental Action Plan (NEAP). NEAPs are currently being prepared or implemented with World Bank support by most African countries. They should contain strategies for addressing all of the issues of the nexus. The NEAP concept is multisectoral in approach, and oriented to bottom-up participatory planning and implementation. It provides a framework for integrating environmental concerns with social and economic planning within a country. The objective is to identify priority areas and actions, develop institutional awareness and processes, and mobilize popular participation through an intensive consultation process with NGOs and community representatives. Donor collaboration can also be effectively mobilized in this manner.

A successful national approach to environmental concerns involves several important steps:

- Establishing policies and legislation for resource conservation and environmental protection that are integrated into the macroeconomic framework and, if possible, assessing the costs of degradation. These were, for example, estimated to be between 5 and 15 percent of GNP [gross national product] in Madagascar and more than 5 percent of GDP [gross domestic product] in Ghana.
- Setting up the institutional framework, usually involving a ministerial or higher-level environmental policy body, developing mechanisms for coordination between agencies, building concern in these agencies, balancing private and public sector concerns, decentralizing environmental management, and assuring continuous contact with local people. The preparation of regional land use plans could be an important component. The basic framework needed to guide the implementation of land tenure reform, forest policy reform, and other elements discussed above can also be included in NEAPs.
- Strengthening national capacity to carry out environmental assessments and establishing environmental information systems. This can be done to some extent by restructuring existing data and making them available to users. Pilot demand-driven information systems should also be initiated to strengthen national capacity to monitor and manage environmental resources. Local and regional research capacity will be crucial to the development of plant varieties and technologies which are truly adapted to local conditions.
- Developing human resources through formal and on-the-job training; introducing environmental concerns into educational curricula and agricultural extension messages; and increasing public awareness through media coverage, general awareness campaigns, and extension services.
- Establishing Geographical Information Systems (GISs) that incorporate adequate environmental information. Lack of operationally meaningful and reliable environmental data is a major problem. It tends to result

in misconceptions about natural resource problems and the consequent risk that policy measures will be misdirected. Urgent needs include assessments of forest cover, soil erosion and soil capability, desertification risks, and the distribution of human and livestock populations. This is clearly an area in which donors can provide support and expertise and governments need to act. It is important to develop national capacity to gather and analyze information in-country: properly designed and operated Geographical Information Systems can be extremely helpful in this regard. GISs make use of aerial photography, remote sensing, and actual ground inspections and data collection. GISs will be particularly useful not only to monitor the progress of natural resource degradation and destruction, but—more importantly—to assess land capability for various uses and, thus, to provide the basis for sound land use planning.

NEAPs are intended to be evolutionary—developing policies through field experience as well as national-level analysis. They should lead to the empowerment of the nongovernmental sector, not just by providing funds for small-scale community activities through national environmental funds, but also by drawing large numbers of village and district representatives into consultative forums. A nongovernmental advisory body was part of the institutional arrangements set up, for example, under the Lesotho NEAP.

Considerable external support has been provided for the NEAP process, from bilateral and multilateral agencies and NGOs [nongovernmental organizations] (such as the World Wildlife Fund, the World Resources Institute, and the International Institute for Environment and Development). External expertise is made available to the countries undertaking NEAP preparation, and aid agency policies are coordinated in the process, with the NEAP forming the basis for coordination. Where NEAPs have led to the preparation of national environmental investment plans (as in Madagascar and Mauritius), donors have substantially oversubscribed the programs. A National Environmental Action Plan can therefore become the major preparatory instrument for addressing the issues discussed [here].

Thomas J. Bassett and
Koli Bi Zuéli

 NO

Environmental Discourses
and the Ivorian Savanna

The image of an entire continent physically disintegrating due to the destructive land-use practices of its inhabitants conveys the magnitude of Africa's environmental problems—at least in the eyes of the World Bank. Yet there remains considerable uncertainty about the very processes generating this assumed degradation of the environment. As the Bank notes for Côte d'Ivoire. . . , "little data exist to confirm this fact." This is also the case for other parts of Africa (Watts 1987; Stocking 1987, 1996). Despite a lack of reliable evidence, the World Bank considers environmental degradation to be so widespread, that "the business" of environmental planning and regulation is now seen as a global affair, and one that falls within its own purview (Falloux and Talbot 1993: xiii–xiv). Indeed, since the late 1980s, the Bank has required low-income countries that receive International Development Association (IDA) funding to draw up national environmental-action plans (NEAPs).

As demonstrated in World Bank policy papers and country reports, the link between environmental planning and development assistance is articulated within the discourse of sustainable development (Williams 1995). The fuzzy green notion of sustainable development is readily adopted by the Bank because of its compatibility with its basic "technocratic, managerial, capitalistic, and modernist ideology" (Adams 1995: 93). Under the banner of sustainable development, the Bank now promotes a "win-win" strategy of combining economic growth with environmental conservation (World Bank 1992: 2–3; Biot et al. 1995). Never considering that its past policies and interventions are in any way implicated in the so-called environmental crisis, the Bank presents itself as an impartial observer and promoter of good stewardship. It is currently assisting dozens of African governments to develop NEAPs which, in assembly-line fashion, are being produced according to a blueprint (Greve et al. 1995). NEAPS are heralded as modern vehicles that will lead its member countries down the road to rational and orderly sustainable development.

In this [selection], we examine the contents of the NEAP for Côte d'Ivoire with special attention given to how environmental problems are constructed for the northern savanna region. Our objectives are [two]fold. The first is to highlight the problem of data gaps in the environmental-planning and sustainable-development discourses. Determining if an environmental problem exists would appear to be a critical first step in the planning process. Yet what

From *Annals of the Association of American Geographers*, March 2000, pp. 67–68, 71, 74, 76–77, 89–91. Copyright © 2000 by Blackwell Publishing, Ltd. Reprinted by permission. www.blackwell-synergy.com

is striking about the NEAP process is how quickly environmental problems are identified and prioritized on the basis of so little data. We confront this data problem by contrasting the image of a highly degraded savanna environment found in Côte d'Ivoire NEAP reports with the actual landscape as experienced by farmers and herders and confirmed by our analysis of aerial photographs and land-cover changes.

Our second objective is to address some of the policy implications related to the disjuncture between local and regional patterns of environmental change and national and global environmental discourses. One result of this disjointed scale problem is that the actual dynamics of environmental change are being overlooked. We consider, in turn, the ecological and human consequences of ignoring ongoing biophysical changes while planners are busy addressing imaginary environmental problems. . . .

Research Area and Methods

. . . We have collected information on land-cover and land-use patterns using a variety of field research and analytical techniques. Survey-research methods were used to administer a questionnaire on environmental perceptions to a sample of 38 Senufo and Jula households in Katiali and to 42 Senufo households in the Tagbanga region. Group interviews were also held with Fulbe pastoralists in the Katiali area. To assess whether local perceptions of environmental change were congruent with scientific findings, we reviewed the specialist literature on human-induced modifications of savanna vegetation. We then examined aerial photographs located in Côte d'Ivoire and France for different time periods to compare land use/cover patterns for the two research sites. Geographic information systems (GIS) techniques were utilized to quantify land-cover trends. To gain a clearer understanding of vegetation change dynamics on the ground, we inventoried species along 50-m transects and in 10 3 10-meter plots following the contact-point method adapted from Daget and Poissonnet (1971) by César and Zoumana (1995). Finally, we collected environmental policy and planning documents and interviewed individuals involved in the NEAP process in government ministries and at the World Bank's regional headquarters in Abidjan. . . .

Discourses on Environmental Change

Before examining the contents of the Ivorian NEAP, it is useful to provide some information on its origins.

The NEAP Process

According to the World Bank, the NEAP process involves four stages: the identification of environmental problems and their underlying causes; setting priorities; establishing goals and objectives; and proposing new policies, institutional and legal reforms, and priority actions. The Bank considers this process to be straightforward. "It is relatively easy to identify problems and formulate appropriate responses to them" (Greve et al. 1995: 8–16). The more difficult phase, it argues, centers around the implementation of reforms and other policy actions.

The elaboration of a National Environmental Action Plan for Côte d'Ivoire began on the eve of the U.N.-sponsored conference on the environment and development held in Rio de Janeiro, June 3–4, 1992. The Ministry of the Environment and Tourism organized a national conference (May 19–21, 1992) during which a rationale for a NEAP was presented. The World Bank worked closely with and helped to train the staff members who organized this meeting and who subsequently carried out the first "civilian phase" in the preparation of the NEAP (World Bank 1994: 4). This stage involved holding regional meetings at which local civic and political leaders, government officials, and selected farmers and herders were invited to present their views on regional environmental issues. This form of "participatory planning" did not involve consultations with ordinary men and women living in rural areas about what they considered to be the most important environmental issues. At the Korhogo regional meeting, a small number of peasants were invited to participate in a setting that was dominated by civil servants representing the agricultural services, planning, and rural development. If "participation" means "the ability of people to share, influence, or control design, decision-making, and authority in development projects and programs which affect their lives and resources" (Peters 1996: 22), then this so-called civilian phase of the Ivorian NEAP process involved very limited participation. As the Korhogo region NEAP report reveals (see below), the voices that were heard and the stories that were ultimately accepted suggests that "participatory" planning in the NEAP process is more rhetoric than reality.

A second national conference took place on November 28–30, 1994, where the NEAP coordinating committee presented its *White Paper on the Environment* that summarized the results of these regional meetings (RCI 1994a). This document became the basis of the Côte d'Ivoire National Environmental Action Plan [NEAP-CI] whose appearance in June 1995 capped the second phase of the NEAP process. At the same meeting, the World Bank presented its own report on Ivorian environmental problems and policy recommendations, *Côte d'Ivoire: Towards Sustainable Development*, which it later revised and distributed in December 1994 (World Bank 1994). A comparison of the outlines and content of the two reports suggests that both the Bank and NEAP coordinating committee worked closely together. The Ivorian government approved the NEAP in 1996, thus bringing the formal planning phases to completion. The execution of the plan, however, quickly ran aground when the Ministry of Housing and the Environment established its own environmental agency to coordinate environmental projects estimated to cost $112 million. Aid donors, led by the World Bank, were critical of the structure of the agency, especially the lack of inter-Ministry coordination and the exclusion of NGOs [Nongovernmental Organizations] from its operations. They also expressed serious concerns about the competence of the individuals appointed by the Minister to head the agency (World Bank 1998). The NEAP proposed the establishment of a National Environmental Agency that would be placed under the control of a Management Council, comprising twelve representatives from government and the private sector, including a representative of Ivorian NGOs. The NEAP process also envisioned the creation of regional commissions and departmental committees in which different social groups would participate in various environmental planning activities. In contrast to this partially decentralized planning apparatus, the Minister of the Environment "viewed environmental planning as a *business* and could only see millions of dollars falling from the sky," according to a well-placed member of the World Bank (World Bank 1998).

Discourse 1: The NEAP Report

What image of environmental change in the savanna emerged from this NEAP process? The most detailed picture is contained in the report summarizing the findings of the northern regional meeting held in Korhogo and published in March 1994. The Korhogo report presents a grim scene of environmental degradation in which peasants and pastoralists are blamed for the deforestation of wooded savannas. According to the report's authors, "vegetative cover is declining due to the practice of shifting cultivation, bush fires, and the anarchic exploitation of forests and overgrazing" (RCI 1994b: 14). This change in plant cover is specifically characterized by "a replacement of the tree savanna by the grass savanna." The report goes on to paint a portentous picture of this process:

> More generally, the progressive widening towards the south of (grassy) plant formations has climatic repercussions (temperature, rainfall. . .) which in turn affects vegetation cycles. To compensate for the corresponding lowering of productivity, the one recourse has been to use chemical fertilizers which engenders certain problems such as soil acidification, and the contamination of surface and subsurface waters (RCI 1994b: 14).

This image of a southerly advancing boundary of a vegetation type associated with more arid climates is similar to the "marching desert" view found in the desertification literature. That is, in the absence of field studies, it is assumed that the forms of environmental transformation purportedly taking place in the Sahel are also occurring in humid savannas. Bush fires and indigenous land-rights systems are signaled out as major forces in this assumed environmental devastation:

> We are increasingly witnessing a decline in vegetation cover, essentially due to bush fires used in an intensive and excessive manner leading to the disappearance of certain varieties . . . these assaults on the environment are essentially linked to the abuses of customary rights, the exaggerated interpretation of the declarations of [the former] President Félix Houphouet-Boigny such as *"Land belongs to the person who improves it"* and *"that which has been planted by the hand of man must not be destroyed, no matter where;"* and especially the absence of a rural land code (RCI 1994b: 12).

According to this analysis, and that of the World Bank (Cleaver and Schreiber 1994: 8–10), "traditional" land-rights systems are inadequate for the task of modern environmental planning. They may have worked in the past, but contemporary land conflicts and insecurity have prevented farmers from investing in land improvements that might increase agricultural output and conservation practices. The assumption is that only when customary rights give way to modern (i.e., freehold) tenure systems will the incentive to conserve natural resources exist. Indeed, the transformation of land-holding systems to freehold arrangements is considered in the Ivorian NEAP to be an important step towards addressing all sorts of environmental problems. [T]his modernization model of tenure change, environmental conservation, and agricultural growth, which informs the Ivorian NEAP and which is at the heart of World Bank rural-development policies in Africa. The model points to the extent to which environmental crises are integral to neoliberal development discourses. These policies only have meaning with reference to agricultural stagnation and/or environmental decline. The desertification narrative serves such a need. This is not to suggest that environmental degradation is not occurring in sub-Saharan Africa. There is ample evidence of it (Batterbury and Bebbington 1998), whether it be soil erosion on the Borana plateau of southern Ethiopia (Coppock 1993), soil-fertility decline in southwestern Burkina Faso (Gray 1997), or rangeland degradation in southern Botswana (Abel and Blaikie 1989). Yet all of these examples are situated in local-level dynamics of resource access, control, and management. They emphasize, as do the case studies of environmental conservation in the Kano Close-Settled Zone of northern Nigeria (Mortimore 1998) and in Machakos District, Kenya (Tiffen et al. 1994), the importance of approaching natural resource management at multiple and nested scales (both biophysical and social). In the policy arena, these examples point to the need to provide "locationally and culturally appropriate technical and economic options" to different groups of land users and the necessity of moving away from "regulation and intrusive administration" (Mortimore 1998: 190–93). In contrast, blueprint development and cookie-cutter planning models like NEAP tend to be highly regulatory and intrusive. The case of Côte d'Ivoire's NEAP is indicative.

With reference to preserving the country's biodiversity, the Ivorian NEAP makes a number of forestry policy recommendations. These include outlawing logging (*l'exploitation forestière*) above the eighth parallel, intensifying village tree planting, controlling bush fires, and creating a Forestry Police to enforce these new regulations (RCI 1996). The first recommendation is strikingly reminiscent of E. P. Stebbing's shelterbelt scheme, proposed more than sixty years ago (Stebbing 1935). The link between bush fires and desertification is commonly made in Côte d'Ivoire newspapers. An editorial in the ruling party's newspaper warned that dry-season bush fires "each year contribute to the desert's advance in our country" (Gooré Bi 1999). A National Committee for Forest Protection and Bush Fire Control was organized in 1996 to raise public awareness about the assumed social and environmental costs of bush fires. The committee organizes a national awareness day each year in which statements are made linking bush fires with desertification. A national arbor day is also held each year, during which public officials and billboards urge citizens to plant trees to stop the purportedly advancing desert.

The image of an increasingly degraded wooded savanna giving way to a grass savanna and, ultimately, desert-like conditions not only persists in the minds of environmental planners, journalists, and public officials but is also firmly implanted in the perception of Ivorian environmental nongovernmental organizations (ENGOs). For example, Côte d'Ivoire's leading ENGO, the Green Cross of Côte d'Ivoire, devoted a special issue of its monthly information magazine to bush fires and forests. In his editorial, Green Cross President Gomé Gnohité Hilaire emphasized the importance of educating the citizens of Côte d'Ivoire about the urgency of protecting the nation's remaining forests. He exclaimed that the paucity of funds going to environmental education was having disastrous consequences:

> We have forgotten that raising awareness, that environmental education, is a daily and unending task. We have continued more than ever to utilize the forest as the green gold of our development without concerning ourselves with the consequences. Our forest ecosystem has continued to degrade, forests are savannized. The savannas are desertified (Gomé Gnohité 1998).

How accurate is this image of environmental change in the northern savanna of Côte d'Ivoire found in national environmental planning documents and in the pages of NGO publications? Has the expansion of livestock raising and the area under cultivation led to an increase in grass savannas and a decline in tree cover? Is fire the great destructive force that environmental planners and NGOs believe it to be? . . .

The Lessons of the Katiali and Tagbanga Case Studies

A major finding of this comparative research on land-cover changes in the Katiali and Tagbanga areas is that, contrary to received wisdom, the savanna has become more wooded over the past thirty years. This finding runs counter to the dominant narrative, which assumes that the savanna has become less wooded and increasingly dominated by grass savannas. It also extends, both geographically and analytically, the findings of Fairhead and Leach on the expansion of wooded landscapes in the forest-savanna transition zone of Guinée (Fairhead and Leach 1996) to the sudanian savanna.

A second finding points to the diversity of savanna vegetation communities in the Korhogo region. The similarities and differences in the transformation of the Tagbanga and Katiali savanna areas underscore the importance of temporal and spatial variations in environmental change. This finding conforms to the scientific literature on savanna ecology that points to a wide range of plant communities, which are commonly distributed in mosaic form across the landscape. The most important factors influencing the nature and direction of vegetation change are farming systems, grazing pressure, population density, and changing fire regimes. These factors, which are themselves linked to changing political and economic processes extending beyond the region (e.g., cotton-development policies, immigration of Fulbe herders, or farmer-herder conflicts), interact with a host of biophysical factors such as soil type, slope, and rainfall to create temporally and locationally specific outcomes.

A third finding of this research is its relevance to environmental planning. Despite its problematic scientific status, the desertification narrative currently guides environmental policy. For example, NEAP-CI recommendations to combat the assumed reduction in tree cover include the regulation of bush fires through a range of increasingly coercive measures, restrictions on wood cutting, and the promotion of village-level tree planting (RCI 1994a). In light of the findings of this case study, such policy recommendations can be seen as misconceived and a waste of limited resources. The disjuncture between national and global environmental discourses and actual vegetation-change patterns is alarming. Our findings show that although desertification is not taking place, heavy grazing and early fires have significantly reduced the quality of the savanna for livestock raising. Tree and shrub invasion and a highly degraded herbaceous layer were evident in both the Katiali and Tagbanga study areas. Since livestock development is a priority of the Ministry of Agriculture, one would think that rangeland rehabilitation would be a center-piece of the Côte d'Ivoire NEAP. Not surprisingly, it is nowhere to be found in NEAP documents which are more concerned with reforestation than range condition. While environmental analysts and planners are occupied with an imaginary environmental problem, tree and bush encroachment continues unabated. This disjointed scale problem also produces its contradictions. For example, the Ivorian NEAP's recommended regulation, permitting only *early*-dry-season fires, would result in further bush invasion. To improve range conditions, degraded areas will have to be protected from grazing for at least two or three years, and woody growth must be controlled by extremely hot (i.e., *late*) bush fires (César 1994).

Conclusion

Given the extraordinary amount of environmental planning currently underway in Africa and its far-reaching implications on land use, access and manage-ment, one obvious conclusion of this study is that further research on environmental-change dynamics is of utmost importance. Indeed, the World Bank places the identification of environmental problems and their underly-ing causes as the first step in the NEAP process. Yet, from all indications, the Bank does not consider this to be a particularly challenging phase. Despite the glaring gaps in our knowledge, the Bank believes that most environmental issues are easy to identify and can be classified along a simple color scheme. A conclusion of this [selection] is that identifying environmental problems and their causes is one of the most difficult and time-consuming stages in environmental planning and policy making.

One of the challenges in confronting the environmental-data problem is that so little data exist with any meaningful time depth. Even where data like aerial photographs do exist, their relatively small scale rarely permits one to make little more than very general statements. This situation demands that multiple approaches be pursued to determine the spatial and temporal dynamics of environmental change that are not apparent in aerial photos. In this study, we have combined household-survey research focused on farming systems and environmental perceptions with aerial-photo interpretation and vegetation transects to identify the general trends in vegetation change. This multiscale, multimethod approach yielded different results from the so-called "participatory approach" followed in the NEAP process, in which the opinions of selected individuals from different social strata were solicited in public meetings. Not surprisingly, peasants and herders were reticent in such fora.

A third point centers on competing discourses on environmental change. In contrasting the environmental narratives expressed in World Bank and NEAP documents with those of rural land users, it would be misleading to suggest that a homogeneous view prevails on either side. For example, peasant farmers downplayed their own role in transforming savanna vegetation through their agricultural activities by pointing their finger at Fulbe herders as the primary agents of environmental change. This tendency to "blame" the Fulbe must be contextualized in the often bitter conflicts that exist between farmers and herders in northern Côte d'Ivoire. Similarly, the tendency of the Fulbe to deny their use of fire as a range management tool and to "blame" farmers and hunters for bush fires must be seen in light of these land-use conflicts.

Fourth, it is also clear that the environmental-crisis lexicon is widespread. Despite the disparate goals of the World Bank, the Ministry of the Environment, and environmental nongovernmental organizations, they share an environmental-crisis imaginary that gives meaning and an immediacy to their missions. The visual imagery of an expanding desert is a powerful framing device that demands equally dramatic solutions, such as the establishment of green belts along the eighth parallel and imprisonment as punishment for lighting bush fires.

Finally, there are striking historical parallels between colonial-era writings on land degradation and control and contemporary environmental planning. Both blame farmers and herders for recklessly destroying the land and altering local climates, programmatic statements abound while good data are hard to come by, and proposed conservation measures invariably involve increased state intervention in the countryside with an emphasis on transforming land-rights systems, specifically the exclusion of local people from protected areas. These recurring themes, principal players, and silences regarding the goals and resource management strategies of farmers and herders suggest that we are operating within a regional discursive formation. What is different between the 1930s and the 1990s is the number of contestants involved in environmental management. In addition to the state, there are NGOs and development-aid organizations seeking to establish their authority and legitimacy as environmental advocates and stewards. The desertification narrative persists in part because it serves to mobilize support for these groups' varied agendas. This [selection] has privileged the voices and experiences of farmers and herders whose understanding of environmental change is more nuanced and sophisticated than the dominant narrative. From all indications, this local understanding of the nature and direction of environmental change is not reflected in the Côte d'Ivoire National Environmental Action Plan. As in the past and despite the rhetoric of decentralization and participatory planning (Little 1994; Ribot 1999; Schroeder 1999), this case study shows that the perceptions of ordinary men and women are marginalized in contemporary environmental planning in sub-Saharan Africa.

POSTSCRIPT

Is Sub-Saharan Africa Experiencing a Deforestation Crisis?

It is important to note that while Bassett and Zuéli question the accuracy of perceptions of deforestation in northern Côte d'Ivoire, they acknowledge that grassland degradation is occurring. The distinction they make between deforestation and degradation is critical because it is often assumed that deforestation equates with degradation, and that afforestation is a positive environmental trend. In the Ivorian savanna, the increase in woody species may actually be undermining the health of grasslands. As Bassett and Zuéli suggest, misperceived forest cover trends in the Ivorian savanna may, ironically, lead to policy prescriptions that exacerbate grassland degradation.

Another significant issue to keep in mind when evaluating these two selections is the question of scale. Cleaver and Schreiber are discussing deforestation at the scale of the African continent, whereas Bassett and Zuéli are examining vegetation trends at the scale of the savanna ecosystem in northern Ivory Coast. Is it possible that deforestation is occurring at the broad, continental scale while quite different, and even contrary, trends are operating in specific bioregions and localities? As Bassett and Zuéli suggest, it is critical not to assume that macro-scale trends are always reflected at the local level.

The findings of Bassett and Zuéli are not inconsistent with others who have come out in recent years with books and articles reassessing landscape change in Africa. Examples of these works include those by James Fairhead and Melissa Leach, *Misreading the African Landscape* (Cambridge University Press, 1996); Michael Mortimore, *Roots in the African Dust* (Cambridge University Press, 1998); and Jeremy Swift, "Desertification: Narratives, Winners and Losers," in Melissa Leach and Robin Mearns, eds., *The Lie of the Land: Challenging Received Wisdom on the African Environment* (Oxford & Heinemann, 1996). Newer work on African savannas suggests that, in addition to misrepresented biomass trends, the character of these ecosystems has been misunderstood. For example, a volume edited by Roy H. Behnke, Ian Scoones, and Carol Kervan, entitled *Range Ecology at Disequilibrium: New Models of Natural Variability and Pastoral Adaptation in African Savannas* (Westview Press, 1993), argues that African savannas may actually be more resilient than originally perceived. The book further asserts that transhuman pastoral livelihoods, rather than European modes of livestock rearing, are better suited to handle the inherent variability of African savannas.

Despite emerging new evidence to the contrary, Cleaver and Schreiber are in the majority when they sound the alarm about deforestation in Africa. Environmental organizations and the World Bank have been the most outspoken about their deforestation concerns. Examples of recent books and articles expressing apprehension about deforestation trends in Africa include Uma Lele et al., *The World Bank Forest Strategy: Striking the Right Balance* (World Bank, 2000); K. Boahene, "The Challenge of Deforestation in Tropical Africa" (1998); Claude R. Heimo et al., *Strategy for the Forest Sector in Sub-Saharan Africa* (World Bank, 1994); and Alan Durning, *Saving the Forest: What Will It Take* (Worldwatch Institute, 1993).

Wherever the truth may lie, the contrasting perspectives presented in this set of selections suggest that it is important not to make assumptions about forest cover change in Africa. Among other issues, students may more thoughtfully read assessments of environmental change in Africa by paying attention to the scale of analysis and suppositions regarding appearance of degradation on the landscape.

Internet References . . .

Minnesota State University's E-Museum, African Cultures Section

This site offers useful background information on over 60 ethnic groups in Africa. It includes information on each group's geographic location, language, history, religion and typical livelihood strategies.

http://www.mnsu.edu/emuseum/cultural/oldworld/
africa.html

Population Council: Africa

The Population Council's Africa page explains population and family planning issues, reproductive health, HIV/AIDS, and other issues by country and for the African continent as a whole.

http://www.popcouncil.org/africa/index.html

Washington Post: AIDS in Africa

The Washington Post has an ongoing "Special Report" on the HIV/AIDS issue that contains news on the HIV/AIDS epidemic from African countries, debate and information on U.S. actions to fight the epidemic, and world HIV/AIDS information.

http://www.washingtonpost.com/wp-dyn/world/
issues/aidsinafrica/index.html

World Health Organization

The World Health Organization offers information on diseases and epidemiological facts for African countries (as well as other areas of the world).

http://www.who.int/en/

The University of Pennsylvania's African Studies Center, Women's Issues

The women's issues page of this website offers links to several other reputable sites dealing with women and gender.

http://www.africa.upenn.edu/About_African/
ww_wmen.html

Social Issues

*P*erhaps more than any other set of contested African issues, those pertaining to the social sphere tend to provoke deep-seated emotional responses. This is also an area where differences in perspective between Africanists and non-Africanists tend to be more apparent. Such a degree of contestation is not surprising as these are, after all, deeply personal and culturally specific issues dealing with sexuality, gender roles, intra-household dynamics, and customs. Despite the highly private nature of some of the topics, this is also a realm that has come under incredible public scrutiny given concern about the global AIDS pandemic and the increasingly global nature of the human rights and feminist movements. Even debt relief has increasingly been cast as a human rights issue.

- Should Female Genital Cutting Be Accepted as a Cultural Practice?

- Are Women in a Position to Challenge Male Power Structures in Africa?

- Is the International Community Focusing on HIV/AIDS Treatment at the Expense of Prevention in Africa?

- Should Developed Countries Provide Debt Relief to the Poorest, Indebted African Nations?

ISSUE 12

Should Female Genital Cutting Be Accepted as a Cultural Practice?

YES: Fuambai Ahmadu, from "Rites and Wrongs: Excision and Power among Kono Women of Sierra Leone," in B. Shell-Duncan and Y. Hernlund, eds., *Female 'Circumcision' Africa: Culture, Controversy, and Change* (Lynne Reiner, 2001)

NO: Liz Creel et al., from "Abandoning Female Genital Cutting: Prevalence, Attitudes, and Efforts to End the Practice," A Report of the Population Reference Bureau (August 2001)

ISSUE SUMMARY

YES: Fuambai Ahmadu, an anthropologist at the London School of Economics, finds it increasingly challenging to reconcile her own experiences with female initiation and circumcision and prevailing (largely negative) global discourses on these practices. Her main concern with most studies on female initiation is the insistence that the practice is necessarily harmful or that there is an urgent need to stop female genital mutilation in communities where it is done. She suggests that "the aversion of some writers to the practice of female circumcision has more to do with deeply imbedded western cultural assumptions regarding women's bodies and their sexuality than with disputable health effects of genital operations on African women."

NO: Liz Creel, senior policy analyst at the Population Reference Bureau, and her colleagues argue that female genital cutting (FGC), while it must be dealt with in a culturally sensitive manner, is a practice that is detrimental to the health of girls and women, as well as a violation of human rights in most instances. Creel et al. recommend that African governments pass anti-FGC laws, and that programs be expanded to educate communities about FGC and human rights.

When examining the issue of female genital cutting in Africa (also known as female circumcision, female genital mutilation, or female genital alteration), it is difficult for many Westerners not to have an emotional reaction. In order to carefully evaluate the topic, the reader should try to keep as open a mind as possible.

This issue tugs at a deeper debate between those who believe there are certain universal rights and wrongs, and that female genital cutting is just wrong, irrespective of the cultural context, and cultural pluralists who believe we need to evaluate a practice within its own cultural context. Advocates of the universality of certain norms often depict female genital cutting as a violation of basic human rights. They may further disparage defenders of female genital cutting as cultural relativists. Cultural relativism is often cast as problematic because it may be used as an excuse to say that anything goes. For example, some individuals have and continue to argue that slavery is appropriate in some cultural contexts.

Others would argue that, despite one's personal objections to the practice, that female genital cutting must be viewed within the context of cultural pluralism. Cultural pluralists assert that there are separate and valid cultural and moral systems that may involve social mores that are not easily reconcilable with one another. In contrast to cultural relativists, however, cultural pluralists would argue that everything does not go, and that there are certain universal norms (e.g., murder is wrong). The challenge for cultural pluralists is to determine if a practice violates a universal norm when it is viewed in its proper cultural context (rather than in the cultural context of another). The result of this deep philosophical divide is that we often see Western feminists pitted against multiculturalists (two groups that frequently function as intellectual allies in the North American context) over this controversial African issue.

In this issue, Fuambai Ahmadu, an anthropologist at the London School of Economics, reflects on her own position as a Western trained academic, as a member of an ethnic group that practices female initiation and as someone who underwent the procedure herself. She is troubled by the ethnocentric insistence of outsiders that the practice is necessarily harmful or that there is an urgent need to stop female genital cutting in communities where it is done. Research and personal experience lead her to conclude that the positive aspects of initiation outweigh the negative ones. She argues that "initiation was the 'acting out' and celebration of women's preeminent roles in history and society." She believes the practice should not be banned, but medicalized. Liz Creel et al. argue that female genital cutting (FGC), while it must be dealt with in a culturally sensitive manner, is a practice that is detrimental to the health of girls and women, as well as a violation of human rights in most instances. They recommend that African governments pass anti-FGC laws and that programs be expanded to educate communities about FGC and human rights. They also believe that the use of medical professionals to perform the procedure should be discouraged.

YES

Fuambai Ahmadu

Rites and Wrongs: Excision and Power among Kono Women of Sierra Leone

The issue of female initiation and circumcision is of significant intellectual and personal interest to me. Like previous anthropologists, I am fascinated by social, ideological and religious/symbolic dimensions of these rituals, particularly from indigenous perspectives. I also share with feminist scholars and activists campaigning against the practice a concern for womens physical, psychological and sexual well-being, as well as with the implications of these traditional rituals for womens status and power in society. Coming from an ethnic group in which female (and male) initiation and circumcision are institutionalized and a central feature of culture and society and having myself undergone this traditional process of becoming a "woman," I find it increasingly challenging to reconcile my own experiences with prevailing global discourses on female circumcision.

Most studies on FGC [female genital cutting] in Africa have been conducted by "outsiders" or individuals who are not from the societies they analyze and who have no personal experience of any form of the operation. The limited number of African women who have written about FGC either come from ethnic groups where female genital operations are not practiced (i.e. Thiam, Dorkenoo, Koso-Thomas) or have never undergone the procedures themselves (Toubia, El-Nadeer). There is an unfortunate and perturbing silence among African women intellectuals who have experienced initiation and circumcision. This reticence however is understandable given the venomous tone of the "debate" and unswerving demand that a definitive stance be taken—evidently, if one is educated—*against* the practice. However, "insider" voices from initiated/circumcised African women scholars can go a long way in providing fresh approaches to our understanding of these practices and their continued significance to the bulk of African women.

This essay is an attempt at reconciling "insider" representations with "outsider" perspectives. I seek to contextualize my own experience within the broader framework of initiation in Sierra Leones Kono society and then contrast dominant Kono paradigms with conflicting international debates which focus on female circumcision as a peculiar manifestation of womens global subordination.

My main quarrel with most studies on female initiation and the significance of genital cutting relates to the continued insistence that the latter is necessarily "harmful" or that "there is an urgent need to stop female genital mutilation in communities where it is done." . . . Both of these assertions are based on the alleged physical, psychological and sexual effects of female genital cutting. I offer, however, that the aversion of some writers to the practice of female circumcision has more to do with deeply imbedded western cultural assumptions regarding womens bodies and their sexuality than with disputable health effects of genital operations on African women. For example, one universalized assumption is that human bodies are "complete" and that sex is "given" at birth. A second assumption is that the clitoris represents an integral aspect of femininity and has a central erotic function in women's sexuality. And, finally, through theoretical extension, patriarchy is assumed to be the culprit—that is, women are seen as blindly and wholeheartedly accepting "mutilation" because they are victims of male political, economic and social domination. According to this line of analysis, excision is necessary to patriarchy because of its presumed negative impact on womens sexuality. Removal of the clitoris is alleged to make women sexually passive, thus enabling them to remain chaste prior to marriage and faithful to their husbands in polygynous households. This supposedly ensures a husband sole sexual access to a woman as well as certainty of his paternity over any children she produces. As victims, then, women actively engage in "dangerous" practices such as "female genital mutilation" to increase their marriageability . . . , which would ultimately enable them to fulfill their honored, if socially inferior, destiny of motherhood.

When attempting to reconcile Kono practice with dominant anti-"FGM" discourses, a number of problems arise, starting with the alleged physical harm resulting from the practice. Part of the problem . . . is the unjustified conflation of varied practices of female genital cutting and the resulting overemphasis on infibulation, a rare practice which is associated with a specific region and interpretation of Muslim *purdah* ideology. Kono women practice *excision*, removal of the clitoris and labia minorae. . . . The purported long-term physical side-effects of this procedure may have been exaggerated. It can be argued, as well, that although there are short-term risks, these can be virtually eliminated through improved medical technology. . . .

Furthermore, among the Kono there is no cultural obsession with feminine chastity, virginity nor with womens sexual fidelity, perhaps because the role of the biological father is considered marginal and peripheral to the central "matricentric unit." Finally, Kono culture promulgates a dual-sex ideology, which is manifested in political and social organization, sexual division of labor and, notably, the presence of powerful female and male secret societies. The existence and power of *Bundu*, the womens secret sodality, suggest positive links between excision, womens religious ideology, their power in domestic relations, and their high profile in the "public" arena.

The Kono example makes evident underlying biases of such culturally loaded notions as the "natural" vagina or "natural female body." The word "natural" is uncritically tossed around in the Female Genital Mutilation (FGM) literature to describe an uncircumcised woman when actually it needs definition and clarification. Kono concepts of "nature" and "culture" differ significantly from western assumptions and it is these local understandings which compel female (and male) genital cutting. In essence, what this paper amounts to is a critique of a profound tendency in western writing on female circumcision in Africa to deliver male-centered explanations and assumptions. Scholars must be wary of imposing western religious, philosophical and intellectual assumptions which tend to place enormous emphasis on masculinity and its symbols in the creation of culture itself. In traditional African societies, as is the case with the Kono, womb symbolism and imagery of feminine reproductive contributions form the basis of meanings of the universe, of human bodies, of society and its institutions—social organization, the economy, and even political organization can be viewed as extensions of the "matricentric core" or base of society. Female excision, I propose, is a negation of the masculine in feminine creative potential, and in the remainder of this essay I will show how the Kono case study demonstrates this hypothesis.

This paper is a culmination of several years of informal inquiry as well as formal research into the meaning of female circumcision and initiation, particularly among my parental ethnic group, the Kono, in northeastern Sierra Leone. This study constitutes an analysis of five stages: (1) my subjective experience of initiation in December/January 1991–92 which lasted just over month; (2) indigenous interpretations from other participants, mainly ritual leaders and their assistants, recorded at the time; (3) later academic study, when I returned to Kono for an additional 2 months in December 1994 and December 1996; (4) a total of nine months conducting formal and informal interviews among Kono immigrants in and around the Washington, D.C. area; and finally, (5) approximately three months spent between January and July of 1998 traveling back and forth between Conakry and Freetown talking to Kono refugees and women activists, mainly about their more immediate survival concerns but also about circumcision, initiation, and the future of womens secret societies. These discussions included informal interviews, as well as formal semi-structured interviews with three ritual officials: two traditional circumcisers, or *Soko* priestesses, and one *digba*, or ranking assistant to the *Soko*.

The cumulative data is drawn from interviews with a broad range of Kono men and women: young, old, university educated professionals in Freetown and in the U.S., as well as illiterate villagers and traditional rulers in Kono. If I have sacrificed quantification, it has been for the benefit of collecting detailed qualitative data which would enable my search for meaning and significance, both of which I felt could be best obtained through carefully selected, knowledgeable informants. What this study attempts to explain are the views, beliefs, and rationales of *supporters* of initiation and circumcision. The extent to which these attitudes reflect those of all or the majority of Kono women is left open for future research. . . .

The "Debate": Physical, Sexual and Psychological Effects

Anthropologists have not been the only ones interested in initiation and female genital cutting. In the last decade or so many others—feminists, politicians, international aid organizations, international medical community etc. within Africa and without—have produced a plethora of literature and convened conferences and the like on the subject of the effects of various forms of genital cutting on womens bodies, their sexuality and psychological well-being. My intention in this section is to interrogate some of the major assumptions in prevailing international discourses on female circumcision in light of my own experiences and the data collected from other Kono women, primarily but not limited to immigrants residing in the U.S.

First, as regards the health implications of excision, several short and long-term risks have been associated with the practice. . . . I have personally interviewed several male and female Sierra Leonean gynecologists who profess that although they regard excision as "medically unnecessary" the practice does not pose any significant adverse long-term effects to women and that, moreover, traditional circumcisers are on the whole "very well trained" and are "experts" at what they do. None had personally treated women with long-term problems related to excision but all stated that they had come across "reports" of horror cases.

Each of the doctors I have spoken to, irrespective of their position on the legitimacy of the practice, agree that short-term risks can be significantly reduced if not altogether eliminated through the use of antiseptic instruments, anesthetics to reduce pain, and skilled traditional officials. Also, it must be noted that most Kono women I have spoken to maintain that excision has existed in their society for hundreds of years and the practice has not adversely affected their fertility nor has it been giving their womenfolk the types of gynecological or obstetrical problems which have been over the past decade become associated with the operation. Thus, if some medical practitioners are saying that safe excisions are possible under the right conditions and if many Kono women do not attribute gynecological/obstetrical problems to their operations and choose to continue to uphold their tradition, a genuine case for limited medicalization can be made on this basis. . . . Such steps may reduce the immediate risks of the operation for young girls, until such a time that women are collectively convinced to give up the practice.

Second, my research and my experience contradict received knowledge regarding the supposed negative impact of removing the clitoris on womens sexuality. Much of this taken for granted information comes perhaps from popular misconceptions about the biological significance of the clitoris as the source of female orgasms. It is probable that such myths evolved as a result of the heightened focus on female clitoris during the 1960s sexual revolution and subsequent discourses regarding womens sexual autonomy. The clitoris has come to be seen in western societies as not only the paramount organ responsible for womens sexual pleasure but it has also been elevated as *the* symbol of womens sexual independence—the latter suited womens objectives in asserting their sexual agency and rejecting previous constraining notions of their roles as wives and mothers.

However, the presumptions which inform Kono womens values regarding female sexuality, as in other aspects of socio-cultural life, emphasize sexual interdependence and complimentarity, principles which are profoundly heterosexual. Western womens notions of the importance of the clitoris to female sexual autonomy can be contrasted with *Bundu* officials stress on vaginal stimulation which implies male penetration, and this glaringly suggests heterosexual intercourse which, because the latter leads to reproduction, is considered the socially ideal form of sexual relations. My informants consider vaginal orgasm as independent of the clitoris but still fundamental to a womans sexuality. Perhaps because women believe that the "internal" vagina is the appropriate locus of womens sexual pleasure, they profess that the clitoris is redundant and leads to excessive "sexiness." Also, as the clitoris is associated with androgyny and "nature," its presence signifies lack of self-control or self-discipline which are attributes of "culture." *Bundu* officials insist that the clitoris is "no good" and that it leads to uncontrolled masturbation in girls and sexual insatiability in adult women. It is believed to be a purely superfluous erotic organ, unlike a "proper" adult penis, its sex-corollary, which at least has reproductive functions. It is thus understandable, even if one does not agree, how some Kono women can claim that while excision curbs a womans desire for sex, the operation itself does not reduce her enjoyment of sexual pleasure.

. . . There can be no way to "objectively" test the evidence regarding the impact of excision on womens sexuality as the latter is subjective and individually variable. Notwithstanding, an interesting finding in the Hite report is that the external clitoris constitutes a small fraction of total nerve endings which account for sensations for the entire appendage. . . . This suggests that excision leaves uncut most of the nerve endings which are beneath the vaginal surface. Thus, paradoxically, even according to "objective" biological science, it is possible for a womans sensitivity to remain for the most part undiminished after excision. This would probably explain how it is that many women who had sexual experiences *prior* to excision, the author included, perceive either no difference or increased sexual satisfaction following their operation. In any case, most contemporary, urban educated as well as rural Kono women are just as interested in their sexuality as are their counterparts in western countries, and they do not perceive of excision as inhibiting them in any way. Also it is worth noting, especially since it is usually omitted, that significant numbers of western women, despite having their clitorises intact, experience their own difficulties in achieving any kind of orgasm, clitoral or vaginal.

Finally, as regards to the psychological well-being of young girls and women who have undergone initiation and excision, more research is needed before any credible generalizations can be made. A small but growing number of African female activists against various forms of circumcision have detailed the pain and trauma they underwent and the lasting impact such negative experiences have had on their lives and thus, they campaign against what they rightfully believe to be an affront to their human rights and womanhood. I have spoken to a few young Kono women who are adamantly opposed to initiation because of their experiences of pain, abuse and maltreatment by female elders in the "bush." However, the bulk of women I have interviewed fervently support the practice and my ground observations confirm that not only do most girls continue to look forward to their initiation but, further, they demonstrate their on-going support for the practice by actively participating in later ceremonies involving younger female friends and relations.

Conclusion

The question is often put to me: "How can a Western-bred and educated African woman *support* a practice which degrades women and deprives them of their humanity?" Notwithstanding the ethnocentrism in this remark, and the fact that I prefer to consider myself "neutral" in terms of the continuation of the practice, I am aware of many educated, professional circumcised African women gracefully negotiating their way through culturally distinct settings. There are those, the author included, who refuse to privilege one presumably objective, scientific model of personhood over supposedly "misguided" local interpretations but, rather, seek to juggle "modern" and "traditional" identities according to appropriate cultural context. Educated circumcised African women, like most people of multicultural heritage, maneuver multiple identities depending on the specific circumstances in which they find themselves. Personally, I do not see any conflict or contradiction in being educated and being circumcised, as the contexts which require each of these cultural idiosyncracies are separate and distinct.

For me, the negative aspect of excision was that it was a physically excruciating experience, for which, given my relatively cushioned Western upbringing, I was neither emotionally nor psychologically prepared. This is in contrast to most of the prepubescent Kono girls with whom I was "joined." As with the young Mandinka girls in the Gambia among whom I am currently conducting fieldwork, they "took" excision "bonically" (Krio term used to describe sheer human strength, strength of the flesh) and in a few hours were up, laughing and playing. After one or two days, they were jumping up and down dancing the "bird dance" to the rhythm of makeshift drums in preparation for their big "coming out" dance. To impose on my research what was my own experience of "pain" would be a gross distortion of the experiences of most of the other novices and thus, a certain disservice to anthropological knowledge in general.

The positive aspects have been much more profound. Initiation was the "acting out" and celebration of womens preeminent roles in history and society. Although I could not at the time put together all the pieces, I felt I was participating in a fear-inspiring world, controlled and dominated by women, which nonetheless fascinated me because I was becoming a part of it. In the years since, I have managed to make sense of much of the ritual symbolism and acting-out, enough to understand that women claim sole credit for everything from procreation to the creation of culture, society and its institutions, and, most important, they maintain a "myth of male dominance" so that their fundamental prerogatives are not threatened by increasing masculinization of religion, culture and society in Africa.

One such prerogative is the virtual deification of mothers among the Kono (and most African societies for that matter). This is not only symbolically important for women, but it gives them "real" power in inter- and intra-domestic lineage and immediate family relations, by virtue of the moral privilege women have over sons and daughters. I agree with Diops assertion that the greatest abomination of any African, male or female, high or low, is the curse of his or her mother. This could also explain the findings of Skramstad and Hernlund indicating that Gambian Mandinka women continue "circumcision" first and foremost out of respect for their mothers and grandmothers. Even for the few Kono women who have second thoughts about "joining" their own daughters, the idea of eradication never comes up. It is not so much that an unexcised woman is unfathomable to them, but the public defiance and condemnation that abolition campaigns require would constitute a most unfathomable "insult" against their mothers and grandmothers.

Another feature of excision is the way in which the scar itself symbolizes womens sameness or common female identity. In effect, the operation rite is what defines and, thus, essentializes womanhood. Unlike in Western society, there is no confusion or fruitless intellectualizing about the definition of "woman." Among the Kono, a woman is a woman by virtue of the fact that she has been initiated and nothing else. But initiation also creates a hierarchical ordering of women in society. At the apex is, of course, the *Soko*, the mother of the community, then an individuals mother, after which is her mother-in-law, and then all other older women in the community. A womans equals are her age-mates, those with whom she was initiated and/or those falling within the same age group. Thus, sameness is not always tantamount to equality, and neither does it imply strict conformity to dominant values of womanhood, such as motherhood. For example, my grandmother often nags me about not yet having children and about the importance of motherhood to a woman but, for her, as for the entire community, it was my initiation which "made" me into a "woman". This is perhaps how it is possible for some circumcised African women to be educated, westernized and yet not view the practice as an affront to their womanhood. In short, initiation/excision has the positive value of creating sameness among all women and maintaining equality within age-groups as well as a general hierarchy of female authority in society.

Other advantages of initiation include beliefs about womens esoteric knowledge and their monopoly over powerful "medicines." Although excision cannot be said to be a marker of ethnicity today (most ethnic groups in Sierra Leone practice excision), what does distinguish Kono *Bundu* from those of other groups are the "medicines" which are used. According to a high-ranking *Bundu* official, even more important than excision itself is women's "medicine" which is used in ritual. The more powerful a sodality's "medicine" is reputed to be, the more feared, and thus, influential are the women leaders of such a group. Kono women often assert the power of their own "medicine" and claim that this is how they dominate their men and "keep them home." Also, it is believed that the medicine which is used for the novices during initiation will protect them against all sorts of witchcraft and other malevolent supernatural practices which may be aimed at them throughout their lives.

Finally, and more subjective, is my shared view of the aesthetics of excision and (male) circumcision. I propose that the basis of Kono appreciation of male/female genital modifications is the latters compatibility and harmony with basic principles of complimentarity and interdependence. These ideals underpin cosmological beliefs regarding sex and gender difference and are manifested in the dual-sex organization of culture and society. As long as there are deeply implanted mental associations of the clitoris with masculinity, then the former will continue to be regarded as dirty, abnormal, unclean, and harmful by a culture which sees "male" and "female" as fundamentally separate and distinct moral categories.

To Cut or Not to Cut?: The Future of Excision

While location and identity may establish who is an "outsider" as opposed to an "insider" with respect to studies on FGC, these factors do not automatically determine the position of any writer regarding abolition. For example, not a few anthropologists—who are by discipline western scholars and often by nationality "outsiders"—have been bitterly criticized for their attempts to represent the cultural viewpoints and values of their informants. Conversely, indigenous African female activists or "insiders," fighting against "FGM" often promulgate the same messages contained in global discourses that link the practice to women's social, sexual and psychological oppression. What is certain is that the future of FGC will depend on the extent to which "insiders" themselves are convinced of purported negative effects of the practice.

The medical evidence as well as the speculations regarding adverse effects on womens sexuality do not tally with the experiences of most Kono women. It is the immediate physical pain and risk of infection which concern most mothers and both of these hazards can be reduced, if not eliminated, through medicalization, education and general modernization of the operation. A compelling point has been made, however, that all the eradication mechanisms, such as policies of international organizations and local NGOs devoted to change peoples attitudes and behaviors, have already been set in place and that most likely there can be no going back. . . . But the virtually universal resistance to change after several decades of international and internationally sponsored local campaigning, conferencing and legislating suggests that what is seriously needed is a re-thinking of previous eradication strategies and a deeper appreciation of the historical and cultural relevance of this ancient practice and its symbolically dynamic and fluid links to womens changing sources and notions of power.

In my opinion, if eradication has become an irreversible "international" political compulsion, then the ideal of "ritual without cutting" . . . seems to be a reasonable middle-ground. The ritual without cutting model positively values many cultural aspects and beliefs underlying female genital operations and initiation while attempting to eliminate the actual physical cutting. Perhaps what *is* needed to replace the physical act of cutting is an equally dynamic symbolic performance which will retain the same fluidity in associated meanings, that is eschewal of masculinity, womanhood, fertility, equality, hierarchy, motherhood, and sexual restraint. However, for rural Kono women in particular, the "cutting" and "medicine" are all-important. Also, as I discussed earlier, "ritual without cutting" can be very dangerous when taken out of context such as in the recruitment and "training" of child rebels in Kono.

I continue to support, however, the goal of medicalizing and modernizing initiation and "circumcision"—not necessarily in a full sense of institutionalizing female circumcision or transferring the practice from the "bush" to hospitals, as in male circumcisions today, because this would reduce the power and authority of female ritual leaders and female elders—but rather by making available basic, modern hygienic equipment and medications to traditional officials to use during rituals. I support change which will promote safe, sanitary environments, so that initiates are given adequate, modern medical assistance to reduce pain and risks of infection. The position that this only legitimizes the practice is dangerously arrogant: the practice is already seen as legitimate by its proponents, who have themselves undergone excision, and denying them the benefits of medicalization only continues to endanger the health and lives of innocent young girls. Modernization should also include impartial, neutral education within primary and secondary schools. Such education should entail both positive historical and cultural significance of initiation/circumcision as well as possible negative health effects. Emphasis should be on preparing young girls to make informed choices about their futures and the futures of their own girl-children.

What direction individual women take should be left to them and their immediate family members. Just as much as die-hard "traditionalists" must relinquish their insistence that uncircumcised women are not socially and culturally "women" who therefore must be denied legal rights and dignity within society, hard-line efforts by abolitionists to coerce women against the practice and stigmatize those who uphold their ancestral traditions as "illiterate," backward, and against "womens rights" and "progress" are unacceptable. It is the bulk of circumcised African women who are unfortunately caught between a rock and a hard place, as the adage goes: Either break traditional customary laws and face the consequences of "not belonging," or ignore increasing efforts to ban the practice and face possible legal penalties instigated by eradicators at the national and international level. Today, it seems that the pressure on circumcised African women, educated or not, is to choose between these two extremist positions—to be either "anti-culture" or "anti-progress."

Change may indeed be occurring gradually, but I do not believe this is necessarily a direct result of "anti-FGM" campaigning. In my grandmothers days, excision was a universal *rite-de-passage*. For my educated, Christian mother who has spent over thirty years in the United States, initiating her daughters was a matter of judgment, an expedient choice to enable us to easily navigate between worlds. My generation is faced with a dramatically different and greater complexity of issues and other priorities (i.e. the complete destruction of Kono through civil war) and, as a result, initiation and excision can hardly be said to be the most pressing preoccupation of young, contemporary Kono women. In the event that I ever have a daughter I would like her to be well-informed about the socio-cultural and historical significance of the operation as well as its purported medical risks so that she can make up her own mind, like I had the opportunity to do. Mbiti has noted regarding female initiation and circumcision in Africa: "If they are to die out, they will die a long and painful death." However, through more culturally sensitive and appropriate "education" as well as limited medicalization strategies, the "death" of female circumcision could be more gradual, more natural, and a lot less painful for millions of future African women and girls. . . .

Abandoning Female Genital Cutting: Prevalence, Attitudes, and Efforts to End the Practice

Introduction

More than 130 million girls and women worldwide have undergone female genital cutting [FGC]—also known as female circumcision and female genital mutilation—and nearly 2 million more girls are at risk each year. The practice often serves as a rite of passage to womanhood or defines a girl or woman within the social norms of her ethnic group or tribe. The tradition may have originated 2,000 years ago in southern Egypt or northern Sudan, but in many parts of West Africa, the practice began in the 19th or 20th century. No definitive evidence exists to document exactly when or why FGC began. FGC is an ancient practice but has also been recently adopted, for example, among adolescents in Chad.

FGC is generally performed on girls between ages 4 and 12, although it is practiced in some cultures as early as a few days after birth or as late as just prior to marriage, during pregnancy, or after the first birth. Girls may be circumcised alone or with a group of peers from their community or village. Typically, traditional elders (male barbers and female circumcisers) carry out the procedure, sometimes for pay. In some cases, it is not remuneration but the prestige and power of the position that compels practitioners to continue. The practitioner may or may not have health training, use anesthesia, or sterilize the circumcision instruments. Instruments used for the procedure include razor blades, glass, kitchen knives, sharp rocks, scissors, and scalpels. A discouraging trend is the use of medical professionals (physicians, nurses, and midwives) in some countries (e.g., Egypt, Kenya, Mali, and Sudan) to perform the procedure due to growing recognition of the health risks associated with FGC and heightened concern regarding the possible role of FGC in HIV transmission. WHO [World Health Organization] has strongly advised that FGC, in any of its forms, should not be practiced by any health professional in any setting—including hospitals and other health centers.

FGC has health risks, most notably for women who have undergone more extreme forms of the procedure (see Box 1). Immediate potential side effects include severe pain, hemorrhage, injury to the adjacent tissue and

From *A Report of the Population Reference Bureau*, August 2001, pp. 3–7, 25–26. Copyright © 2001 by Population Reference Bureau. Reprinted by permission.

organs, shock, infection, urinary retention and tetanus—some of these side effects can lead to death. Long-term effects may include cysts and abscesses, urinary incontinence, psychological and sexual problems, and difficulty with childbirth. Obstructed labor may occur if a woman has been infibulated. This involves cutting off the external genitalia and sewing together the two sides of the vulva, leaving a small hole for urination and menstruation. If the woman's genitalia is not cut open (defibulated) during delivery, labor may be obstructed and cause life-threatening complications for both the mother and the child, including perineal lacerations, bleeding and infection, possible brain damage to infants, and fistula formation.

TYPES OF FEMALE GENITAL CUTTING

Female genital cutting (FGC) refers to a variety of operations involving partial or total removal of female external genitalia. The female external genital organ consists of the vulva, which is comprised of the labia majora, labia minora, and the clitoris covered by its hood in front of the urinary and vaginal openings. In 1995, the World Health Organization classified FGC operations into four broad categories described below:

Type 1 or **Clitoridectomy:** Excision (removal) of the clitoral hood with or without removal of the clitoris.

Type 2 or **Excision:** Removal of the clitoris together with part or all of the labia minora.

Type 3 or **Infibulation:** Removal of part or all of the external genitalia (clitoris, labia minora, and labia majora) and stitching and/or narrowing of the vaginal opening, leaving a small hole for urine and menstrual flow.

Type 4 or **Unclassified:** All other operations on the female genitalia including

- pricking, piercing, stretching, or incising of the clitoris and/or labia;
- cauterization by burning the clitoris and surrounding tissues;
- incisions to the vaginal wall; scraping or cutting of the vagina and surrounding tissues; and introduction of corrosive substances or herbs into the vagina.

Note:
1. World Health Organization, *Female Genital Mutilation: Report of a Technical Working Group* (Geneva: WHO, 1996): 9.

All of these possible side effects may damage a girl's lifetime health, although the type and severity of consequences depend on the type of procedure performed (see Box 1). Infibulation or Type 3 is the most invasive and damaging type of FGC. Operations research studies conducted in Burkina Faso and Mali have shown that women who were infibulated were nearly two and a half times more likely to have a gynecological complication than those with a Type 2 or Type 1 cut. Risks during childbirth also increased according to the severity of the procedure. For instance, in Burkina Faso, women with

Types 2 or 3 cutting had a higher likelihood of experiencing hemorrhaging or perineal tearing during delivery.

While it is difficult to determine both the number of women who have undergone FGC and how many have undergone each type of circumcision, WHO has estimated that clitoridectomy, which accounts for up to 80 percent of all cases, is the most common procedure. Fifteen percent of all circumcised women have been infibulated—the most severe form of circumcision.

FGC is practiced in at least 28 countries in sub-Saharan and north-eastern Africa but not in southern Africa or in the Arabic-speaking nations of North Africa, with the exception of Egypt. It is practiced at all educational levels and in all social classes and occurs among many religious groups (Muslims, Christians, animists, and one Jewish sect), although no religion mandates it. For countries presented here with DHS [Demographic and Health Surveys] data, prevalence varies from 18 percent in Tanzania to nearly 90 percent or more in Egypt, Eritrea, Mali, and Sudan. According to WHO estimates, 18 African countries have prevalence rates of 50 percent or more. Through migration, the practice has also spread to Europe, North and South America, Australia, and New Zealand. Although doctors, colonial administrators, and social scientists have documented the adverse effects of FGC for many years, governments and funding donors have become increasingly interested in the practice because of the public health and human rights implications.

Global efforts to end FGC have used legislation to provide legitimacy for project activities, to protect women, and to discourage circumcisers and families who fear prosecution. In the 1960s, WHO was the first United Nations (UN) specialized agency to take a position against female genital cutting. It began efforts to promote the abandonment of harmful traditional practices like FGC in the 1970s, focusing largely on gathering information about FGC's epidemiology and health consequences and speaking out about FGC at international, regional, and national levels. In 1982, WHO issued a formal statement to the UN Commission on Human Rights and recommended several actions:

- Governments should adopt clear national policies to end FGC, and educate and inform the public about its harmful aspects.
- Anti-FGC programs must consider the practice's association with difficult social and economic conditions and respond to women's needs and problems.
- Women's organizations at the local level should be encouraged to take action.

In 1988, WHO began to integrate FGC into the development context of primary health care. Over the intervening years, WHO shifted its position on FGC from addressing the practice only in terms of health to acknowledging it as both a health and human rights issue. In the 1990s, FGC gained recognition as a health and human rights issue among African governments, the international community, women's organizations, and professional associations. The 1993 Vienna Human Rights Convention, the 1994 International

Conference on Population and Development, and the 1995 Fourth World Conference on Women called for an end to the practice. When performed on girls and nonconsenting women, FGC violates a number of recognized human rights protected in international conventions and conferences, such as the Convention on Children's Rights, the Convention on the Elimination of All Forms of Discrimination against Women, and recommendations of the Committee on the Elimination of Discrimination against Women (CEDAW). These conventions explicitly recognize harmful traditional practices such as FGC as violations of human rights, including the right to nondiscrimination, the right to life and physical integrity, the right to health, and the right of the child to special protections.

Respect for international human rights law does not require that every culture use an identical approach to abandoning FGC. One Muslim scholar suggested that respecting different cultures means accepting "the right of all people to choose among alternatives equally respectful of human rights," and that human rights must include life, liberty, and dignity for every person or group of people.

In Africa, 10 countries–Burkina Faso, the Central African Republic (CAR), Côte d'Ivoire, Djibouti, Ghana, Guinea, Niger, Senegal, Tanzania, and Togo—have enacted laws that criminalize the practice of FGC. The penalties range from a minimum of six months to a maximum of life in prison. In Nigeria, three of 36 states (as of 2000) had also enacted legislation regarding FGC. In Burkina Faso, Ghana, and Senegal, these laws are enforced and circumcisers are imprisoned. In these countries, various groups educate the public about the law, use a variety of strategies (e.g., public service announcements and watchdog committees) to denounce FGC, and stop circumcisers by going to the police. Several countries also impose fines. In Egypt, the Ministry of Health issued a decree declaring FGC unlawful and punishable under the Penal Code. There have been several prosecutions under this law, which include jail time and fines. In addition, seven more developed countries that receive immigrants from countries where FGC is practiced—Australia, Canada, New Zealand, Norway, Sweden, the United Kingdom, and the United States—have passed laws outlawing the practice. Enforcement of these laws, however, is extremely uneven. France, on the other hand, consistently enforces general penal code provisions against providers of FGC but has not adopted specific legislation regarding FGC.

Why is FGC Performed?

The traditions surrounding FGC vary from one society to another. In some communities, FGC is a rite of passage to womanhood and is performed at puberty or at the time of marriage. In other communities, it may be performed on girls at a younger age for other reasons such as a celebration of womanhood, preservation of custom or tradition, or as a symbol of ethnic identity. The ritual cutting is often an integral part of ceremonies, which may occur over several weeks, in which girls are feted and showered with presents and their families are honored. It is described as a joyous time with many visitors, feasting, dancing, good food, and an atmosphere of freedom for the girls. The ritual serves as an act of socialization into cultural values and an important connection to family, community, and earlier generations. The ceremonies often involve three interrelated aspects:

- **Educational** A girl learns her place in society and her role as woman, wife, and mother.
- **Physical** A girl must undergo physical pain to prove she is capable of assuming her new role courageously without showing suffering or pain; the pain is experienced both through the actual cutting and through punishment received by girls in complete submission throughout weeks of initiation.
- **Vow of silence** Each girl must make a solemn pledge not to speak about her experience during the ceremony.

The reasons for performing FGC differ, but many practicing communities believe that it preserves the girl's virginity and protects marital fidelity because it diminishes her sexual desire. Practicing communities cite reasons such as giving pleasure to the husband, religious mandate, cleanliness, identity, maintaining good health, and achieving good social standing. At the heart of all this is rendering a woman marriageable, which is important in societies where women get their support from male family members, especially husbands. A circumcised woman will also attract a favorable bride price, thus benefiting her family. The practice is perceived as an act of love for daughters. Parents want to provide a stable life for their daughters and ensure their full participation in the community. Many girls and women receive little formal education and are valued primarily for their role as sources of labor and future producers of children. For many girls and women, being uncircumcised means that they have no access to status or a voice in their community. Because of strong adherence to these traditions, many women who say they disapprove of FGC still submit themselves and their daughters to the practice.

Understanding Why the Practice Continues

FGC is a cultural practice. Efforts to end it require understanding and changing the beliefs and perceptions that have sustained the practice over the centuries. Irrespective of how, where, and when the practice began, those who practice it share similar beliefs—a "mental map"—that present compelling reasons why the clitoris and other external genitalia should be removed. The details of these mental maps vary across countries, and there are distinctive features to each culture that providers, community workers, and others involved with anti-FGC campaigns need to take into consideration.

Figure 1 provides a conceptual framework for understanding the role of FGC in society. This mental map shows the psychological and social reasons, and the religious, societal, and personal (hygienic and aesthetic) beliefs that contribute to the practice. These beliefs involve continuing long-standing

Figure 1

Why the Practice of FGC Continues: A Mental Map

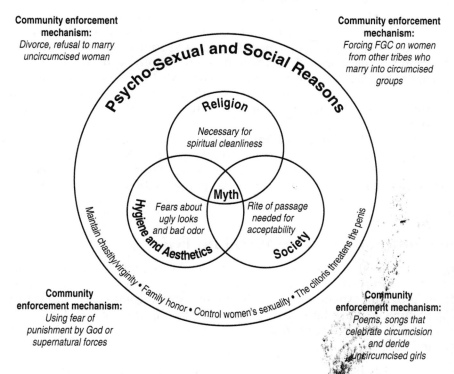

Community enforcement
mechanism:
*Divorce, refusal to marry
uncircumcised woman*

Community enforcement
mechanism:
*Forcing FGC on women
from other tribes who
marry into circumcised
groups*

**Community
enforcement mechanism:**
*Using fear of
punishment by God or
supernatural forces*

**Community
enforcement mechanism:**
*Poems, songs that
celebrate circumcision
and deride
uncircumcised girls*

Source: Asha Mohamud, Nancy Ali, Nancy Yinger, World Health Organization and Program for Appropriate Technology in Health (WHO/PATH), *FGM Programs to Date: What Works and What Doesn't* (Geneva: WHO, 1999):7.

custom and tradition; maintaining cleanliness, chastity, and virginity; upholding family honor (and sometimes perceived religious dictates); and controlling women's sexuality in order to protect the entire community. In the countries surveyed by Demographic and Health Surveys, good custom/tradition is the most frequently cited reason for approving of FGC. Bad custom/ tradition is also mentioned as one of the primary reasons for discontinuing the practice.

To encourage abandonment of FGC, health care providers, community workers, and others involved with anti-FGC programming need to understand the mental map in the communities where they are working. Communities have a range of enforcement mechanisms to ensure that the majority of women comply with FGC. These include fear of punishment from God, men's unwillingness to marry uncircumcised women, insistence that women from other tribes get circumcised when they marry into the group, as well as local poems and songs that reinforce the importance of the ritual. In some cases, women who are not circumcised may face immediate divorce or forced excision.

Girls who do undergo FGC sometime receive rewards, including public recognition and celebrations, gifts, potential for marriage, respect and the opportunity to engage in adult social functions. In other instances, girls and women are cut without an accompanying ceremony; thus, importance is attached to being circumcised rather than to having gone through a ritual.

The desire to conform to peer norms leads many girls to undergo circumcision voluntarily, yet frequently girls (and sometimes infants) have no choice in whether they are circumcised. A girl's family—typically her mother, father, or elder female relatives—often decides whether she will undergo FGC. Due to the influence of tradition, many girls accept, and even perpetuate, the practice. In Eritrea, men are more likely than women to favor ending the practice.

FGC could continue indefinitely unless effective interventions convince millions of men and women to abandon the practice. Many African activists, development and health workers, and people following traditional ways of life recognize the need for change but have not yet achieved such an extensive social transformation. . . .

Recommended Actions to End FGC

Data on attitudes, practices, and prevalence can provide important background information on opportunities for intervention. In addition, lessons from program experiences provide an important context for formulating abandonment campaigns. PATH [Program for Appropriate Technology in Health] and WHO developed the following recommendations for policymakers and program managers.

Recommendations for Policymakers

Policymakers are those who are in a position to influence policies and provide funding related to FGC.

> 1. *Governments and donors need to support the groundswell of agencies involved in FGC abandonment with financial and technical assistance.*

An increasing number of agencies, especially NGOs [nongovernmental organizations], are involved in efforts to end FGC. However, programs tend to be small, rely heavily on volunteers and funds from foreign donors, and reach a small proportion of the people in need. Additional support is needed to make the growing network of agencies more effective and expand their reach.

In Egypt, 15 NGOs, including the Egyptian Fertility Care Society, the Task Force Against FGM, the Cairo Institute for Human Rights Studies, and CEOSS [Coptic Evangelical Organization for Social Services] have been instrumental in advocating the abandonment of FGC. In order to become more effective, these groups need to collaborate with one another, enhance training in advocacy and communications skill building, and evaluate the impact of their programs.

2. Governments must enact and use anti-FGC laws to protect girls and educate communities about FGC and human rights.

Passing anti-FGC legislation is one of the most controversial aspects of the FGC abandonment movement. It is extremely difficult to enforce anti-FGC laws. There is fear that heavy-handed enforcement may drive the practice underground. In fact, this has occurred in some countries. Still, most program planners and activists agree that anti-FGC legislation can demarcate right from wrong, provide official legal support for project activities, offer legal protection for women, and ultimately, discourage circumcisers and families for fear of prosecution. The key is to use the law in a positive fashion—as a vehicle for public education about and community action against FGC.

3. National governments need to be active both in setting policy and in expanding existing programs.

A key role for governments is to "scale up" successful community-based FGC abandonment activities. To date, most governments have provided support in the form of in-kind contributions to NGOs working in the communities. The excellent program models that NGOs have carried out on a pilot basis need to be expanded, either by direct government interventions or by increased support for the NGO networks.

4. To sustain programs, governments need to institutionalize FGC abandonment efforts in all relevant ministries.

Currently, none of the anti-FGC efforts underway are sustainable over the long run, in part because they have failed to change the social norms underlying FGC. The integration of FGC issues into government programs, however, has met with some success. In Burkina Faso, the National Committee to Fight Against the Practice of FGC has effectively promoted FGC abandonment through participation in national events such as the international day of population, by integrating FGC abandonment into all of the relevant ministries, and through training and awareness raising activities.

Efforts in other countries, such as Mali, have encountered more difficulties. While various ministries have expressed their support for anti-FGC activities, they have not been integrated into the relevant ministries, particularly in programs carried out by Mali's Ministry of Health. The primary nursing and medical schools in Mali do not include FGC as an adverse health practice in their curricula. Presently, PRIME II, a partnership of U.S.-based organizations, is working with the Ministry of Health to develop a national curriculum integrating FGC.

Governments have a responsibility to make political decisions and place FGC abandonment in the mainstream of reproductive health and development programs. Limited success has been achieved through increased fundraising, greater integration of anti-FGC activities into government and civil society programs, and through solicitation of community support.

> *5. Health providers at all levels need to receive training and financial support to treat FGC complications and to prevent FGC.*

A key foundation for FGC abandonment is to make health providers aware of the extent and severity of FGC-related complications and to give them the skills and resources to treat these problems. Health providers often encounter women and girls suffering from FGC-related complications, yet they are often not prepared to treat and counsel women, or to prevent recurrence of the circumcision practice. Because there is limited training on clinical treatments for circumcised women or counseling women suffering from psychological or sexual problems, women lack access to high quality, relevant services in most countries.

A 1998 operations research study in Mali sought to assess the use of health personnel to address FGC. The study, which was conducted by an NGO, Association de Soutien au Developpement des Activités de Population (ASDAPO), and the Ministry of Health, evaluated the effectiveness of a three-day training course on identifying and treating medical complications related to FGC and counseling patients about the problem. The study focused on 14 urban and rural health centers in Bamako and the Ségou region and included 107 health providers from experimental and control sites. Results indicated that the course was highly effective in changing provider attitudes toward FGC. After receiving training, three in four trained providers knew at least three immediate and long-term complications of FGC. The study also indicated that providers felt they had limited competence in caring for FGC complications (even after receiving training) and needed further training in how to discuss FGC with their clients.

> *6. Governments, donors, and NGOs working on FGC abandonment should continue to coordinate their efforts.*

Findings from field assessments reveal an impressive array of cooperative efforts and exchanges of information and resources among NGOs, government institutions, and donors. Agencies typically invite each other to meetings and training activities and coordinate at program sites to avoid duplication of efforts. Although occasional conflicts arise over funding and strategies, they should not discourage agencies from continuing to coordinate and build on each other's strengths.

> *7. International agencies should assist staff of NGOs and government to develop their advocacy skills.*

Advocacy is essential to ensuring that FGC abandonment programs are established and maintained until the practice of FGC ceases. Agencies involved in abandonment efforts increasingly use advocacy for public education and to influence legislation, but they need to improve their skills.

POSTSCRIPT

Should Female Genital Cutting Be Accepted as a Cultural Practice?

After reading the different arguments in this issue, there are at least five different points that one may want to ponder before taking an informed stance on topic. First, female genital cutting covers a very broad range of practices in the African context. In some instances, apparently contradictory statements from either author may have as much to do with the specific practices they have in mind as with the fact that they have differing views on the general topic.

Second, the whole notion of choice, the prospect of giving girls and women the option of undergoing or not undergoing the procedure, implies that they are aware that there is a choice. Many girls and women may just assume that this is what is done, or what is normal.

Third, if a girl or young women opts not to undergo female genital cutting, there could be serious social consequences in some settings. Within the context of the educational programs advocated by Creel et al., is there an obligation to make sure individuals are made aware of the medical dangers of the procedure as well as the social consequences of not being initiated?

Fourth, some African countries (e.g., Kenya) have a mix of ethnic groups that may or may not practice female genital cutting. In other nations, such as Mali or Eritrea, the vast majority ethnic groups, and the population in general, practice female genital cutting. This level of homogeneity or heterogeneity could have implications for people's exposure to different practices (particularly in urban areas where ethnic groups tend to mix) as well as the chances of success or failure of education programs in this domain.

Finally, the different authors have very different views on medicalizing FGC in Africa. Ahmadu contends that this will minimize health problems whereas Creel et al. fear that this may help perpetuate the practice. How likely is making the procedure safer going to contribute to its spread?

For more information on this debate, see Richard Scweder's article "What about 'Female Genital Mutilation'?" and "Why Understanding Culture Matters in the First Place" in *Daedalus* (Fall 2000) or Monica Antonazzo's paper "Problems with Criminalizing Female Genital Cutting" in *Peace Review* (2003). For a publication questioning the medical evidence against female genital surgeries, see an article by Carla M. Obermeyer in *Medical Anthropology Quarterly* (no. 13, 1999) with the title "Female Genital Surgeries: The Known, The Unknown, and the Unknowable." Finally, for more of an anti-FGM perspective, see *Eradicating Female Genital Mutilation: Lessons for Donors* (by Susan Rich and Stephanie Joyce, Wallace Global Fund for a Sustainable Future, 1990).

ISSUE 13

Are Women in a Position to Challenge Male Power Structures in Africa?

YES: Richard A. Schroeder, from *Shady Practices: Agroforestry and Gender Politics in The Gambia* (University of California Press, 1999)

NO: Human Rights Watch, from "Double Standards: Women's Property Rights Violations in Kenya," A Report of Human Rights Watch (March 2003)

ISSUE SUMMARY

YES: Richard A. Schroeder, an associate professor of geography at Rutgers University, presents a case study of a group of female gardeners in The Gambia who, because of their growing economic clout, began to challenge male power structures. Women, who were the traditional gardeners in the community studied, came to have greater income-earning capacity than men as the urban market for garden produce grew. Furthermore, women could meet their needs and wants without recourse to their husbands because of this newly found economic power.

NO: Human Rights Watch, a nonprofit organization, describes how women in Kenya have property rights unequal to those of men, and how even these limited rights are frequently violated. It is further explained how women have little awareness of their rights, that those "who try to fight back are often beaten, raped, or ostracized," and how the Kenyan government has done little to address the situation.

$\mathbf{A}$s is the case in other parts of the world, African women suffer from discrimination and inequality. According to the World Bank, the female adult illiteracy rate in Africa in 2001 was 46 percent as compared to 38 percent for the general population. Girls also continue to attend primary school in lower numbers than boys in many African countries (although this ranges from near equality in nations such as South Africa, Zimbabwe, and Namibia to great disparities in countries like Benin, Chad, and Guinea). Despite these disadvantages, women are the backbone of the rural economy in many African settings where it is estimated that they produce, on average, 70 percent of the food supply.

The inequities faced by many women in the African context led to the rise of the women in development (WID) movement in aid circles in the late 1970s and 1980s. These WID programs were also instigated because of a general recognition that many aid programs had not addressed the needs of women or had excluded them entirely. Many agricultural development programs catered almost exclusively to men. In many instances, such programs exacerbated economic disparities between men and women. WID programs were specifically designed to counteract these problems, including a number of initiatives related to gardening, income generation, health care, and education.

In promoting these initiatives, development agencies occasionally exploited the image of African women as a downtrodden class of people who undertake a disproportionate share of the work, yet are severely disadvantaged in terms of access to education, health care, land, and legal protection. While there may be some truth to this generalization, it is problematic because it denies African women "agency." In other words, it could negate or understate the ability of African women to change their situation. This is not to say that African women should not form alliances with outside groups to work for transformation, but those peddling the assistance need to be careful that they are not trafficking images and stereotypes that may be disempowering.

In this issue, Richard A. Schroeder presents a case study of a group of female gardeners in The Gambia. These women, who were the traditional gardeners in the community, benefited from outside funding for fencing and wells during the heyday of WID programming in the 1980s. They eventually came to have greater income-earning capacity than men as the urban market for garden produce grew, and they adeptly intensified production. As a result, men were often forced to turn to their wives for loans. This allowed women to "purchase" freedom of movement and social interaction. Furthermore, women with growing economic clout could challenge male power structures because they were capable of meeting their needs and wants without recourse to their husbands. They also were less susceptible to the threat of divorce (which historically implied the nearly impossible obligation of repaying one's bride-price) because women were now capable of repaying their bride-price with their gardening income.

In contrast, the selection from Human Rights Watch contains the assertion that in Kenya "discriminatory property laws and practices impoverish women and their dependents, put their lives at risk by increasing their vulnerability to HIV/AIDS and other diseases, drive them into abhorrent living conditions, subject them to violence, and relegate them to dependence on men and social inequality." The Kenyan government is castigated for having done little to address this situation.

YES

Richard A. Schroeder

Shady Practices: Agroforestry and Gender Politics in The Gambia

Introduction

Some sixty kilometers upriver along the North Bank of The River Gambia lies the Mandinka-speaking community of Kerewan (ke´-re-wan). The dusty head-quarters of The Gambia's North Bank Division is located on a low rise over-looking rice and mangrove swamps and a ferry transport depot that facilitates motor vehicle transport across Jowara Creek (Jowara Bolong), one of The River Gambia's principal tributaries. Since the Kerewan area was dominated by opposition political parties throughout the nearly thirty-year reign of The Gambia's first president, Al-Haji Sir Dawda Jawara (1965–1994), it became something of a developmental backwater. Before 1990, Kerewan town had no electricity or running water beyond a few public standpipes. For a community of 2,500 residents, there were no restaurants and only a poorly stocked market that lacked fresh meat. Indeed, from the standpoint of the civil servants assigned to the North Bank Division, Kerewan was considered a hardship post. Mandinka speakers sarcastically referred to the divisional seat as "Kaira-wan," a place where "peace" (Mandinka: *kaira*) reigned to the point of overbearing stagnation. Neighboring Wolof speakers, meanwhile, disparaged the commu-nity by dubbing it "Kerr Waaru"—"the place of frustration."

Kerewan's reputation was only partially deserved, however, for the community was actually the center of a great deal of productive economic activity. Over two decades beginning in the mid-1970s, the town's women transformed the surrounding lowlands into one of the key sites of a lucrative, female-controlled, cash-crop market garden sector. A visitor to Kerewan as recently as 1980, when I made my first trip to The Gambia, would have found that vegetable production on the swamp fringes ringing Kerewan on three sides was decidedly small-scale. Most gardeners, virtually all of whom were women, worked single plots that were individually fenced with local thorn bushes or woven mats. Outside assistance in obtaining tools, fences, and wells was minimal. Seed suppliers were not yet operating on a significant scale, and petty commodity production was largely confined to tomatoes, chili peppers, and onions. The market season, accordingly, stretched only a few weeks, and sales outlets were all but nonexistent. Most Kerewan produce was sold directly to end users in the nearby Jokadu District by women who transported their fresh vegetables by horse or donkey cart and then toted them door to door on their heads (a marketing strategy known as *kankulaaroo*).

By 1991, when I completed the principal phase of research for [my] book, large gardens on the outskirts of Kerewan had come to dominate the landscape. Each morning and evening during the October–June dry season, caravans of women plied the footpaths connecting a dozen different fenced perimeters to the village proper. Over the course of nearly twenty years, the number of women engaged in commercial production rose precipitously from the 30 selected to take part in a pilot onion project in the early 1970s to over 400 registered during an expansion project in 1984, and some 540 recorded in my own 1991 census. The arrival of the first consignments of tools and construction materials donated by developers for fencing and wells in 1978 initiated an expansion period which saw the area under cultivation more than triple in size, growing from 5.0 ha to 16.2 ha in ten years. Between 1987 and 1995, a second wave of enclosures nearly doubled that area again. At least a dozen separate projects were funded by international NGOs, voluntary agencies, and private donors. These donations were used toward the construction of thousands of meters of fence line and roughly twenty concrete-lined irrigation wells. In addition, there were some 1,370 hand-dug wells and nearly 4,000 fruit trees incorporated within Kerewan's garden perimeters. Growers purchased seed, fertilizer, and other inputs directly from an FAO [Food and Agriculture Organization]-sponsored dealership in the community and sent truckloads of fresh produce to market outlets located up and down the Gambia-Senegal border, which thrived on the vegetable trade. In sum, the Kerewan area developed over two decades into one of the most intensive vegetable-producing enclaves in the country. . . .

Theories Connecting Gender, Development, and the Environment

The image most widely used to capture the "plight" of Third World women is that of an African peasant woman toting an improbably large and unwieldy bundle of firewood on her head. She may or may not have a young child tied to her back, but the image is always meant to convey that she has traveled a great distance to gather her load. As a metaphor, this feminine icon suggests the incredible burdens women shoulder, and the great lengths they go to, to satisfy the multiple and competing demands society and their families place on them. The implication is that women suffer these conditions universally, as a class, and that pure, selfless motives drive them to undertake routinely dull, repetitive, and ultimately thankless tasks. At the same time, the graphic portrayal of firewood collectors is meant to underscore the idea that close connections exist between women and the natural environment. It suggests that women forced to gather wood from the countryside lead a hand-to-mouth existence, where knowledge of the landscape is bred of necessity and deep personal experience, and where the vagaries of climate and ecology have profound and immediate implications for human well-being. Thus, by virtue of their collective lot in a singular division of labor, women mediate the relation-ship between nature and society, and they feel the brunt of natural forces as a consequence.

Such images convey a stark reality: life for peasant women is often filled with considerable toil and drudgery. Yet if these women suffer a common plight, it resides not in any particular niche in some all-encompassing divi-sion of labor but in the countless ways the range and variety of their lived experiences are distorted in the words and images conveyed by outsiders. The wood-gathering icon represents Third World women as Africans, African women as peasants, and peasant women as a single type. There is no geo-graphical detail at either localized or macropolitical scales that might serve as an explanation for the plight thus portrayed. Moreover, to render such women as beasts of burden, dumb, stolid, unwavering in their support of their fami-lies, unstinting in their service of same, is to acquiesce in the notion that they are perpetual victims, steeped in need, and incapable or disinclined to contest their lot creatively.

This tension between images of women as victims and women as auton-omous actors traces back to the earliest efforts of developers to promote Women in Development (WID) programs in the Third World. The United Nations–sponsored convocation in Mexico City in 1975 proclaimed an Inter-national Decade for Women and initiated efforts within the major develop-ment agencies to address a broad agenda of issues deemed especially pertinent to Third World women. . . .

Gone to Their Second Husbands: Domestic Politics and the Garden Boom

One of the offshoots of the surge in female incomes and the intense demands on female labor produced by the garden boom was an escalation of gender politics centered on the reworking of what [Anne] Whitehead once called the "conjugal contract." In Kerewan, the political engagement between gardeners and their husbands can be divided into two phases. The first phase, compris-ing the early years of the garden boom, was characterized by a sometimes bit-ter war of words. In the context of these discursive politics, men whose wives seemed preoccupied with gardening claimed that gardens dominated women's lives to such a degree that the plots themselves had become the women's "second husbands." Returning the charge, their wives replied, in effect, that they may as well be married to their gardens: the financial crisis of the early 1980s had so undermined male cash-crop production and, by exten-sion, husbands' contributions to household finances, that gardens were often women's only means of financial support during this period.

As the boom intensified, so, too, did intra-household politics. The focus of conflict in the second phase—which extended into the mid-1990s—was the role of garden income in meeting household budgetary obligations. Several studies have examined "non-pooling" households in Africa, that is, households in which men and women tend to engage in distinctly different economic activities and control their own incomes from these enterprises. The garden boom offers a case study in which women, by virtue of their new incomes, entered into intra-household negotiations over labor allocation and income disposition with certain economic advantages. The upshot of these negotiations was not, however, quite so simple. In terms of budgetary obligations, women in the garden districts assumed a broad range of new responsibilities from their husbands. Moreover, they frequently gave their husbands part of their earnings in the form of cash gifts. This outcome appears in some respects as a capitulation on the part of gardeners. I argue, . . . however, that it can also be read as symbolic deference designed to purchase the freedom of movement and social interaction that garden production and marketing entailed. In effect, gardeners used the strategic deployment of garden incomes to win for themselves significant autonomy and new measures of power and prestige, albeit not always at a price of their own choosing.

. . . Before the garden boom, men in Mandinka society had powerful economic levers at their disposal which they could, and did, use to "discipline" their wives. They controlled what little cash flowed through the rural economy due to their dominant position in groundnut production and were able to fulfill or deny a range of their wives' expressed needs at will. These included such basic requirements as clothing, ceremonial expenses (naming ceremonies, circumcisions, and marriages for each individual woman's children), housing amenities, and furnishings. The power vested in control over cash income was only enhanced by polygamous marital practices and the opportunities they afforded to play wives off against one another. A second advantage was derived from the husband's rights in divorce proceedings. In the event of a divorce, Mandinka customary law requires that the bride's family refund bridewealth payments. Consequently, when marital relations reach an impasse, divorce is not automatic; the financial arrangement between the two families must first be undone. Typically, the woman flees or is sent back to her family so that they can ascertain to their own satisfaction whether she has made a good faith effort to make her marriage work. The onus is on the woman to prove her case, however, and she is not infrequently admonished by her own family to improve her behavior before being returned to her husband.

The advent of a female cash-crop system reduced the significance of both these sources of leverage, not least because women's incomes had outstripped their husbands' in many cases. A rough comparison of the garden incomes of women in Kerewan and Niumi Lameng and the earnings their husbands reported from groundnut sales showed that 81 percent and 47 percent of women in the Niumi Lameng and Kerewan samples, respectively, earned more cash than their husbands from sales of these crops. This reversal of fortunes changed fundamentally the way male residents of the garden districts dealt with their wives:

> Before gardening started here, if you saw that your wife had ten dalasis you
> would ask her where she got it. At that time, there was no other source of
> income for women except their husbands. . . . But nowadays a woman can save
> more than two thousand dalasis while the husband does not even have ten

dalasis to his name. So now men cannot ask their wives where they get their money, because of their garden produce.

—Gardener's husband

Indeed, the garden boom reduced male authority ("If she realizes she is getting more money than her husband, she may not respect him"), and the extent of gardeners' economic influence expanded proportionately. The simple fact that women could largely provide for themselves ("If we join [our husbands] at home and forget [our gardens in] the bush, we would all suffer. . . . Even if he doesn't give you [what you want], as long as you are doing your garden work, you can survive") constituted a serious challenge to the material and symbolic bases of male power. In the first phase of conflict brought on by the boom, men openly expressed their resentment in pointed references to female shirking and selfishness. Their feelings were also made plain in actions taken by a small minority who forbade their wives to garden, or agitated at the village level to have gardening banned altogether. In the second phase, men dropped their oppositional rhetoric, became more generally cooperative, and began exploring ways to benefit personally from the garden boom. Sensing the shift in tenor of conjugal relations, women, accordingly, began a prolonged attempt to secure the goodwill necessary to sustain production on a more secure basis.

. . . Survey data show that both senior members of garden work units and women working on their own took on many economic responsibilities that were traditionally ascribed to men. Fifty-six percent of the women in the Kerewan sample, for example, claimed to have purchased at least one bag of rice in 1991 for their families. The great majority bought all of their own (95%), and their children's (84%), clothing and most of the furnishings for their own houses. Large numbers took over responsibility for ceremonial costs from their husbands, such as the purchase of feast day clothing (80%), or the provision of animals for religious sacrifice. Many paid their children's school expenses. In a handful of cases, gardeners undertook major or unusual expenditures such as roofing their family's living quarters, providing loans to their husbands for purchasing draught animals and farming equipment, or paying the house tax to government officials. There are, once again, unfortunately no baseline data that could be used to gain historical perspective on this information. Nonetheless, several male informants stated unequivocally that, were it not for garden incomes, many of the marriages in the village would simply fail on the grounds of "non-support.". . .

Gone to Their Second Husbands

It is fair to say that domestic budgetary battles did not originate with the garden boom in Mandinka society; nor are they wholly unique to either The Gambia or Africa. Nonetheless, the Gambian garden boom clearly produced dramatic changes in the normative expectations and practices of marital partners in the country's garden districts. . . .

The price of autonomy notwithstanding, women in The Gambia's garden districts succeeded in producing a striking new social landscape—by embracing the challenges of the garden boom, they placed themselves in a position to carefully extricate themselves from some of the more onerous demands of marital obligations. Indeed, in a very real sense, they won for themselves "second husbands" by rewriting the rules governing the conjugal contract. Thus the product of lengthy intra-household negotiations brought on by the garden boom was not the simple reproduction of patriarchal privilege and prestige; it was instead a new, carefully crafted autonomy that carried with it obligations and considerable social freedoms.

Double Standards: Women's Property Rights Violations in Kenya

Summary

Shortly after Emily Owino's husband died, her in-laws took all her possessions—including farm equipment, livestock, household goods, and clothing. The in-laws insisted that she be "cleansed" by having sex with a social outcast, a custom in her region, as a condition of staying in her home. They paid a herdsman to have sex with Owino, against her will and without a condom. They later took over her farmland. She sought help from the local elder and chief, who did nothing. Her in-laws forced her out of her home, and she and her children were homeless until someone offered her a small, leaky shack. No longer able to afford school fees, her children dropped out of school.

—Interview with Emily Owino, Siaya, November 2, 2002

When Susan Wagitangu's parents died, her brothers inherited the family land. "My sister and I didn't inherit," said Wagitangu, a fifty-three-year-old Kikuyu woman. "Traditionally, in my culture, once a woman gets married, she does not inherit from her father. The assumption is that once a woman gets married she will be given land where she got married." This was not the case for Wagitangu: when her husband died, her brothers-in-law forced her off that homestead and took her cows. Wagitangu now lives in a Nairobi slum. "Nairobi has advantages," she said. "If I don't have food, I can scavenge in the garbage dump."

—Interview with Susan Wagitangu, Nairobi, October 29, 2002

Women's rights to property are unequal to those of men in Kenya. Their rights to own, inherit, manage, and dispose of property are under constant attack from customs, laws, and individuals—including government officials—who believe that women cannot be trusted with or do not deserve property. The devastating effects of property rights violations—including poverty, disease, violence, and homelessness—harm women, their children, and Kenya's overall development. For decades, the government has ignored this problem. Kenya's new government, which took office in January 2003, must immediately act to eliminate this insidious form of discrimination, or it will see its fight against HIV/AIDS (human immuno-deficiency virus/acquired immune deficiency syndrome), its economic and social reforms, and its development agenda stagger and fail.

This report recounts the experiences of women from various regions, ethnic groups, religions, and social classes in Kenya who have one thing in common: because they are women, their property rights have been trampled. Many women are excluded from inheriting, evicted from their lands and homes by in-laws, stripped of their possessions, and forced to engage in risky sexual practices in order to keep their property. When they divorce or separate from their husbands, they are often expelled from their homes with only their clothing. Married women can seldom stop their husbands from selling family property. A woman's access to property usually hinges on her relationship to a man. When the relationship ends, the woman stands a good chance of losing her home, land, livestock, household goods, money, vehicles, and other property. These violations have the intent and effect of perpetuating women's dependence on men and undercutting their social and economic status.

Women's property rights violations are not only discriminatory, they may prove fatal. The deadly HIV/AIDS epidemic magnifies the devastation of women's property violations in Kenya, where approximately 15 percent of the population between the ages of fifteen and forty-nine is infected with HIV. Widows who are coerced into the customary practices of "wife inheritance" or ritual "cleansing" (which usually involve unprotected sex) run a clear risk of contracting and spreading HIV. The region where these practices are most common has Kenya's highest AIDS prevalence; the HIV infection rate in girls and young women there is six times higher than that of their male counterparts. AIDS deaths expected in the coming years will result in millions more women becoming widows at younger ages than would otherwise be the case. These women and their children (who may end up AIDS orphans) are likely to face not only social stigma against people affected by HIV/AIDS but also deprivations caused by property rights violations.

A complex mix of cultural, legal, and social factors underlies women's property rights violations. Kenya's customary laws—largely unwritten but influential local norms that coexist with formal laws—are based on patriarchal traditions in which men inherited and largely controlled land and other property, and women were "protected" but had lesser property rights. Past practices permeate contemporary customs that deprive women of property rights and silence them when those rights are infringed. Kenya's constitution prohibits discrimination on the basis of sex, but undermines this protection by condoning discrimination under personal and customary laws. The few statutes that could advance women's property rights defer to religious and customary property laws that privilege men over women. Sexist attitudes are infused in Kenyan society: men that Human Rights Watch interviewed said that women are untrustworthy, incapable of handling property, and in need of male protection. The guise of male "protection" does not obscure the fact that stripping women of their property is a way of asserting control over women's autonomy, bodies, and labor—and enriches their "protectors."

Currently, women find it almost hopeless to pursue remedies for property rights violations. Traditional leaders and governmental authorities often ignore women's property claims and sometimes make the problems worse. Courts overlook and misinterpret family property and succession laws. Women often have little awareness of their rights and seldom have means to enforce them. Women who try to fight back are often beaten, raped, or ostracized. In response to all of this, the Kenyan government has done almost nothing: bills that could improve women's property rights have languished in parliament and government ministries have no programs to promote equal property rights. At every level, government officials shrug off this injustice, saying they do not want to interfere with culture.

As important as cultural diversity and respecting customs may be, if customs are a source of discrimination against women, they—like any other norm—must evolve. This is crucial not only for the sake of women's equality, but because there are real social consequences to depriving half the population of their property rights. International organizations have identified women's insecure property rights as contributing to low agricultural production, food shortages, underemployment, and rural poverty. In Kenya, more than half of the population lives in poverty, the economy is a disaster, and HIV/AIDS rates are high. The agricultural sector, which contributes a quarter of Kenya's gross domestic product and depends on women's labor, is stagnant. If Kenya is to meet its development aims, it must address the property inequalities that hold women back.

Unequal property rights and harmful customary practices violate international law. Kenya has ratified international treaties requiring it to eliminate all forms of discrimination against women (including discrimination in marriage and family relations), guarantee equality before the law and the equal protection of the law, and ensure that women have effective remedies if their rights are violated. International law also obliges states to modify discriminatory social and cultural patterns of conduct. Kenya is violating those obligations.

With a new government in office and a new draft constitution containing provisions that would enhance women's property rights set for debate, this is a pivotal time for Kenya to confront the deep property inequalities in its society. It must develop a program of legal and institutional reforms and educational outreach initiatives that systematically eliminates obstacles to the fulfillment of women's property rights.

Conclusion

Women's property issues touch deeply the ways people live, think, and organize their social and economic lives. It's not just a matter of getting a few women in parliament. People feel threatened.

—Professor Yash Pal Ghai, chairman, Constitution of Kenya Review
Commission, Nairobi, October 23, 2002

Property rights abuses inflicted on women in Kenya should be recognized for what they are: gross violations of women's human rights. Discriminatory property laws and practices impoverish women and their dependents, put their lives at risk by increasing their vulnerability to HIV/AIDS and other diseases, drive them into abhorrent living conditions, subject them to violence, and relegate them to dependence on men and social inequality.

Despite the slow recognition that property rights violations harm not just women and their dependents but Kenya's development as a whole, little has been done to prevent and redress these violations. Averting these abuses in a country where dispossessing women is considered normal will be difficult. A concerted effort is needed not just to improve legal protections, but to modify customary laws and practices and ultimately to change people's minds. With extreme poverty, a moribund economy, rampant violence, and catastrophic HIV/AIDS rates, Kenya can no longer afford to ignore women's property rights violations. Eliminating discrimination against women with respect to property rights is not only a human rights obligation; for many women, it is a matter of life and death.

POSTSCRIPT

Are Women in a Position to Challenge Male Power Structures in Africa?

In many ways, the viewpoints presented in this issue get at a deeper debate about social change and the best way to improve the situation of women in Africa. The selection by Human Rights Watch presents the local situation for women in Kenya as deplorable and intractable, suggesting that a top-down, legislative solution is the best course of action. Critics of this approach might argue that, while this is all well and good, it is largely ineffectual as the reach of government is fairly limited in many African contexts. The case study presented by Schroeder about women in The Gambia provides ammunition for those who suggest that a bottom-up approach that is focused on economic empowerment is the best avenue to greater gender equality in Africa. Imagine, for example, what type of social change might occur in the United States if women earned more on average than men (the situation in Kerawan). This can be compared with U.S. Bureau of Labor Statistics survey results showing that American women earned 77 percent of their male counterparts' salaries in 1999. However, it should be noted that a reading of Schroeder's entire volume (of which a small portion was excerpted for this issue) reveals that the situation was later constrained because women's access to land for gardening was somewhat tenuous. Many men who had temporarily loaned land to women for gardening began reasserting their rights to these plots in the 1990s. As such, it may be that both top-down (i.e., legislative) and bottom-up approaches are needed in order to improve the situation of women in Africa.

The case presented by Schroeder is not an isolated incident of economically empowered women in Africa. Another classic example concerns the "Nanas-Benz" of Togo who are wealthy cloth merchants. They are emblematic of how successful women can be in the West African marketplace. *Nanas* means "established woman" or "woman of means." Benz refers to the type of auto preferred by these market women. The most successful of these merchants can turn over about $600,000 in cloth per month. They act as agents between importers and wide-ranging clientele in West Africa. Successful Nanas-Benz make sure that their children attend a university. The girls study economics, management and administration while the boys become architects, teachers, and bankers. The business is often passed down to a woman's female children.

While WID programs still exist today, there has been an effort to move beyond stand-alone programs focused on women to attention and awareness of the situation and needs of women in all types of programs and policy initiatives. This broader approach is often simply referred to as "gender" or "gender and development." For examples of the WID and gender approaches, see relevant sections of the Web sites of the United States Agency for International Development `http://www.usaid.gov/wid/links.htm` and the World Bank `http://www.worldbank.org/gender/`.

ISSUE 14

Is the International Community Focusing on HIV/AIDS Treatment at the Expense of Prevention in Africa?

YES: Andrew Creese, Katherine Floyd, Anita Alban, and Lorna Guinness, from "Cost-Effectiveness of HIV/AIDS Interventions in Africa: A Systematic Review of the Evidence," *The Lancet* (2002)

NO: Philip J. Hilts, from "Changing Minds: Botswana Beats Back AIDS," in *Rx for Survival: Why We Must Rise to the Global Challenge* (Penguin Books, 2005)

ISSUE SUMMARY

YES: Andrew Creese and his colleagues, who work for the World Health Organization (WHO) and European Universities, suggest that cost-effectiveness is an important criterion for deciding how to allocate scarce health care funding. A case of HIV/AIDS can be prevented for $11 by selective blood safety measures and targeted condom distribution with treatment of sexually transmitted diseases. In contrast, antiretroviral treatment for adults can cost several thousand dollars. They argue that a strong economic case exists for prioritizing preventive interventions and TB treatment.

NO: Philip J. Hilts, who teaches journalism at Boston University, describes a comprehensive HIV/AIDS program in Botswana. This program not only offered preventive care, but sophisticated triple drug AIDS treatments to all people of the nation, free of charge. By 2005, the program was treating 43,000 people and the cost of treatment is one-tenth of what it is in the United States.

Slowing the spread and impact of HIV/AIDS is one of the greatest challenges facing contemporary Africa. Unlike some other diseases, AIDS is particularly problematic because it strikes the working-age population and thus has serious economic and social consequences. In 1999 AIDS became the leading cause of death in Africa, overtaking malaria. As of 2007, the Joint United

Nations Programme on HIV/ADIS (UNAIDS) reported that 22.5 million adults and children were living with the HIV virus in Sub-Saharan Africa (SSA), which accounts for 68 percent of the infected population worldwide. SSA also accounted for more than three-quarters of AIDS related deaths in 2007, as well as 68 percent of new infections (1.7 of 2.5 million). Unlike other world regions, the majority of people living with HIV in SSA are women (61%). The overall infection rate in SSA is estimated at 5 percent as compared to .8 percent worldwide.

Southern Africa is the worst affected region with eight countries with a national adult prevalency rate that exceeded 15 percent in 2005 (including Botswana, Lesotho, Mozambique, Namibia, South Africa, Swaziland, Zambia, and Zimbabwe). South Africa is the country in the world with the most HIV infections, but like many other countries in Sub-Saharan Africa (SSA), its adult prevalency rate is stable or declining.

The spatial pattern of the disease has changed over time. Initially, it was distributed along major highways and in the urban centers of eastern and southern Africa. In the 1990s, the epicenter of the virus moved to southern Africa. In Africa, the disease is largely transmitted through unprotected heterosexual sex and unsafe medical practices. Truck drivers, sex workers, and military personnel all have above-average infection rates and are believed to play a significant role in the spread of the virus.

Until the 2000s, much of the HIV/AIDS work in Africa focused on prevention as opposed to treatment. Uganda was touted as an example of a country that aggressively pursued prevention and was able to dramatically reduce its rate of new infections. The exorbitant costs of antiretroviral drugs also seemed to make such expenditures unrealistic. But increasingly, access to such drugs at affordable prices began to be framed as a human rights issue. It was also argued that African countries could not afford to lose so much human capital to early death.

In this issue, Andrew Creese and coauthors, who work for the World Health Organization (WHO) and European Universities, suggest that cost-effectiveness is an important criterion for deciding how to allocate scarce health care funding. A case of HIV/AIDS can be prevented for $11 by selective blood safety measures and targeted condom distribution with treatment of sexually transmitted diseases. In contrast, antiretroviral treatment for adults can cost several thousand dollars. They argue that a strong economic case exists for prioritizing preventive interventions and TB treatment. Cost-effectiveness criteria could also be used to decide between different types of treatment.

Philip Hilts, who teaches journalism at Boston University, describes a comprehensive HIV/AIDS program in Botswana. This program not only offered preventive care, but sophisticated triple drug AIDS treatments to all people of the nation, free of charge. By 2005, the program was treating 43,000 people and the cost of treatment is one-tenth of what it is in the United States. This program benefited from substantial levels of external funding from the Merck pharmaceutical company.

YES ⤶

Andrew Creese, Katherine Floyd, Anita Alban, and Lorna Guinness

Cost-Effectiveness of HIV/AIDS Interventions in Africa: A Systematic Review of the Evidence

Introduction

HIV/AIDS accounts for about 20% of all deaths and disability-adjusted life-years (DALYs) lost in Africa, which makes it the biggest single component of the continent's disease burden. The epidemic has reduced life expectancy in the worst affected countries by more than 10 years, and its social and economic consequences have been devastating.

Substantial new resources are becoming available for prevention, care, and support. The European Commission is committed to a major increase in spending on the diseases of poverty, including HIV/AIDS. A global fund to fight AIDS, tuberculosis, and malaria became operational in January, 2002; so far pledges are in the region of US$2 billion. . . .

To ensure that any new resources have the maximum possible effect on the epidemic, cost-effectiveness should be considered in the design of strategies for prevention, care, and support. As Kahn and Marseille have pointed out, the scale of the HIV/AIDS epidemic combined with scarcity of resources makes cost-effectiveness especially important in developing countries. Up to now, however, cost-effectiveness has been well documented only for industrialised countries. For low-income and middle-income countries, we could identify only one detailed review, which addressed interventions to reduce mother-to-child transmission. For Africa, investigators focused on individual HIV/AIDS-related interventions. We could not identify any published report that brought together the evidence base in a standardised way that allowed comparison among interventions.

We report a critical assessment of studies of the cost-effectiveness of HIV/AIDS interventions in Africa, and present their results in a standard form.

Methods

Review of Published Work

We searched Medline, Popline, and EconLit databases for 1984–2000 using the key words HIV, AIDS, and HIV/AIDS in combination with each of the terms: costs; cost-effectiveness; cost-benefit analysis; economics; and Africa. Citations and reference lists were then reviewed to identify any additional relevant studies. Abstracts from international conferences were searched but were not included because they provided insufficient detail. Unpublished data were obtained through contact with experts in HIV/AIDS. A total of 57 studies and nine reviews were identified, including several unpublished reports and presentations.

Criteria for Inclusion and Exclusion of Identified Studies

We assessed each study using a standard checklist. We then decided in three stages about inclusion in our review. First, we included any study that met all these five criteria: (i) the report contained data for Africa; (ii) it measured both cost and effectiveness; (iii) it seemed to use standard methods for estimating costs and outcomes, (iv) it seemed to include all major cost items, and (v) it allowed a generic measure of outcome (either HIV infections prevented or DALYs gained) to be calculated. We focused on studies in which investigators had analysed costs and effects together, rather than reviewing evidence on costs and effects separately, because the two items are not independent of each other.

Second, studies that met these inclusion criteria were excluded if (a) they were about regimens that are now out of date, such as long-course zidovudine for prevention of mother-to-child transmission; (b) they had estimated the effectiveness of an intervention before clinical trial results were available, and subsequent cost-effectiveness studies had used clinical trial results in their effectiveness estimates; or (c) drug prices had altered substantially since publication. We therefore excluded three studies of interventions to reduce mother-to-child transmission (table 1).

Third, we identified interventions not covered by studies meeting the five initial inclusion criteria, but for which some cost and effectiveness data existed. We identified two such interventions—highly active antiretroviral treatment (HAART) for HIV-positive adults, and promotion of female condoms. In view of the current importance of antiretroviral treatment, we decided to include a study that used only drug costs, even though drug prices have fallen since its publication, and we could only calculate a cost per life-year gained rather than a cost per DALY gained from the data presented. To provide a more recent estimate of cost-effectiveness, we used laboratory test costs for antiretroviral therapy in adults enrolled in the HIV drugs access initiatives in Uganda and Côte d'Ivoire, and the cost of drugs cited by Médecins Sans Frontières in 2001. An unpublished study of promotion of female condoms was included only after written communication with its authors.

Standardisation of Studies Meeting Inclusion Criteria

Thus, we included 24 of the initial 66 studies identified. Data from these studies spanned 13 years (1988–2000), and differed widely in their methods and assumptions. A few studies had primary data for both costs and outcomes, but most used epidemiological models to estimate effectiveness. In the modelling, some studies included analysis of the secondary infections prevented by an intervention, whereas others did not; and different values were used for some variables (eg, the efficiency of HIV transmission) that determine effectiveness. Several studies included an analysis of treatment-cost savings but most did not; others also included savings from averting loss of productivity in their calculations. In most studies, investigators focused on costs from a provider perspective only, but a few also looked at costs incurred by patients. Different prices were used, particularly for antiretroviral drugs, whose prices and regimens have changed substantially in the past 5 years. Discount rates, effectiveness measures, the reporting of costs and effects, assumed life expectancy at birth, and the year in which costs were assessed also varied.

To ensure the widest possible comparability among interventions, we standardised both cost and effectiveness data; therefore, the figures we report differ from the results shown in the original publications. Standardisation of cost data included the year of prices, the price of 1 year of triple combination therapy, how costs were assessed, and savings related to averted treatment costs and productivity losses. For effectiveness, we undertook no new modelling. However, we standardised the discount rate used to estimate the present value of future health gains; life expectancy at birth; average age at HIV infection; assumptions for tuberculosis treatment, including years of life gained through cure and death rates in the absence of treatment; the disability weighting associated with years of life lived with AIDS; and the frequency of home-based care visits.

For all studies we calculated unit costs and effectiveness. Once both had been standardized, we calculated two measures of cost-effectiveness: (1) cost per HIV infection averted (for the preventive interventions) and (2) cost per DALY gained (for all interventions). Sensitivity analyses were excluded if they were based on variable measurements (eg, life expectancy at birth, discount rate) for which we had already standardised results, or if there was too little detail to allow recalculation of figures. . . .

Results

Cost per HIV Infection Prevented

There was a wide range in the cost per HIV infection prevented. Costs for condom distribution ranged from as little as $11 to over $2000. Measures to improve blood safety cost between just under $20 and about $1000 to prevent one case of HIV. There was especially large variation in the different strategies to reduce mother-to-child transmission. Breastfeeding and formula-feeding interventions cost from around $4000 to over $20 000 per infection prevented, whereas single-dose nevirapine cost much less—about $20–341. Diagnosis and treatment of sexually transmitted infections cost just over $270 per infection prevented, and the figure for voluntary counselling and testing (VCT) was higher, at around $400–500.

Cost per DALY Gained

The cost per DALY gained by interventions ranged from around $1 for a combined treatment of sexually-transmitted disease (STD) and condom promotion programme and for blood screening, to well over $1000 for HAART in adults. Blood safety measures, and single-dose nevirapine for prevention of mother-to-child transmission, cost as little as $10 per DALY gained. Tuberculosis treatment could also be less than $10 per DALY gained, but as high as $68 when inpatient care was involved. VCT and co-trimoxazole prophylaxis for HIV-positive patients with tuberculosis cost around or below $20. Home-based care varied from around $100 to $1000, with community based care programmes having a lower cost per DALY than programmes organised from health facilities.

Discussion

Our results show that there are few studies of the cost-effectiveness of HIV/ AIDS prevention, treatment, and care interventions in Africa, and there is considerable variability in the cost-effectiveness of such interventions. The most cost-effective interventions are for prevention of HIV/AIDS and treatment of tuberculosis, whereas HAART for adults, and home based care organised from health facilities, are the least cost effective. For some interventions, such as prevention of mother-to-child transmission, tuberculosis treatment, and home based care, there are particular strategies that provide the best value for money (best buy).

This review has several limitations. For five interventions, only one study was identified, and the maximum number of studies—for mother-to-child transmission—was four. In no one country were all interventions assessed, which made unbiased comparison of interventions difficult. Cost data were not always comprehensive, and were sometimes too few for standardised sensitivity analysis. The cost of HAART was underestimated, because data for only a very restricted subset of costs were considered. There were no data for the costs of use and strengthening of general health services necessary for provision of HAART. The effect of some interventions on HIV prevention might have been underestimated because some potential effects that are difficult to measure— such as reduced stigma arising from increased knowledge of status—were not accounted for. None of the studies on interventions to reduce vertical transmission looked at the effect of VCT on horizontal transmission. The effectiveness of HAART might have been underestimated because we had insufficient data to measure its effect on transmission through lowering viral loads. It could also have been overestimated. First, its use might increase transmission since risky behaviour by HIV-positive people with improved life expectancy could be encouraged. Second, side-effects mean that the value of 1 year of life is likely to be less than the 1 DALY assumed here. Some studies are based on project implementation at only a few sites (for example the study of VCT), or on theoretical analyses of interventions (eg, some studies of mother-to-child transmission). Thus, costs and effects in practice and on a large scale might be different from those shown. Finally, some interventions may complement each other in ways that are missed in analyses of individual interventions.

These limitations mean that both generalisability and interpretation should be viewed with caution. Ideally, we would have data for every intervention from several studies in similar settings—both income levels and prevalence rates can distort comparisons within and between countries. Salaries are linked to average national income and can thus affect costs. HIV prevalence does not affect the cost-effectiveness of every intervention but, where costs are incurred in diagnosis of a case of HIV (such as with VCT), the lower the prevalence, the higher the cost per HIV-positive case detected. For example, all studies of prevention of mother-to-child transmission show a relation between prevalence rates and cost-effectiveness.

Our review includes data from low-income countries in each intervention group, typically with high HIV prevalence. For mother-to-child transmission and tuberculosis treatment, we included data from both low-income and middle-income countries with a wide range in HIV prevalence, and the rankings of the types of intervention were consistent. For some other interventions, such as tuberculosis prevention, costs are likely to be higher in wealthier countries with lower rates of HIV infection. Two possible exceptions are blood safety and VCT. For blood safety, the major costs are probably supplies and equipment, which are likely to be similar across countries. For VCT, the estimated cost was similar to other estimates that have been made for Africa. A drawback to the VCT data is that the study used an index for HIV transmission efficiency that was ten times that typically used by the UN programme on HIV/AIDS. Together with very high rates of reported behaviour change, we might have overstated the effectiveness of this intervention elsewhere.

The evidence base could be improved by more cost-effectiveness studies that included all economic costs and used standard methods. Guidelines for cost-effectiveness analysis, including those for HIV/AIDS prevention, should be more widely and rigorously used. Ideally, analyses for several interventions in a single setting should be undertaken. In view of the powerful advocacy for access to antiretroviral therapy for HIV-infected adults, and the poor evidence currently available, work on the cost and effectiveness of such treatment in African settings is a priority. But in five other intervention areas—peer education for prostitutes, diagnosis and treatment of STDs, VCT, prevention therapy for tuberculosis, and co-trimoxazole prophylaxis for HIV-positive patients with tuberculosis—we depend on the results of only one study. Moreover, apart from tuberculosis, there are no data for treatment of opportunistic infections. New analysis could initially focus on interventions for which we have effectiveness data, but for which costs are not documented, and vice versa.

How can the existing data be used to inform policy? Cost-effectiveness rankings do not, on their own, indicate which health interventions are priorities for public funding. A recent framework based on seven questions has proposed that an intervention should be publicly funded if it is cost effective and it is (1) a public good; or (2) associated with important externalities and demand is inadequate; or (3) represents a catastrophic cost and insurance is not available; or (4) beneficiaries are poor.

Table 2 shows how this economic framework supplements the cost-effectiveness data we have collated. The use of a more comprehensive framework makes little difference. No intervention is ruled out with the first six questions, and the determining factor for public finance is cost-effectiveness.

Table 1

HIV/AIDS Intervention Groups, Individual Interventions, and Standardised Cost-Effectiveness Results, US$ for Year 2000

Intervention groups (numbered) and individual interventions	Place and year of publication	Cost per HIV infection prevented	Cost per DALY gained
Prevention			
1. Condom distribution			
Condom distribution plus STD treatment for prostitutes	Sub-Saharan Africa, 1991	11–17	1
Female condoms targeted to:			
Prostitutes	Kenya, 1999	275	12
High-risk women	Kenya, 1999	1066	48
Medium-risk women	Kenya, 1999	2188	99
2. Blood safety			
Hospital based screening	Tanzania, 1999	18	1
	Zambia, 1995	107	5
Strengthening blood transfusion services through:			
Defer high risk donors	Zimbabwe, 1995	18–107	1–5
Test and defer high risk donors	Zimbabwe, 1995	48–74	2–3
Rapid test	Zimbabwe, 1995	62	3
Improved transfusion safety with outreach	Zimbabwe, 2000	208–256	10–12
Improved blood collection and transfusion	Tanzania, 1999	950	43
3. Peer education for prostitutes	Cameroon, 1998	79–160	4–7
4. Prevention of mother-to-child transmission			
Single dose nevirapine-targeted	Sub-Saharan Africa, 2000	20–341	1–12
	Uganda, 1999	308	10
Single-dose nevirapine-universal	Uganda, 1999	143	5
	Sub-Saharan Africa	268	9
Petra regimen	South Africa, 1999	268	9
ZDV CDC Thai regimen	South Africa, 2000	949–2198	33–75
	South Africa, 1999	2356	81
Formula recommendation	South Africa, 1999	3834	131
Breastfeeding 3 months	South Africa, 1999	5006	171
Formula provision	South Africa, 1999	6355	218
Breastfeeding 6 months	South Africa, 1999	21 355	731
5. Diagnosis and treatment of STIs	Tanzania, 1997	271	12
6. Voluntary counselling and testing	Kenya and Tanzania, 2000	393–482	18–22

(Continued)

Table 1   *(Continued)*

Intervention groups (numbered) and individual interventions	Place and year of publication	Cost per HIV infection prevented	Cost per DALY gained
Treatment and care			
7. Short-course tuberculosis treatment for new sputum-smear positive pulmonary patients			
Ambulatory care	Malawi, Mozambique, Tanzania, 1991	n/a	2–3
	Uganda, 1995	n/a	2–4
	South Africa, 1997	n/a	8–16
IUATLD model (involves 2 months hospitalisation at treatment outset followed by monthly visits to a health clinic to collect drugs) Community-based DOT	Uganda, 1995	n/a	3–4
	Malawi, Mozambique, Tanzania, 1991	n/a	4–8
	South Africa, 1997	n/a	34–68
	South Africa, 1997	n/a	14–21
8. Co-trimoxazole prophylaxis for HIV+ tuberculosis patients	Hypothetical low income country, sub-Saharan Africa	n/a	6
9. Home-based care			
Community-based programme	Tanzania, 2000	n/a	77
	Zambia, 1994	n/a	99
Health facility based programme	Zambia, 1994	n/a	681
	Tanzania, 2000	n/a	786
	Zimbabwe, 1998	n/a	469–1230
10. Preventive therapy for tuberculosis			
Isoniazid for 6 months	Uganda, 1999	n/a	169
Rifampicin plus pyrazinamide, 2 months	Uganda, 1999	n/a	282
Isoniazid plus rifampicin, 3 months	Uganda, 1999	n/a	288
11. Antiretroviral therapy for adults	Senegal and Côte D'Ivoire, 2000	n/a	1100
	South Africa, 2000	n/a	1800

Despite the limitations of our review and difficulties with generalisation, cost-effectiveness can be used for some broad prioritisation among interventions. The World Development Report of 1993 suggested that any intervention achieving a DALY gain for $50 or less ($62 in year 2000 prices) was highly cost effective in the context of the poorest countries. The general inference was that these interventions should be made available to all those in need before less cost-effective options are provided to a few. On this basis, several preventive interventions (targeted condom distribution, blood screening, nevirapine for the prevention of mother-to-child transmission and STD treatment), and two treatment interventions (co-trimoxazole prophylaxis for patients with HIV and tuberculosis) and tuberculosis treatment should have first call on new funds for HIV/AIDS in Africa. Within intervention categories first priority should be given to the intervention that is a clear best buy—for example, short-course nevirapine treatment for mothers and babies, and targeted condom distribution.

Table 2

Economic Factors Affecting Priority of Health Interventions for Public Funding

	Public good?	Important externalities	Adequate demand?	Catastrophic cost?	Voluntary Insurance available for catastrophic cost?	Benefit group poor?	Cost effective (US$ cost per DALY)
Condom distribution	No	Yes	No	No	N/a	Yes	1–99
Blood safety	No	Yes	Yes	No	N/a	Yes	1–43
Peer education for prostitutes	No	Yes	No	No	N/a	Yes	4–7
MTCT	No	No	?	No	N/a	Yes	1–731
STDs	No	Yes	No	No	N/a	Yes	12
VCT	No	Yes?	No	No	N/a	Yes	18–22
TB short course	No	Yes	Yes	Yes	N/a	Yes	2–68
Co-trimoxazole prophylaxis	No	No	?	No	N/a	Yes	6
Home care	No	No	?	Yes	No	Yes	77–1230
TB preventive therapy	No	Yes	No	?	No	Yes	169–288
ARV therapy	No	?	Yes	Yes	No	Yes	1100–1800

Reading from left to right, answers to the seven questions included in the framework[1,49] are suggested, in the order in which they should be asked. ARV=antiretroviral therapy, MTCT=mother-to-child transmission, TB=tuberculosis, VCT=voluntary counselling and testing. N/a=not applicable.

In practice, cost-effectiveness will need to be balanced with several other considerations. Affordability is one important issue; in the context of health budgets, a cost-effective intervention is not necessarily affordable when it is relevant to many people, and public funding will result in high demand. In Africa, this concern is most likely to apply to interventions to prevent mother-to-child transmission. Even with only restricted provision of antiretroviral treatment to HIV-positive adults, it could also become relevant for VCT services. Antiretroviral treatment for HIV-positive adults may not be as cost-effective as some other interventions, but the overwhelming pressure being placed on governments to provide such care is impossible to ignore. Recent estimates are that 20%, 40%, and 50% of health resources are already being consumed by HIV infected persons in Malawi, Zambia, and Zimbabwe, respectively.

In addition, HIV-infected people and the non-governmental organisations assisting them represent an increasingly important political force. Therefore, provision of care and support is more politically attractive, at least in the short term. Furthermore, care and support are essential parts of an enabling environment (in which people are empowered to address their difficulties) that is required to reduce discrimination and stigmatisation. By contrast, people at risk of becoming infected, the young in particular, are a more disparate and less easily organised group, with no clear cut or well articulated interests, and weak advocates. Prioritisation of care can be reinforced by difficulties in implementing or expanding the more cost-effective preventive interventions. Effective prevention strategies for the most vulnerable populations are still not scaled up to levels that could have a major impact on the HIV epidemic, even where funds are available.

The kind of cost-effectiveness evidence presented here can, however, help to inform policy decisions on resource allocation between prevention and care. For example, the results and estimates of the reachable population (ie, the population size that is feasible to cover with each intervention) have been used to explore the consequences of alternative ways to use an additional $400 million per year. At a WHO workshop (HSI/WHO/HQ, WHO/AFRO, UNAIDS. Costing and prioritisation of WHO's contribution to the International Partnership Against AIDS in Africa. Geneva, Sept 4–5, 2000), participants estimated that with this increase in funding, about 750 000 more people with HIV/AIDS in Africa could be treated every year, and almost one million infections prevented (17.9 million DALYs gained). A 10% spending reallocation from treatment towards more prevention (defined as management of STDs, blood safety, VCT, prevention of mother-to-child transmission, and preventive programmes among prostitutes) would increase the total DALYs gained by over 15%.

Allocation of new funds for HIV/AIDS requires more than rankings of cost-effectiveness. Nevertheless, value for money is important, especially in African countries, where resources are particularly scarce and needs are so great. Existing cost-effectiveness data are few, and much more high quality research is needed for detailed planning and programming. Yet even the available data make it clear that a spending programme for HIV/AIDS relief in Africa that neglects to bring cost-effectiveness evidence into the consultation process risks unnecessary sacrifice of hundreds of thousands of prevention opportunities, treatment opportunities, and lives.

Philip J. Hilts

Changing Minds: Botswana Beats Back AIDS

The greatest public health challenge in our time is AIDS, and the place it has wreaked the most havoc is in Africa. Sub-Saharan Africa has about 10 percent of the world's people, but about 60 percent of the people infected with HIV; in more than a dozen countries, it has become common practice to hire two or even three people to fill each job because of the certainty that workers will die within a short time after training. About 26 million people in Southern Africa are infected now, and that means, even with future successes, the epidemic will be a major presence for many years to come. If a new global health campaign is to be waged, the defeat of AIDS in Africa must be a priority. The myths about AIDS in Africa persist—that money to fight AIDS is lost to corruption, that Africans have resisted condoms and behavior change more than others. The truth is progress has been made in several places in Africa, and much more progress is expected as sophisticated HIV treatments become more accessible to Africans. The most remarkable case of progress against HIV in Africa has been in Botswana, which is now leading what has been called the "decade of treatment" in Africa.

Whoever called Africa the dark continent must have been blind, because there is very little of Africa that could be called dark. Here in the great southern expanses of the continent, day after day, the sky is empty of clouds; intense light fills the whole blue bowl. . . .

When Botswana was declared independent in 1966 its prospects were grim. It was one of the two or three poorest nations in the world, with its citizens earning fewer than two dollars per day, and nothing to give hope for more.

It sits up on high tableland, grass and bush savannah mostly, with a great desert—the Kalahari—in the middle and west of the country. There is too little rain for agriculture in most of the country, just enough to grow grasses for cattle. At the time of independence, the nation, the size of Texas, had a total of four miles of road, essentially no electricity, and no telephones. The airport was a dirt strip with a shack sometimes housing an attendant. From the shack it was a hefty hike to the new capital city, Gaborone.

But from that low state, everything changed. Diamonds were unearthed soon after; the best and purest cache in the world lay beneath the country's red and ochre soil. Many nations have rich resources and squander them; not so in Botswana. The government planned wisely and built a parliamentary democracy strong on merit and clean of corruption. With the diamond money the government built schools, roads, clinics, and wells across the dry nation.

Botswana soon was the star of Africa—with the highest growth rate in the world, 9.2 percent—between 1966 and 1996. Average life spans shot up over a similar period, from 46 to 67.5 years expectancy in 1999. School enrollment went up from about 40 percent of children to 98.4 percent. Literacy went up to over 80 percent, among men and women equally. Ninety-seven percent of the Botswana have safe drinking water within 2.5 kilometers of home. Child immunization for five diseases rose to up over 95 percent.

There were problems amid the prosperity, of course. The wealth was not evenly divided. Wealth is measured in cattle in Botswana, and a little over 2.5 percent of Botswana own 40 percent of the nation's cattle. Two-thirds of the women and one-third of the men have no cattle at all. In a country with no industry and very tough farming, that is serious. Even in the midst of prosperity, unemployment remained high—it's estimated to be 40 percent. Half the people still earn less than a dollar a day, though because land is communally held and essentially free for citizens, most everyone has a place to go to lay her head, even if it's only a hut on parched ground.

At first, it looked like the horseman of pestilence would pass Botswana by. The epidemic of AIDS flared up in the United States, then in the Caribbean, then Europe, and finally it became its most intense across a belt in the middle of Africa, from Kenya to Uganda and down to Zambia. Until about 1993, Botswana was spared.

Then the epidemic struck hard, like a silent storm sweeping down the eastern boundary of the nation, dropping an unwelcome viral rain. By 2000, Botswana found itself with almost 40 percent of its adult population infected with HIV, one of the highest rates of infection ever recorded for any disease. Some towns had even higher rates—up to 52 percent in one town that serves as a way station on the truck route from Zimbabwe.

This small, successful country thus became the worst spot in what is arguably the worst epidemic in human history. The people, led by President Festus Mogae, an Oxford-trained development economist and a former official of the World Bank, began to worry about the future of the nation. As Mogae himself said, this is the worst thing that had ever happened there, bar none.

Just as matters got to their worst, a plan emerged.

The bold project in Botswana started with an idea inside the executive offices at Merck & Co. in Whitehouse Station, New Jersey, in talks with experts at the Harvard AIDS Institute and Harvard University.

The plan was to tackle an entire nation at once. Too many AIDS projects were short or limited to one aspect of the problem, such as counseling for those infected, or providing condoms, or writing educational materials. Why not take one nation and try to provide a complete set of services, from education in schools to prevention messages in the media, to condom distribution, to testing for HIV, to counseling, to full AIDS treatment in hospitals and clinics? It would be most unusual particularly because it would offer sophisticated triple-drug AIDS treatments to all the people of the nation, free of charge, permanently. Could such a comprehensive effort turn back the epidemic? That was the bet.

Merck was at the top of the pharmaceutical industry, hugely profitable. But there was trouble ahead; the entire pharmaceutical industry was beginning a terrible slide in the eyes of the public.

The drugs beginning to come on the market in 1996 were the greatest breakthrough in AIDS treatment since the beginning of the epidemic. They were a new category of drugs called "protease inhibitors." These, combined with earlier drugs, made a potent antiviral "cocktail."

The excitement over the drugs was uncontainable. Even before they were released patients were clamoring for them. People who had three hundred thousand to a million virus particles per deciliter of their blood found that the drugs knocked those counts to zero. Some small numbers of viruses undoubtedly remained, but they could not be detected.

The physical consequences of it was dramatic. Lazarus stories began to be reported of patients who were within days or hours of death when they got the drugs. Two weeks later they were up and about, gaining weight and getting ready to go back to work. Over time, the miracle was confirmed. As many as 90 percent of those infected were able to knock out the virus and restart their lives; it is now estimated that the drugs can add ten, and possibly many more, healthy years onto the life of an infected person.

There were fifty-one thousand deaths from AIDS in the United States in 1995. After the drugs appeared in the United States the death rate dropped immediately and soon was down to fifteen thousand per year, and is still dropping in 2005. Doctors are cautious about pronouncements like this, but they began to say that near normal life spans might be ahead for many of those infected with HIV.

The industry had avoided getting into the business of researching and producing AIDS drugs. But when they did, the companies made a strategic blunder. They decided to set prices for AIDS drugs at extremely high levels, enough to produce gasps even in the business press.

These drugs were true lifesavers. But the companies set their prices between ten and fifteen thousand dollars per person for a year's supply. That did not take into account the other thousands of dollars needed for medicines and doctors by people infected with HIV, and it was a price that would have to be paid every year into the future.

Worse, when the companies were asked to send the drugs to Africa and Asia for cheaper prices, they flatly refused. They feared that if there were two prices their arguments that high prices were justified would be undermined. Soon, generic manufacturers were defying Western patents and making the drug cocktails for less than $150 for a year's supply *and still making a profit.* Thus it was clear just how inflated the Western drug company prices were.

The companies made further blunders, arguing that a good price wouldn't matter in Africa because those countries didn't have the infrastructure—doctors and clinics and refrigerators—to handle proper distribution of the drugs anyway, so high prices weren't important.

Famously, Andrew Natsios, the head of the U.S. Agency for International Development, testified in Congress that Africans shouldn't get the drugs.

> If we had [the drugs] today, we could not distribute them. We could not administer the program because we do not have the doctors, we do not have the roads, we do not have the cold chain. . . . If you have traveled to rural Africa you know this, this is not a criticism, just a different world. People do not know what watches and clocks are. They do not use western means for telling the time. They use the sun. These drugs have to be administered during a certain sequence of time during the day and when you say take it at 10:00, people will say, what do you mean by 10:00?

The argument was made that if the drugs were not taken properly, and doses were missed, then the virus could quickly become resistant. That could render them useless for all.

The reaction to all this was outrage. A Harris poll showed that the drug companies were popular and respected up until 1997, when their rating by the public was 79 percent favorable. By 2000, it had dropped to 59 percent, and did not stop there. By 2004 it had sunk to 44 percent favorable and 48 percent unfavorable. People were now saying the companies were greedy and drug prices were too high. No industry in the poll's history had ever fallen so far and so fast in the public esteem.

Roy Vagelos, by then former chairman of Merck, began to condemn the companies outright. "This industry delivered miracles, and now they're throwing it all away," he said. "They just don't get it." As if to reinforce Vagelos's comments, Pat Kelly, president of Pfizer's American drug division, said when told the drug companies were now esteemed as low as cigarette companies, "We find it incredible that we could be equated to an industry that kills people as opposed to cures them."

Poorer nations said that they could not afford the drugs, but they had real AIDS emergencies and they had no choice but to seize the formulas for the drugs and make cheap copies themselves to give to their people. Brazil and India started making and using emergency "generic" AIDS drugs. In South Africa the law allowed the government to force pharmaceutical companies to grant licenses for making the drugs during an emergency. The drug companies took the South African government to court to maintain control over the drugs and their prices; and the companies lost.

Merck officials were feeling the pinch of the criticism. This was particularly difficult for Merck, which had a reputation for charitable instincts, and its executives routinely quoted their founder's remarks about how health was first and profits second.

The company had just succeeded in a philanthropic venture that was the most remarkable in the history of the pharmaceutical industry. The company has a drug that is a very powerful antiparasite medicine; it was the top seller among veterinary drugs. Scientists inside the company knew that it would also be useful against parasites in humans, but unfortunately the humans infected with parasites were not in major markets. The patients who needed the drug couldn't pay the price, so Merck at first did not make a human version of it.

In the end, Merck decided to make the drug and donate it to the people who needed it. Further, they offered to create a delivery system. By the late 1990s 25 million people per year were getting the drug. Some areas, where half the people had in the past been infected with river blindness now saw essentially no cases. (River blindness is a parasitic disease passed by the bites of black flies: the flies thrive near rivers which are also the most fertile farmland, but which must be abandoned for higher ground when too many people go blind from the bites.) The gains turned out to be more than health. Farm output jumped up, as people were able to work more and in areas previously off-limits because of infestations of worm-carrying black flies.

Another Merck project done in combination with the Harvard AIDS Institute was the "enhancing care initiative," a project to understand how best to deliver AIDS care in developing countries. It soon became clear that piecemeal projects by universities, NGOs, and governments, with poor communication among the groups, would be ineffective in addressing the epidemic.

Gradually, Merck executives and Harvard public health doctors were learning that even if the price problem could be resolved, the harder issue would be finding ways of delivering the drugs. "Improving infrastructure was key to making a difference in HIV," said Guy Macdonald, then Merck vice president. "Just donating drugs is not enough." He said it was frustrating that the public debate was about unconscionable prices, when he knew that even if the prices drop to zero, the drugs still would not get to the people who need them.

Macdonald and other executives had become so isolated from mainstream opinion that they had lost sight of the main point—whether AIDS was a tough problem in other ways wasn't the issue. Setting high prices was an act that on its own was unconscionable.

In the middle of the public relations crisis over AIDS drug prices, in August 1999, Macdonald went to a Merck management committee saying that Merck should go beyond the previous "enhancing care" project and do something bolder on AIDS. The Gates Foundation surprised Merck by offering to put in $50 million if Merck would match it. So, the scale of the project was set at $100 million, to be spent over five years in some nation that needed an anti-HIV program.

The five countries that on paper appeared to be the best candidates were those in Africa hard-hit by HIV—Uganda, Malawi, Senegal, Rwanda, and Botswana. The country chosen had to have both an HIV problem and, far more important, a government willing to tackle it. That left out many countries immediately, most especially South Africa, where the government refused to build an AIDS treatment program and rejected Western drugs.

Botswana was the smallest and likely the most manageable spot for a project. What decided the matter finally was President Festus Mogae, who told Merck and Gates at their first meeting that the project should have started yesterday; a sense of urgency was needed.

Then CEO Ray Gilmartin and Vice President Guy Mcdonald made the announcement on July 10, 2000.

What began in Botswana in 2000 soon grew into the most important experiment on AIDS ever done. No one had tackled an entire nation before with a comprehensive program including the most sophisticated AIDS drugs, especially not in Africa. It became the largest and longest running public health project on the African continent.

It was also in a new and growing category of aid, called "public-private partnerships," in which international private groups become partners with governments to carry out large projects.

The plan raised startlingly clear questions: It was said the price of the drugs was killing tens of thousands—what if the drugs were free? It was said that even if the drugs were shipped to developing nations, they could not get them to patients because governments were ineffective. It was said that even if the drugs were offered on all street corners, people wouldn't take them because they did not even want to know if they were infected, and besides they didn't believe in Western treatments. This bold project would answer those questions and more.

⋅⊙⋅

Why Botswana? It seems strange that such a small, peaceful country should be the center of a firestorm, the nation to reach the highest level of infection anywhere on earth. People puzzled over it for a few years, from a dozen different perspectives.

It was an unusual conjunction of three dark stars over the time and the place—unusual happenings in love, in the virus itself, and in the movement of the people along the roads that made the difference.

First, one of the worst pieces of biological news in recent decades has been the finding that HIV changes routinely. Gene trading with other bugs, it has developed a new, more troublesome strain in southern Africa. The viral type that began the HIV epidemic in America, Africa, and Europe in the early 1980s was one that came to be called HIV-1b. The kinds most common in Central and East Africa have been HIV-1a and HIV-1d. Only a decade later did a new one, HIV-1c, spread in southern Africa. This one spreads and multiplies faster than any previous type. Upon genetic examination, it has been found to have at least two features that make it more dangerous than its predecessors. First, it has an ability to latch onto the surface of vaginal and penile skin cells more readily than other strains. Second, it multiplies more readily than other strains. More particles more able to attach to skin cells may make the C strain more adept at spreading.

At the peak of the epidemic in Uganda, 15 to 20 percent of pregnant women, who are the sentinel group, were infected at the peak of the epidemic in Uganda with A and D types. But in the countries infected with the C type the rates are double and triple that.

A second feature of the epidemic alighting in southern Africa is that the people in Botswana and neighboring areas are extremely mobile for people of a traditional culture. They move constantly, from farm to cattle post to city and back again, thus assuring that couples are constantly apart and vulnerable to second loves.

This mobility is at least partly a legacy of colonialism. When the British were making colonies all around Botswana, they needed labor. The solution was to impose a "hut tax" on the Tswana tribes, payable only in British money. People who would normally pay in cattle or goats were thus forced to get "paying" work. That paying work, of course, was not in their local villages. It was in the mines of South Africa, or on distant estates of white settlers. So the Botswana got use to husbands on the move and family members in general traveling to get work.

The impact of this high mobility is that there is no settled family life. Typically, mothers and fathers do not raise their children themselves; grandmothers and aunts raise the children. Young couples are often away from each other, and during these times they develop other relationships.

This leads to the most important reason why AIDS in southern Africa runs at a higher rate: It is fractured relationships. Not sex, but relationships.

Despite the mythology to the contrary, Africans are not more promiscuous than other people. As researchers have discovered in recent years, the term "promiscuity" has little meaning in the real world, as patterns of behavior are mixed everywhere.

Relationships and sex are different. To start with the sexual habits of two rather different groups—Americans and Botswana—it is clear that the Botswana are in general *not* more promiscuous. Studies show that the peoples with the greatest number of sexual partners are the Americans, French, and Germans, while Asians and Africans lag in both the number of partners and the frequency of sex. The Americans have more sexual partners than the Africans do, and their sexual adventures are more abrupt—more one-night stands and sudden runs of activity. The number of sex partners is not the essential problem in southern Africa. It is something more fundamental.

In traditional Africa the basic standard is, in fact, the standard of the Old Testament. Faithfulness is valued, but male authority is paramount. A man who is prosperous enough traditionally may have a mistress or a second wife, as in the Bible.

In Tswana tradition both man and woman have a responsibility to be faithful. It was assumed that men tended toward infidelity and wives were counseled in the marriage ceremony itself to accept their husband's straying. The old saying was "A man, like a bull, cannot be confined in a *kraal* [corral]." The modern version now heard in discussions of faithfulness uses the two local staples of the diet—cornmeal and rice—to make the metaphor: "A man cannot live on *pap* all his life, but must sometimes have rice."

The infidelities of men and women were not treated as equally serious in the old culture, but a man did have a duty to care for his wife, including faithfulness in most situations. He could be punished for affairs.

What has gotten lost in the mix of Western and African culture is the punishment for unfaithfulness for husbands. Families are now fractured in time and space, and tribal authority to rein in the behavior of men has dissipated.

The logic and cohesiveness of the culture has developed fissures. Now, this ancient version of "faithfulness" has become dangerous.

﹡⟨❂⟩﹡

Roads in Africa are the streams that carry HIV—where the roads go, the virus can follow. When HIV first began to move in Africa, it was the trans-African highway from Kenya, through Uganda, to the Congo that carried this live cargo. It was hauled in the cabs of the trucks, inside the bodies of the drivers. They made stops and deposited swarms of particles along the way, from whence the virus spread to cities and rural areas surrounding the truck routes. . . .

Unfaithfulness exists in all cultures, but there are several different patterns. In some places, such as the United States and Europe, multiple sex partners are common, but mostly the partnerships are serial—people don't usually go with more than one partner at a time. This is referred to as "serial monogamy." In Asia a somewhat similar pattern exists, but with an emphasis on flings. Dalliances with other partners occur, but partners return to their main squeeze after short affairs. In these situations, HIV can be passed easily, but not so quickly.

Unfortunately, add a dollop of faith*ful*ness to the mix, and you have the pattern of stable but overlapping relationships common in southern Africa. In Botswana, polygamy is outlawed and infidelity is frowned upon. But at the same time, the traditional marriage ceremony still carries this counseling for the bride: Wives are advised that for a happy marriage it is important not to ask a husband where he has been at night. Loyalty is more important, lest a woman create mistrust. The same advice is not passed on to the groom.

Thus, Africans are caught in transition between two African values— faithfulness and male authority.

What has been learned from this collision of values has meaning for those who want to stop the HIV epidemic. It suggests that from a purely practical point of view the two warring factions who emphasize abstinence and faithfulness or condoms and knowledge have both been right in some ways.

Faithfulness is vital. But also, condoms can be very effective. And in both cases, knowledge and testing are indispensable.

In the three successful cases of prevention documented around the world—in Senegal, Thailand, and Uganda—there were two key factors. People reduced the number of partners they had, and increased their condom use. There are fancier ways of saying these things: "Be faithful" and "change your behavior" emphasize a different approach to loving, while "condomize" and "safe sex" emphasize practical precautions.

﹡⟨❂⟩﹡

When the international team arrived to begin their challenge to AIDS in Botswana, they started with a plan that read precisely like something from a corporate office. What's needed? Computers, IT plans, counselors, doctors, trucks, refrigerators. How long it would take to bring them in? How long would the training take? How much it would cost?

It said that in Botswana, a nation of about 1.5 million people, something more than 300,000 adults were infected with HIV. They had calculated that not all were equally sick, but that about 110,000 of them were already in need of triple-drug treatment. The project would treat 19,000 the first year, and then ramp up to the full 110,000 over the next four years.

Some 108 new doctors, nurses, and pharmacists would be brought in. An array of new prefab clinic buildings would be put up. Training by experts would be provided for all the key people in Botswana's health system, from social workers to counselors and MDs. Condoms would be provided in the millions, both free and through discounted "social marketing" plans. Education would be brought in to the public schools from grade school to university. Market research, including focus groups and other polling methods, would be used to create the right messages and deliver them to the right citizens. The center of the system would be a computer network that would keep track of all patients, from the time they came forward for tests, all over the country on an instantaneous basis. That way, when a patient showed up at a clinic, his or her updated record would be in hand at any place.

The system was built to address the problems they expected to see: difficulty ensuring that patients took their medicines; effort needed to visit patients in their homes as well as waiting for them in the clinic; full counseling for the difficult problems of stigma; and effective public messages about HIV and the project itself.

The experts who worked in Botswana were completely unprepared for what they actually faced. If they had known, they probably would have first hired some experts on Botswana culture and begun with visits to tribal chiefs in the villages and bureaucrats in the city. They learned, of course, but it was a painful process with long, long delays.

While it was tough going, the project was something never really tried before, and it led the way in Africa. It did prove that critics were wrong about bringing sophisticated medicines to Africa; Africans take their medicine as well as or better than Westerners, and the drugs are just as effective as anywhere else, even considering that the patients coming in are sicker in Africa.

The obstacles were not the expected logistical difficulties—from watches to strict routines of medicine taking—but cultural, and the full array of expensive clinics, doctors, and nurses once thought to be essential could actually be a hindrance to delivering lifesaving treatment. The Botswana experiment lit up the path that other countries in Africa and Asia have now started following.

Donald de Korte, a Dutch doctor who had been Merck's managing director in South Africa for some years, was brought on to lead the grand experiment. He is a tall man, with sandy, gray-streaked hair and a ruddy complexion.

He became the director of what was named ACHAP, for the African Comprehensive HIV/AIDS Partnership. He is blunt, impatient with those not working to speed, but has a sense of humor about life and the difficulties ahead. . . .

De Korte was aware that the project was a risk, for Botswana, for Merck, and for himself personally because of the chance of failure. And after laying the ground for the plan for months, he had already encountered unexpected trouble.

De Korte found that there were widespread vacancies in Botswana's health staff—perhaps as many as 25 percent of the positions were unfilled. But the ministries that had failed to fill the jobs, the government now insisted, would also be in charge of recruiting the 108 new doctors, pharmacists, and nurses needed in the new program. De Korte asked to hire the 108 separately, fresh staff to work alongside current staff, rather than filling current holes in the system.

But as time went on, intransigence increased. The parallel staff was not only disapproved, but after de Korte had recruited dozens of doctors and nurses from other African countries, the usual process took over and destroyed recruitment.

The usual procedures—two interviews spaced months apart, approval by several ministries, finding funds from the treasury—would normally take a year and a half before a new hire could come to work. Needless to say, doctors in Africa, much in demand, cannot keep their lives and families on hold while waiting for consultations to be followed in careful order in Botswana. So in the second year of the program, more than forty prospective doctors had been recruited—and then were lost to the system because of delay.

It took two and a half years after the announcement of the program in Botswana to begin bringing doctors in. And when they arrived there were still disputes among government officials, and the doctors went for months without pay.

When it came to building a little prefabricated clinic on the grounds of the main hospital, Princess Marina in the capital, de Korte was told to allow the government to build it through the usual system. Eighteen months later nothing had been done, De Korte pleaded with the president himself, and was finally given power to build the clinic; it was up in less than three months.

The normal operation of the government was set by old cultural habits. The tribes had an unusually democratic way of governing themselves. They were led by chiefs, but all major decisions traditionally have been submitted to the whole population of the village. That meant meeting at the *kgotla*—a public space under a large tree where all villagers could assemble. At such meetings, which could last for days or weeks, each citizen was expected to speak his piece and debate the matter at hand. Then the chief would make a decision, usually based on what he felt the consensus was. This type of consultation before decisions is a conservative mechanism that has served the tribes well for eight hundred years, keeping them stable and peaceful.

The principle is one of consultation (*therisanyo* in Setswana, one language used in Botswana). The dignity of each person in society is maintained by recognizing his position, as shown by the gesture to get his consent when a matter is at issue.

Translated into modern government, that means that many officials have the right to be heard from, and to give or withhold support for the measure going forward. The effect is of a system that is careful to follow rules and works well to weed out corruption and renegade decision makers.

The doctor hired to lead the toughest challenge, building the drug treatment program for the nation, was Ernest Darkoh. His family is from Ghana, but he was raised in Kenya and Tanzania, and then went to school in the United States. He earned his MD from Harvard, but felt that ordinary medicine really didn't address the larger problems of the world, so he decided to study public health. After gaining his MPH, he realized that the big problems in health all have major parts that are about management and money. So he took an MBA from Oxford. Then, to get real world experience, he took a job with the McKinsey consulting firm, well known for its work in health systems.

Eventually, he was asked to take on the challenge of Botswana.

When he arrived one of his first encounters was with the board appointed by the government to oversee the big project. He jumped in enthusiastically, talking about rolling out plans.

But he found that the government-appointed board had not been authorized to make any decisions. It was a board built, in the midst of a raging epidemic, to discuss matters. He was told the board had no mandate yet, could not hire or fire or make any lasting decisions.

"The sole reason for creating the team was to be empowered and to make decisions," Darkoh said, but in fact what was created was another layer of bureaucracy even before the work started. "It was literally very scary," he said. "This was not the way to run a national emergency. From the beginning it was ten steps forward, twelve steps back. You have major victories, and then the next day you're ready to pack up and go."

A central problem was also encouraging people to get HIV tests. Under the elaborate system developed on the American model, testing involved multiple trips and permissions and counseling, raising great barriers to getting lifesaving drugs to the people. The solution proposed was to change the whole approach to testing, removing the elaborate counseling sessions and visits, and creating rather a routine medical procedure done whenever a patient shows up at the hospital. Patients had the right to refuse, but if they didn't object, they would get HIV tests.

Darkoh said that the policy was controversial because it went against policies established over years in the West built to guarantee consent and confidentiality. It was built in the years when disclosure of infection would bring down stigma, alienation, and potential job loss. Because there had been no good treatments, and the government had not offered care to the sick, it had been clear that forced testing could have led to harm, and would have done little good for the infected.

But by the time the epidemic had swept Botswana, the situation had changed greatly. The stigma was still present, but the government was offering lifesaving drugs and full care, at no cost. And with more than a third of the whole nation infected, it was a vital state interest to find out who was infected and to try to treat them and counsel them not to spread the disease further. It was President Mogae who broke the jam over testing, and he pressed through the new "routine testing" policy.

Two years into the project the infrastructure was still being built, and the 19,000 patients treated in the first year turned out to be much less—3,200 after eighteen months, and most of that was done by a handful of doctors working absurd hours because manpower recruitment was still caught in the hands of multiple, slow decision makers.

By 2003, de Korte was frustrated and under great stress. He had become a customer for pharmaceuticals himself: He started on Prozac. Darkoh had been ready to resign more than once.

Eventually the friction got to be too much. The board relieved de Korte of command in the fall of 2003, in hopes that the conflicts had to do with de Korte's tough personality and demands for performance. Few of those watching thought much would have been done at all without de Korte's pressure. But to prevent a complete and public breakdown of the project, Merck and Gates took the prudent step of bringing in a manager from within Botswana, Tsetsele Fantan, who had been the manager of the HIV program at the nation's largest mine, was appointed director of the Merck-Gates project.

⋅⊙⋅

Harriet would have appeared stately if she were able to stand to her full height, but she was still a little weak. She has been on the new drugs only a short time. Less than four weeks before, she was on a pallet in a dark room at the back of her mother's house. She could not walk.

Most healthy people have immune system cell counts of about 1,000; hers were down to 35 and diving to zero. By contrast, her blood was swarming with more than 300,000 HIV particles per deciliter of blood, and that count was rising. Her medical counts, in any clinic around the world at the time, were the numbers of death.

She was ready for it. She said she could do nothing more for her children. She had stopped weeping over her youngest daughter who had HIV, as she didn't have even the moisture in her eyes to make tears.

But one afternoon a friend who worked at the hospital came by to get her. She brooked no arguments, but simply lifted Harriet up and with some help carried her to a car, and then into the hospital. She was given a round of tests, though she was semiconscious and barely cared.

Within weeks she regained her appetite both for food and life. She started to walk again. Reporters in the capital of Botswana were keeping count, and they said that Harriet was the fifth person in the entire nation to openly admit being infected.

On the other side of the coin was a schoolteacher from a village south of the capital who asked that reporters not use his name. He understood about the disease and how it was passed. He knew in looking over his last few years that he had taken risks with girlfriends. He suspected he might well have the virus. But when he faced the terrible moment of going to get tested he realized with crystal clarity what it was all about.

He knew that he would likely walk into the testing center as one person, relatively healthy and well liked, a young man with friends, a good job, and a family, and walk out of the center as a ghost, a man whose friends did not want to touch him, whose neighbors would turn away in the street. His job would be in danger. It was as if he were being asked to end his life as a human and become a monster, some kind of shamed creature, all voluntarily. Death didn't seem so serious a consequence compared to a life of being humiliated daily.

After many attempts and great pressure from his wife, he finally did get tested. But now that he knows he has the virus, he still keeps it a secret from his friends and the school where he works.

⋅⟨◉⟩⋅

Botswana has no medical school, so all the Botswana who are doctors must go abroad for training. Not all come back, and among those who do, few ever went to work for the government. The pay is low and there has been little effort to recruit them. It is a significant loss for the country.

Ndwapi Ndwapi, born in a village in northern Botswana and schooled in the capital, spent ten years being trained in medicine in the United States. When he came back his training was perfect—infectious diseases—for him to be grabbed up by his nation's emergency AIDS program.

He is a tall young man with round cheeks and a small mustache. His gaze is intense. When he speaks he sounds like a man in the trenches, under constant fire. He is now head of the largest HIV clinic in Botswana, in the hospital in the capital. He had to fight his own government to get there.

When he arrived back from his training in the United States, he says, "They were very glad to see me" at the ministry of health. But they took some months before giving him an assignment; they wanted him to take his place at the bottom of the ladder in Botswana—a posting in a low-ranking job two hundred miles from the capital at a salary of about $2,500 per year. He could have earned about $120,000 to start in the United States and could have moved quickly into his specialty; accounting for cost of living differences, a $30,000 salary would be expected in Botswana.

"It's completely nuts," he says, "and it's symptomatic of the system."

Having left and come back, he can see Botswana in the light of other ways of doing things. So his first response to his treatment when he returned was anger and frustration. He was in some ways in the same position as the outsiders from ACHAP who were fighting to make things happen on an emergency basis. He had to battle for his job in an AIDS program even though it was desperately short of doctors, especially doctors who understood Botswana culture and language.

He says, frustrated as he was, that he understood where the slowness came from. Now that he was back he felt it was his duty to help change the dysfunctional things about the slow system in Botswana.

It is a cultural inheritance with a distinguished past now caught in an emergency that makes it break down.

In emergencies, it fails, says Ndwapi. "The money's there, the will is there, the know-how is there, but somehow, you can't hire the people you want to hire.

We know for a fact that there are doctors throughout Africa and other places in the world that would love to do this job. And yet, somehow, it just doesn't happen," he says.

To protest, to fight the dignified system of respect and consultation is considered shameful, putting your personal interests above the good of the group. But Ndwapi began to argue loudly for quick decision making, and for bypassing some usual procedures. "I was more than willing, and I still am more than willing, to take responsibility for whatever happens," he says, "for whatever comes down on my head."

"If I make decisions on my own sometimes, I can sleep at night because I know that the alternative is a hundred times worse than anything I can do. The alternative is doing nothing."

As we sat in a tiny cubicle at the Princess Marina Hospital, near a long corridor lined on both sides by patients who have been waiting for several hours, he says that the war on HIV must come down to this, in some ways, everywhere: fighting to make a system not set up to handle health emergencies take them on aggressively.

He mentions the prefab clinic that had been the subject of fights between ACHAP and the government. It was finally built, he says, "but you know it's not being used yet."

"Why?"

"Because there are no phones. Because there is no paper. In Botswana, we run out of paper." There is money to buy paper, but it doesn't get bought and delivered. The supply office refers to the ministry that controls procurement, and that ministry refers to another ministry, which says it has not sent supply money because it's been asked to close its books to end the fiscal period by another ministry. When you get to the ministry of finance, they say the folks are wrong, they are still supposed to be buying paper.

"You see what I mean?"

But on a day in May 2003, the prefab clinic does, finally, open for business. Gradually, changes happen. Slowly, new ways of doing things are installed.

Ndwapi is a man struggling to push his culture forward much faster than it wants to go. In the face of years of success that suggests the culture has done well, he must argue that it is now stumbling. It is a struggle not just for the lives of those in the hallway, but for the future of the country, and for a way nations can work together.

It's tough, there are fights and suspicions, but it is the best way to do it, Ndwapi says. "The best way is to bring in an organization like ACHAP. Charge it with the responsibility of doing this, okay? And just give them the mission of setting it up and then integrating it into this nation." They must start it, hire and train local people, and then turn it over, he says. "Any time in the past two years we got anything significant done, it was because ACHAP has been involved. They took charge."

By 2004, the original leader, Donald de Korte was gone, and Darkoh and Ndwapi were beleaguered, but the fights had begun to pay off. All of the clinics envisioned in the original plan were finally up and running, albeit three years late. After the decision to make testing easier, those infected began coming forward in larger and larger numbers.

"We're going to take off," Ndwapi says. "This is beginning to work. You know, this is a country that is good with the big things. The little things on the ground are not so good, but the big things, knowing which way to go, we get those right."

The program did take off, finally. The number of people who were tested, enrolled in regular AIDS care, and getting the HIV drugs rose from 3,000 in early 2003, to 20,000 in mid 2004, to 43,000 by early 2005, and it is still rising.

The project has now surpassed all other African and Asian countries in its delivery of HIV care and drugs. Following Botswana's lead, twelve other African nations have now started bringing drug treatment to their HIV-infected citizens, and this time in Africa has been dubbed "the decade of treatment" for Africa, when the world's drugs and expertise finally began to turn to those who need them most.

A United Nations project called "3 by 5," has begun working toward the goal of treating three million people in the poor countries with top-end AIDS drugs by the end of 2005. The goal will not be met, but the pressure is on, and it is estimated that one million or more HIV-infected people in poor countries will be under treatment by that date.

Ernest Darkoh, after three years before the mast in Botswana, now says that there are strong lessons for others to follow when delivering AIDS drugs to poor countries. First, don't expect to see results quickly; development is not linear, it takes time to build up and learn what the real problems are before it takes off. Second, though it is natural to think of bringing on a treatment program slowly, beginning with central clinics in the capital, it is a mistake. The sickest patients come forward first, and because they need ten times more help than others, they overwhelm the system. There is also little to be gained from a slow scale-up—the problems at each new village clinic are the same as the previous ones, and must be learned anew at each place. So, he says, go for it. Scale up quickly, go to the rural areas nearest the patients' homes all at once. Then, bring in experts to work in each place for six months to train those who will have to take over.

Another lesson: Make testing as easy as possible, because you need to get to patients before they are at their sickest, and they can be better treated and returned to work the earlier they come in.

The final message is that "patients will spend ninety-nine percent of their lives in their communities, not at a hospital or a health facility." Therefore, it is possibly wasteful and dangerous to emphasize the building of a "brick-and-mortar health care infrastructure." In fact, drugs can be delivered from the back of a truck if need be. But the vital job is to track the patients and their conditions.

"Therefore," says Darkoh, "for any new program, the highest priority and the bulk of the initial effort should go toward establishing a robust and reliable patient-tracking, monitoring, and evaluation system," with or without walls.

Along the way, the data from Botswana have proved skeptics wrong—Africans actually take their medicines much better than Westerners. On average, Africans take 90 percent of all their pills, compared to Americans, who take about 70 percent of their prescribed dose. In addition, in testing verbal reports, researchers found that Africans are more truthful when telling how many pills they missed compared to Americans. The Africans overestimate by 3 percent, whereas Americans overestimate their compliancy by 20 percent.

The cost of treating the Botswana, even though it was the first program and emphasized the need for high-level training and fully qualified doctors and nurses, cost about one-tenth or less than treatment in the United States. In Botswana treatment cost has so far ranged from $580 to $1,580 per person for a year. The cost is expected to drop considerably in coming years. . . .

From Botswana and from each of the other successes I have described, there are fundamentals to be learned about the new "smart aid" approach.

First, in each case, there was strong leadership present—Fazle Abed and his coworkers at BRAC in Bangladesh, Ram Shrestha and his colleagues in Nepal, David Heymann and the polio team in India and elsewhere, and the combination of President Festus Mogae and the team at the African Comprehensive HIV/AIDS Partnership in Botswana. This does not exhaust the list of leaders on these projects, for good leaders tend to attract others who are effective. In each of these stories, one of the key issues leaders emphasize is a commitment to get results no matter what the obstacles or number of years it takes. These leaders believe there is simply nothing more important for their nations than to deliver on this work. There can be no higher ambition than to make them succeed even if the work is hard and requires many tries to get each part of the project right. Blunders were made in each case, as I hope I have spelled out.

A further feature in common is that in three cases, the work was accomplished with inexpensive medicine and local volunteers. The fourth case, Botswana, used medicine that is not so cheap but still is a bargain relative to its cost in the developed nations. In each case, there is a high health impact for the money spent.

One thing that is vital is that scientific research was used effectively, coupled with good management, in each instance. None of these results would have been possible without scientific experiments showing what was effective, because people in the past have often made reasonable but quite incorrect guesses about what works in health. Scientific backup is indispensable.

Some of this is not obvious. We thought we knew a great deal about vitamin A, how the body uses it, what its chemistry is, and so forth. When scientists did the research, they discovered that we knew nothing about the single most vital fact about this body chemical. In Bangladesh, Fazle Abed, after three decades of work in the villages, has found that no matter how well he thought he knew the culture and how to get people organized, he didn't really know until he tried. In that regard, development is like science—it requires actual experimentation, data collection, and analysis to get things done, even when it's assumed things work a specific way. A good case in point is the topic of maternal mortality and infant mortality during the day of birth; in Western countries we think we know what's important for health at birth. But we have been wrong. We are just now discovering how to deliver babies with high success rates. For example, we know that germs can cause infection for both mother and baby at birth, but our Western solution has been a kind of blanket hygiene of the entire birth environment. However, in most places that is not possible. So now we must find out what the important parts of hygiene at birth are. Is it clean hands for the birth attendant? In many countries, probably not, because the midwives do not examine and handle mothers and babies in the intrusive way we do in most developed nations; the chances of infection are smaller from that route. But it turns out that how and when the cord is cut might be vital. Or putting the baby to the mother's breast immediately—not common in medical settings—may save many infants from dying due to lack of warmth or early nutrition. In new settings, we need new science.

The good management part of any project should go without saying, as successful work in any field requires it. In delivering aid it is important to keep in mind that culture is critical, and so local workers and a sense of local values must be present.

Another point worth making is that each project went forward with explicit plans to build up local infrastructure and systems for the long haul. Good programs don't come and go; they come and stay. This is one reason why they are so cost-effective.

The best practitioners say the essence of successful development is a humility before challenging work and a commitment to learn what is the right thing to do—not in general, but in this intervention, in this week or month. The other important factors—science, monitoring, management, cautious spending—all follow from this.

POSTSCRIPT

Is the International Community Focusing on HIV/AIDS Treatment at the Expense of Prevention in Africa?

There are a number of interesting points that arise from these selections. First, one of early concerns about widespread HIV/AIDS treatment programs in Africa was related to the belief that African patients would not take their medicine regularly, or that limited health infrastructure would lead to lax surveillance of patients. Siddhartha Mukherjee, for example, made this argument in a 2000 article in *The New Republic* entitled "Take Your Medicine." As the Hilts study of the Botswana case showed, Africans took 90 percent of all their pills as compared to 70 percent for Americans.

Second, the problems of AIDS orphans and mother-to-child transmission clearly seem relevant to this debate as well. Sub-Saharan Africa has the largest population of AIDS orphans in the world, that is, children for whom both parents have died of AIDS. Clearly, drugs that prolong the life of a parent also enhance the life of a child. Drugs taken shortly before the birth of a child by an HIV-infected mother greatly reduce the chances of transmission. For more on the issue of mother-to-child transmission, see a 2001 World Health Organization technical consultation entitled "New Data on the Prevention of Mother-to-Child Transmission of HIV and Their Policy Implications." A good book on the AIDS orphan problem in Uganda, Zambia, and South Africa is Emma Guest's *Children of AIDS: Africa's Orphan Crisis* (Pluto Press, 2001).

Finally, it is sobering to think that hundreds of HIV/AIDS cases could be prevented for the cost of treating one person with the disease (even as the cost of treatment falls). This is a terrible choice for a government to have to make, and ideally government budgets would be large enough to do both. Many African government health department budgets were reduced drastically in the 1980s and 1990s as the result of IMF and World Bank imposed structural adjustment policies. Debt service payments (with several African countries ranking amongst the most indebted in the world) also reduce the amount of current spending on social services. In the face of such a horrendous epidemic, some have argued for debt forgiveness if it is tied to increases in public health spending (see, e.g., a 2005 United Nations University Research Paper #2005/9, by Addison, Mavrotas, and McGillivray, entitled "Aid, Debt Relief and New Sources of Finance for Meeting the Millennium Development Goals"). For additional general information on the HIV/AIDS issue see, UNAIDS' "2007 AIDS Epidemic Update" (http://data.unaids.org/pub/EPISlides/2007/2007_epiupdate_en.pdf).

ISSUE 15

Should Developed Countries Provide Debt Relief to the Poorest, Indebted African Nations?

YES: Dorothy Logie and Michael Rowson, from "Poverty and Health: Debt Relief Could Help Achieve Human Rights Objectives," *Health and Human Rights* (1998)

NO: Robert Snyder, from "Proclaiming Jubilee—for Whom?" *The Christian Century* (June 1999)

ISSUE SUMMARY

YES: Dorothy Logie, a general practitioner and active member of Medact, and Michael Rowson, assistant director of Medact, argue that debt is a human rights issue because debt and related structural adjustment policies reduce the state's ability to address discrimination, vulnerability, and inequality. Debt relief, if channeled in the right direction, could help reduce poverty and promote health.

NO: Robert Snyder, faculty in the department of biology at the College of the Ozarks, argues that debt cancellation will only work if the factors that created debt in the first place are addressed. He uses a case study of Rwanda to demonstrate why political and social change must occur for debt forgiveness to work.

$\mathbf{A}$s Logie and Rowson note in their article, 34 of the 41 most indebted nations in the world are found in Africa. Furthermore, these same authors note that 23 percent of new aid receipts in Africa are spent on debt repayment. Responsibility for the debt crisis in Africa is complex and fairly difficult to attribute to any single group of individuals or entity. Resolution of this problem is hugely controversial, and it has been a matter of intense debate over the past several years.

Debt has accumulated to African governments for a number of reasons. First, many African governments pursued a policy known as import substitution in the 1960s and 1970s. Rather than importing manufactured and processed goods from abroad, the idea was that African governments should foster like enterprises within their own national borders to produce goods that would "substitute" for imports. This approach, conceptualized by the Latin American economist Raul Prebisch, was designed as an antidote to the perpetual quandary of developing countries trading inexpensive commodities for expensive manufactured goods (see a discussion of this in the Postscript to Issue 1). The problem was that these state-run enterprises were often relatively uncompetitive at best (i.e., they produced goods at a cost higher than the imported competition) or a serious drain on state resources at worst (especially if they were used as sources of patronage by the ruling elite). As a consequence, the privatization of inefficient state-run enterprises was an important aim of the structural adjustment policies discussed in Issue 3.

Second, even though many African economies grew rapidly in the 1960s and early 1970s, this growth began to temper significantly in the late 1970s and 1980s. Part of this slowdown in growth has been attributed to a global rise in petroleum prices at the time—a problem for the majority of African nations, which were (and are) petroleum importers. Even after African economies began to slow down, commercial banks and public lenders often lent to African governments based on previous levels of growth—contributing to unhealthy levels of indebtedness. Third, the loan officers at commercial banks, and even at multilateral institutions like the World Bank, were (and are) often under a certain amount of pressure to make loans. This meant that creditors encouraged African governments, in some instances, to obtain loans they really should not have been taking. Finally, some African government officials inappropriately used borrowed monies, making it difficult to pay these back in a timely fashion.

The current high level of indebtedness in many African countries has led NGOs, think tanks, and religious organizations to call for debt forgiveness. Others have warned about the dangerous messages that debt forgiveness will send to future borrowers. In this issue, Dorothy Logie, a general practitioner and active member of Medact (an organization of health professionals challenging barriers to health), and Michael Rowson, assistant director of Medact, argue that debt is a human rights issue because debt, and related structural adjustment policies, reduce the state's ability to address discrimination, vulnerability, and inequality. Debt relief, if channeled in the right direction, could help reduce poverty and promote health. In contrast, Robert Snyder, an associate professor of biology at Greenville College, argues that debt cancellation only will work if the factors that created debt in the first place are addressed. He uses a case study of Rwanda to demonstrate why political and social change must occur for debt forgiveness to work.

YES

**Dorothy Logie and
Michael Rowson**

Poverty and Health: Debt Relief Could Help Achieve Human Rights Objectives

UDHR [Universal Declaration of Human Rights] Article 25

1. Everyone has the right to a standard of living adequate for the health and well-being of himself and of his family, including food, clothing, housing and medical care and necessary social services, and the right to security in the event of unemployment, sickness, disability, widowhood, old age or other lack of livelihood in circumstances beyond his control.

2. Motherhood and childhood are entitled to special care and assistance. All children, whether born in or out of wedlock, shall enjoy the same social protection.

. . . [O]n the fiftieth anniversary of the UDHR [Universal Declaration of Human Rights], human rights activists still confront the bitter reality of widespread hunger, disease and discrimination in the context of a global economy characterized by widening inequality and poverty. Although the preamble to the UDHR reaffirms the worth of each individual person and the equal rights of men and women to progress towards a better standard of living, and although the idea of freedom from poverty has been in human rights law and discourse since the adoption of the UDHR, poverty-related issues have not been given priority in the human rights agenda. This anniversary represents both an opportunity to push poverty to the front of that agenda, and to promote action that might enable its reduction.

Poverty and Ill-Health

Poverty, in both its absolute and relative forms, is the single most important driver of ill-health in the world today. This is hardly surprising. In developing countries, the pathways by which low levels of economic and social well-being affect health are easily found and are the daily reality of hundreds of millions. These pathways include: lack of access to safe water (experienced by 1.2 billion people); lack of adequate sanitation; poor housing; low income (at least 1.3 billion people live on under $US1 per day), and lack of access to health

From *Health and Human Rights*, vol. 3, no. 2, 1998, pp. 82–97. Copyright © 1998 by Francois-Xavier Bagnoud Center for Health and Human Rights. Reprinted by permission.

services (faced by 800 million people). Discrimination against women, the elderly, ethnic minorities, refugees, the disabled and other marginalized groups both causes and magnifies these problems. Many other factors, such as conflict and adverse climate changes, for example, can also contribute to poverty and ill-health. Another contributor can be the skewed spending priorities of governments which may have high levels of military expenditure or may devote most of their health budgets to secondary health care for urban citizens, at the expense of primary and preventative health services.

Human Rights Response

Faced by such diverse causes of poverty and ill-health, human rights activists obviously need to work at international, national and community levels, and both within and outside the health sector, to make their anti-poverty agenda effective and credible. . . . Here we will focus our attention at the level of the international economy.

The anniversary of the UDHR is taking place in the midst of a widespread economic crisis, which threatens to lead to a global recession. . . . For many countries, a new recession may be only the latest stage in a downward economic record—since 1980, 100 countries have experienced economic decline or stagnation, and 1.6 billion people have seen their incomes reduced. This decline has been most obvious in sub-Saharan Africa. . . .

Debt and Economic Adjustment

Today a large burden of foreign debt is carried by over 40 of the world's poorest countries. This potentially has multiple effects on their economies and acts as a significant constraint to improvements in international health. First, it undermines prospects for economic growth (and thus poverty reduction) by discouraging public and private investment; private investors, in particular, fear the higher taxes, higher inflation and currency speculation that an unsustainable debt burden can bring. Second, debt repayments siphon away precious foreign exchange needed to buy the imports essential for economic growth and the maintenance of health systems. Third, debt repayments divert money from government budgets which could be used for health, education and poverty reduction initiatives. And fourth, they use up sources of foreign exchange (other than export revenues) such as grants and loans from government and multilateral donors. For poor countries, the accumulation of a large foreign debt can thus be the prelude to a catalogue of economic disasters.

The Scale of Sub-Saharan African Debt

> Many states in Africa lack the financial capital needed to address basic expectations and fundamental needs. This is one of the central crises in Africa today, and one that is due in large measure to the problem of African public sector debt.[1]

In the early 1980s, the developing world as a whole faced foreign debts of around US$800 billion—the results of a decade of irresponsible actions on the part of both creditors and borrowers. Today, total debt stands at over two trillion US dollars, despite large repayments in the intervening years. Sub-Saharan Africa, containing 34 of the 41 most heavily indebted poor countries, is worst affected. Taken together, its US$230 billion debt is small compared to debt in other parts of the world, but compared to its earnings from exports or its total GDP [gross domestic product], the debt represents an overwhelming burden. More money is spent on interest payments than on health and education, and many countries are unable to afford even the most basic annual health package, estimated by the World Bank to cost around US$12 per capita. In Uganda, with one of the highest infant and maternal morality rates (and an AIDS epidemic), the government spends annually only US$2.50 per capita on health. Several other heavily-indebted countries are spending equally small amounts on health, leading to an increasing reliance on cost-recovery mechanisms (such as user charges) to cover the widening gap between health needs and budgetary capacity.

Many countries in the region are literally bankrupt, and are in the process of building up huge arrears of debts that can never be repaid. What repayment they do manage is financed by revenues from exports and other money from the domestic budget, new loans (thus incurring further debts), and grants from aid donors. It is sobering to note that in 1996, twenty-three percent of all aid given to sub-Saharan Africa was spent on debt repayments to financial institutions and governments in the North.

Structural Adjustment Policies

In return for either delaying debt repayments or lending more money, international donors such as the World Bank and IMF [International Monetary Fund] have demanded that countries undertake policy reforms, known as structural adjustment programs, aimed at reducing domestic demand by raising interest rates, devaluing currencies and reducing public expenditure. They also recommend that the state's role in public life be reduced by, for example, eliminating subsidies for food and fertilizers, relaxing foreign investment regulations, privatizing state-run industries and services, and cutting government bureaucracy (including in the health sector). . . .

Economic Crisis, Adjustment and Vulnerable Groups

Article 25 of the UDHR specifically points to mothers and children as social groups needing special attention. Today we might extend this concern to other vulnerable groups such as women, the disabled and people living with HIV/AIDS. These groups are at greater risk of suffering during economic crises for a range of reasons, most notably related to discrimination. Debt and inappropriate economic adjustment can reduce the state's capacity to intervene to correct discrimination, vulnerability and inequality, thus putting these groups at even greater disadvantage in difficult times. . . .

Due in part to the lack of funds which can result from the constraints debt and adjustment impose on social sector spending, international and national plans for improving the health of women and children remain to be fully carried out. For example, 40 African countries have prepared National Plans of Action in response to the global Plan of Action emanating from the 1990 World Summit for Children which incorporated priority health goals for children and for women. These plans include raising immunization rates, improving oral hydration, eliminating iodine and Vitamin A deficiencies and encouraging breastfeeding. But implementation has been slow or nonexistent due to lack of both money and political will.

. . . Africa is the only part of the world in which the number of children out of school is increasing. In Niger, for example, fewer than one-quarter of children attend primary school, and less than 20 percent of these are girls. Where it exists, school often means a mud hut with a leaking roof, classes of 40 or more students and a chronic lack of teaching materials. In Zambia, expenditure on primary schools is now at less than half its mid-1980s level. This is a denial of the right to education as stated in Article 26 of the UDHR and also of Article 15 of the Convention on the Rights of the Child (which has been ratified by all of the governments of Africa except Somalia).

Reproductive Health

Article 25 throws the spotlight on motherhood as a condition during which women require "special care." However, in what has been described as "the health scandal of our time," 585,000 women still die each year from pregnancy-related causes and many times that number are incapacitated as a result of child-bearing. In parts of sub-Saharan Africa maternal mortality is still rising and, a decade after the introduction of the 1987 Safe Motherhood Initiative, its implementation remains frustrated not only by lack of funds and political will but also by continuing discrimination against women.

. . . Low levels of spending on health can result in inadequate medical and physical infrastructure, maternal malnutrition, user charges, poor-quality staff training and motivation, unreliable blood supplies and lack of drugs. . . .

HIV/AIDS

AIDS has become a marker for injustice, discrimination and lack of realization of human rights. The virus thrives on poverty, social disruption, ignorance and accelerated urbanization: its spread is encouraged by lack of resources, lack of clean water, commercial sex, and rapidly declining health services. Each of these factors is potentially exacerbated when adjustment policies lead to budget cuts, unemployment, and migration. . . .

Using Debt Relief to Promote Gains in Health

After a decade of vociferous pressure from NGOs [nongovernmental organizations] and others, both creditor governments and the international financial institutions have moved to a point where they have agreed to put a mechanism into place (the Highly Indebted Poor Countries Initiative) which will cancel some low-income country debts. It is believed that by relieving a proportion of foreign debt, economic growth will be encouraged and, if the relief is deep enough, this should free resources that governments could then use to tackle some of the enormous health problems outlined above. However, the process is slow, the relief is offered to too few countries and, even where provided, the relief is often not extensive enough to make a significant impact on human development problems. Oxfam has put forward a scheme which would require countries, in return for faster and deeper debt cancellation, to use the gains from debt relief to implement national development priorities agreed to by governments, civil society, and donors. They have also shown that for some highly-indebted poor countries, debt cancellation could provide a significant portion of the external finance needed to implement the National Plans of Action agreed to after the World Summit for Children.

In the long-term, debt relief could reduce the need for countries to undertake economic adjustment—with its technical-fix approach to health as a commodity and the resulting emphasis on introducing user charges, competition, and other market mechanisms into the delivery of health care. Countries could then be free to reorient their vision of health towards universal primary health care (as contained in the Alma Ata Declaration) and to emphasize a preventative public health agenda.

The Problem of Conditionality

. . . [H]uman rights activists and health professionals might link up to ensure that debt relief does help to reduce poverty and promote health, and that it does so in a fair way. For example they might:

- work to ensure that the debt relief process is open and accountable and not dominated by the interests and agendas of creditors, but also includes the concerns of governments and civil society representatives;
- help to highlight and build upon schemes proposed by developing countries themselves—schemes that use debt relief to achieve human rights objectives. In fact, several poor countries (such as Uganda) already have human-development-oriented schemes waiting in the wings to be financed by the proceeds from debt relief;
- make sure that debt relief is not conditional on health or economic system reforms that are potentially harmful to health outcomes; and
- press for governments that have ratified human rights instruments (such as the Convention on the Rights of the Child) and the World Bank and IMF (which are components of the UN system) to modify their policies in accordance with these international obligations.

Conclusions

Debt relief is not a solution on its own, but if channeled in the right direction, and with the active involvement of civil society, it can achieve progress in reaching human development targets. There is a responsibility, and a legal obligation, for governments and international financial institutions to address the determinants of health (including income, education, safe water and food, and all human rights) in order to achieve lasting health improvement.

Human rights activists and health professionals should work toward addressing these issues by pressing for swift and generous debt relief. . . .

The fiftieth anniversary of the UDHR is a time to call again for poverty reduction and health equality to be at the center of development strategies. In the meantime, the UDHR remains a living document, a standard by which we can measure the world's imperfections and work towards righting wrongs—past, present and future. The more people—health professionals, nongovernmental organizations and activists—understand what human rights instruments have to say about poverty and health, the more these instruments can be used to lever change.

Note

1. K. Annan, from the "Report to the Security Council on the Causes of Conflict and the Promotion of Durable Peace and Sustainable Development in Africa," April 1998, quoted in Oxfam's submission to the UN Committee on the Rights of the Child, *Violating the Rights of the Child: Debt and Poverty in Africa* (Oxford: Oxfam, May 1998).

Robert Snyder

Proclaiming Jubilee—for Whom?

Jubilee 2000 is gaining momentum. Centers for the movement have arisen in more than 40 countries, and numerous churches and nongovernmental organizations have signed on to the campaign. The goals of this movement, which seems to have originated with the All Africa Conference of Churches and is now centered in the United Kingdom, are best summed up in the apostolic letter issued by Pope John Paul II in 1994. It states: "In the spirit of the Book of Leviticus (25:8-12), Christians will have to raise their voice on behalf of all the poor of the world, proposing the Jubilee as an appropriate time to give thought, among other things, to reducing substantially, if not canceling outright, the international debt which seriously threatens the future of many nations." . . .

The idea is appealing. After all, there is no such thing as an international bankruptcy court which allows hopelessly indebted countries to declare themselves insolvent. Countries that have no hope of ever paying off their debt languish in a state of perpetual penury. The people of these countries barely eke out a living, while the banks owned by the wealthy prosper.

The world's financial institutions have recognized that something needs to be done to change this situation. The International Monetary Fund (IMF) recently started the Heavily Indebted Poor Country (HIPC) initiative, which singles out countries undergoing extreme financial stress. On the list are many African nations, including Rwanda, Burundi, Kenya and the Democratic Republic of Congo. Each country must pass a second screening to be eligible to receive some debt relief.

The Jubilee 2000 people claim that the relief proposed by the IMF is not enough. It does indeed seem to fall far short of what is needed. However, the concept proposed by Jubilee 2000 is riddled with pitfalls; to apply it universally would be naïve.

The economies of the heavily indebted countries would clearly benefit from debt relief. In countries with benevolent governments, the citizenry on the whole would gain. However, the socioeconomic structure of some of the heavily indebted nations is such that, in the long term, debt relief might only aggravate the condition of the poor.

As a former agricultural missionary in east and central Africa, I've learned that quick fixes can sometimes become excuses for not dealing with the more painful fundamentals of international and national problems. A poorly

From *The Christian Century*, June 30–July 7, 1999. Copyright © 1999 by Christian Century. Reprinted by permission. Subscriptions: $49/year from PO Box 378, Mt. Morris, IL 61054. 1-800-208-4097.

executed act of sympathy can exacerbate the problem that it is meant to solve. Consider Rwanda.

Until 1994 Rwanda was under the rule of President Juvénal Habyarimana. Generally, Westerners liked him. From the perspective of international agencies, he was at worst a benevolent dictator, at best a progressive peacemaker promoting development. Compared to many African countries, Rwanda experienced a time of stability and growth during Habyarimana's rule. We now realize, however, that he was a cunning power broker and, to a certain degree, a racist. He made sure that the benefits of international aid projects accrued mainly either to his extended family or to the northwestern region of Rwanda from which he came.

The people of Rwanda's southern half were well aware of this inequity. All Rwandans had to carry identity cards that showed their ethnicity. If you were Tutsi, you faced discrimination whether you were from the north or the south. Though 10 to 15 percent of the population was Tutsi, no Tutsi was allowed to hold a leadership position in government or the military. A small group of Tutsi ran profitable business enterprises, but they were well aware that the price for the freedom to carry on business was not to interfere with or criticize Habyarimana's dictatorial hold. Rwanda's leaders drained the economy into their own bank accounts, while making sure that no opponent could get enough political strength to challenge the status quo. Habyarimana manicured his image for Western donors, and aid dollars poured in. The government and the army put on a friendly face to those of us working in the country.

The Rwandans were not fooled by this political masquerade. They understood the rules of the game, according to the former Rwandan minister of defense, James Gasana, who escaped from Rwanda in 1993. An insightful moderate, he would probably have been killed for his political stance by the powers that eventually led to the 1994 genocide. In a paper presented at the Ecumenical Institute in Bossey, Switzerland, in 1996, Gasana stated that the Rwandan army served only one purpose: to protect the power elite. This is not unique to Rwanda. Says Steven Were Omamo of Kenya's leader: "[Daniel arap] Moi's government . . . is widely viewed as an engine of domination instead of the agent of the popular will, more interested in maintaining old forms of influence and patronage for a minority than in expanding opportunity for the majority. This, I believe, is the root of our current troubles." Wangari Maathai, the legendary leader of the Green Belt Movement in Kenya, states: "Leadership in Africa has been . . . concerned with the opportunity to control the state and all its resources. Such leadership sees the power, prestige and comfortable lifestyles that the national resources can support. It is the sort of leadership that has built armies and security networks to protect itself against its own citizens."

❦

In countries such as these, the army and secret service are part of the political machine. They silence their opposition and prevent any broad-based power sharing. When I lived in Rwanda, one of my employees told me that his elderly mother had tried to vote against the continuation of the Habyarimana regime and been prevented from doing so. When she then stated that an old woman with mud on her feet from the fields ought to be allowed to vote against the official who drives his Mercedes Benz to the polling booth, she was arrested.

Though it is hard to prove, it is widely accepted that some African leaders promote ethnic violence during election times or when their power is challenged. The powerful are willing to injure and kill people so that they can continue to feed unhindered on the country's resources. Mobutu Sese Seko, the former president of Zaire (now the Democratic Republic of Congo), so ferociously plundered his country's resources that at his death his estimated worth stood at between $5 billion and $10 billion. His country's national debt was $14 billion.

Even some of the church leaders in such countries become involved in power games and ethnic divisiveness instead of serving as champions of justice. They, too, may have a vested interest in maintaining the status quo. We only need to consider our own history of race relations to understand how this can happen. Sometimes the flow of international charitable aid into the church attracts self-interested people into the institution; not all church leaders are oriented to serving the people. Many courageous men and women of the church have fought for justice, but many others have manipulated the system for their own gain.

Do we need to do something to help deeply indebted countries? Absolutely. Is the industrialized world partly responsible for their plight? Absolutely. Do we want to encourage corrupt leaders by giving them money that will enable them to pretend to be benevolent lovers of the people? Absolutely not. If we are going to forgive debt, let us not fool ourselves into thinking that we can outsmart the cunning men and women who are experienced at manipulating the international community for their own benefit. These leaders who are so good at sleight of hand will empty our pockets while they throw a few crumbs to the poor, and then laugh as their own bank accounts grow.

If a country is governed by a small, corrupt power elite and the national debt is really the debt of that elite, then let them face their people without foreign aid. The international community placed strong economic sanctions on the former white South African government. Even though those sanctions also impacted the poor, no one called for their discontinuation. Everyone agreed that ending the evil of apartheid required stern measures. Why can't we see that apartheid-like policies also exist in other countries? The world has shut its eyes to the racist policies of Rwanda and Burundi. Instead of imposing sanctions, we want to forgive their debts. When Kenya's leaders stir the country's racial tensions into riots, we look the other way and then talk about forgiving the government's debts.

***

Some will accuse me of paternalism and of ignoring our own guilt. But anyone who has lived among the people of countries with corrupt regimes has seen what happens when money comes in from the outside. The Jubilee 2000 campaigners claim to be aware of dictatorial and international power cliques. They state, "Jubilee 2000 calls for co-responsibility of debtors and creditors for the debt crisis. Remission of debt should be worked out through a fair and transparent process ensuring full participation of debtors in negotiations on debt relief." But can there be such a thing as "transparent processes" in countries where spies and guns counter any threat to the status quo? Why does it take a coup d'etat to change most African governments?

We will only increase our guilt if we inhibit necessary, fundamental changes from occurring in these countries. We recognized this in dealing with the former Rhodesia and South Africa. But not with Rwanda. We seem to be blind to black-on-black racism and corruption. Only fundamental change would have prevented the genocide in Rwanda. Only fundamental change will stop the incessant coups d'etat in nations where one group after another seeks to grow fat on the country's resources.

A groundswell of opposition to corrupt leaders is rising in several African nations. The West must not provide the leaders of such nations with the means to mollify their populations temporarily while they solidify their positions of power. Where the church is in bed with the government, it should also be considered suspect. At the same time, the church in the West must educate itself about our history of foreign political manipulation focused on protecting our own self-interests. This understanding should be a prerequisite to joining campaigns like that of Jubilee 2000.

Forgiving debts is a worthwhile enterprise, consistent with biblical teachings. But the admonition to fight for the oppressed must equally be kept in mind. Forgiving a national debt and freeing the oppressed are not necessarily the same thing. In fact, they may be opposites. Let us proceed cautiously. We should not help any poor country that has a large, internally focused military or secret service. We must deal with more than the superficial issue of debt relief. The West must acknowledge its role in creating and supporting corrupt dictatorships. The economic powers need to help poor countries ruled by benevolent governments to get a sure footing in the international economic system.

Ultimately, we must realize that we in the West cannot "fix" the problems of the poor countries. The people themselves must rise up and say no to their corrupt power elites. They must say no to the petty corruption that occurs at every police station and customs office. They must say no to benefiting from the ill-gotten funds of family members with access to power. They must say no to preying on ethnic groups who are outside of the power clique. They must say no to corrupt spiritual leaders. Until this is done, debt relief will provide only a temporary respite, a time when leaders can rest more peacefully in their expensive villas. It will only camouflage the slow, under-the-surface boil in countries ruled by corrupt dictators and their minions.

The church must not look to economic cures while ignoring systemic disease. We must not swing the odds against our brothers and sisters who are fighting for change. They understand the need for changed hearts. To paraphrase Bakole Wa Ilunga's book *The Paths of Liberation: A Third World Spirituality:* The path of liberation is long and winding, but it always must go through the heart of humanity.

POSTSCRIPT

Should Developed Countries Provide Debt Relief to the Poorest, Indebted African Nations?

Snyder argues that one of the main problems with debt relief is that it does not make African governments accountable to their own people. In his case study of Rwanda, he suggests that, more often than not, excessive debt exists in African countries because of corruption and mismanagement. Other arguments against debt relief have tended to focus on the turmoil that debt relief would create in the international financial system. There is a fear among public and private lenders that if one country is allowed to default on its loans without serious repercussions, then there will be a raft of other countries that will quickly follow suit. Proponents of debt relief would argue that both of these perspectives ignore the role that lenders have played in exacerbating the African debt crisis.

Although Logie and Rowson certainly do not agree with Snyder, it is interesting to note that the former only see debt relief as useful given certain circumstances. Similarly, Snyder seems willing to accept debt relief if certain conditions are met. In other words, both sides find debt relief useful given the right circumstances (although the conditions advocated by both sides are fairly different). According to Logie and Rowson, the debt relief process must be transparent, and not "dominated by the interests and agendas of creditors," or "conditional on health or economic system reforms that are potentially harmful to health outcomes." Snyder calls on the developed countries not to provide debt relief to nations with corrupt governments, a problem he hints at being pervasive throughout much of Africa. He fears that debt relief to such nations will only allow their corrupt leaders to remain in power longer.

One major debt relief program under way since 1996 is the World Bank and IMF's Heavily Indebted Poor Countries (HIPC) initiative. The program is significant because it is the first time in the 50-year history of these institutions that they allowed some of their debt to be written off. The program also allows for debt to be reduced from bilateral donors on a block basis (rather than forcing debtor nations to negotiate individually with each creditor). The Paris Club, an informal group of bilateral creditors, helped develop this program along with the World Bank and IMF. Of the 42 countries eligible for HIPC debt relief, seven African countries have qualified to date, including Benin, Burkina Faso, Mauritania, Mali, Mozambique, Tanzania, and Uganda. Since its inception, the HIPC initiative has come under heavy attack from critics because of the conditions it imposes on debtor nations wishing to receive relief. According to the World Bank (www.worldbank.org/hipc/about/hipcbr/hipcbr.htm), in order to receive relief, countries must "face an unsustainable debt burden, beyond available debt relief mechanisms"; and "establish a track record of reform and sound policies through IMF and World Bank supported programs." It is the second condition in particular that has angered many debt-relief advocates.

One of the largest debt-relief groups is Jubilee Research (formerly Jubilee 2000). The Jubilee 2000 movement originated in the early 1990s with the All Africa Conference of Churches and slowly gained momentum since that time, especially in the United Kingdom. The Jubilee 2000 Petition was launched during the 1998 G8 Summit in Birmingham, England, where 70,000 people linked in a chain of arms to persuade leaders to provide debt relief to the world's poorest countries. See www.jubilee2000uk.org for more information on the Jubilee 2000 movement. The five-year anniversary of the Birmingham human chain recently was marked at the meeting of the G8 in Evian, France (June 2003). Critics of the HIPC initiative continue to call for the relaxation of privatization and liberalization conditions that are linked to debt relief.

Internet References . . .

AllAfrica Global Media

AllAfrica Global Media is the largest provider of African news online with offices in Johannesburg, Dakar, Abuja and Washington, D.C. Over seven hundred stories are posted daily in French and English, in addition to multimedia content.

http://allafrica.com/

African Governments on the WWW

African Governments on the WWW catalogues Internet links to many government organizations in Africa.

http://www.gksoft.com/govt/en/africa.html

Africa Action

Africa Action provides information on political movements related to a wide variety of African issues. It hosts its own information and contains links to other Internet sites.

http://www.africaaction.org/index.php

Centre for Democracy and Development

The Centre for Democracy and Development is a U.K. based non-governmental organization (NGO) promoting democracy, peace, and human rights in Africa.

http://www.cddwestafrica.org/

African Union

The website of Africa's premier pan-African organization, the African Union (formerly the Organization of African States)

http://www.africa-union.org/

Politics, Governance, and Conflict Resolution

*T*he terrain of politics, governance, and conflict resolution is simultaneously one of the most hopeful and distressing realms in contemporary African studies. While more contested elections have been held in the last 15 years than at any other time in the post-colonial period, the African continent also suffers from more instances of civil strife than other world regions. Scholars and commentators intensely debate the connections between contemporary political developments, historical patterns of governance, global geo-politics, and local traditions of decision making, public discourse, and conflict resolution.

- Is Multi-Party Democracy Taking Hold in Africa?
- Is Foreign Assistance Useful for Fostering Democracy in Africa?
- Is Corruption the Result of Poor African Leadership?
- Are African Led Peacekeeping Missions More Effective than International Peacekeeping Efforts in Africa?

ISSUE 16

Is Multi-Party Democracy
Taking Hold in Africa?

YES: Michael Bratton and Robert Mattes, from "Support for Democracy in Africa: Intrinsic or Instrumental?" *British Journal of Political Science* (July 2001)

NO: Joel D. Barkan, from "The Many Faces of Africa: Democracy Across a Varied Continent," *Harvard International Review* (Summer 2002)

ISSUE SUMMARY

YES: Michael Bratton, professor of political science at Michigan State University, and Robert Mattes, associate professor of political studies and director of the Democracy in Africa Research Unit at the University of Cape Town, find as much popular support for democracy in Zambia, South Africa, and Ghana as in other regions of the developing world, despite the fact that the citizens of these countries tend to be less satisfied with the economic performance of their elected governments.

NO: Joel D. Barkan, professor of political science at the University of Iowa and senior consultant on governance at the World Bank, takes a less sanguine view of the situation in Africa. He suggests that one can be cautiously optimistic about the situation in roughly one-third of the states on the African continent, nations he classifies as consolidated democracies and as aspiring democracies. He asserts that one must be realistic about the possibilities for the remainder of African nations, countries he classifies into three groups: stalled democracies, those that are not free, and those that are mired in civil war.

There was a great deal of enthusiasm among Africanists in the early 1960s when more than 40 African nations gained independence and formed popularly elected governments. This enthusiasm was tempered when a large proportion of these countries succumbed to one-party rule or military regimes by the end of the decade. The 1970s and 1980s were largely characterized by the persistence of undemocratic forms of governance. Lacking popular support, undemocratic regimes and guerilla movements often sought Soviet or American patronage within the context of the cold war. The United States, in the name of anti-communism, financially and militarily backed a number of unsavory political leaders and guerilla insurgents during this period. These ranged from Mabuto Sese Seko in former Zaire to UNITA rebels in Angola. Seko, perhaps one of the most corrupt of African dictators, plundered his country for over 20 years during the cold war with the full support of the United States. In Angola, the U.S. and then-white-ruled South Africa sustained a bloody civil war by supporting UNITA rebels in the late 1980s.

The end of the cold war largely led to the end of perverse outside intervention in African affairs. Combined with this change in the external environment was a groundswell of internal support for political reform, which some commentators attribute to the democratic changes occurring in Eastern Europe in the late 1980s that many Africans observed through the international media. The result has often been referred to as Africa's "second wave" of democratization in which, between 1991 and 2000, multiparty elections were held in all but 5 of Africa's 47 states.

In this issue, Michael Bratton and Robert Mattes find as much popular support for democracy in Zambia, South Africa, and Ghana as in other regions of the developing world. However, citizens of these countries tend to be less satisfied with the performance of their elected governments than those in comparable non-African nations. The authors interpret these results to mean that support for democracy in Africa is more intrinsic (an end in itself) than instrumental (a means to an end—such as improving material standards of living). This finding highlights the importance that Africans attach to the basic political rights afforded by democracy. It also contradicts other research indicating that governments in new democracies mainly legitimate themselves through economic performance.

In contrast, Joel D. Barkan takes a more sober view of the situation in Africa. He states that those assessing the political situation in Africa roughly break down into two camps, the optimists and the realists. These two groups tend to draw very different conclusions because they focus their attention on different countries in Africa. Barkan contends that one can be cautiously optimistic about the situation in roughly one-third of the states on the African continent, nations he classifies as consolidated democracies (Botswana, Mauritius, and South Africa) and as aspiring democracies (15 countries). The prospects for the remainder of African nations are much more uncertain. Barkan classifies these states into three groups, the stalled democracies (13 countries), those that are not free (10 countries), and those that are mired in civil war (roughly 6 countries). As a realist, he believes that there is a tendency to over celebrate progress in the first two groups and to retreat from the challenges in the third, fourth, and fifth groups.

YES

**Michael Bratton
and Robert Mattes**

Support for Democracy in Africa: Intrinsic or Instrumental?

Popular support for a political regime is the essence of its consolidation. By voluntarily endorsing the rules that govern them, citizens endow a regime with an elusive but indispensable quality: political legitimacy. The most widely accepted definition of the consolidation of democracy equates it squarely with legitimation. In a memorable turn of phrase, Linz and Stepan speak of democratic consolidation as a process by which all political actors come to regard democracy as 'the only game in town'. In other words, democracy is consolidated when citizens and leaders alike conclude that no alternative form of regime has any greater subjective validity or stronger objective claim to their allegiance.

This article explores how the general public in new multiparty political regimes in sub-Saharan Africa is oriented towards democracy. What, if anything, do Africans understand by the concept? Do they resemble citizens in new democracies elsewhere in the world in their willingness to support a regime based on human rights, competing parties and open elections? And beyond democracy as a model set of rights and institutions, are citizens in Africa satisfied with the way that elected regimes operate in practice? All of these questions are coloured by the fact that many of Africa's democratic experiments are taking place in countries with agrarian economies, low per capita incomes and minuscule middle classes. Under such unpropitious conditions, observers have every reason to wonder whether elected governments have the capacity to meet citizen expectations and, if they cannot, whether citizens may therefore quickly lose faith in democracy.

We assume that citizens will extend tentative support to neo-democracies, if only because they promise change from failed authoritarian formulae of the past. But what is the nature of any such support? Is it *intrinsic*, based on an appreciation of the political freedoms and equal rights that democracy embodies when valued as an end in itself? Or does support reflect a more *instrumental* calculation in which regime change is a means to other ends, most commonly the alleviation of poverty and the improvement of living standards?

The resolution of this issue has direct implications for regime consolidation. Intrinsic support is a commitment to democracy 'for better or worse'; as

From *British Journal of Political Science*, July 2001, pp. 447–450, 453–460, 469–473. Copyright © 2001 by Michael Bratton and Robert Mattes. Reprinted by permission of the authors.

such, it has the potential to sustain a fragile political regime even in the face of economic downturn or social upheaval. By contrast, instrumental support is conditional. It is granted, and may be easily withdrawn, according to the temper of the times. If citizens evaluate regimes mainly in terms of their capacity to deliver consumable benefits or to rectify material inequalities, then they may also succumb to the siren song of populist leaders who argue that economic development requires the sacrifice of political liberties.

Let us be clear. We do not dispute that evaluations of democracy in new multiparty regimes are likely to be based in good part on the performance of the government of the day. After all, it is very unlikely that citizens in neo-democracies would possess a reservoir of favourable affective dispositions arising from a lifetime of exposure to democratic norms. If democracy is a novel experience, how could such socialization have taken place? Instead of bestowing 'diffuse support', citizens fall back on performance-based judge-ments of what democracy actually does for them.

We wish to divide regime performance, however, into distinct baskets of goods: an *economic* basket (that includes economic assets, jobs and an array of basic social services) and a *political* basket (that contains peace, civil liberties, political rights, human dignity and equality before the law). The African cases provide a critical test of the importance of political goods to evaluations of democracy. If the denizens of the world's poorest continent make 'separate and correct' distinctions between 'a basket of economic goods (which may be deteriorating) and a basket of political goods (which may be improving)', then citizens everywhere are likely to do so. And if political goods seem to matter more than economic goods in judging democracy, then we can cast light on the 'intrinsic v. instrumental' debate. If democracy is valued by citi-zens as an end in itself in Africa, then this generalization probably holds good universally.

In this study we find that citizen orientations to democracy in Africa are most fully explained with reference to both baskets of goods. With one inter-esting country exception, satisfaction with democracy (the way elected gov-ernments actually work) is driven just as much by guarantees of political rights as by the quest for material benefit. Support for democracy (as a pre-ferred form of government) is rooted even more deeply in an appreciation of new-found political freedoms, a finding that runs counter to the conventional view that the continent's deep economic crisis precludes regime consolida-tion. At least so far, new democratic regimes in Africa have been able to legiti-mate themselves by delivering political goods.

Scope of the Study

Our substantive focus is intentionally restricted—to attitudes to democracy, among masses rather than elites—because our geographical coverage is broader than most studies in Africa. This article uses standard survey items to compare political attitudes in Ghana, Zambia and South Africa, thus bridging the major regions of the sub-Saharan sub-continent and situating public opinion in Africa in relation to other new democracies in the world.

All three countries underwent an electoral transition to multi-party democracy during the last decade but their political trajectories have since diverged. Both of South Africa's competitive polls (in April 1994 and June 1999) were ruled substantially free and fair by independent observers. By contrast, Zambia's founding elections of October 1991 were far more credible than its dubious second contest of November 1996. For its part, Ghana experienced improved electoral quality, with flawed elections in November 1992 being followed by a December 1996 poll that drew almost universal praise. Thus, with reference to the institution of elections alone, South Africa's democracy has stabilized, Ghana's is gradually consolidating, and Zambia's is slowly dying.

In reality, democracy is a fragile species throughout Africa. It is far from clear that a pervasive political culture exists to promote and defend open elections, let alone any other democratic institution. Regime transitions in Africa commonly resulted from intense struggles between incumbent and opposition elites, whose interest in self-enrichment was sometimes more palpable than their commitment to democracy. Even elected leaders have tampered with constitutional rules in order to prolong a term of office or to sideline rivals. And the armed forces continue to lurk threateningly in the wings: about half a dozen of Africa's new democracies succumbed to military intervention within five years of transition. Only in places like South Africa in 1994 (and possibly Nigeria in 1999), where transitions were lubricated by pacts among powerful insiders, are there signs that a culture of compromise and accommodation has penetrated the ranks of the political elite.

The extent to which a commitment to democracy has radiated through the populace is also open to question. After all, regime transitions in Africa were sparked by popular protests that were rooted in economic and political grievances. While the protesters had clear ideas about what they were *against* (the repressions and predations of big-man rule) they did not articulate an elaborate or coherent vision of what they were *for*. Judging by the issues raised in the streets, people seemed to want accountability of leaders and to eliminate the inequities arising from official corruption. To be sure, these preferences loosely embodied core democratic principles. And multiparty elections quickly became a useful rallying cry for would-be political leaders. But, during the tumult of transition, relatively little attention was paid to the institutional design of the polity. Emerging from life under military and one-party rule, citizens could hardly be expected to have in mind a full set of democratic rules or to evince a deep attachment to them.

This article takes stock of what has been learned from the first generation of research on political attitudes in new African democracies in the 1990s. . . .

The Meaning of Democracy in Africa

In considering the meaning of 'democracy' in Africa, the first possibility is that the term has not entered popular discourse, especially where indigenous languages contain no direct semantic equivalent. Some cultural interpretations emphasize that the word changes its meaning in translation, sometimes even signifying consensual constructs like community or unity. Or, because African languages borrow new terminology from others, a phonetic adaptation from a European language (like 'demokrasi') may have become common currency.

In one form or another, democracy seems to have entered the vocabulary of most African citizens. When the 1997 Ghanaian survey asked respondents 'What is the first thing that comes to mind . . . when you think of living in a democracy?', 61.5 per cent were able to provide a meaningful response, rising to 75 per cent in 1999. Interestingly, even more respondents felt that Ghana was a democracy in 1997, implying that some people who could not specify a meaning for democracy could nevertheless recognize one if they saw one. In both countries, the salience of the concept was a function of education, with democracy having meaning in direct proportion to a respondent's years of schooling.

Contrary to cultural interpretations, we contend that standard liberal ideas of civil and political rights lie at the core of African understandings of democracy. In Zambia in 1993 and 1994, participants in two rounds of focus groups were asked 'What does democracy mean to you?' In the ensuing discussions, democracy was most commonly decoded in terms of the political procedure of competitive elections in which 'people are free to vote if they want to' and 'have a right to choose their own leaders'. Informants described how they resented having been forced to vote for the former ruling United National Independence Party (UNIP) and decried the political intimidation exerted by the party's youth wing. They favourably compared a choice of candidates under a multi-party regime with the system of 'appointed representatives' under a one-party state.

An open-ended question in the 1999 survey in Ghana about 'the first thing that comes to your mind . . . when you hear the word "democracy"' elicited the following responses, in frequency order: civil liberties and personal freedoms (28 per cent of all respondents), 'government by the people' (22 per cent), and voting rights (9.2 per cent). The only other major response was 'Don't know' (24.8 per cent) and very few respondents offered a materialistic interpretation (2.5 percent). These findings seem to suggest that Ghanaians view democracy almost exclusively in political terms, with an emphasis on selected civil liberties (especially free speech), collective decision-making and political representation.

Survey findings point to a much more materialistic world view in South Africa. In 1995, South Africans were asked to choose from a list of diverse meanings (both political and economic) that are sometimes attached to democracy. At the top of the popular rankings, 91.3 per cent of respondents equated democracy with 'equal access to houses, jobs and a decent income' (with 48.3 per cent seeing these goods as 'essential' to democracy). This earthy image of democracy far outstripped all other representations: for example, regular elections (67.7 per cent), at least two strong parties (59.4 per cent), and minority rights (54.5 per cent). To be sure, a majority of South Africans did associate democracy with procedures to guarantee political competition and political participation, but their endorsement of these political goods was far less ringing than the almost unanimous association of democracy with improved material welfare. Tellingly, only small minorities found it 'essential' to democracy to hold regular elections (26.5 per cent) or guarantee minority rights (20.6 per cent).

Because South Africa is a deeply divided society with mutually reinforcing fault lines of race and class, one would expect that various social groups would hold disparate views of democracy. We have noted elsewhere 'massive racial differences in agreement with regime norms'. Whites are much more likely than blacks to agree that regular elections, free speech, party competition and minority rights are essential to democracy. This procedural interpretation of democracy most likely reflects their own minority status and their reliance for protection on constitutional and legal rules. South African blacks, for their part, attach just as much or more importance to narrowing the gap between rich and poor. And while many South Africans of all races say they accept the necessity of redistributing jobs, houses and incomes, blacks seem to focus more on 'equality of results' while whites stress 'equality of opportunity'.

We reach four working conclusions based on recent research on citizen conceptions of democracy in three African countries. First, Africans here are more likely to associate democracy with individual liberties than with communal solidarity, especially if they live in urban areas. Secondly, popular conceptions of democracy have *both* procedural *and* substantive dimensions, though the former conception is more common than the latter. Thirdly, citizens rank procedural and substantive attributes in different order across countries. Zambians place political rules at the top of the list of democratic attributes, whereas South Africans relegate such guarantees behind improvements in material living standards. Finally, rankings differ even within the category of political goods: whereas Zambians (and to a lesser extent South Africans) grant primacy to elections, Ghanaians elevate freedom of speech to the top of their own bill of democratic rights.

These cross-national differences can be interpreted in terms of the life experiences of citizens under each country's old regime. Zambians may regard democracy mainly in terms of competitive multi-party elections because of their disappointing experiences with the ritual of 'elections without choice' under Kenneth Kaunda's one-party state. Ghanaians, for their part, emphasize freedom of speech as a reaction against the tight controls over communication imposed by the previous military regime, whose populist ideology was the only approved form of political discourse. Finally, South Africans place socio-economic considerations at the heart of their notion of democracy because of the integrated structure of oppression experienced under apartheid. Impoverished under the old regime, they see the attainment of political freedom as only the first step in rectifying manifold inequalities in society. In this conception, democracy has an inclusive meaning; it is as much a means to social transformation as a politically desirable end in itself.

Support for Democracy in Africa

The best way to ask questions about popular support for democracy is in concrete terms and in the form of comparisons with plausible alternatives. Since democracy has motley meanings, it is not useful to ask whether people support it in the abstract. It is far better to elicit opinions about a real regime with distinctive institutional attributes, such as a 'system of governing with free elections and many parties'. And if citizens support democracy as the 'least worst' system (the so-called 'Churchill hypothesis'), it is worth testing their levels of commitment against other regime forms that they have recently experienced or could conceive of encountering in the future.

Table 1 reports results of survey questions of this sort from various world regions, with sub-Saharan Africa represented by Ghana, Zambia and South Africa. In so far as these countries are representative of the region, Table 1 shows that the level of public commitment to democracy is much the same in Africa as in other regions of the world that have recently undergone regime change. Excluding Southern Europe, almost two out of three citizens in new democracies extend legitimacy to elected government as their preferred political regime: the relevant mean figures are 65 per cent for East and Central Europe, 63 per cent for South America, and 64 per cent for the three countries of sub-Saharan Africa. Indeed, the average level of support in Africa (64.3 per cent) is virtually identical to the combined mean for Latin America and post-Communist Europe (64.2 per cent).

Table 1

Public Attitudes to Democracy: Preliminary Cross-National Comparisons

	Support democracy	Satisfied with democracy	Supportive and satisfied	Supportive but not satisfied
European Union	78	53	—	—
Southern Europe	84	57	79	11
Greece	90	52	84	11
Portugal	83	60	77	9
Spain	78	60	75	12
East and Central Europe	65	60	72	6
Czech	77	56	70	8
Poland	76	61	70	4
Romania	61	77	68	4
Bulgaria	66	61	75	2
Slovakia	61	49	62	14
Hungary	50	53	79	4
South America	63	50	45	22
Uruguay	80	54	57	29
Argentina	77	53	55	28
Chile	53	48	38	17
Brazil	41	46	32	16
Sub-Saharan Africa	64	48	41	18
Ghana (1997)	74	53	46	13
Zambia (1996)	63	53	49	14
South Africa (1997)	56	38	29	13
South Africa (blacks)	61	45	35	11
South Africa (whites)	39	7	5	18

Note: Regional means are raw estimates, uncorrected for proportional population size of countries. Further fnn. to Table 1 can be found in the electronic version of the journal available at www.cup.cam.ac.uk

Moreover, deviation in support for democracy around the regional mean is lower for the three African countries than for other parts of the world. The countries with the lowest and highest levels of support for democracy are separated by just 18 percentage points in the African cases, but by 27 points for Eastern Europe and 39 points in South America. We interpret this to mean that authoritarian regimes have been widely discredited across the continent. Although the citizens of Ghana and Zambia may not have committed themselves to democracy as firmly as the citizens in Uruguay and the Czech Republic, they evince less nostalgia for hardline rule than citizens in Hungary and Brazil. Once again, though, South Africa is an exception. And we would need many more confirming cases before we could be sure that legitimating sentiments are evenly spread across all African countries.

Indeed, variations are evident within Africa in the extent to which citizens support new regimes. Of the three cases under review, Ghana displays the highest levels of citizen commitment to democracy. In 1997, fully 73.5 per cent of citizens thought it somewhat or very important for Ghana to 'have at least two political parties competing in an election'. The intensity of this support appears to be strong, as reflected by the 55.9 per cent of respondents who thought these institutions 'very important'. And the quality and depth of this support is underlined by the even higher proportions who granted importance to the right of citizens to form parties representing diverse viewpoints (82.5 per cent), to the openness of the mass media to political debate (89.3 per cent), and to the regular conduct of honest elections (92.7 per cent). While there is some possibility that respondents are acquiescing here to non-controversial 'motherhood' questions, Ghanaians nonetheless appear to consistently favour a full basket of liberal political rights.

Among the countries considered, legitimation of the new regime was lowest in South Africa, where citizens do not yet feel a widespread attitudinal commitment to democracy. A 1997 survey asked respondents to choose between the following statements: '[When] democracy does not work . . . some say you need a strong leader who does not have to worry with elections. Others say democracy is always best'. Since only a bare majority chose the democratic option (56.3 per cent, up from 47 per cent in 1995, but dropping back again below 50 per cent in 1998), support for democracy appeared to be weaker there than in the other African countries. Other responses underscore the shallowness of democratic legitimacy and the appeal of authoritarian alternatives in South Africa. In 1997, about one-third of the population thought that, under democracy, 'the economic system runs badly' (29 per cent), order is poorly maintained (30.2 per cent), and leaders are 'indecisive and have too much squabbling' (35.1 per cent). And more than half of all South Africans (53.8 per cent) stated that they would be 'willing to give up regular elections if a non-elected government or leader could impose law and order and deliver jobs and houses'.

Thus, the potential constituency for forceful rule appears to be larger in South Africa than in South America, where an average of just 15 per cent of citizens considers that 'in some circumstances an authoritarian government can be preferable to a democratic [one]'. Sentiments for a strong man were higher in South Africa (30.8 per cent) than in Chile (19 per cent) and Brazil (21 per cent), where authoritarian nostalgia is usually considered to be high. Question wording may have had a significant effect, with the cue of higher material living standards ('jobs and houses') inducing even some of democracy's supporters to abandon it. But, at minimum, this finding draws attention to the role of instrumental calculations in the assessments of democracy by many South African citizens.

South Africa's deviance is explicable again, however, in terms of its cultural diversity. White South Africans were much less likely to judge that 'democracy is always best' (39 per cent) than the country's African citizens (61 per cent). And, while 'coloureds' situated themselves between blacks and whites when granting such support to democracy (53 per cent), Asian South Africans were the least supportive of all (27 per cent). Thus the cautious, even retrogressive, attitudes of ethnic minorities tended to depress overall levels of commitment to democracy in South Africa. Examined alone, African citizens can be seen to support this form of regime at the highest level of any ethnic group in South Africa (61 per cent), a level not too different from citizens in Zambia (63 per cent) and the sub-Sahara region as a whole (64 per cent).

In Zambia, the question on support for democracy differed slightly, while still focusing on a political system featuring elections and posing a comparison with a realistic alternative regime. Respondents were asked to choose: Is 'the best form of government . . . a government elected by its people' or 'a government that gets things done'? On the assumption that support erodes as regimes mature, especially if citizens' expectations are not fully realized, we thought that support for 'elected government' would decline over time. To date this has not happened in Zambia. Public support for democracy held steady, at 63.4 per cent in 1993 and 62.9 per cent in 1996. As in Ghana, other related items bespoke an electorate with a relatively firm syndrome of democratic commitments. In 1996, 73 per cent preferred 'a choice of political parties and candidates' to 'a return to a system of single-party rule'.

Satisfaction With Democracy in Africa

Democracy looks better in theory than in practice. In elected regimes worldwide, more citizens support democracy as their preferred form of government than express satisfaction with the way that it actually works. This generalization holds true not only for Third Wave neo-democracies but, even more so, for the established regimes of Western Europe. . . .

Unlike support for democracy, satisfaction with democracy is not as widespread in the three African countries as it is in South America and Eastern Europe. Satisfaction lags support by a wider margin in the sub-Saharan region (16 per centage points) than in the other two world regions (13 and 5 per centage points respectively). Substantively, fewer than half (48 per cent) of the citizens in these new African democracies report satisfaction with key aspects of the performance of elected regimes. Once more, the African average is pulled down by South Africa, with Ghana and Zambia displaying popular approval of regime performance at levels similar to consolidating democracies like Uruguay and Argentina. Although different racial groups in South Africa again evince distinct levels of satisfaction (45 per cent for blacks versus just 7 per cent for whites), black South Africans in this instance trail their fellow citizens elsewhere on the continent in their contentment with democracy in practice (39 per cent). Instead, they tend to more closely resemble the citizens of Brazil (41 per cent), more of whom are unhappy with democracy than are satisfied with it. . . .

Explaining Satisfaction With Democracy

. . . Satisfaction with democracy among African citizens appears to depend upon their assessment of the performance of government, particularly its performance at delivering *both* economic *and* political goods. Taken together, these factors explain between a quarter and two-fifths of the variance in expressed satisfaction in three African countries. Apart from social background, no set of factors—whether general performance, economic goods or political goods—can be discarded without a significant loss of explanatory power. Any ecumenical explanation of satisfaction with democracy in Africa must make reference to government performance in *both* its political *and* economic dimensions.

But what about the relative weight of economic and political explanations? We note that the delivery of economic goods sometimes has large independent effects on satisfaction with democracy in individual countries. Crossnationally, however, such effects are rather inconsistent. We therefore conclude that economic effects are subject to the exigencies of time and place, such as gradual economic recovery in Ghana and persistent economic crisis in Zambia. We therefore doubt that a general explanation of satisfaction with democracy can be constructed from economic data alone. At the same time, we note that the effects of political factors, while occasionally weaker than those of economic factors, prevail more consistently across countries. This observation suggests that the delivery of political goods is a more reliable general predictor of satisfaction with democracy and a more promising foundation on which to construct a theory of democratic consolidation. This line of argument is explored further in the next section.

Explaining Support for Democracy

We turn, finally, to explain support for democracy as a preferred regime type. As Table 2 shows, our analysis accounts for 12 to 17 per cent of the variance in popular support (see adjusted R^2 statistics). Our explanation was less complete in this case perhaps because of the impalpability of the issue at hand: citizens may find it more difficult to assess the qualities of abstract constitutional rules than the concrete performance of actual governments. In any event, public opinion in Africa seems to be less fully formed, and more contradictory, when it comes to support for democracy.

Nevertheless, Table 2 does reveal interesting findings. First, it reconfirms that attitudes to democracy cannot be inferred from standard social background

Table 2

Multiple Regression Estimates of Support for Democracy

	S. Africa			Ghana			Zambia		
	B	(s.e.)	Beta	B	(s.e.)	Beta	B	(s.e.)	Beta
Social background factors									
Gender			0.028			−0.014			0.048
Age			−0.019			0.000			0.042
Education			−0.009			0.001	0.064	(0.010)	0.200***
General performance factors									
Approval of government performance	0.084	(0.014)	0.145***	0.368	(0.064)	0.169***	0.122	(0.030)	0.128***
Satisfaction with democracy	0.082	(0.011)	0.196***	0.393	(0.052)	0.195***			−0.010
Economic factors									
Assessment of current economic conditions			−0.013			0.038			0.001
Assessment of current personal QOL			−0.017			0.023			−0.021
Assessment of future personal QOL	0.035	(0.011)	0.077***			−0.023			0.067
Support for market reforms			0.038			−0.006			0.017
Delivery of economic goods			−0.002	0.066	(0.031)	0.062***			0.059
Political factors									
Interest in politics	0.054	(0.015)	0.077***			0.015	0.115	(0.025)	0.144***
Trust in government institutions			0.032			−0.003			0.018
Perception of government responsiveness			0.031			−0.008			0.012
Perception of official corruption			−0.003	−0.140	(0.072)	−0.045*			−0.020
Delivery of political goods			0.028	0.158	(0.025)	0.153***	0.461	(0.080)	0.181***
N		3,500			2,005			1,182	
R		0.349			0.417			0.382	
R^2		0.122			0.174			0.146	
Adjusted R^2		0.120			0.171			0.142	

(*)Significant at 0.05
(**)Significant at 0.01
(***)Significant at 0.001

characteristics. Again, gender and age were irrelevant to the legitimation of democracy in all countries studied and education had a positive impact only in Zambia. These findings are consistent with the observations that 'the more education a person has, the more likely he or she is to reject undemocratic alternatives' but that, overall, 'social structure [has] little influence . . . on attitudes towards the new regime'. If African societies do not contain entrenched pockets of generational or gender-based resistance to democratization, then the prospects for the consolidation of democratic regimes would seem to be slightly brighter than is sometimes thought.

Secondly, regime legitimacy in Africa depends upon popular appraisals of government performance. Consistently, in all three countries, support for democracy was strongest among citizens who felt that elected governments were generally doing a good job. But approval of government performance was closely connected to party identification, with supporters of the ruling party in each country being much more approving. Thus we must investigate further whether citizens are accrediting government performance—and thereby supporting democracy—out of 'knee-jerk' loyalty to a ruling party rather than a rational calculation that democratic governments deserve legitimation because they are more effective.

In Ghana and South Africa, support for democracy also was accompanied by expressions of satisfaction with democracy. We take this as further evidence that regime legitimation in Africa rests squarely upon performance considerations. On the up-side, popular demand for government performance increases the likelihood that citizens will make use of the rules of democratic governance to hold their leaders accountable. On the down-side, it also raises the possibility that citizens may conflate the performance of governments (that is, the achievements of incumbent groups of elected officials) with the performance of regimes (that is, the rules by which governments are constituted). The risk thus arises that, faced with continued mismanagement by ineffective governments, Africans may throw the baby out with the bath-water. By punishing government under-performance, they may inadvertently dismiss democracy.

Thirdly, and notwithstanding what has just been said about performance, we find little systematic evidence from Africa that citizens predicate support for democracy on the delivery of economic goods. Generally speaking, the legitimation of democratic regimes does not depend on citizen assessments of personal or national economic conditions, either now or for the future. Only in South Africa are assessments of future personal conditions linked positively to support for democracy. Strikingly too, when other relevant factors are controlled for, citizen perceptions of economic delivery have no discernible effects on the endorsement of democracy in either Zambia or South Africa. The delivery of economic goods only seems to matter in Ghana, though the influence of this instrumental consideration is far from the strongest in the Ghana model.

Instead, we are led back again to the impact of political factors. For the first time, we find that citizen interest in politics had a positive effect on attitudes to democracy in two out of the three countries (Zambia and South

Africa). It stands to reason that democracy will not consolidate where citizens remain disinterested in, and detached from, the political process; before people can actively become democracy's champions, they must orient themselves towards involvement in political life. One wonders why Ghanaians, who display the highest levels of interest in politics among the Africans surveyed, do not automatically support democracy. The answer appears to lie, at least in part, in the popular perception of rampant official corruption in that country. Many persons who are predisposed by their interest in politics to become active citizens are 'turned off' from democracy by what they see as the illicit machinations of civilian politicians. As one would expect, perceptions of official corruption are negatively associated with support for democracy in all three African countries; only in Ghana, however, is this relationship statistically significant.

Finally, and most importantly, the delivery of political goods bears a strong and significant relationship to the popular legitimation of democracy. In judging democracy, the Africans that we surveyed think of government performance first and foremost in political terms. Unlike the delivery of economic goods, a factor that is relevant in only one country, this relationship holds in at least two country cases. . . .

Conclusion

In this [selection,] we have established that levels of popular support for democracy are roughly similar in three neo-democracies of sub-Saharan Africa as in other Third Wave countries. Almost two-thirds of eligible voters in these African countries say that they feel some measure of attachment to democratic rules and values. Under these circumstances, the popular consolidation of democracy in at least some African countries does not seem an entirely far-fetched prospect.

Yet the African cases stand apart from other new democracies in terms of lower levels of mass satisfaction with actual regime performance. The fact that African survey respondents support democracy while being far from content with its concrete achievements suggests a measure of intrinsic support for the democratic regime form that supersedes instrumental considerations. But, although support for democracy may be quite broad, we cannot confirm that it is deep. We do not yet know if citizens will vigorously defend the political regime if economic conditions take a decisive turn for the worse or if rulers begin to backtrack on hard-won freedoms.

Joel D. Barkan

The Many Faces of Africa: Democracy Across a Varied Continent

A decade ago, seasoned observers of African politics including Larry Diamond and Richard Joseph argued that the continent was on the cusp of its "second liberation." Rising popular demand for political reform across Africa, multiparty elections, transitions of power in several countries, and negotiations toward a new political framework in South Africa led these experts to conclude that the prospects for democratization were good. Today, these same observers are not so sure. They describe Africa's current experience with democratization in terms of "electoral democracy," "virtual democracy," or "illiberal democracy," and are far more cautious about predicting what is to come. What is the true state of African democracy? And what is its future?

Governance Before the 1990s

Africa's first liberation was precipitated by the transition from colonial to independent rule that swept much of the continent, except the south, between 1957 and 1964. The West hoped that the transition would be to democratic rule, and more than 40 new states with democratic constitutions emerged following multiparty elections that brought new African-led governments to power. The regimes established by this process, however, soon collapsed or reverted to authoritarian rule—what Samuel Huntington has termed a "reverse wave" of democratization. By the mid-1960s, roughly half of all African countries had seen their elected governments toppled by military coups.

In the other half, elected regimes degenerated into one-party rule. In what was to become a familiar scenario, nationalist political parties formed the first governments. The leaders of these parties then destroyed or marginalized the opposition through a combination of carrot-and-stick policies. The result was a series of clientelist regimes that served as instruments for neo-patrimonial or personal rule by the likes of Mobutu Sese Seko in Zaire or Daniel Arap Moi in Kenya—regimes built around a political boss, rather than founded in a strong party apparatus and the realization of a coherent program or ideology.

This pattern, and its military variant (as with Sani Abacha in Nigeria), became the modal type of African governance from the mid-1960s until the early 1990s. These regimes depended on a continuous and increasing flow of

From *Harvard International Review*, Summer 2002, pp. 72–77. Copyright © 2002 by the President of Harvard College. Reprinted by permission.

patronage and slush money for survival; there was little else binding them together. Inflationary patronage led to unprecedented levels of corruption, unsustainable macroeconomic policies that caused persistent budget and current account deficits, and state decay, including the decline of the civil service. Most African governments still struggle with this structural and normative legacy, which has obstructed the process of building democracy.

Decade of Democratization?

Africa's second liberation began with the historic 1991 multiparty election in Benin that resulted in the defeat of the incumbent president, an outcome that was replicated in Malawi and Zambia in the same year. The results of these elections raised expectations and created hopes for the restoration of democracy and improved governance across the continent. By the end of 2000, multiparty elections had been held in all but five of Africa's 47 states—Comoros, the Democratic Republic of Congo, Equatorial Guinea, Rwanda, and Somalia.

Along with the new states of the former Soviet Union, Africa was the last region to be swept by the so-called "third wave" of democratization, and as with many of the successor states of the former Soviet Union, the record since has been mixed. In stark contrast to the democratic transitions that occurred in the 1970s and 1980s in Southern and Eastern Europe and Latin America (excluding Mexico), most African transitions have not been marked by a breakthrough election that definitively ended an authoritarian regime by bringing a group of political reformers to power. While this type of transition has occurred in a small number of states, most notably Benin and South Africa, the more typical pattern has been a process of protracted transition: a mix of electoral democracy and political liberalization combined with elements of authoritarian rule and, more fundamentally, the perpetuation of clientelist rule. In this context, politics is a three-cornered struggle between authoritarians, patronage-seekers, and reformers. Authoritarians attempt to retain power by permitting greater liberalization and elections while selectively allocating patronage to those who remain loyal. Meanwhile, patronage-seekers attempt to obtain the spoils of office via electoral means, as reformers pursue the establishment of democratic rule. The boundaries between the first and second of these groups, and sometimes between the second and third, can be blurred because political alignments are very fluid. Liberal democracy is unlikely to be consolidated until reformers ascend to power.

The result is what Thomas Carothers has termed a "gray zone" of polities, describing countries where continued progress toward democracy beyond elections is limited and where the consolidation of democracy, if it does occur, will unfold over a long period, perhaps decades. This characterization does not necessarily mean that the third wave of democratization is over in Africa. Rather, we should expect Africa's democratic transitions to be similar to those of India or Mexico. In the former, the party that led the country to independence did not lose an election for three decades, and periodic alternation of power between parties did not occur until after 40 years. In the latter, the end of one-party rule and its replacement by an opposition committed to democratic principles played out over five elections spanning 13 years rather than a single founding election. Such appears to be the pattern in Africa, where two-thirds of founding and second elections have returned incumbent authoritarians to power, but where each iteration of the electoral process has usually resulted in a significant incremental advance in the development of civil society, electoral fairness, and the overall political process.

That many African polities fall into the gray zone is confirmed by the most recent annual *Freedom in the World* survey conducted by Freedom House. Of the 47 states that comprise sub-Saharan Africa, 23 were classified by the survey as "partly free" based on the extent of their political freedoms and civil liberties. Only eight (Benin, Botswana, Cape Verde, Ghana, Mali, Mauritius, Namibia, and South Africa) were classified as "free" while 16, including eight war-torn societies (Angola, Burundi, the Democratic Republic of Congo, Ethiopia, Eritrea, Liberia, Rwanda, and Sudan) were deemed "not free."

The overall picture revealed by these numbers is sobering. Less than one-fifth of all African countries were classified as free, and of these, only two or three (Botswana, Mauritius, and perhaps South Africa) can be termed consolidated democracies. On the other hand, if one excludes states in the midst of civil war, one-fifth of Africa's countries are free, one-fifth not free, and three-fifths fall in-between. That is to say, four-fifths of those not enmeshed in civil war are partly free or free, a significant advance over the continent's condition a decade ago. Only a handful are consolidated democracies, but few are harsh dictatorships of the type that dominated Africa from the mid-1960s to the beginning of the 1990s. As noted by Ghana's E. Gyimah-Boadi, "Illiberalism has persisted, but is not on the rise. Authoritarianism is alive in Africa today, but is not well."

Optimists and Realists

The current status of democracy in Africa varies greatly from one country to the next, and one should resist generalizations that apply to all 47 of the continent's states; one size does not fit all. Notwithstanding this reality, those who track events in Africa have divided themselves into two distinct camps: optimists and realists. Those in the United States who take an optimistic view—mainly government officials involved in efforts to promote democratization abroad, former members of President Bill Clinton's administration responsible for Africa, members of the Congressional Black Caucus, and the staff of some Africa-oriented nongovernmental organizations—trumpet the fact that multiparty elections have been held in nearly 90 percent of all African states. They note that most African countries have now held competitive elections twice and that some, including Benin, Ghana, and Senegal, have held genuine elections three times, at least one of which has resulted in a change of government. The optimists further note that the quality of these elections has improved in some countries, both in terms of efficiency and of fairness. Electoral commissions seem to have been more independent, even-handed, and professional in recent elections than in the early 1990s. Opposition candidates and parties have greater freedom to campaign and have faced less harassment from incumbent governments. The presence of election observers, both foreign and domestic, is now widely accepted as part of the process. Perhaps most significant, citizen participation in elections has been fairly high, averaging just under two-thirds of all registered voters.

Recognizing that elections are a necessary but insufficient condition for the consolidation of democracy, the optimists also point to advances in several areas, listed below in their approximate order of accomplishment. First, there has been a re-emergence and proliferation of civil society organizations after their systematic suppression during the era of single-party and military rule. Second, an independent and free press has also re-emerged, spurred on by the privatization of broadcast media in several countries. Third, members of the legislature have increasingly asserted themselves in policy-making and overseeing the executive branch. Fourth, the judiciary and the rule of law have been strengthened in countries such as Tanzania, and human rights abuses have also declined. Fifth, there have been new experiments with federalism—the delegation or devolution of authority from the central government to local authorities—to enhance governmental accountability to the public and defuse the potential for ethnic conflict, most notably in Nigeria but also in Ethiopia, Ghana, Tanzania, Uganda, and South Africa. One or more of these trends, especially the first two and perhaps the third, can be found in most African countries that are not trapped in civil war.

Optimists also point to less exclusive membership in the governing elite, which has expanded into the upper-middle sector of society far more than during the era of authoritarian rule. In country after country, repeated multi-party elections have resulted in significant turnover in the national legislatures and local government bodies, sometimes as high as 40 percent per cycle. While the quality of elected officials at the local level remains poor, members of national legislatures are younger, better educated, and more independent in their political approach than the older generation they have displaced. Although further research is needed to confirm any major change in the composition of these bodies, new politicians and legislators also appear more likely than their predecessors to be democrats and to focus on issues of public policy and less likely to be patronage seekers.

Finally, public opinion across Africa appears to prefer democracy over any authoritarian alternatives. Surveys undertaken for the Afrobarometer project in 12 African countries between 1999 and 2001 found that a mean of 69 percent of all respondents regarded democracy as "preferable to any other kind of government," while only 12 percent agreed with the proposition that "in certain situations, a non-democratic government can be preferable." Moreover, 58 percent of all respondents stated that they were "fairly satisfied" or "very satisfied" with the "way democracy works" in their country.

Realists—who criticize what they contend was a moralistic approach to US foreign policy by the Clinton administration and disparage the use of democratization as a foreign policy goal—take a far more cautious view of what is occurring on the continent. Considering the same six developments that optimists cite as examples of democratic advances, realists note that all six are present in fewer than six countries. They also see much less progress than the optimists when nations are considered one by one. First, regular multiparty elections across the continent have resulted in an alternation of government in only one-third of the countries that have held votes. Moreover, only about one-half of these elections have been regarded as free and fair, with results accepted by those who have lost. It is also debatable in most of these countries whether recent elections have been of higher quality than those held in the early 1990s.

Second, although the re-emergence of civil society and the free press is a significant advance from the era of authoritarian rule when both were barely tolerated or systematically suppressed, civil society remains very weak in Africa compared to other regions and is concentrated in urban areas. Political parties are especially weak and rarely differentiate themselves from one another on the basis of policy. Apart from the church, farmers' organizations, or community self-help groups in a smattering of countries (such as Kenya, Côte d'Ivoire, and Nigeria), civil society barely exists in rural areas where most of the population resides. The press, especially the print media, is similarly concentrated in urban areas and thus reaches a relatively small proportion of the entire population. Only the broadcast media penetrates the countryside, but it is largely state-owned. Although private broadcasting has grown in recent years, especially in television and FM radio, stations cater almost exclusively to urban audiences. With a few exceptions, AM and short- and medium-wave radio—the chief sources of information for the rural population—remain state monopolies.

Third, while the legislature holds out the promise of becoming an institution of countervailing power in some countries, it remains weak and has rarely managed to effectively check executive power. Fourth, the judicial system in most countries is ineffectual, either because its members are corrupt or because it has too few magistrates and too poor an infrastructure to keep pace with the number of cases. Human rights abuses also continue, though less frequently and with less intensity than a decade ago. Fifth, Africa's experiments with federalism, though apparently successful, are confined to six states. Finally, the extent to which Africans have internalized democratic values is hard to judge. Although the Afrobarometer surveys indicate broad support for democracy, the results also suggest that such support is "a mile wide and an inch deep." An average of only 23 percent of respondents in each country described their country as "completely democratic."

Both optimists and realists are correct in their assessments of what is occurring in Africa. But how can both views be valid? The answer is that each presents only one side of the story. On a continent where the record of democratization is one of partial advance in over one-half of the cases, those assessing progress toward democratization, or lack of it, tend to dwell either on what has been accomplished or on what has yet to be achieved. These divergent assessments are proverbial examples of those who view the glass as either half-full or half-empty. Optimists and realists also draw their conclusions from slightly different samples. Whereas optimists focus mainly on states that are partly free or free, realists concentrate on states that are partly free or not free.

Optimists and realists are also both right because there are several Africas rather than one. In fact, at least five Africas cut across the three broad categories of the Freedom House survey. First are the consolidated and semi-consolidated democracies—a much smaller group of counties than those classified as free. This category presently consists of only two or three cases, such as Botswana, Mauritius, and perhaps South Africa. The second group consists of approximately 15 aspiring democracies, including the remaining five classified by Freedom House as free but not yet consolidated democracies plus roughly 10 classified as partly free where the transition to democracy has not stalled. All these states have exhibited slow but continuous progress toward a more liberal and institutionalized form of democratic politics. In this group are Benin, Ghana, Madagascar, Mali, Senegal, and possibly Kenya, Malawi, Tanzania, and Zambia. Third are semi-authoritarian states, countries classified as partly free where the transition to democracy has stalled. This category consists of approximately 13 countries including Uganda, the Central African Republic, and possibly Zimbabwe. Fourth are countries that are not free, with little or no prospect for a democratic transition in the near future. About 10 countries make up this group, including Cameroon, Chad, Eritrea, Ethiopia, Rwanda, and Togo. Finally, there are the states mired in civil war, such as Angola, Congo, Liberia, and Sudan. Each of these five Africas presents a different context for the pursuit of democracy.

Inhibiting Democracy

Several conditions peculiar to the continent make Africa a difficult place to sustain democratic practice. They explain why Africa lags behind other regions in its extent of democratic advance, why political party organizations are weak, and why the ties between leaders and followers are usually based on clientelist relationships. These conditions in turn create pressures for more and more patronage, a situation that undermines electoral accountability and leads to corruption.

Africa is the poorest of the world's principal regions: per capita income averages US$490 per year. This condition does not affect the emergence of democracy but does impact its sustainability. On average, democracies with per capita incomes of less than US$1,000 last 8.5 years while those with per capita incomes of over US$6,000 endure for 99. The reasons for this are straightforward. Relatively wealthy countries are better able to allocate their resources to most or all groups making claims on the state, while poor countries are not. The result is that politics in a poor country is likely to be a zero-sum game, a reality that does not foster bargaining and compromise between competing interests or a willingness to play by democratic rules.

Almost all African countries remain agrarian societies. With few exceptions like South Africa, Gabon, and Nigeria, 65 percent to 90 percent of the national populations reside in rural areas where most people are peasant farmers. Consequently, most Africans maintain strong attachments to their places of residence and to fellow citizens within their communities. Norms of reciprocity also shape social relations to a much greater degree than in urban industrial societies. In this context, Africans usually define their political interests—that is to say, their interests as citizens vis-à-vis the state—in terms of where they live and their affective ties to neighbors, rather than on the basis of occupation or socio-economic class.

With the exceptions of Botswana and Somalia, all African countries are multi-ethnic societies where each group inhabits a distinct territorial home-land. Africans' tendency to define their political interests in terms of where they live is thus accentuated by the fact that residents of different areas are often members of different ethnic groups or sub-groups.

Finally, African states provide much larger proportions of wage employment, particularly middle-class employment, than states in other regions do. African states have also historically been large mobilizers of capital, though to a lesser extent recently. Few countries have given rise to a middle class that does not depend on the state for its own employment and reproduction. In this context, people seek political office for the resources it confers, for their clients' benefit, and for the chance to enhance their own status. In the words of a well known Nigerian party slogan, "I chop, you chop," literally, "I eat, you eat."

POSTSCRIPT

Is Multi-Party Democracy Taking Hold in Africa?

In addition to the factors raised by Barkan as inhibiting democracy in Africa, which some would dispute, there are other conditions frequently evoked to foreground a discussion of multiparty democracy in Africa. First, prior to independence, most African nations had little to no experience with democracy (as it is conceived in the West) at the national scale. If anything, the colonial period served to reinforce undemocratic tendencies, as the main purpose of unelected colonial administrations was to extract resources. Second, most African nations inherited national borders from the colonial era that cut across ethnic boundaries. The "unnaturalness" of these boundaries has made African states more difficult to govern. Third, and a point alluded to in the introduction to this issue, external powers have meddled in African affairs, often to the detriment of more representative government. The French, in particular, have intervened on a number of occasions in their former colonies when the leadership was not supportive of French interests. Finally, the role of the military is very poorly defined in many African contexts. In the absence of strong civilian rule, there is a tendency for this institution to assert control when there are economic or political problems. Here again, the way in which the military was used in the colonial era probably has contributed to this ill-defined role. While some scholars are highly cognizant of the aforementioned factors when assessing political change in Africa, others assert that attempts to put the "blame" for Africa's nontransition to democracy on outsiders or former colonial powers is simply a convenient excuse for the corruption and mismanagement of African leaders.

For those interested in further reading, Claude Ake offers a different perspective on African democracy than Bratton and Mattes, arguing that "the democracy movement in Africa will emphasize concrete economic and social rights rather than abstract political rights." See *Democracy and Development in Africa* (The Brookings Institution, 1997). A good example of a more thoroughly pessimistic view (or realistic depending on your perspective) of the prospects for democracy in Africa is George Ayittey's *Africa in Chaos* (St. Martin's Press, 1998).

ISSUE 17

Is Foreign Assistance Useful for Fostering Democracy in Africa?

YES: Arthur A. Goldsmith, from "Donors, Dictators, and Democrats in Africa," *The Journal of Modern African Studies* (2001)

NO: Julie Hearn, from "Aiding Democracy? Donors and Civil Society in South Africa," *Third World Quarterly* (2000)

ISSUE SUMMARY

YES: Arthur A. Goldsmith, professor of management at the University of Massachusetts in Boston, examines the relationship between the amount of development assistance given to sub-Saharan African countries in the 1990s and the evolution of their political systems. He suggests that there is a positive, but small, correlation between donor assistance and democratization during this period. He views aid as insurance to prevent countries from sliding back into one-party or military rule.

NO: Julie Hearn, with the department of politics and international relations at Lancaster University, investigates democracy assistance in South Africa. She critically examines the role assigned to civil society by donors, questioning the "emancipatory potential" of the kind of democracy being promoted.

Starting in the early 1990s the international aid community began to more explicitly link donor assistance to democratic reform in Africa. This was in part due to a realization that, in the quest for constancy in strategically important African nations, the United States and other donor nations had often perpetuated the existence of corrupt and antidemocratic regimes that ultimately were unstable. Furthermore, the end of the cold war and the disintegration of the Soviet Union meant that the competing one-party, socialist ideology had lost most of its steam. Finally, there was a growing conceptual assertion that good governance was essential for economic growth and enhanced international trade. The way in which donors openly began to work to shape political structures in Africa was unprecedented. While covert attempts to influence the internal politics of African nations had always existed, it was once considered an infringement of national sovereignty for one nation to work actively and openly at shaping the political discourse in another.

The link between foreign assistance and democratic reform has taken two major forms to date. The first is "political conditionality," which links general foreign assistance (for all types of programs) to governance and democracy criteria. In other words, a country must meet certain standards of democracy as a condition for receiving any type of assistance. So, for example, the World Bank now requires its loan applicants to meet certain governance and economic criteria before it will release funds. The second type of assistance is designed specifically to promote the development and strengthening of democratic institutions and practices (often through technical assistance programs). For example, the United States Agency of International Development (USAID) works to advance democracy in Africa by funding programs that facilitate: 1) free and fair elections, 2) the rule of law, 3) a greater advocacy role for civil society, and 4) transparent, accountable, and participatory governance.

Proponents of this approach argue that it is better to rely on governance criteria than geopolitical considerations when dispensing aid. Critics suggest that the former is just a thinly veiled rationale for the latter, which will always dictate who receives foreign assistance and how much. Furthermore, they assert that democratic and economic conditionalities are now tightly woven into one package promoting a global neoliberal agenda that favors the interests of the wealthy nations over those of the poor.

In this issue, Arthur A. Goldsmith examines the relationship between the amount of development assistance given to sub-Saharan African countries in the 1990s and their levels of democratic reform. His assessment of such reform is based on a number of measures, including the staging of elections, electoral challenges to incumbent leaders, voter participation, the number of coup d'etats, and political indices (Freedom House index of political freedom and a democracy index). He states that there is a positive, but small, correlation between donor assistance and democratization during this period. Goldsmith views aid as analogous to "'maintenance therapy'—the long-term use of foreign assistance to forestall or postpone re-emergent authoritarian rule."

In contrast, Julie Hearn examines democracy assistance in South Africa and suggests that Western donors are largely concerned with establishing forms of governance that help maintain the international system. She asserts that U.S. assistance effectively has changed the debate on democracy in South Africa among civil society organizations, encouraging a focus on procedural democracy, and minimizing discourse related to economic justice. She is critical of this type of assistance because it has led to the maintenance of an "intensely exploitative economic system" in South Africa.

YES

Arthur A. Goldsmith

Donors, Dictators, and Democrats in Africa

Introduction

Sub-Saharan Africa (henceforth simply Africa) is marked by weak, often dictatorial states. They are also disproportionately among the states that receive the most aid per capita in the world. Is there a connection? A growing opinion assumes that there must be. It is probably no surprise when Doug Bandow (1997) of the libertarian Cato Institute asserts that fifty years experience proves that aid usually hurts political reform. More surprising, perhaps, is a study sponsored by the Swedish Foreign Ministry that documents how large amounts of aid delivered over long periods may reduce accountability and democratic decision-making among recipient states (Bräutigam 2000). Even the World Bank (1998: 84–8) raises questions about aid's impact on governments, concluding that the Bank has often given too much money to ineffective regimes and in the process has sometimes undermined their administrative capacity.

A common theme in these criticisms is that aid is like a narcotic, fostering addictive behaviour among states that receive it. States are thought to exhibit the symptoms of dependence—a short-run benefit from aid, but increasing need for external support that does lasting damage to the country (Azam et al. 1999). By feeding this 'addiction', the aid donors have supposedly weakened the resolve of African states to act on behalf of their citizens. Development assistance, in other words, has had the perverse and unintended political effect of reinforcing despotic rule in the region. The implication is that countries need to 'kick the habit' of aid before they can turn to the task of building authentic democratic institutions.

This article takes a sceptical look at these convictions, asking whether it is true that heavy reliance on aid has blocked democratic development in Africa. It focuses on the period after 1990, when many donors started making democratisation an explicit object of policy. Dissenting from the prevailing critique of aid, it finds that aid dependency has not systematically set back Africa's political evolution. The evidence suggests, to the contrary, that aid may have had a small favourable effect over the past decade, encouraging more responsible self-government in some countries. . . . Getting Africa off the donor assistance 'drug' is a commendable goal, but it does not appear to

From *The Journal of Modern African Studies*, September 2001. Copyright © 2001 by Cambridge University Press. Reprinted by permission.

be a prerequisite for democratisation in the region, as some people assume is true. Weaning countries abruptly from external financing and technical assistance might well have the opposite effect.

Foreign aid is an international transfer of resources that would not have taken place as the result of market forces. It includes grants and loans made at subsidised interest rates, provided by governments or by international financial institutions. It also includes technical assistance and debt relief. One goal of these transfers has been to encourage democracy, or pluralistic national political systems where people are reasonably free to express their political demands and to hold rulers to account. Democracy in this sense is not identical with competitive elections, held at regular intervals. The two do overlap, however, and elections are often the best tangible evidence of the extent to which a democratic system is in place. Accordingly, the discussion will concentrate on election procedures and outcomes.

The article starts by documenting the ways in which international donors have attempted to boost democracy in the region. Donors' forays into government reform have been criticised as inconsequential or counterproductive. However, analysis of the data suggests a clear, though small, correlation between the amount of aid received by a country in the 1990s, and the extent to which its political system opened up to greater accountability and competition. The issue for many African countries is how to consolidate and extend these moderate reforms on their own, with less external support.

Foreign Aid for Democracy

Africa has been using large amounts of foreign aid for years. Depending on the definition of aid, the average African country took between $600 and $1,500 (in 1995 prices) in aid per capita between the mid-1970s and mid-1990s. Starting about 1990, international donors began to link these resources expressly to democratic reform. Representative government had disappeared in most African countries following independence. Too often, African governments ignored or repressed their people. They failed to supply critical public goods—or if they did, they redirected them to the regime's narrow base of supporters. During the Cold War, the rich democracies were reluctant to say or do much about these governmental problems for fear of driving African countries into the socialist camp. The changed geopolitical scene in the late 1980s altered those calculations and freed public lenders to use their clout to extract domestic political concessions in Africa (Olson 1998).

The new official consensus on democratisation was clearly reflected in the Development Assistance Committee (DAC) policy statement in 1993. For the first time, the DAC specifically advocated that developing countries lay down procedures whereby ordinary people can help shape the policies that affect their lives. Communities and private organisations must be empowered so they can check the risk of arbitrary government, according to the DAC. Thus, client states should be encouraged to build institutions that assure the consent of the governed—and that allow the governed to withhold their consent so that their political leaders can be peacefully replaced (OECD 1993: 9–12).

To take at face value any official developed country policy statement about the importance of democratic government in a developing country would be naive. Since 1975, an amendment to the Foreign Assistance Act has made US aid conditional on respect for human rights and civil liberties. Yet, *realpolitik* often meant that human rights violations were overlooked, while national security issues dominated who got aid (Hook 1998). An oft-cited example was Zaire's Mobutu Sese Sekou, whose corrupt but reliably anti-communist regime for decades received American backing. With the 'Evil Empire' defeated, however, US foreign assistance policy turned more seriously to human rights as a basis for determining how to allocate resources (Meernik et al. 1998; Apodaca & Stohl 1999; Blanton 2000). The United States suspended aid to Mobutu in 1992.

There was economic logic behind making legislative and administrative reforms a centre of attention in development assistance. Greater participation and more debate in public life, the donors argued, would provide a sounder institutional grounding for economic advancement. Not only did democracy offer a better way to aggregate and employ local knowledge, the climate of open discussion would help move resources to their most productive uses. Democracy's built-in checks and balances can lead to greater public account-ability, responsiveness and transparency—which can enhance the business and investment climate, and perhaps eventually make foreign assistance less important. Empirical evidence also exists that democracy helps less-developed countries make better use of the aid that they do get (Svensson 1995).

This is not the classic political defence of civil liberties and free and fair elections. The usual instrumental arguments for democratic procedures are that they give voice to majority demands and that they are a peaceful means for recruiting new leadership talent. The economic argument put forth by international financial institutions and bilateral aid agencies in the 1990s is different. Without denying the political advantages of pluralistic competi-tion, the donors' economic argument concentrates on improving the environ-ment for private investment and innovation.

How Aid Affects Recipient Country Politics

Foreign aid can help shape African domestic politics in four ways. The first way happens by accident. Some of the pressure for government reforms in Africa is a by-product of donor-inspired economic austerity schemes, also known as structural adjustment. Imposed with increasingly frequency since the 1980s, these market-based reforms aim to shake up moribund African economies. Yet, they also encourage political shake-ups by curbing the power of the state to pay off its partners and confidants in the private sector. Africa's hitherto 'silent majority' has been energised to begin exercising its voice—though ironically, it is sometimes to speak against the hardship associated with structural adjustment. Democratic political reforms may thus inadvert-ently undermine pro-market economic policies, and contradict the donors' economic aims for their African clients (Baylies 1995). Still, the political effect often is for greater mass participation in public life, especially among urban groups who have tended to see themselves as net losers under structural adjustment.

The second mode of donor political influence is through direct aid for political reform. A recent example is Chad, which held a constitutional referendum and a presidential contest in 1996. France provided the logistical support that allowed co-ordination of voting nation-wide. France also underwrote the cost of Chad's elections (May & Massey 2000: 122). The amounts the donors give directly for governance and civil service reform are limited—only 4.4 per cent of all bilateral official development assistance (ODA) commitments made world-wide in 1998 (DAC 1999, Table 19). The World Bank (1999, Appendix 12) reports that its cumulative spending for public sector management in Africa amounted to just 3.8 per cent of lending to the region as of 1999.

However, these figures grossly understate the degree of external support for political reform. They do not include additional resources that go to support non-government organisations (NGOs). NGOs are a third avenue for aid's influence on democratisation. Official donors are taking steps to strengthen these voluntary and community groups in Africa (Robinson 1995). About half the World Bank's development projects have some involvement of local and international NGOs, for example. Many bilateral donors make even greater use of NGOs. Worldwide, about $9 billion in official aid is funnelled annually through these groups, or 15 per cent of all aid, not including the private funds that NGOs raise and spend on charitable activities (Gibbs et al. 1999). These groups often advocate on behalf of underrepresented groups in society, which may lead to demands for changes in political institutions and procedures.

Modifying the political system is not usually the donors' immediate objective when they enter partnerships with NGOs. Sometimes the aid may have the opposite effect of politically neutralising the recipient groups by making them look like foreign agents (Robinson 1993). Critics charge that too many domestic democracy movements in Africa rely on external support for resources and validation (Ihonvbere 1996). Yet, over time, such groups may add to the domestic organisational endowment and social capital that are important foundations for democratic government. Case studies in Ghana, Uganda and South Africa find that aid-supported groups can become key players in setting the course of national political reform (Hearne 1999).

The fourth, and perhaps most important, way in which aid can affect a recipient country's politics is through specific political conditionalities. Donors put political strings on loans for seemingly unrelated projects and programmes, using the financial resources as a reward and punishment to induce political reform. Often working in collaboration, donors make plain to the client state that it must shape up politically or lose access to credit. Such pressure is common. After Niger's President Ibrahim Maïnassara was killed in a coup in April 1999, for example, France immediately cut off development assistance, pending a return to civilian rule. France, which is Niger's largest international patron, restored its support seven months later, after successful completion of the presidential election. When a recent study looked at World Bank and International Monetary Fund (IMF) programmes in Africa from

1997 to 1999, it found that nearly three fourths of the loan conditions (or about 80 per country) pertained to governance (Kapur & Webb 2000).

Direct political aid, NGO support, and political conditionalities are often used in concert to try to bring about a favourable result, as illustrated by Zimbabwe. The IMF and the World Bank suspended aid to Zimbabwe in 1998. There were several reasons, the most serious being the sending of troops to the Democratic Republic of Congo (DRC), which compromised efforts to control Zimbabwe's budget deficit. The IMF and World Bank offered to restore the money only if Zimbabwe showed a serious effort to curb its military and to undertake other administrative and political reforms.

President Robert Mugabe's subsequent land policies hardened the donors' position. In an effort to buttress political support in the run-up to legislative elections in 2000, Mugabe openly sanctioned illegal seizures of commercial farms. His government also drew up a list of properties to be taken officially without compensation. Opposition groups charged that these farms were earmarked for government cronies instead of people who really needed land. Britain signalled its willingness to release funds for land reforms and to organise a conference to solicit support from other Western countries to redistribute farms to the truly landless. However, first all unauthorised land invasions had to stop and legal procedures be restored.

The US Agency for International Development (AID) forged links in Zimbabwe with private groups on grounds that government institutions were too politicised to be effective. For the 2000 national elections, the US government funded the training of 10,000 domestic election monitors and helped the semi-independent Electoral Supervisory Commission to cope with the administrative demands of election logistics. In Washington, the United States Congress considered the Zimbabwe Democracy Bill. It would impose an embargo on the country pending a certified return to the rule of law, respect for ownership of property, and freedom of speech and association.

Doubts and Controversies

How effective have such activities been? Official statements usually reflect self-assurance. In recent testimony before Congress, for example, AID's assistant administrator for Africa, Vivian Lowery Derryck (1999) expressed the following position:

> As a whole, Africa has made major progress towards expanding and consolidating democracy during the past ten years. The widespread increases in freedom of speech and the media, freedom of assembly and association, competitive national and local elections, and the growth of civil society have given more Africans greater freedom and stability in their lives than at any time in the recent past . . . USAID has been involved in many of these transitions, and we are proud of the achievements of these new democracies.

When policymakers speak for themselves, however, they typically sound less confident about the political outcome of their work. Former chief economist at the World Bank, Joseph Stiglitz (1999) has said that policy conditionalities actually tend to undermine participatory processes in developing countries, which should be building their own capacity to make democratic decisions. Ex-deputy administrator for AID Carol Lancaster (1999: 66) goes farther, suggesting that foreign aid in Africa has encouraged poor governance, by giving dishonest and incompetent regimes a sense of security.

It is not hard to find anecdotal evidence to support scepticism about foreign aid's beneficial political impact. Consider the Zimbabwe case, just cited. Despite the pressure, President Mugabe remained defiant. He charged that the opposition Movement for Democratic Change was the surrogate of the British and American governments. Foreign observers were turned away from the 2000 elections. Challenger candidates and their supporters were intimidated. Zimbabwe defaulted on its foreign debt that year. The government refused to obey court rulings against the land seizures, and it kept its troops engaged in the DRC. World Bank and IMF credits remained on hold. Political conditionalities appear to work best when they are in response to a specific event or tip the balance towards domestic opposition groups (Crawford 1997)—neither of which were evidently the case in Zimbabwe.

Nor have donors been completely consistent about whom they help. They have pushed harder for civil rights with some clients than others. In June 1990, French President François Mitterrand warned African heads of state that French aid would henceforth be conditional on progress in the direction of democracy. France pointedly did not intervene to protect the dictator Hissène Habré of Chad in a coup six months later, despite having troops in his country. Yet France ignored human rights abuses by Habré's successor, Idriss Déby.

The problem with negative anecdotes like these is that one can find others that cast foreign pressure and support for democratisation in a more positive light. Though it never received much direct financial assistance, South Africa is perhaps the best example of how the international community has helped give birth to a liberal constitution and multiparty political system in Africa. To assess aid's political impact systematically, we cannot rely just on stories from selected countries; we need to look specifically for two things: (a) comprehensive indications of the degree of democratisation across Africa; and (b), if democratisation can be substantiated, for signs that aid contributed to it. . . .

Evidence of Democratisation

Political scientists who specialise on Africa tend to question the authenticity and depth of democracy in the region. The social context of electoral rules obviously differs from what is found in Europe or North America, and superficially similar institutions and procedures may hold very different meanings south of the Sahara. With most African political reforms so new, no one can make confident predictions about where they are heading. Nonetheless, three types of evidence can be cited in support of a bona fide democratic tendency. One indication is that across the sub-continent more liberal rules of political engagement are being adopted. Second, is the growing number and competitiveness of elections in recent years. Third, are overall indexes of political freedom, which, because they capture the previous two types of evidence, have been on the rise in Africa. . . .

This article has looked into the relationship between foreign aid and steps towards democracy in African countries over the past decade and earlier. Among specialists in international relations, it is often considered axiomatic that aid has an addictive effect on government that subtly reinforces repression in countries with single party rule, even if the opposite result is intended. Many area experts also doubt the ability and good will of outsiders to sponsor human rights and authentic multiparty competition in Africa. The result is seen as 'donor democracy' without significant domestic bloodlines. Civil society critics of the international economic regime, such as the Fifty Years is Enough Coalition or the Jubilee 2000 movement, are apt to agree that aid (at least in its current forms) is anti-democratic in character. Even the donors sometimes concede the point that their efforts in Africa have been politically counterproductive.

This article's analysis suggests a somewhat more favourable outlook. First, the data indicates that democratisation is more than a false front put up for donors. In some countries, at least, meaningful though tenuous changes in governing style and substance look as if they are taking place. Second, while we must be cautious about attributing causation, foreign assistance appears to have a positive association with these welcome political trends. This conclusion is supported by statistical analysis of quantitative data. Donors, it seems, can work with some client states or with civil society groups to obtain somewhat greater democratisation in Africa. There is no evidence here for the prevalent view that the 'compulsive use' of aid has net perverse political effect, or that 'going cold turkey' with less aid would speed the pace of democratic reform. Rather than the metaphor of addiction, a closer analogy may be 'maintenance therapy'—the long-term use of foreign assistance to forestall or postpone re-emergent authoritarian rule.

The difficulty for development policymakers is that aid's political benefit appears to be quite small and perhaps transient. Local opposition to arbitrary leadership and public corruption seems far more important. With many other factors pulling against democratic reform, any gains won with the help of development funds can easily be undone. At issue for many African countries is whether they can find the means to use official assistance to greater political effect, consolidating and extending the modest progress made since 1990. Given pressure from the developed world to break the cycle of aid dependence in Africa, these societies probably will soon have far less external help for their efforts to head for more responsive and open systems of government.

Julie Hearn

 NO

Aiding Democracy? Donors and Civil Society in South Africa

Democracy Assistance: Promoting Stability

During the 1980s a new branch of the aid industry was born, democracy assistance. Although 'democracy' often entered the foreign-policy-making vocabulary of the North in the postwar period, it was not the dominant form in which the North related to the South. The principal form was the development of strategic alliances with authoritarian regimes. The new industry arose out of a major reconsideration of Western foreign policy towards the South, particularly within the USA. With the US defeat in Vietnam, the Nicaraguan revolution and other nationalist victories in the South, US foreign policy towards the Third World had reached crisis-point by the late 1970s. It had failed to stop popular anti-US regimes taking power in South East Asia, Central America and Southern Africa and its capacity to shape events abroad appeared severely curtailed. By the early 1980s, a new consensus began to emerge among policy-makers around the strategy of 'democracy promotion'. This involved two key elements.

First was the recognition that coercive political arrangements had failed to deal with the social movements that had challenged authoritarian rule and that formal liberal democracies were better able to absorb social dissent and conflict. It is important to understand that the rationale for turning to liberal democracy was that it was perceived to be a better guarantor of stability. The goal remained the same: social stability, it was simply that the means to achieve the end had changed. This becomes clear when we examine the kind of democracy being promoted in the Third World. It is about creating political structures that most effectively maintain the international system. It has no more to do with radical change than its predecessor, authoritarianism does. As Samuel Huntington, one of the most influential proponents of formal democracy, clearly states: 'The maintenance of democratic politics and the reconstruction of the social order are fundamentally incompatible.' At its core, the contemporary political and industry is about effective system maintenance.

The second point is that, where earlier foreign policy had focused almost exclusively on the strength of the client state and its governmental apparatus, the new democracy strategy began to recognise the important role of civil society. It was from within civil society that opposition to authoritarian rule

From *Third World Quarterly*, vol. 21, no. 5, 2000, pp. 815–817, 819, 821, 823–825. Copyright © 2000 by Taylor & Francis Journals. Reprinted by permission.

had emerged and therefore it was imperative 'to penetrate civil society and *from therein* assure control over popular mobilization' (emphasis in original). [William I.] Robinson continues:

> The composition and balance of power in civil society in a given Third World country is now just as important to US and transnational interests as who controls the governments of those countries. This is a shift from social control 'from above' to social control 'from below . . . '

This is an important part of democracy assistance. Aid is targeted at a country's most influential, modern, advocacy-orientated civil society organs which include: women's organisations, human rights groups, national or sectoral NGO [nongovernmental organization] for business associations, private policy institutes, youth and student organisations, and professional media associations. As commentators, including those who direct the new political aid, have pointed out, this is not very different from what the CIA used to do, particularly within the context of counter-insurgency and 'low-intensity conflict'. However, former CIA director William Colby makes a key point: 'Many of the programs which . . . were conducted as covert operations [can now be] conducted quite openly, and consequently, without controversy'.

As Robinson points out: 'Transferring political intervention from the covert to the overt realm does not change its character, but it does make it easier for policymakers to build domestic and international support for this intervention.' This is the trump-card of democracy promotion, it diffuses opposition to Northern intervention. Advisor to the State Department and academic, [Howard] Wiarda, clearly sums up:

> A US stance in favor of democracy helps get the Congress, the bureaucracy, the media, the public, and elite opinion to back US policy. It helps ameliorate the domestic debate, disarms critics (who could be against democracy?) . . . The democracy agenda enables us, additionally, to merge and fudge over some issues that would otherwise be troublesome. It helps bridge the gap between our fundamental geopolitical and strategic interests . . . and our need to clothe those security concerns in moralistic language . . . The democracy agenda, in short, is a kind of legitimacy cover for our more basic strategic objectives.

Since its inception in the early 1980s, democracy assistance has continued its take-off. In the 1990s this was fuelled by three important developments: the academic and donor preoccupation with 'governance' as the root of underdevelopment, the practice of political conditionality, that is, making aid conditional on political reforms, and the changing balance of power in North–South relations. During the 1980s an orthodoxy developed that Africa's development crisis was precipitated by a failure of the state and that 'governance' had to be reconstructed, from the bottom up. Shaping civil society became the road to reforming the state. Making aid dependent on such changes has been the site of sharp confrontations between the governments of many sub-Saharan African countries and donors. In South Africa, no such crude coercion was needed. As international opponents of apartheid, including Western states, united with domestic combatants, a broad consensus was forged over the form that a new liberal democracy would take. With the demise of nationalist and socialist ideologies, such foreign, overtly political, interference was no longer viewed with the same levels of distrust. The latter has allowed the North to intervene in the (civil) societies of the South with an unprecedented degree of perceived legitimacy.

South Africa has had a long history of Western support to civil society. The highly conflictual politics of apartheid, particularly of the late 1970s and 1980s, generated a 'vast array of more or less popular, more or less institutionalised organisations and initiatives in broad opposition to the apartheid state'. These included trade unions, community organisations, sectorally mobilised movements of youth, students and women, as well as business, lawyers and religious associations. It is these kinds of civil society organisations (CSOs) (although they were hardly ever referred to as such) that donors funded. This support began with Denmark in the mid-1960s and was followed by Norway and Sweden in the 1970s. It culminated in the mid-1980s with the imposition of sanctions by Western governments and the international isolation of the apartheid regime. The Nordic countries were joined at this time by the European Union and the USA, who each provided an unprecedented $340 million over a nine year period to CSOs, before the end of apartheid and the 1994 elections. Despite such a significant involvement, a comprehensive account of foreign assistance to civil society in this period is still to be written, not least because of the covert nature of that support. With the election of an internationally recognised government, foreign donors began to provide aid to the new South African state as well as continuing some funding to civil society, though on a smaller scale. Although this loss of finance has had a considerable impact, it has not been fully analysed and thus there is substantial dispute as to how much funding was withdrawn and how significant this was.

This article examines foreign assistance to civil society in South Africa since 1994. The premise of this research is that political aid is 'political', that it is about consciously influencing the 'rules of the game'. . . .

The Importance of Democracy Assistance

Unlike in other African countries, democracy assistance forms a major part of foreign aid to South Africa. The principal objective of aid programmes to the country is to influence the political transition and to focus on democratic consolidation. This kind of aid is in stark contrast to other donor programmes on the continent, which primarily supplement the meagre national budget of African governments so that they can provide basic services in the areas of welfare, agriculture, energy and infrastructure. These are the predominant categories of aid in most African countries, where democracy assistance on average accounts for less than 5% of total aid. South Africa, with an average per capita GNP [gross national product] of about $3200, is categorised as an upper middle income country, along with Brazil and Chile. As such it would normally be disqualified as an aid recipient. Danish aid, for example, is restricted to countries with an average GNP per capita of less than $2000. Aid to the country is seen as a temporary measure, because, as USAID/South Africa points out: 'South Africa has substantial resources to address its problems over the long term.' Donor programmes are termed 'transitional', mirroring South Africa's own transition, and were to end soon after the 1999 elections, commonly perceived as the formal end-point of the passage from one political system to another. In South Africa, nation-wide poverty is not the motivating force behind donor activity. The whole thrust of aid involvement is about deepening the political changes that have taken place since 1994 and ensuring that, as far as possible, 'a point of irreversibility' is reached before the ending of external assistance. Foreign aid to South Africa is very much a case of democracy assistance, and if we wished to study contemporary foreign intervention in a country's democratisation process, South Africa could not be a better case study. . . .

Such a strong emphasis on political aid in South Africa is hardly surprising. Since the beginning of the century, South Africa has been important to the West, both politically and economically. It has been described as 'a reliable, if junior, member of the Northern club'. The West's relationship with Africa was largely predicated on a long-term strategic alliance with the apartheid regime in South Africa. This continued throughout the 1970s and into the 1980s. At the same time South African capital, some of which was in the same league as that of any Northern-based corporation, became thoroughly intermeshed with capital originating in Europe, the USA and Japan. As globalisation advanced, South Africa became a key outpost of international capital. However, with the political unrest that began with the 1976 Soweto uprising, capital outside South Africa began to push its South African counterparts to search for a political solution that would involve a transition from racial to non-racial capitalism. . . . [P]riority [was] given to democracy building in South Africa by the West after 1994. . . .

In the situation proffered by 1994, civil society was not a priority. There are a number of reasons for this. In other African countries, aid to civil society is about establishing something that is not there. It is about creating a modern, advocacy-orientated civil society. In South Africa this already exists. Using the lowest common denominator of pluralist theory, which says the more civil society groups, the better, South Africa scores highly. It has a dense, long-standing associational life. Second, this associational life is modern, a key characteristic of the donor model. Third, it is strongly advocacy-orientated and has proven its lobbying abilities on the world stage. Fourth, in South Africa, in 1994 at least, donors did not need to convince the new government that civil society had a legitimate role to play and that the government must give it the political space in which to operate. That was already what the government believed, since many new government officials came from the NGO sector, and as a result there were unusually close and sympathetic relationships between civil society and the government.

However, perhaps most importantly, many donors had established close links with civil society throughout the 1980s and early 1990s. For example, a large number supported the work of IDASA [Institute for a Democratic South Africa] in the late 1980s and early 1990s. IDASA is arguably one of the most professional, effective and high profile CSOs in South Africa today, and thoroughly steeped in democratic liberalism. A 1994 annual report states that the 'personal credibility with international donors' of cofounder, Boraine, 'was pivotal in securing a generous funding base for the organisation, allowing it to expand country-wide and make interventions with national impact'. After the 1994 elections, IDASA was renamed the Institute for Democracy in South Africa. It now runs some 12 national programmes and projects and has a staff of 140. This close association with donors continues today, possibly making it the most donor-associated democracy NGO in South Africa. We have indicated how the German foundations developed strategic relationships with sections of civil society, how the Nordic countries were stalwart supporters of an underground civil society, and the enormous resources that the USA spent on cultivating links with CSOs. Already from the mid-1980s the USA had grasped the pivotal role that civil society would play in shaping the new South Africa. Subsequently, it began to attempt to influence it, checking the growing radicalism among the black population by developing counterweight forces conducive to the establishment of a liberal order. This was achieved by supporting an emergent black middle class of professionals who could be incorporated into a post-apartheid order; developing a network of grassroots community leaders who could compete with more radical leadership; and cultivating a black business class that would have a stake in stable South African capitalism. From the standpoint of 1994, donors had already made an impact in civil society. The next section suggests one important role that donors are financing civil society to play in the new South Africa.

What Role for Civil Society?

A report on the democratic outlook for South Africa by an influential South African think-tank concludes that the chief threat to democratic consolidation is:

> the limited capacity of the state to govern—and, more particularly, to cement a 'social contract' with society in which government protects the rights of citizens who, in turn, meet their obligations to democratic government.

The US National Democratic Institute (NDI) describes the situation facing South Africa in the following terms: 'the twin challenges of rebuilding a new united South Africa while simultaneously developing the institutions that will conduct the daily business of government'. We have shown how foreign aid has prioritised the institutional development of government, thereby attempting to meet the need to build the capacity of the state to govern. However, as both analysts note, the other side of the equation is to link society with this new institutional framework, to cement the social contract and to build, in the words of the then Deputy President, Thabo Mbeki, 'a democratized political culture'. This is where the role of civil society is so important to the architects, both domestic and external, of the new South Africa. It is a particular kind of civil society that can help to legitimise the new state in the eyes of the South African citizenry and help to build a culture where citizens meet their obligations to liberal democratic government. First we show why this is needed in South Africa if liberal democracy is to succeed. Then we examine which civil society institutions are available to fulfil this function and how donor organisations are supporting this very role for civil society.

The same South African report writes about 'widespread citizen non-compliance—reflected in, among other indicators, crime and widespread non-payment for public services'. It continues: 'A variety of factors produce outcomes in which citizen dissatisfaction is expressed in withdrawal from the public arena and in attempts to evade the reach of government'. It concludes: 'This threatens democracy as much as overt resistance to democratic order . . . ' An annual review of political developments in South Africa in 1997, produced for the quarterly journal of the South African Coalition of NGOs and Interfund, a consortium of Northern NGOs, mainly Nordic, provides the following commentary:

> Whether currently higher or merely consistent with historical trends, crime rates in South Africa are unusually high . . . Public insecurity aside, the effect of crime is to reduce citizens' confidence in public institutions at a point when the success of the democratic transition requires enhanced trust and participation.

And a report written for the consortium of non-governmental donors, Interfund, writes:

> A key challenge for actors in civil society is to capture and steer rising (and probably inevitable) frustration into constructive, non-violent forms of conflict, namely political pressure channeled through social movements.

The purpose of the transition was to provide the political settlement that would allow the passage from racial to non-racial capitalism in South Africa. As we have noted, aid programmes have maintained this focus on political stability rather than on socioeconomic transformation, as a result of which South Africa continues to be a highly unequal society with areas of extreme deprivation. Indeed [Robert] Mattes and [Hermann] Thiel assert that the inequality is worsening. [Hein] Marais points out how the kind of instability facing South Africa, described by the above commentators, is 'symptomatic of the extreme inequalities that scar the society'. In a situation of such contradiction between economic inequality and political stability, political stability or 'democracy' will be simply about managing that tension. Civil society is the lynchpin in holding together that tension by fostering support among citizens for a government that maintains the inequality that undermines their lives. This, in effect, is recognised by the above report where it identifies the need for civil society to capture and steer the rising frustration. Obviously, social concessions will be made from time to time to maintain stability, but the primary function of political society, that is the state and civil society, will be to manage the tension between the economic and political spheres. Constituents of civil society must understand that this is their function in the political economy of South Africa in the eyes of those who wish to maintain capitalism, and ask themselves is this the role that they want to play?

Civil society plays this role in two ways. First it is the key mediator between the new state in South Africa and its citizens. From the following ratings we can see how urgently this is needed. . . . [A]pproval of the government's performance dropped between 1995 and 1997. The national government's aparting fell from 57% to 47%; parliament's went from 53% to 46%; and over-all approval of all the provincial governments declined from 42% to 36%. In 1997 the approval rating for the new local governments introduced at the beginning of 1996 stood at a meagre 30%. No wonder then that the Konrad Adenauer foundation asserts that 'if democracy is to be understood and accepted by South Africans it must be seen to work well, particularly at the local level'. Second, the CPS [Centre for Policy Studies] report points out that democratic consolidation can only occur when there is widespread agreement among political elites and citizens on institutional rules. They cite political development theorists [Juan] Linz and [Alfred] Stepan who see democracy as consolidated when democratic rules become 'the only game in town'. Civil society has a key role to play in creating among the population an adherence to the values of liberal democracy and an acceptance of the rules of the game. Mattes and Thiel argue that, as well as structural features, an attitudinal commitment to democracy is essential. They write: 'The level of elite and citizen commitment to democratic processes is the single direct determinant of the probability of democratic endurance or consolidation.' In their analysis of public opinion polls taken on 'democracy' they comment: 'The results raise important questions about South Africans' understanding of democracy.' While only 27% rated as 'essential' such key procedural elements of democracy as reg-ular elections, 48% said that equal access to houses, jobs and a decent income was 'essential' to democracy. They go on to explain why this might be so:

> While 'one man, one vote' was always the goal, the key liberation movements subscribed to and spread to their poverty-stricken followers an economic, as opposed to a procedural view of democracy.

This is disturbing to the authors and, of course, to those, within and outside the country, who wish to maintain the distinction between the politi-cal and economic sphere and maintain the tension between gross inequality and political stability. This is the wrong kind of democracy. The authors advise the following re-education:

> Thus one might urge South Africa's educational system, civil society, and political parties to shift their emphasis . . . to the . . . task of teaching people to value democratic institutions and processes more for their own sake than for what they may deliver in terms of immediate and tangible benefits.

What is interesting in South Africa, compared with other African countries, is the number and calibre of CSOs geared towards doing precisely that, encouraging a popular commitment to procedural democracy. What is more, these kinds of CSOs feature predominantly in donor political aid programmes. In our research we asked over a dozen different foreign donors what kind of civil society organisations they funded through their democracy assistance. There were five main categories: democracy organisations, concerned with the overall relationship between states and citizens; human rights and legal aid groups; conflict resolution agencies; organisations servicing or representing the nongovernmental sector; and think-tanks. Of these categories, democracy organisations were the largest. Not only were they the most numerous, but they also received the largest amounts of aid and were supported by the broadest cross-section of donors.

This is not to suggest that donor focus on the other categories, particularly in the human rights and legal aid field, is unimportant. For example, the National Institute for Public Interest Law & Research (NIPLAR), a consortium, received $3.25 million from USAID between 1996 and 1998 to create 18 human rights and democracy centres nation-wide. Along with the Legal Resource Centre (LRC) and the Black Sash Trust, NIPLAR receives donor funds to provide free legal advice. Between 1996 and 1999 USAID funded the Independent Mediation Service of South Africa (IMSSA) with $3 million as an umbrella grantee providing subgrants to conflict resolution NGOs working with local government. Another significant grant from the USA in 1997 went to the Free Market Foundation, a core partner of the German liberal Friedrich Naumann Foundation. This was to fund a programme promoting market-orientated economic policies in the South African parliament and administration. Many of these internationally funded projects form part of a broad liberal democratic discourse; however, it is crucial to investigate what the specific category of democracy organisations do in civil society.

The most prominent is IDASA. It is fully committed to procedural democracy, for example, the manager of the public opinion service at IDASA co-wrote the above article. As we mentioned, it is now an organisation with a staff of 140. It is probably also the most donor-funded CSO in South Africa. The other organisations are the Institute for Multiparty Democracy, whose name could not be more indicative of procedural democracy, and Khululekani Institute for Democracy, aimed at bringing parliament closer to the people. A fourth, the Electoral Institute of South Africa, deals with that key aspect of procedural democracy. A fifth, the Helen Suzman foundation, undertakes similar democracy surveys to those of IDASA, and has a map of Southern Africa on the back of its quarterly enblazoned with 'promoting liberal democracy'. A sixth, the South African Institute of Race Relations has a foreign donor-funded Free Society project which aims to monitor South Africa's democratic development and to promote the rule of law, ethics, justice, the concept of limited government and economic freedom. As a 1995 project description, written by one of its foreign funders, the US National Endowment for Democracy, explains: the programme will inform key government and non-government officials on activities that hinder the development of a free society. The project seeks to achieve these aims through three principal means: (1) publishing *'Frontiers of Freedom'*, a quarterly newsletter; (2) sponsoring specific research projects; and (3) hosting and attending special events, including briefings and lectures, frequently in conjunction with other non-profit institutions. It is interesting to note how some of the language has changed in the 1997 project description, which introduces the relatively new term 'civil society organisations', talks explicitly about researching 'public policy alternatives', and replaces the ideologically unambiguous 'limited government' with the much more ambiguous and widely accepted term, 'good governance'.

It is not altogether surprising to find out that these civil society organisations at the forefront of promoting procedural democracy are very much part of the South African liberal landscape. The South African Institute of Race Relations is one of the oldest liberal institutions in the country. The Helen Suzman foundation is named after arguably the most prominent South African liberal politician. IDASA was started in 1987 by van Zyl Slabbert, former leader of the opposition and Alex Boraine, former Progressive Federal Party MP. What these CSOs have done is to put procedural democracy high up on the agenda for civil society, and for the nation, and to establish the terms of the debate. This is not surprising given the resources allocated to them by the international donor community. IDASA has received grants not simply of tens of thousands of dollars, but of $1 million. In 1996 it received $1.165 million from the Ford Foundation. This is an exceptionally large grant by the Foundation's standards, which normally provides grants from $200 000 to $50 000 to CSOs in Africa, and is by far the largest grant to any grantee in South Africa. At the same time IDASA received a $1 million grant from USAID for a two-year period. The South African Institute of Race Relations and the Institute for Multi-Party Democracy received similar grants from USAID over the same period.

Conclusion

As we have seen, since 1994 South Africa has received an unprecedented amount of international political aid aimed at consolidating its liberal democracy. Even without the benefit of an in-depth, detailed study, one can safely conclude that there are few, if any, aspects of the new South African political system that have not been shaped by donor input. The external involvement in the construction of the new South African state raises important questions. What is the nature of the state of a middle income country that has been so extensively 'advised' by a myriad of international players? How do we understand such a state within existing theoretical frameworks? Does a state that is so permeable and malleable to external shapers exhibit the same autonomy as the states of advanced economies? Does it change the nature of the state? Is it a case of autonomy compromised? What impact does it have on the state's foreign policy and, perhaps even more pertinently, on its domestic policy?

And what of civil society? This article suggests that political aid to civil society has had two major consequences. First it has changed the debate on democracy. During the past five years, it is possible to see a process in which democracy has been redefined. Although half of South Africans still believe that access to housing, jobs and a decent income are essential components of a democratic society, this residual belief in social democracy is being eroded and replaced by the norms and practice of procedural democracy. It is our argument that the North has played its role in this process by funding the liberal proponents of procedural democracy in civil society, and that, subsequently, political aid has successfully 'influenced the rules of the game'. The second consequence is that this has facilitated a newly legitimatised South African state to preside over the same intensely exploitative economic system, but this time unchallenged. External and domestic support for procedural democracy has successfully removed all challenges to the system. It has ensured that democracy in the new South Africa is not about reconstructing the social order but about effective system maintenance.

POSTSCRIPT

Is Foreign Assistance Useful for Fostering Democracy in Africa?

One aspect to be aware of when interpreting these articles is that Goldsmith's research was funded by USAID, the foreign assistance arm of the U.S. government that funds a number of democracy programs in Africa. The reader should also note that some of the differences in assessment boil down to fundamentally different views on the way democracy should be conceptualized.

Many scholars are critical of the type of democracy and governance assistance being offered by USAID in Africa. A major concern is that the United States has one particular view of what democracy is and how it should function. Many believe that it is culturally presumptuous for Western nations and international financial institutions to seek the universal imposition of one type of political system.

In many African countries, district- and provincial-level officials are appointed by a central government. As such these are, relatively speaking, highly centralized political and administrative systems. While this level of centralization is not an uncommon situation in some European countries, e.g., France, this is different than the federal system in the United States where local and state officials are directly elected. This type of reform is being pushed by donors (mainly the U.S. and international financial institutions) in Africa because of a belief that decentralized government is more efficient and more responsive to the people. Critics of these policies argue that it is less about transferring power to the people than an opportunity for central government to shed its responsibilities.

For those interested in further reading, Mark Robinson has written a paper concerning donor assistance to civil society organizations entitled "Strengthening Civil Society in Africa: The Role of Foreign Political Aid," *IDS Bulletin* (no. 26, 1995). Kent Glenzer also has a very interesting book chapter, under the title "State, Donor NGO Configurations in Malian Development 1960–1999," in which he looks at the decentralization question in Mali. See B. I. Logan, ed., *Globalization, the Third World State, and Poverty-Alleviation in the Twenty-First Century* (Ashgate 2002). Finally, Kempe Hope examines a new African initiative, the New Partnership for African Development (NEPAD), designed to foster good governance and democracy in Africa in an article in *African Affairs* (2002) entitled "From Crisis to Renewal: Towards a Successful Implementation of the New Partnership for Africa's Development." Gorm Rye Olsen describes how the European Union has backed away from direct support for the promotion of democracy in Africa in a 2002 article in *International Politics* entitled "Promoting Democracy, Preventing Conflict: The European Union and Africa."

ISSUE 18

Is Corruption the Result of Poor African Leadership?

YES: Robert I. Rotberg, from "The Roots of Africa's Leadership Deficit," *Compass* (2003)

NO: Arthur A. Goldsmith, from "Risk, Rule, and Reason: Leadership in Africa," *Public Administration and Development* (2001)

ISSUE SUMMARY

YES: Robert I. Rotberg, director of the Program on Intrastate Conflict and Conflict Resolution at Harvard University's John F. Kennedy School of Government, holds African leaders responsible for the plight of their continent. He laments the large number of corrupt African leaders, seeing South Africa's Mandela and Botswana's Khama as notable exceptions. According to Rotberg, the problem is that "African leaders and their followers largely believe that the people are there to serve their rulers, rather than the other way around."

NO: Arthur A. Goldsmith, professor of management at the University of Massachusetts—Boston, suggests that African leaders are not innately corrupt but are responding rationally to incentives created by their environment. He argues that high levels of risk encourage leaders to pursue short-term, economically destructive policies. In countries where leaders face less risk, there is less perceived political corruption.

$\mathbf{R}$ightly or wrongly, corruption is perceived to be a major obstacle to development in Africa. Transparency International's annual corruptions perceptions index (a survey of surveys on this issue) ranked Chad, Nigeria, Equatorial Guinea, Ivory Coast, Angola, and the Democratic Republic of Congo among the top ten countries perceived to be the most corrupt in the world in 2005. Chad tied for first with Bangladesh as the worst in the world of the 159 countries surveyed. Among those countries perceived to be the least corrupt in Africa were Botswana, Tunisia, South Africa, and Namibia.

Arguments about the genesis of corruption in Africa typically break into those that emphasize internal factors and those that stress structural or political economic conditions (often termed externalist explanations). The first type of argument typically looks to aspects of African culture, society, and tradition to explain the presence and persistence of corruption. For example, regional ties, ethnic allegiances, obligations to the extended family, patron-client relationships, and (occasionally) moralistic explanations are used to elucidate why corruption takes place in Africa. In contrast, structural arguments begin with the premise that a proclivity for corruption is universal, but that history and macro-level political economic conditions have created or reinforced opportunities for corruption in Africa. Examples of such factors include a colonial experience that reinforced anti-democratic traditions, cash-strapped governments that cannot afford to pay civil servants a living wage, or predatory international corporations that seek to access markets and resources through bribery rather than normal government channels. The two points of view presented in this issue represent the two sides of this debate, yet they approach a middle ground of explanation that is slightly more nuanced than the typical arguments heard from either side.

In this issue, Robert I. Rotberg, director of the Program on Intrastate Conflict and Conflict Resolution at Harvard University's John F. Kennedy School of Government, holds Africa's kleptocratic, patrimonial leaders, like Robert Mugabe of Zimbabwe, responsible for giving Africa a bad name, creating poverty and despair, and inciting civil wars and ethnic conflict. He attributes this problem to several factors, including the tendency of the African electorate to "acquiesce for long periods to the autocratic actions of their leaders," the lack of a hegemonic bourgeoisie that is independent of government, a weak civil society, little expectation for political leaders to be fair, and presidents who believe they are the embodiment of the state. He praises the ethical leadership of Botswana's Khama, South Africa's Mandela, and Mauritius' Ramgoolam.

Arthur A. Goldsmith, professor of management at the University of Massachusetts—Boston, suggests that African leaders are not innately corrupt, but are responding rationally to incentives created by their environment. In finding that there is a correlation between political risk and corruption, and between low political risk and liberal economic reform, he argues that high levels of risk encourage leaders to pursue short-term, economically destructive policies. He suggests that the risks of governing may be reduced by the spread of multi-party democracy, a form of governance that will make transitions in power more orderly and reduce the chances of execution or imprisonment for leaders upon departure from office.

YES

Robert I. Rotberg

The Roots of Africa's Leadership Deficit

Leadership in Africa is typified more by disfiguring examples—the Idi Amins and Robert Mugabes—than by positive role models such as Nelson Mandela and Seretse Khama. Other clusters of developing nations, such as Southeast Asia or Latin America, exhibit wide variations in leadership quality, but none is so extreme in its range. During the past three decades roughly 90 percent of sub-Saharan Africa's leaders have behaved despotically, governed poorly, eliminated their people's human and civil rights, initiated or exacerbated existing civil conflicts, decelerated per capita economic growth, and proved corrupt.

Why should sub-Saharan Africa show such an extensive disparity between the many nation-states that have been and are poorly led and those few that consistently have been led well? Are the distinctions particularly African? Are they a product of colonial misrule? Do they reflect a common problem of transition from dependency to independence? Do they emanate from deep-rooted poverty and a lack of economic growth? Is sub-Saharan Africa's lamentable leadership record, in other words, attributable to exogenous variables beyond its control, or does Africa respond less favorably to a leadership challenge of the same order as every other region's?

The positive examples of African leadership stand out because of their clear-minded strength of character, their adherence to participatory democratic principles, and their rarity. In contrast, the negative examples include so many varieties—predatory kleptocrats; autocrats, whether democratically elected or militarily installed; simple-minded looters; economic illiterates; and puffed-up posturers—that caricaturing or merely dismissing them would mislead. These single-minded, often narcissistic leaders are many and share common characteristics: they are focused on power itself, not on the uses of power for good; they are indifferent to the well-being of their citizens but anxious to receive their adulation; they are frequently destructive to and within their own countries, home regions excepted; unreachable by reason, they are quick to exploit social or racial ideologies for political and personal purposes; and they are partial to scapegoating, blame-shifting, and hypocrisy.

Good leaders globally, not only in sub-Saharan Africa, guide governments of nation-states to perform effectively for their citizens. They deliver high security for the state and the person; a functioning rule of law; education; health; and a framework conducive to economic growth. They ensure effective arteries of commerce and enshrine personal and human freedoms. They empower civil society and protect the environmental commons. Crucially, good leaders also provide their citizens with a sense of belonging to a national enterprise of which everyone can be proud. They knit rather than unravel their nations and seek to be remembered for how they have bettered the real lives of the ruled rather than the fortunes of the few.

Less benevolent, even malevolent, leaders deliver far less by way of performance. Under their stewardship, roads fall into disrepair, currencies depreciate and real prices inflate, health services weaken, life expectancies slump, people go hungry, schooling standards fall, civil society becomes more beleaguered, the quest for personal and national prosperity slows, crime rates accelerate, and overall security becomes more tenuous. Corruption grows. Funds flow out of the country into hidden bank accounts. Discrimination against minorities (and occasionally majorities) becomes prevalent. Civil wars begin.

It is easy in theory and in practice to distinguish among good, less-good, bad, and despicable leaders everywhere, especially in sub-Saharan Africa. Good leaders improve the lives of their followers and make those followers proud of being a part of a new Camelot. Good leaders produce results, whether in terms of enhanced standards of living, basic development indicators, abundant new sources of personal opportunity, enriched schooling, skilled medical care, freedom from crime, or strengthened infrastructures. Bad and despicable leaders tear down the social and economic fabric of the lands; they immiserate their increasingly downtrodden citizens. Despicable rulers, particularly, oppress their own fellow nationals, depriving them of liberty, prosperity, and happiness.

Poverty within the context of resource abundance, as in oil-rich Nigeria from 1975 to 1999, indicates inadequate leadership. Despicable leadership is exemplified by Mugabe's Zimbabwe, a rich country reduced to the edge of starvation, penury, and fear. Economic growth from a low base in the aftermath of civil war and in a context of human resource scarcity, as in contemporary Mozambique, signals effective leadership. The opening of a long-repressed society, with attention to education and a removal of barriers to economic entrepreneurship, as in post-dictatorship Kenya, is another sign of progressive leadership.

Botswana is the paragon of leadership excellence in Africa. Long before diamonds were discovered, the dirt-poor, long-neglected desert protectorate demonstrated an affinity for participation, integrity, tolerance of difference and dissent, entrepreneurial initiative, and the rule of law. The relative linguistic homogeneity of Botswana may have helped (but compare Somalia, where everyone speaks Somali, is Muslim, and there are clans but no separate ethnic groups). So would the tradition of chieftainship and the chiefly search for consensus after discussion among a *kgotla*, or assembly of elders. The century-old, deeply ingrained teachings of the congregational London Missionary Society mattered, too, and infected the country's dominant political culture. Botswana stands out in sub-Saharan Africa as the foremost country (along with Mauritius and South Africa) to have remained democratic in form and spirit continuously since its independence (in 1966). Throughout the intervening years it has conspicuously adhered strictly to the rule of law, punctiliously observed human rights and civil liberties, and vigorously attempted to enable its citizens to better their social and economic standings. A numerically small population (1.6 million) doubtless contributes to Botswana's relative success, and exploiting the world's richest gem diamond lodes—since 1975—has hardly made achieving strong results more difficult. But Angola, Gabon, and Nigeria all have abundant petroleum, without the same striking returns for their peoples.

Any examination of Botswana, especially before 1975, shows the value of well-intentioned, clear-eyed visionary leadership. Seretse Khama, heir to the paramount chieftaincy of the country's most important and largest ethnic polity, completed his bachelor's degree at Fort Hare College in South Africa in 1944, spent a year reading law at Balliol College, University of Oxford, and then studied for the bar at the Inner Temple in London. In 1948, he married Ruth Williams, a Briton, and returned home to take up his chieftainship. But the British colonial authorities prevented him from exercising the rights of paramountcy, and he and Ruth were exiled to Britain in 1951. Five years later, they were allowed to return, officially as commoners.

Khama came from a family of Bamangwato chiefs who were well regarded for their benevolence and integrity. His studies and his marriage may conceivably have reinforced those family traits. Being exiled might have embittered him, but Khama seems instead to have viewed exile as a mere bump along the road to leadership within the evolving context of Botswana's maturity from protectorate to nation. Whatever the combination of nature and nurture, when Khama (later Sir Seretse Khama) founded the Botswana Democratic Party (BDP) in 1961 and led his country to independence, he already held dear those values of deliberative democracy and market economic performance that proved a recipe for his young country's political, social, and economic success. Modest, without obvious narcissism, non-ostentatious as a chief and leader (unlike so many of his African contemporaries), and conscious of achieving a national, enduring legacy, Sir Seretse was able to forge a political culture for the emergent Botswana—a system of values governing the conduct of political affairs—that has endured during the peaceful and increasingly prosperous presidencies of Sir Ketumile Masire and Festus Mogae, his successors.

Sir Seretse had a largely implicit, understated, but nevertheless substantial program for his people and his country. He put that program into place gradually, never succumbing to external political whims (such as the affinity for Afro-socialism or crypto-Marxism that infected his peers elsewhere in Africa), instant panaceas (such as nationalizing his productive mineral industries in the disastrous manner of neighboring Zambia), or posturing ineffectively against the hideous crimes of apartheid in nearby South Africa. Indeed, Sir Seretse and Sir Ketumile were deft and decisive in their disapproving but non-antagonistic approach to South Africa. Sir Seretse engineered his control of Botswana's diamond resources without frightening off or limiting investment from South Africa. He trained his own Botswanan successors and empowered them, but gradually, and without overstretching indigenous human resource capacities. Sir Seretse took no shortcuts. He and his successors abided no abridgements of citizen rights.

Sir Seretse could have done otherwise. As a paramount chief beloved by his people and respected for his learning, he could have behaved as so many of his African peers behaved during the 1960s and 1970s. If he had arrogated more and more power to himself, "for the good of his people," there would have been few critics. The rest of Africa had largely followed President Kwame Nkrumah, Ghana's first president from 1957–1966, in renouncing colonial traditions of representative government and becoming autocrats. Even gentle Julius Nyerere of Tanzania and equally gentle, modest Kenneth Kaunda of Zambia by the 1970s were abandoning inherited democratic forms and substituting single-party, single-man rule in place of broad participation. They were depriving judiciaries of independence and legislatures of autonomy. Objectors were jailed. Newspapers were banned or bought out. State radio broadcast only the words of the rulers.

Not Sir Seretse. He adhered to the nostrums that were no longer in current use in nearly all of Africa. For him, there was an ethic of performance and good governance to which he adhered. Sir Seretse was conscious every day that he could do better than the leaders of next-door South Africa, where whites oppressed the majority and deprived most inhabitants of their human rights and civil liberties. For whatever set of personal and pragmatic reasons, Sir Seretse epitomized world-class qualities of leadership.

In very different circumstances, Sir Seewoosagur Ramgoolam, the first leader of Mauritius (an offshore member of the African Union), operated under the same internalized leadership rules as Sir Seretse. Ramgoolam was more explicit in charting his vision, however—more in the manner of Lee Kuan Yew of Singapore. When Sir Seewoosagur took the Mauritian prime ministerial reins immediately after independence in 1968 (remaining prime minister until 1976), he understood that the island nation's mélange of colors and peoples—a plurality of Tamil-speaking Hindu Indians, Urdu- and Hindi-speaking Muslims from India and Pakistan, Chinese, and indigenous Creole-speaking Franco-Mauritians, most of whom were descended from slaves—could not long survive in peace if he or others were anything but transparently democratic. He stressed open politics, nurtured social capital, welcomed a free press, and strengthened the rule of law inherited from Britain, and earlier from France. Sir Seewoosagur also sensed that Mauritius' economy, hitherto based entirely on exporting raw sugar, would have to be diversified and grow. He attracted new investors from Asia. Soon Mauritius was a major world textile manufacturer; an island without sheep became a dominant supplier of wool garments.

Once again, leadership was central to Mauritius' post-independence transition from a potentially explosive racial hothouse and a primary producer subject to the fluctuations of world markets into a bustling, prosperous, politically hectic sustainable democracy. Sir Seewoosagur could have attempted to follow the other possible road to peace and growth on a crowded island of 1.2 million—strong, single-man rule of the Lee Kuan Yew variety. But the tactics that worked so well among overseas Chinese in Singapore might have been incendiary in Mauritius's multiethnic mix.

Likewise, without Nelson Mandela's inclusive leadership, black-run South Africa after 1994 would have been much more fractured and less successful in governing its apartheid-damaged peoples. Mandela's vision insisted on full rights for the majority, but without too abrupt a removal of minority economic privileges. It strengthened the rule of law, greatly broadened the delivery of essential services, largely maintained existing pillars of the economy such as transportation and communications networks, and slowly shifted away from the dominant command economy toward one that was more market driven.

Mandela, Khama, and Ramgoolam all led their nations democratically when they could have aggregated personal power. Their leadership model might have been more Asian—top-down, less open, less constitutional, and less multi-ethnic and multi-tribal—and still benevolent and thus accomplished. Instead, they demonstrated what few of their fellow African leaders then or since have demonstrated: that Africans are perfectly capable of building nations, developing sustainable democratic political cultures, and modernizing and growing their economies effectively. Given these particular individuals' disparate human and ethnic origins, and given their respective nations' very diverse colonial legacies, it makes no sense to assert that African traditional culture somehow inhibits the exercise of democratic leadership.

There must be other reasons for leadership gone wrong in Africa, especially for those men who begin as promising democrats and then emerge a term or two later as corrupt autocrats. Take Bakili Muluzi, president of Malawi, for example. After the thirty-year dictatorship of Dr. Hastings K. Banda ended, Muluzi led the new United Democratic Front (UDF) against Banda and his associates, promising a return to full-fledged democracy. Overwhelmingly victorious, the UDP and Muluzi took power in 1994 and governed reasonably effectively during their first five-year term. Educational and health services were expanded, civil society and an open press were embraced, the judges were released from their fetters, and serious steps were taken to improve the very poor country's economic performance. Muluzi presided genially over this peaceful and welcomed transition from autocracy in his country of twelve million people.

Muluzi's second term, from 1999, began well enough, although the sticky stain of corruption soon began to spread through the upper echelons of government and around the state house. Economic growth stagnated, not least because of decisions not made by the president and the arrangement of special deals for presidential associates. In 2002, he decided that Malawi would be better off if he broke the constitutional provision against a third presidential term, beginning in 2004. (President Frederick Chiluba, in Zambia, another post-dictatorial reformer, tried the same argument to keep his presidency, but was rebuffed by Parliament and the citizenry. In Namibia, however, President Sam Nujoma successfully breached his country's constitution and now serves a third term.)

Malawi's Parliament denied Muluzi the needed constitutional amendments twice, and Muluzi reluctantly backed away from a third-term attempt in 2003. Instead, he bulldozed the ruling party's executive committee into letting him hand-pick a questionable successor (illegal by party rules), and then compelled a suddenly called meeting of the UDF to amend the party's by-laws to give him that authority, and also to make him permanent chair of the party, in control of its finances. Key cabinet ministers resigned, and Malawi's politics were soon thrown into turmoil—all local matters which concern us little here. The main question is what causes a democrat to turn autocratic? Is it simply that absolute power corrupts absolutely, as Lord Acton said long ago?

Mugabe is another of many African leaders who began by governing plausibly (in 1980, in Mugabe's case), only to turn venal later. Admittedly, within a few years of assuming power in Zimbabwe, he had used a special military brigade to kill 20,000 to 30,000 followers of a key opponent. But the first eighteen years of Mugabe's prime ministerial and presidential leadership (the title changed in 1987) also brought enlarged educational and medical opportunities, economic growth, relatively modest levels of official corruption, and comparatively calm relations between the tiny white commercial farming community and black Africans. Throughout the period, Mugabe astutely gained more and more personal power. He used official terror to remove challengers, and state-supplied patronage to keep senior supporters in line. From about 1991, his onetime key backers say, Mugabe began behaving with more and more omnipotence and arrogance. He was reelected frequently as president, and his largely obedient party dominated Parliament. Every now and again one or two outspoken dissidents were tolerated.

By 1998, Mugabe was seventy-four years old, married for the second time, and increasingly cranky that Mandela's release from prison and assumption of the South African presidency had dimmed Mugabe's own attempt to be a major player in all-African politics. His second wife was known, too, to be avaricious, and by 1998 corruption at the highest levels of Zimbabwe had grown in scale and audacity. Mugabe sought to salt away wealth for his extended family. He also gave license to the corrupt activities of others so that he could control them, in the manner of Mobutu Sese Seko of the Congo. Then, in 1998, Mugabe unilaterally decided to send 13,000 soldiers to the Congo, ostensibly to assist Laurent Kabila, the rebel successor to Mobutu, to defend against a Rwandan-organized invasion. Mugabe also wanted to grab the diamonds, cobalt, cadmium, and gold of the Congo for himself.

With Zimbabwean troops in the Congo until 2003, and corruptly acquired funds fleeing to safe havens offshore, Mugabe and his cronies bled Zimbabwe until, by 2000, the foreign exchange coffers were largely empty and food and fuel shortages began to recur regularly. By then he had also unleashed thugs against commercial farmers, using an old tactic to mobilize indigenous support. This time, however, it failed to do so, especially in the cities. Mugabe lost a critical constitutional referendum in early 2000. By mid-year he had also come within a few seats of losing his party's parliamentary majority in a national election. The Movement for Democratic Change (MDC), led by Morgan Tsvangirai, had posed a formidable challenge and, indeed, claimed that Mugabe's party had falsified the votes in several key constituencies.

Mugabe lashed out furiously against the MDC, and attacked whites and blacks suspected of supporting the opposition. The country's once formidable rule of law became the law of the jungle, with Mugabe packing the Supreme Court and threatening High Court judges until they retired or resigned. Legions of hired thugs attacked white farmers and forcibly occupied the farms (despite High Court injunctions), thus depressing agricultural productivity. When Tsvangirai stood against Mugabe in the 2002 presidential election, he was defeated in a poll widely believed in Europe, the U.S., and among Zimbabweans to have been rigged. Even after such a disputed triumph, Mugabe persisted in victimizing MDC members and their presumed supporters. Having driven Zimbabwe to the brink of starvation in 2002 and 2003, he and his lackeys sought to deprive areas that had voted for the MDC of relief shipments of food.

By late-2003, Zimbabweans faced constant shortages of food and fuel. Unemployment had reached 80 percent and inflation 500 percent. The U.S. dollar, worth 38 Zimbabwean dollars in 2000, was being traded on the street for 5,000 local dollars. Hospitals operated without basic medicines. Schools were closed. President Bush and Secretary of State Colin Powell called for Mugabe's ouster, an unusual step, and so did Prime Minister Tony Blair. Zimbabwe's Council of Churches also railed at Mugabe, a Jesuit-trained Catholic. Tsvangirai, meanwhile, was indicted for treason and served some time in jail, as did many of his senior MDC colleagues. Mugabe, throughout, resisted entreaties to retire, as the once proud, wealthy country spiraled into decay.

These appalling details are less relevant, here, than seeking to explain why Mugabe and Muluzi, Chiluba and Nujoma, and also former President Daniel arap Moi of Kenya and many other African leaders perform adequately during their early elected terms and then, in their second terms or beyond, become despots. Is it the inevitability of Acton's aphorism, or some law of diminished accountability? Most African leaders, the Botswanan and South African presidents and the Mauritian prime ministers aside, travel in pompous motorcades, put their faces on the local currencies, and expect to see photographs of themselves in every shop and office. Almost invariably, the less legitimate the office and the less robust the country, the more ostentatious their displays and the more stilted their bearing and manner.

Is it the African reverence for "big men," a hangover from pre-colonial reverence for chieftainship, that turns democrats into despots and persuades obedient electorates to support the pretensions of their peers turned potentates? Would it help if the new nations of sub-Saharan Africa abandoned executive presidencies on the American model and reverted to pure parliamentary governing systems with ceremonial heads of state?

African leaders are driven by instincts no baser than those of their colleagues in Asia, Europe, or the U.S. But African electorates tend to acquiesce for long periods to the autocractic actions of their leaders. That acquiescence may stem from the sheer rawness of democracy in Africa, and from the absence of a long period of preparation for democracy, unlike in colonial India or the West Indies. The African press's lack of sophistication and independence is a contributing factor. Civil society is also weaker. Extensive public-sector patronage in most African countries also allows leaders to escape criticism until their leadership excesses are obvious.

Africa for the most part lacks a hegemonic bourgeoisie—a business class that is independent of government and capable of thriving without patronage and contracts; such independence lessens the zero-sum quality of a rule. In those few countries where there is that independence, as in South Africa but not yet Nigeria, a leader approaching the end of his term in office does not have to worry about taking the perquisites with him and looting the country before he and his colleagues go. In many other countries in Africa, especially the poorer ones, the incentives to grab it all are great.

Throughout most of Africa there is little expectation, thus far, that successors will be fair, that an incoming political movement will not necessarily victimize its predecessors, and that there is an acceptable role for former presidents and prime ministers—except, notably, in Mauritius and Botswana. In many places, too, there is as yet no sustainable democratic political culture. That is, whereas American and European politicians might want to behave as autocrats, they are restrained by the norms of their dominant political cultures and the likelihood of being found out. In Africa, shame is less apparent than a kind of entitlement. Once elected, or once chosen by a military junta to rule, the president confuses himself with the state—in some way thinking of himself as embodying and being the state. It is only the exceptional individuals like Khama or Mandela who can escape the deep psychological trap of constant sycophancy. Like Louis XIV, others come to accept their own importance as the suns around which their little countries revolve. Except in a few places like Botswana, where an early leader knew better and emulated President Washington's refusal to be royal, African leaders and their followers largely believe that the people are there to serve their rulers, rather than the other way around.

Fortunately, there are a handful of very new leaders in Africa who espouse an ethic of good governance. They are distinguished from their less democratic peers by a willingness to govern transparently, to consult with interest groups within their populations that are not their own, to create an atmosphere of tolerance and fairness in their official operations, and to strengthen the institutions of their societies. These promising new leaders include Presidents Abdoulaye Wade of Senegal, who had opposed previous methods of rule for decades and now rules consensually; Mwai Kibaki of Kenya, in opposition from 1992 to his election in late 2002; John Kuffour of Ghana, who has begun reducing the corrupt climate of his autocratic predecessor; and Prime Minister Pakalitha Mosisili of tiny Lesotho, who has modernized his country's methods of governance through a process of laborious national consultation.

Africa is not yet ready to parse distinctions between transactional and transformational leadership. It needs leaders in the first instance who serve whole nations, not just their tribes or ethnic groups or extended families. It needs leaders who embrace responsibility for the commonweal, and not for a group of associates who live off and puff up a country's all-commanding autocrat. It desperately needs new leaders who take Khama and Mandela as their models and embrace the Washingtonian-like restraints that they embodied. Once there are a cadre of leaders who espouse and embody in their actions the democratic values that emboldened Khama, Mandela, and Ramgoolam, and now drive their successors and men like Wade, Kibaki, Koffour, and Mosisili, Africa will begin to move from despotism and denials of human rights to the era of democratic leadership. Given the timbre of Africa's younger leaders, and the spread throughout Africa of global bourgeois democratic values, that era may soon be at hand.

Arthur A. Goldsmith

 NO

Risk, Rule, and Reason: Leadership in Africa

Introduction

Sub-Saharan Africa is poorly led. The region has far too many tyrants and 'tropical gangsters', far too few statesmen, let alone merely competent office-holders. Too often, these leaders reject sound policy advice and refuse to take a long and broad view of their job. They persecute suspected political rivals and bleed their economies for personal benefit. With a handful of exceptions, notably South Africa under Nobel laureate Nelson Mandela, countries in the sub-Saharan area are set back by a personalist, neopatrimonial style of national leadership (Aka, 1997).

Better leadership is not the cure-all for Africa's lack of development, but it would be an important step in the right direction. A few years back some observers saw hope in a new generation of supposedly benevolent dictators, such as Isaias Afwerki in Eritrea, Meles Zenawi in Ethiopia, or Yoweri Museveni in Uganda (Madavo and Sarbib, 1997; Connell and Smyth, 1998). Subsequent events (war between Eritrea and Ethiopia, invasion of the Congo Republic by Uganda) chilled the optimism (McPherson and Goldsmith, 1998; Barkan and Gordon, 1998; Ottaway, 1998). In most countries, it seems progressive leadership soon reverts to the more familiar form of autocratic one-man rule.

There is no shortage of macro-level explanations for this pattern. Authoritarian political traditions, lack of national identity, underdeveloped middle classes and widespread economic distress are among the sweeping, impersonal forces cited as factors that produce poor leader after poor leader. Foreign aid may have enabled some of these leaders to hang on longer than they would have otherwise, especially during the Cold War. This article instead takes a micro-level view of leadership. Without denying that macro-level social and economic factors bear on leaders' behaviour, I find it also useful to look at these people as individuals and to speculate about the incentives created by their environment.

In the tradition of political economy, we can begin with the assumption that African leaders are usually trying to do what they think is best for themselves. We can posit that they choose actions that appear to them to produce the greatest benefit at least cost, after making allowances for the degree of risk involved. Such a leader also is capable of learning, and takes cues from what is

From *Public Administration and Development*, vol. 21, 2001, pp. 77–79, 83–86. Copyright © 2001 by John Wiley & Sons, Ltd. Reprinted by permission.

happening to other leaders in neighbouring countries. He can improve his behaviour if he has to.

While no African leader fully exemplifies this rational actor model, all these individuals' behaviour can be illuminated by it. After all, even the best leaders have mixed, sometimes egoistic motives. To the extent that it represents reality, the rational actor model also may suggest how changing the political incentive system might induce African leaders to behave less autocratically.

I start this article by speculating about how these leaders might react to perceived levels of risk in their political environment. Next, I investigate the actual level of risk, guided by a new inventory that covers every major leadership transition in Africa since 1960. Then, I assess how risk appears to have distorted the way African leaders act in office. Finally, I consider the ways in which democratization may be changing political incentives for the better.

Leadership and Individual Motivation

Perhaps the most troubling thing about African leaders is their tendency to reject (or simply not follow through on) conventional economic advice (Scott, 1998). Africa is the graveyard of many well-intended reforms. The vacillating public attitude of Kenya's President Daniel Moi is emblematic. In March 1993, he rejected an International Monetary Fund (IMF) plan for being cruel and unrealistic. One month later, he reversed himself, and agreed to the plan. In June 1997, the IMF cut off lending to Kenya after Moi refused to take aggressive steps to combat corruption. Again, his initial reaction was defiance, swiftly followed by a more accommodating line.

Why are African leaders apt to resist advice to carry out market-friendly reforms that could boost national rates of economic growth? If one accepts the premise that, with sufficient time, open market policies will work in Africa, such a choice can look senseless. Certainly, no African leader would prefer to perpetuate mass poverty and economic stagnation in his country, which can only make governing more difficult. More to the point, perhaps, cooperating with the international financial institutions is the best way to assure continued diplomatic support and financial credit. Yet, many African leaders apparently see political rationality in choosing policies that are economically damaging or irrational. Miles Kahler (1990) refers to this as the 'orthodox paradox.'

Political economy offers a theory of micro-level behaviour that may explain the paradox. Mancur Olson (1993) argues that time is the key. According to this theory, the predicament facing any individual national leader is that the pay-offs to most economic reforms lie in the future, but he also has to hold on to power now. An insecure power base is likely to encourage either reckless gambling for immediate returns or highly cautious strategies to preserve political capital; it is unlikely to promote measured actions to obtain long-range returns. Whether a leader acts for the short or the long term, therefore, is influenced by his sense of the level of threat to his career.

A more technical way to understand a leader's intertemporal choices is to think of a 'political discount rate'. One of political economy's core ideas is that future events have a present value, which one can calculate by using a rate of discount. That rate of discount rises with risk and uncertainty. When an outcome is doubtful over time, it makes sense to mark down its present value. The more doubtful the outcome, the more valuable are alternative activities that yield immediate dividends, even if the expected return of those activities is low. Thus, under conditions of political uncertainty, the narrowly 'rational' leader will systematically forgo promising political 'investments'—ventures whose benefits he may not survive to reap. Whenever he is given a choice, according to this argument, such a leader will usually prefer current political 'consumption'. It follows that free-market reforms look like a poor bargain, requiring immediate political pain in exchange for distant (and therefore questionable) gain.

High political discount rates are also a possible explanation for the extensive and destructive political corruption seen in Africa. The Democratic Republic of Congo's Mobutu Sese Sekou is the archetype. The late dictator erased the line between public and private property, accumulating a vast personal fortune and bankrupting his country. His is an extreme case, yet every national leader has opportunities to profit individually from his office. According to the premises of political economy, it is the leader with the least certainty about his fate who has the strongest incentives to take his rewards now—and to take as much as possible. A more self-assured leader may calculate that it is safe to defer most personal financial gain until after he has left office. Some of the misuse of public office also may be due to the need to buy support from friends and extended family members. Olson (1993), for example, postulates that leaders with an insecure grip on power have an incentive to take steps to patronize favoured ethnic groups, often at the expense of national economic health. This sort of pork-barrelling is well known in Africa.

Political economy thus presents a cogent theory for why African rulers act the way they do. Short-term policy making and political corruption are 'rational' ways of trying to manage the risks associated with governing in an unsettled political system, as we typically find in Africa. According to this thesis, overly cautious or corrupt leaders may simply be attempting to maximize utility under conditions of personal and political uncertainty. Their assessment of risk is affected by their personal experiences and by their perceptions about larger trends in their country and region. Unfortunately for the social welfare, their effort to protect their individual interests has spillovers that hurt everyone else.

The issue for this article is whether the facts support this theory. First, is it true that African leaders face a high degree of risk? We can reasonably assume these people are tolerant of risk, or they would not have chosen political careers. Thus, we need to look for evidence of extraordinary occupational hazards for leaders. The second question is whether political risk in Africa is associated with 'bad' (anti-market) economic policy choices or with corruption. As we will see below, the answers to both questions seem to be affirmative: there is significant physical risk for leaders, and that risk correlates with anti-market policies and with corruption. Those two findings, in turn, suggest scope for enhancing the area's national leadership by reducing the risks of governing, a goal that may be abetted by democratization. . . .

Risk and Leaders' Behaviour

There is little doubt . . . that holding high office in Africa poses acute risks. To what extent do those risks affect leaders' behaviour, specifically their behaviour in the areas of economic reform and corruption? . . . That question is difficult to answer fully without detailed case studies of the individuals involved. In the absence of such information, however, we can look for approximate answers in national indicators of economic policy and corruption. To the extent we believe that country leaders control public policy or set the tone for public honesty, aggregate data may give us clues about how these leaders conduct themselves.

To represent a country's commitment to free market economics, I use the Heritage Foundation's Index of Economic Freedom (Johnson et al., 1999). The index is calculated by aggregating country scores on 10 policy indicators and measures of the business climate. Depending on their scores, countries are categorized as free (none in Africa), mostly free, mostly unfree, or repressed. While I do not see eye to eye with the Heritage Foundation on many subjects, I suspect that these categories offer a good approximation for how fully countries comply with IMF-style structural adjustment programs. My grouping of countries is based on the average economic freedom rating for 1995–1999.

I hypothesized earlier in this article that low-risk environments would tend to produce more reform-minded leaders, or at least leaders who would be more willing to go along with economic reform in exchange for financial credit. . . . [A] correlation exists between the hazards of leadership and the degree of 'economic freedom'. Leaders in the so-called mostly free countries were the least likely to be overthrown, killed, arrested or exiled. Leaders in the mostly unfree and repressed countries, by contrast, experienced a greater number of negative outcomes. Low political risk and liberal economic programmes seem to go together in Africa.

Correlation does not prove causation, especially in making inferences about micro-level behaviour based on macro-level data. We cannot say whether a safer political environment encourages leaders to opt for the market, or conversely, whether leaders who opt for the market make their political environment safer (though the latter possibility seems less likely, at least in the short run). In either case, however, the results are consistent with political economy theory.

What is the relationship between political risk and corruption? For a measure of the latter, I use Transparency International's Corruption Perception Index for 1999. Transparency International is a watchdog organization formed to help raise ethical standards of government around the world. It compiles an annual index that assesses the degree to which public officials and politicians are believed to accept bribes, take illicit payment in public procurement, embezzle public funds, and otherwise use public positions for private gains. The index is based on several international business surveys, using different sampling frames and varying methodologies (Transparency International, 1999). While Transparency International is careful to point out that the rankings only reflect perceptions about corruption, I find it reasonable to assume that they correspond roughly to reality.

I have conjectured that leaders in the riskier African countries would have the greatest propensity to use their public offices for personal ends. Once more, the data lend support to my hypothesis. . . . The pattern is striking. There has never been a successful coup in the less corrupt group of countries. None of their ex-leaders has been arrested or exiled, and only one was killed while in office (South Africa's Verwoerd). The more corrupt countries, by contrast, have many coups and many leaders who suffered personally upon losing power.

As with the economic freedom index, these correlations do not prove that a hazardous political environment encourages leaders to become corrupt. The opposite is also plausible: corrupt rulers seem likely to invite coups and to bring personal suffering on themselves. To the extent that risk and corruption are related, the relationship between the two probably is mutually reinforcing. The important point for this article is that the observed association of risk and corruption conforms to what you would expect, based on the assumption of 'rational' behaviour among national rulers. Without overstating the case, the correlation lends support to a political economy account of poor leadership in Africa.

Democratization and Improved Leadership

Political economy also suggests that one solution to poor leadership is to make the political environment less hazardous. A safer environment would reduce the incentives to engage in political misbehaviour and, in principle, encourage more responsible and forward-looking activity. In this context, Africa's recent moves toward more pluralistic national political systems, where people can express their political opinions and take part in public decisions, are reasons for hope. It is fashionable—and correct—to observe that democracy has shallow roots in most African countries (Joseph, 1997; van de Walle, 1999). Much of the impetus for reform comes from abroad, from the region's creditors. Yet, when we observe the patterns of leadership transitions, it is hard to deny that genuine changes are taking place.

No sitting African leader ever lost an election until 1982, when Sir Seewoosagur Ramgoolam of Mauritius was voted out. Since then, 12 more incumbents have been turned out of office by voters—accounting for about one-sixth of the leadership transitions in the 1990s. The threat of losing an election also may account for the increasing rate of leader retirements—nine in the 1990s versus only eight in the previous three decades.

Democratization appears to be altering the outcomes of the many coups that still occur. In the past, the new heads of military juntas often declared themselves permanent leaders (sometimes after doffing their uniforms and becoming 'civilians'). Now, it is becoming the norm for coup leaders quickly to organize internationally acceptable elections—and, more importantly, to honour the results afterwards (Anene, 1995). Recent examples include Niger and Guinea-Bissau. . . . The fact we see more transitions of this type in the 1990s is an indirect reflection of the region's growing democratization.

[There are] additional reasons to think that contemporary presidential elections are not simply façades in many countries. The entire sub-Saharan region had only 126 elections for top national office in the 30 years through 1989. Most of those were show elections, with an average winner's share of close to 90%. Conditions have changed significantly in the 1990s. There were 73 leadership elections during that decade, or more than half as many as in the three prior decades. All but five of sub-Saharan countries were involved. Equally important, the winner's share dropped to an average of about two-thirds of the votes cast. Such results would be considered landslide victories in the developed world. No president in the history of the United States has ever reached two-thirds of the popular vote. Still, in African terms, the tendency clearly is toward greater competitiveness at the ballot box.

The classic liberal defences of free and fair elections are that they give voice to majority demands and that they are a means for recruiting new leadership talent. Political economy and African experience suggest three additional benefits, all associated with reducing the hazards leaders face.

First, elections have the virtue of softening the penalties of losing political office. The defeated candidate in an election campaign, as opposed to the victim of a coup plot, is far less likely to be executed, jailed or exiled by his successor. By providing a low-risk avenue of exit, elections thus reduce the stakes in political competition. If the arguments in this article are correct, that would free African leaders to take a more purposeful, pragmatic view of their jobs.

A second benefit occurs if elections become institutionalized, and take place according to a schedule. Countries that hold regular elections reduce speculation about when (and how) the next political transition is likely. Again, the probable impact in Africa would be to change the political calculations made by the region's chief power holders, to allow them to worry less about how to hold onto power and to think more about the long term. Predictable political transitions might also reduce anxiety among private investors, and thus mitigate the harmful political business cycle that exists in some countries.

The third benefit stems from the more rapid turnover among national rulers that results when elections become a regular part of political experience. As leaders come to see their jobs less as an entitlement and more as a phase in their careers, that actually may liberate them to 'do the right thing', and not always feel forced to do what is politically expedient. Merilee Grindle and Francisco Thoumi (1993) have remarked on this phenomenon among lame-duck presidents in Latin America. Knowledge that their positions are transitory can, somewhat ironically, concentrate the incumbents' attention on how best to leave a lasting legacy. Similar results are possible in Africa.

Concluding Observations

Before multi-party competition and elections can have these positive effects on leaders, Africa's competitive political systems must become institutionalized. This has yet to happen in most countries, according to the results of

Samuel Huntington's (1968) 'two-turnover test'. Huntington notes that institutionalized democracies prove themselves by repeatedly carrying out peaceful transfers of power through the ballot box. The first time an opposition leader replaces an incumbent power holder does not necessarily establish a tradition of peaceful political change. It is only after the new incumbent is defeated and leaves office that one can begin to be confident that constitutional procedures have taken root.

Second turnovers are almost unheard of in Africa. Botswana has not had one. The same party has ruled that country since independence. Mauritius has had two election-based leadership turnovers, but many observers question whether that island nation properly deserves classification in the region. Bénin is the only other African country where incumbent power holders have twice lost elections. The dictator Mathieu Kérékou fell to Nicéphore Soglo in 1991, but he regained the presidency by defeating Soglo in the election 5 years later. Kérékou's continued role raises some doubt whether Bénin's second transition indicates much other than the persistence of narrow, personalistic politics in that country.

Nonetheless, the last decade does offer hope that some African societies will be able to establish more orderly systems of political competition. That could change the incentives for African leaders, and encourage them to act more responsibly and even-handedly. As a means of redressing decades of oppression and economic stagnation, that cannot happen soon enough.

POSTSCRIPT

Is Corruption the Result of Poor African Leadership?

In this issue, Robert Rotberg attributed Africa's troubles to the fact that "African leaders and their followers largely believe that the people are there to serve their rulers, rather than the other way around." In contrast, Arthur Goldsmith viewed the mismanagement and corruption of African leaders as a structural problem in which individual leaders are responding to the incentive structures around them. These two interpretations of the situation appear to be quite different. Yet, while Rotberg eschewed the political economy or structural perspective, he concluded his argument by both calling for new leaders who will serve whole nations, *and* pointing out the conditions that allow the base instincts of many African leaders to prevail. In pointing to the adage that "absolute power corrupts absolutely," Rotberg evokes a universal rather than particularistic (i.e., conditions unique to Africa) explanation. Furthermore, by asserting that this tendency is unleashed by a weak civil society and the lack of democratic traditions, he acknowledges that the environment in which African leaders operate contributes to the problem. This is quite different than other internalist arguments that often seek to explain corruption in Africa in terms of cultural factors. These conditions are also considered at a scale that is consistent with the micro-level sphere that Goldsmith investigates. In sum, the differences between the two arguments may be more about style and emphasis than substance.

A less-discussed element of corruption is the extent to which international corporations may contribute to the problem in their dealings with African governments. In some instances, it is standard business practice for companies to provide financial incentives (or bribes) to government officials in order to win contracts, obtain permits, or gain certain rights. Interestingly, it is the government officials who are often accused of corruption, while little is heard of the companies' role in this process. An example of an exception to this involves a Canadian company that was convicted by the Lesotho high court for bribing a senior Lesotho government official in order to win contracts on that country's $8 billion Lesotho Highlands Water Project (a joint project of the governments of Lesotho and South Africa). Commenting on the case, a South African official said that it is often assumed that corruption is "a peculiarly African problem. This case shows that such a perception is wrong. It takes two to tango." ("Government Cracks Down on Western Corruption," *New African*, December 2002.)

For those interested in further reading on this topic, good examples of the structural perspective on corruption include an article by M.M. Munyae and M.M. Mulinge in a 1999 issue of the *Journal of Social Development in Africa* entitled "The Centrality of a Historical Perspective to the Analysis of Modern Social Problems in Sub-Saharan Africa: A Tale from Two Case Studies," and an article by N.I. Nwosu in a 1997 issue of the *Scandinavian Journal of Development Alternatives* entitled "Multinational Corporations and the Economy of Third World States." There are roughly two types of particularlistic or internalist explanations regarding corruption in Africa—one is negative and the other is positive. The first, essentially negative perspective, views internal African characteristics as flaws that contribute to a universally accepted problem known as corruption. An example of this perspective is an article by M. Szeftel in a 2000 issue of the *Review of African Political Economy* entitled "Clientelism, Corruption and Catastrophe." The second, more positive or postmodern interpretation often views "corruption" as a relative concept that is culturally defined. In other words, what is viewed as corruption in one culture is not necessarily corruption in another. Examples of this perspective include a volume by Chabel and Daloz entitled *Africa Works: Disorder as Political Instrument* (Indiana University Press, 1999) and a 2001 article by Jeff Popke in the *African Geographical Review* under the title "The 'Politics of the Mirror': On Geography and Afro-Pessimism."

ISSUE 19

Are African-Led Peacekeeping Missions More Effective than International Peacekeeping Efforts in Africa?

YES: David C. Gompert, from "For a Capability to Protect: Mass Killing, the African Union and NATO," *Survival* (Spring 2006)

NO: Nsonurua J. Udombana, from "Still Playing Dice with Lives: Darfur and Security Council Resolution 1706," *Third World Quarterly* (2007)

ISSUE SUMMARY

YES: David C. Gompert, an adviser to Refugees International and a senior fellow at the RAND Corporation, believes that the African Union could be effective in Sudan if adequately supported. He believes that Africans are willing to commit combat forces to stop the killing in Darfur because they are more deeply affected by such abuses than Europe or North America. In fact, the unwillingness of the great powers to create a standing UN peacekeeping force is illustrative of a weak commitment of the West to intervene in Africa.

NO: Nsonurua J. Udombana of Central European University is more critical of the African Union peacekeeping mission in Sudan. He believes this mission has failed in Darfur because it suffers from several weaknesses, including problems of command and control, logistical support, operational practice, and lack of funds.

Certain major powers (most notably the United States, the United Kingdom, and France) and the United Nations (UN) have supported peacekeeping missions in war-torn areas of Africa over the past several decades. The UN has supported a number of such missions in Africa, with the effort in Mozambique often considered to have been more successful, and those in Somalia and Rwanda receiving poor reviews. In light of mixed or bad peacekeeping experiences, the UN Security Council has found it increasingly difficult to authorize new peacekeeping missions. Due to the West's growing reluctance to intervene in Africa, African states have increasingly taken matters into their own hands. Most of these African efforts have been undertaken under the auspices of the African Union (AU).

Any discussion of the AU must be preceded by a brief discussion of its predecessor, the Organization of African Unity (OAU). The OAU was formed in 1963—a time when many African states had recently achieved independence. Its major purpose was to foster unity and provide a collective voice for African nations. The OAU also aimed to eradicate all remaining forms of colonialism on the continent. Some (most notably Kwame Nkrumah of Ghana) even saw the OAU as a vehicle for a federation of African states. The OAU suffered from the fact that it had no real power to enforce its decisions. Its policy of noninterference in the affairs of nonmember states was also problematic. Given its inability to protect basic human rights, and its uncritical acceptance of several dictators on the continent, the OAU was dissolved in 2002. It was replaced by the AU, a supranational organization of 53 African states established in 2001. The AU aims to support democracy, basic human rights, and sustainable economies and to bring an end to conflicts on the continent. It eventually aims to have a single currency (the Afro) and an integrated defense force.

The AU's first peacekeeping mission was to Burundi in 2003. They currently have peacekeepers in the Darfur region of Sudan and in Somalia. The AU began sending peacekeeping troops to Darfur in 2005, and had 7,000 peacekeepers in place in mid-2007. Their mission has been extremely challenging because they must patrol an area roughly the size of France and are poorly funded and badly equipped. In June 2006, the U.S. Congress appropriated $173 million to support the AU peacekeeping force. Many Western advocacy organizations have called for UN peacekeepers to supplement or replace the AU force. In July 2007, the UN Security Council approved a resolution to create a joint African Union and UN peacekeeping mission known as the The United Nations African Union Mission in Darfur (UNAMID). It has a mandate of 12 months and is to begin deploying in October 2007. This 26,000 member force is to be merged with the 7,000 member AU force at the end of 2007.

In this issue, David Gompert, an adviser to Refugees International and a senior fellow at the RAND Corporation, argues that the AU could be effective in Sudan if adequately supported. He notes that the idea of creating a standing UN peacekeeping force has been in discussion for years and gone nowhere. He sees this as illustrative of a weak commitment of West to intervene in Africa. He believes that Africans (and the AU) are willing to commit combat forces to stop the killing in Darfur because they are more deeply affected by such abuses than Europe or North America. He acknowledges, however, that the AU needs the logistical and military support of an organization like NATO.

Nsonurua Udombana of Central European University is more critical of the African Union peacekeeping mission in Sudan, calling it "patently ineffective." He believes this mission has failed in Darfur because it suffers from several weaknesses, including problems of command and control, logistical support, operational practice, and lack of funds. He would rather urge the UN Security Council to unite and compel the government of Sudan to accept a UN deployment of peacekeepers.

YES

David C. Gompert

For a Capability to Protect: Mass Killing, the African Union and NATO

While condemning the Sudanese government and its Janjaweed henchmen for the horrors they have visited on the people of Darfur Province, the United States and its NATO allies have opted to back an African Union (AU) peacekeeping force to stop the atrocities. But the AU force lacks the firepower and authority to succeed. Darfur makes clearer than ever that it takes combat forces, not ordinary peacekeepers, to stop large-scale killing. If the West will not intervene militarily in Africa to prevent future Rwandas and Darfurs, it should help Africans build their own capability to do so.

Meanwhile, the US government's Global Peace Operations Initiative (GPOI) aims to add 75,000 peacekeepers worldwide by 2010, most of them African. While the GPOI is welcome—more peacekeeping capacity is obviously needed—it does not, as conceived, promise to create combat capabilities sufficient to stop mass violence when there is no peace to keep. Now that we know that the scourge of genocide has jumped from the twentieth century into the twenty-first, the world needs multilateral military capabilities for forcible intervention against large-scale atrocities, displacement and death. A partnership between NATO and the AU, with UN support, to develop AU forces able to stop genocide would be a step towards this end. Because the AU is far from having such capabilities today, such a partnership could take years to bear fruit, but by the same token should be launched as soon as possible.

Since the UN's birth after the Second World War, a precondition of peacekeeping has been the consent of the warring parties to accept peacekeepers and honour cease-fire or peace agreements, thus creating permissive conditions and obviating the need for peacekeepers to fight and take casualties. But the forces, legal authority and operating rules of engagement that are adequate for such consensual situations are inadequate for violent ones, such as civil war and state failure, in which mass atrocities usually occur, especially when the local government is complicit.

Repeated crises have shown that peacekeeping is either precluded or, if in place, incapable of stopping mass killing. Peacekeepers did not prevent Serbian ethnic cleansing of Bosnian Muslims or the massacre of Muslim men

From *Survival*, Spring 2006, pp. 7–18. Copyright © 2006 by Taylor & Francis Journals. Reprinted by permission.

and boys at Srebrenica. Peacekeepers could not halt the rampaging of the 'West Side Boys' of Sierra Leone prior to the arrival of British paratroopers, nor prevent the slaughter of Tutsis and moderate Hutus in Rwanda. Peacekeepers of the AU Mission in Sudan (AMIS) may discourage but cannot stop Janjaweed burning, raping and killing in Darfur; indeed, AMIS personnel have been abducted and murdered.

This is not to disparage peacekeeping, which can help prevent conflict and provide security for post-war reconstruction. However, there is an additional requirement for military intervention forces that are strong enough that they do not need the consent of the parties, the cooperation of the offending government, or the self-restraint of killers—strong enough even to deliver violence to killing forces if there is no other way to stop genocide. To limit the international community to the ability to end mass atrocities only under *permissive* conditions is to ignore that mass atrocities occur under *non-permissive* conditions. Peacekeeping might be enough to keep peace between two obliging sovereigns but is not enough to keep a vicious sovereign from warring on its own people.

The Responsibility, Right and Capability to Protect

The persistence of mass killing and the incapacity of traditional peacekeeping to stop it have fuelled political support for important new international legal principles: *the responsibility to protect* and *the right to protect* human beings that are undefended or even slaughtered by their government. The former principle means that states, acting together, *should* intervene to stop atrocities; the latter means that they *may* do so. The concept underlying these principles is that sovereignty cannot be a shield behind which to commit or permit crimes against humanity, especially when illegitimate regimes rely on such crimes to stay in control.

These ideas challenge centuries-old tenets of unqualified sovereignty and prohibition of intervention. Hard-nosed statesmen and pundits may fear that such a compromise of sovereignty will produce international chaos, and authoritarian regimes—China, for instance—sneer at the *responsibility and right to protect* for plainly self-serving reasons. Consequently, the responsibility and right to protect face political, legal and practical hurdles and will likely be debated for years before being broadly accepted.

Yet these disagreements are no reason to delay the development of an international *capability to protect*. Multilateral military forces adequate to stop mass killing would, at the very least, provide the option to act in cases when there is international consensus to do so. Moreover, having such capabilities would increase pressure on states and groups to desist from atrocities and allow international humanitarian intervention or else face forcible action anyway. A government that is condoning or abetting mass killing, like the Sudanese government is today, would likely be more amenable to cooperation if it knew that the international community could act effectively to stop the killing whether it cooperates or not.

Attempts by the UN to extend peacekeeping into non-permissive situations, such as Bosnia and Somalia, have run into institutional and material barriers. Neither the UN Charter nor the peacekeeping capabilities and mandates that are predicated on it enable forcible international action to stop mass atrocities. Consequently, countries (e.g., the United States, the UK, Australia and France) and coalitions (e.g., NATO and ad hoc groupings) with superior military forces are authorised to undertake especially demanding and dangerous interventions, ranging from the liberation of Kuwait to air strikes in Bosnia to British intervention in Sierra Leone to current operations in Afghanistan. In Kosovo, the UN not only lacked the means to stop Serbian ethnic cleansing of Albanian Kosovars, but also could not reach agreement in the Security Council in support of NATO's view that the Belgrade regime's savagery had compromised its sovereignty and justified intervention—forcing NATO to take vigilante action.

Thus, the international community has had to outsource forcible interventions precisely when they are most needed—when innocents are being slain or uprooted in large numbers. The problem, of course, is that nations, including the United States, and coalitions, including NATO, may opt not to intervene in the very situations that involve mass human-rights violations because they are taking place in Africa or other places that are not deemed important enough to warrant forcible intervention on grounds of national interest. As we know, genocide can happen where the powerful Western democracies have no vital interests.

So we have cases like Rwanda and Darfur in which peacekeepers are available but militarily inadequate while militarily adequate forces are unavailable. This suggests a need for multilateral intervention forces, readily available to the UN or the AU—Africa being the focus here—that can stop mass killing and cleansing when an international consensus exists to do so. Such forces would reduce both the burden and reliance on the United States and its allies to use deadly force when they have no vital stakes. This is not to say that the Western democracies should never intervene solely to save lives—they cannot plausibly, or morally, claim that genocide is Africa's problem, not theirs—but rather to point out that counting on them is unwise and, with the right effort, could be unnecessary.

Military Superiority

The scale of this challenge should not be underestimated, because the combat capabilities of intervening forces will now become more critical. Forces dispatched to protect human beings under non-permissive, non-consensual conditions must be militarily superior to those of any of the hostile parties, including a recalcitrant sovereign state. Operational superiority is not a standard that has applied, or need apply, to traditional peacekeepers; because they are not intended to fight, they are generally not equipped, trained or organised to fight. But military superiority is crucial for forcible multilateral humanitarian intervention because of the presumption of armed opposition, the need to deter such opposition, and even the intention of initiating hostilities against killing forces if need be.

The superiority of humanitarian intervention forces over opposing forces is achievable. More often than not, the perpetrators of mass atrocities are killers but not fighters, in the sense of disciplined troops prepared to stand up to combat forces. Rag-tag Bosnian Serbs, machete-wielding Hutus and militia of the old regime in East Timor all folded when confronted by real soldiers. Janjaweed marauders signed up to rape and kill, not to fight and die in Darfur. The notion that intervening forces will face fierce and formidable enemies at great risk of casualties and failure is not borne out by experience or analysis. While there is plenty of evidence that killing forces flee instead of fight Western forces, there are anecdotal indications that they are not keen to shoot it out with good African troops either. With Western help, capable African combat troops—South Africans, Rwandans, Nigerians, Senegalese, Kenyans and others—can be improved and melded into effective multilateral humanitarian-intervention forces. While this would have the effect of making superior African militaries stronger still, it would do so in a multilateral—'denationalised'—framework and under Western influence.

Broadly speaking, military superiority has two components: operationally superior deployed forces, under expected conditions; and escalation dominance, through some combination of deployable reinforcements and deterrent forces. The requirement for superior deployed capabilities implies a need to strengthen the military qualities of forces available to operate under the UN or AU. More specifically, in the context of sizeable non-permissive humanitarian crises, the standard of superiority of intervening forces demands some measure of:

- accurate and persistent strategic awareness;
- fast deployment and employment, e.g., air and high-speed land mobility;
- precision fire-power from land, gunship and other strike systems;
- information dominance: tactical intelligence collection, fusion and dissemination;
- command and control, including deployable communications with adequate bandwidth and connectivity to global grids;
- flexible and ample logistics; and
- able combat leadership, decision-making and cognition at all levels.

Of course, the size and weight (armour) of humanitarian intervention forces must be adequate to ensure their superiority and survivability. However, the better they are in the qualities just listed, the smaller and lighter they can be and still have an operational advantage and escalation dominance. Indeed, small, light, mobile, aware forces can have appreciable operational advantages over large, heavy, ponderous ones in negotiating difficult terrain, covering large territory, responding to warnings of attack, manoeuvring and visiting effective but discriminating fire on opposing forces. All else being equal, speed and knowledge are more important than mass and lethality in operations aimed at stopping dispersed violence in remote areas. The essential quality of humanitarian intervention forces is that they be networked—able to exploit the operating concepts and technologies of the information age.

Over the years, the idea of creating a standing UN peacekeeping force has surfaced but gone nowhere. If there is no consensus to create a UN permanent peacekeeping force for permissive missions, there will surely be none to create a standing humanitarian combat intervention force under supranational control. However, this does not prevent taking action to ensure the availability of such a capability when needed. With the military application of information technology, especially data connectivity, it is becoming increasingly easy to generate forces at relatively short notice that can join up and operate effectively together by virtue of their ability to 'plug and play'. This is especially so if they are light, air-mobile forces at high readiness in training and materiel, and provided arrangements and preparations to generate them have been made and rehearsed.

NATO as Model and Partner for the AU

Generating and using superior military forces cannot be done via the established way of assembling peacekeeping forces, which depends mainly on ad hoc recruitment from sundry countries that offer spare non-combat forces of uneven quality. A better model for force generation can be found by looking at NATO, which maintains few standing military capabilities but has obligations, standards and agreed procedures, frequently exercised, to generate forces quickly for joint action upon warning and a political decision to do so. Because of such preparations, NATO is able to join up earmarked national forces into a coherent multilateral force with reasonable predictability and speed, which adds to deterrence.

In essence, whereas UN members are, fundamentally, obligated only to *abide* in peace and security, NATO members have committed themselves by treaty, under certain circumstances, to *provide* peace and security, even if it means going to war. True, NATO includes a commitment of forces that may go beyond what could be expected for countries that are not formal allies bound to defend one another but instead members of an inclusive international organisation like the AU. However, what is so interesting about NATO is not the legal obligation of its members to furnish forces for common defence of allied territory (under Article 5 of the NATO Treaty) but instead the emerging understandings and procedures for planning and generating forces for expeditionary operations (under Article 4) when there is not a binding commitment. Even as NATO relies increasingly on its members to make good on non-obligatory plans to prepare and provide forces for Article-4 contingencies, Africans and others could learn and borrow from these practices.

Under such an approach, the relevant international organisation—the AU, for our purpose here—would need permanent control of only modest command and control cells and information systems in order to permit quick force generation. It would need to issue quality, readiness and interoperability standards and common communications protocols. Of course, prior political understandings would be needed with at least some members to the effect that they accept the responsibility to protect and, in principle, can be counted upon to provide forces as planned. Such understandings are implicit in the current effort to form regional peacekeeping brigades of the Africa Standby Force under AU auspices, though these forces lack fire-power, deployability, interoperability and efficient force-generation processes. For African humanitarian intervention forces to be able to deploy and fight decisively to stop mass killing, force-generation principles and practices like NATO's would need to be adopted.

Even such arrangements for planning, preparing and generating superior military forces for non-consensual humanitarian intervention might not suffice if unexpectedly strong opposition is encountered or if fighting drags on or expands. This suggests a need for escalation options sufficient to leave no doubt that the international intervention will succeed militarily. Reinforcements may come in the form of additional ground forces, air strikes, intelligence, command and control, and logistical capabilities. It is less crucial that these capabilities be under the control of the AU (or UN) than that their availability be a certainty to all concerned, including hostile forces. Such escalation dominance can and probably must be provided by a powerful partner.

There are, of course, ample military capabilities among the United States and certain European NATO members to establish and if need be exercise escalation dominance in most situations of international intervention to stop mass atrocities. The distance, scale, logistical demands and firepower requirements will determine whether the United States must participate; under many circumstances, the combination of NATO command and non-US forces would lend sufficiently credible escalation dominance. Designation of a lead country would be natural, though a direct relationship between NATO and the AU would broaden participation and enhance (while admittedly also complicating) command and control.

As for escalation strategies, NATO air strikes in Bosnia demonstrated the decisive effect of the use of precision tactical air-power against forces that are interfering with peacekeepers on the ground. If air-power is not enough, the new net-centric capabilities and operating concepts being adopted by NATO militaries can provide joint (air–ground–naval) forces to reinforce African humanitarian intervention forces that find themselves in trouble. This would be a natural mission for the NATO Response Force.

Political understandings would have to be reached prior to an intervention such that adequate forces of NATO or individual members will be ready to escalate. Such understandings, made known, would help ensure the success of intervening forces, deter opposition to them, and even reduce the need for escalation. Mass-killing forces and their leaders will not be eager to face Western military power. The arrival of US Marines in Liberian waters clearly helped convince Charles Taylor to exit the country and permit the UN to insert a peacekeeping force. The concept of a humanitarian-intervention partnership between NATO and the AU offered here would enable the Western powers, including the United States, to become a steady wholesaler instead of an inconsistent retailer of security—a more acceptable and sustainable role politically both in the West and in the view of Africans.

In time, the EU might be in a position to help the AU maintain and use humanitarian intervention forces. For now, it is lacking in experience in forcible military action, in force planning and force generation, in combat command and control, and in escalation capabilities, apart from those of member states that are also members of NATO. More important than these shortcomings is that the EU does not include the United States, the participation of which is important for technical—e.g., its global information grid—and political reasons. Just as it would be a mistake for the United States to pursue a partnership with the AU to the exclusion of its European allies, it would be a mistake for the Europeans to pursue such a partnership to the exclusion of the United States. The aim of supporting the AU is best served by the Atlantic allies working together. . . .

Although NATO and several of its members already have the military capacity to intervene to stop genocide in Africa, neither they nor, for that matter, the Africans favour that option. NATO could help the AU make the capability to protect a reality. As noted earlier, the United States and several European countries now have underway programmes to expand peacekeeping capacity, mainly but not only in Africa. Beyond this, NATO can provide:

- expanded and focused training and other assistance to those AU members prepared to earmark quality *combat* forces for humanitarian military intervention, as many African countries have already agreed to do in connection with the several African regional brigades of the AU's Africa Standby Force (at a minimum, NATO can provide coordination and some military standards among the national assistance programmes of its members);
- sharing of expertise, models and procedures for planning, preparing, generating and integrating stand-by national forces for forcible multilateral action when needed; and
- capabilities and plans for operational support, strengthening of command and control, reinforcement and escalation dominance.

The principal instruments that NATO would use to carry out such a programme are its military commands (under Allied Command Operations), its international staff, and those special operations forces (SOF) of members with competence in developing indigenous forces. In this regard, the US government is considering the idea of proposing a NATO SOF capability. While intended for direct counter-terrorist operations, NATO SOF could also be highly useful for improving and working with African forces, as some are doing on a small scale already. Overall, NATO provides an ideal venue for the Atlantic democracies to pool military efforts to help Africa and other regions where peace often fails and mass suffering occurs. And nothing could be more consistent with NATO's new aim of extending security beyond Europe.

Readers might wonder whether Africans themselves are willing to commit combat forces to stop genocide when the West is not. The answer is that African countries pay a high price for mass human-rights abuses and killing on their continent—a price that European and North American countries do not pay, at least not directly. Flows of hundreds of thousands of refugees, cross-border incursions of militia groups, social and political upheaval, and damage to already struggling economies can hurt entire regions, as has happened in West Africa, Central Africa and the Horn of Africa since the end of the Cold War. As long as wars and mass atrocities continue to destabilise parts of Africa, it makes sense for Africans to play a leading role in intervening to stop them. While they have far to go in building consensus and capabilities to protect their region from conflict, Africans are putting much greater effort into and reliance upon the AU than they ever did its feeble predecessor, the Organisation of African Unity.

Although Africans are indeed taking greater responsibility to stop the killing that has plagued their people and harmed development, they need help to create multilateral military capabilities to stop genocide, especially if the West is disinclined to intervene. To get this right, Africans should not hesitate to look to NATO for assistance. The time is ripe for NATO to respond with a major initiative to help the AU create and stand behind a capability to protect.

Nsonurua J. Udombana

Still Playing Dice with Lives: Darfur and Security Council Resolution 1706

The Darfur genocide is the first in the 21st century and may eventually be the best known in history. 'Never in human history has a genocide in progress been so visible', although it remains invisible to the obdurate and politically motivated doubters. By the time the genocide claims its last victim, the UN Security Council, which has the primary mandate of maintaining international peace and security, will be suffering from resolution fatigue. The Council has already adopted about 10, mostly lame, resolutions bearing on the Darfur crisis. Its latest release was Resolution 1706 of 31 August 2006, adopted by a vote of 12 in favour, none against; China, Russia, and Qatar predictably abstained. These 10 resolutions do not include statements by the Security Council presidents, numerous reports by the UN Secretary-General and the infamous Report of the UN Commission of Inquiry on Darfur. They also exclude resolutions, declarations, and decisions of the African Union (AU) and its Peace and Security Council (PSC).

The avalanche of global and regional resolutions, statements, communiqués and mission reports evidences, in principle, a desire to see an end to the pogrom in Darfur. In practice, these exercises, not to say the several ceasefire and peace agreements signed by belligerents, have done little to stem what the PSC calls 'the ever-deteriorating security situation on the ground'. In the past three years the Security Council has repeatedly expressed its alarm that the violence in Darfur has continued unabated. It expresses 'its utmost concern over the dire consequences of the prolonged conflict for the civilian population in the Darfur region as well as throughout Sudan, in particular the increase in the number of refugees and internally displaced persons'. It condemns 'all violations of human rights and international humanitarian law . . . in particular the continuation of violence against civilians and sexual violence against women and girls'. The Council has expressed every sentiment except a desire to take a strong action to save victims of the Darfur genocide.

Resolution 1706 is expected to change the status quo ante. It authorises the expansion of the UN Mission in Sudan (UNMIS) to Darfur—without prejudice to its existing mandate and operations—and its deployment to replace the patently ineffective African Union (AU) Mission in Sudan (AMIS) and support

From *Third World Quarterly*, vol. 28, no. 1, 2007, pp. 97–106, 110–111, omit notes. Copyright © 2007 by Taylor & Francis Journals. Reprinted by permission.

the effective implementation of the Darfur Peace Agreement (DPA). It requests the Secretary-General to arrange rapid deployment of additional capabilities to enable UNMIS deploy in Darfur and calls on UN member states to ensure such an expeditious deployment—subject to consent by the Government of National Unity (GNU), a euphemism for the National Islamic Front/National Congress Party in Khartoum! The resolution requests the Secretary-General to consult jointly with the AU and with parties to the DPA—including the gnu—on a plan and timetable for a transition from AMIS to UNMIS.

The AU and its PSC welcomes the proposed transition, but the government of Sudan views the move as an encroachment on its sovereignty, an attempt at recolonisation and the climax of efforts to undermine the DPA. Notwithstanding the promise that UNMIS shall have a strong African participation and character, Omar al-Bashir, the strongman of Sudan, threatens an all-out war against the UN should it attempt forcible deployment of peacekeepers in Darfur. Sudan's tough talk 'is a simple matter of bristling at the perceived loss of sovereignty', but it also is an act of resentment against the West for not rewarding Sudan's so-called attempt at modernisation. Khartoum, says *The Economist*, would like to see its co-operation with the Central Intelligence Agency (CIA) in the war against terrorism recognised; its name removed from the US State Department's list of state sponsors of terrorism; and Congress lift its trade embargo. These wishes are not being granted, hence the hard-line posturing over Resolution 1706.

This Article interrogates Resolution 1706 in the context of the continuing mayhem in Darfur and the AU's first major experiment at peacekeeping through AMIS. How well has AMIS performed? Could it have done better with a more robust mandate and enhanced military strength? How correct is it to say that AU member states are incapable of pulling resources together for effective regional peacekeeping? What is the legal basis for the proposed transition from AMIS to UNMIS and what will be the role of the AU and its PSC in this new enterprise? Does Resolution 1706 translate into clear rules of engagement? Given the nature of the Sudanese state, is governmental consent an absolute necessity for troop deployment, or merely desirable? This article attempts to provide answers to these and related questions.

The next part assesses AMIS's experiment at peacekeeping in the context of its mandate. The following section analyses Resolution 1706 and UNMIS. The final part draws some conclusions from the narrative and analysis.

Darfur and the AU Mission in Sudan

Darfur, a large, arid region in western Sudan, is the symbol of a nation's retreat from humanism, the ugly story of a failed state and, by extension, of a failed continent, where so much is, and rightly should be, expected, but which offers so little peace, security, stability and prosperity to its citizens. Darfur is a painful reminder that a peaceful order is still a far cry in Africa, where rulers, intoxicated by the narcotics of power, rule their countries in anger with unrelenting persecution and smite their peoples in wrath with unceasing blows. Death, devastation and displacement have defined Darfur since early 2003, when two rebel movements—the Justice and Equality Movement (JEM) and the Sudan Liberation Movement/Army (SML/A)—attacked government positions in Sudan. In response, the Sudanese government and its Janjaweed criminal alliance unleashed a terrifying violence on Darfur and ethnic Darfurians, aimed clearly at changing the demography of the region.

Darfur is characterised by a criminality of the most unimaginable invention. The narrative 'has become numbingly, terrifyingly familiar': the Janjaweed monsters—the vicious instrument of ethnic destruction—are killing farmers wholesale and cutting down fruit trees; slaughtering innocent civilians and poisoning wells with their corpses; burning villages; raping women; 'cutting babies out of mother's wombs and playing with the foetuses in front of them'. Sudan's aircraft destroy whole villages with impunity. Between 80% and 90% of all villages of the Fur, Massalit, Zaghawa and Birgid tribes have been destroyed, in a conflict that has poisoned inter-ethnic relations and threatened the stability of neighbouring countries, especially Chad. Humanitarian workers remain 'targets of brutal violence, physical harassment and rhetorical vilification'. Over 250 000 civilians have died since the onset of the genocide. Millions have had their livelihoods destroyed and have become refugees and internationally displaced persons (IDPS)—a meaningless classification that ought to have gone with the 20th century. Up to 2000 refugees a day flood into Darfur's camps of despair, many of them 'seriously malnourished, dehydrated or in critical need of medical assistance'. Unfed and thirsty, many sleep without shelter in the dust . . . but why go on?

Suffice to state that Darfur is a byword for human misery. It also exposes the façade of collective regional peacekeeping in Africa, given AMIS's failure to make a real difference to the security situation on ground. This section evaluates the AU's 'pioneering experiment' in peacekeeping, after briefly examining the meaning of the concept in international law.

The Concept of Peacekeeping

Peacekeeping is a mechanism for addressing a wide variety of threats to international peace and security. Boutros-Ghali defines it as 'the deployment of a [UN] presence in the field, hitherto with the consent of all parties concerned, normally involving [UN] military and/or police personnel and frequently civilians as well. Peacekeeping is a technique that expands the possibilities for both the prevention of conflict and the making of peace.' The practice of peacekeeping evolved in response to the cold war deadlock that paralysed the Security Council and prevented it from functioning as designed. The UN Charter made no direct reference to it, thereby creating some difficulties in defining where peacekeeping lies on the spectrum between consent and coercion, between passivity and force. However, Dag Hammarskjøld, the former Secretary-General who proposed the first UN peacekeeping force, described the practice as a 'Chapter Six and a Half' operation, falling in between Chapter VI measures for peaceful resolution of conflicts and Chapter VII enforcement action. The International Court of

Justice (ICJ) also confirmed the legality of peacekeeping actions in 1962, in both Suez and the Congo.

Peacekeeping functions have traditionally ranged from observance of ceasefire, to demarcation lines or withdrawal of force agreements, but the practice has acquired a certain elasticity in recent years, as new circumstances have made new demands on the military capacity of the institutions of security governance. Increasingly modern peacekeeping has become 'a catch-all term', extending to election monitoring, delivery of humanitarian supplies, assisting the national reconciliation process, and rebuilding a state's social, economic and administrative infrastructure. Both before and after the Cold War the UN has consistently employed peacekeeping operations as its primary mechanism for restoring peace and security and the Security Council increasingly mandates such operations to protect civilians. Cox argues that the future credibility of the UN depends on successful peacekeeping operations, but their efficacy as a tool for restoration of peace remains debatable.

Many regional organisations have also undertaken peacekeeping operations, both collaboratively with the UN and independently of it. The proliferation of intra-state conflicts after the Cold War began to weigh down the international security framework, in terms of both finance and logistics, necessitating the need for burden sharing with the UN. Besides, these intra-state conflicts have regional specificities and being grassroots mechanisms, regional bodies are better placed to conduct short, robust stabilisation or peacekeeping and peace-enforcement operations before the UN has the chance to undertake a multidimensional mission. The North Atlantic Treaty Organisation (NATO), for example, has deployed peacekeeping missions in recent years, including the Implementation Force (IFOR) in 1995, Stabilisation Force (SFOR) in 1996 and Kosovo Force (KFOR) in 1999. There are NATO-led missions elsewhere, including—presently—Afghanistan.

One of the key tasks of the AU is to promote peace, security and stability in Africa, which its Constitutive Act acknowledges as a prerequisite for the implementation of Africa's development and integration agenda. One of the AU's organising principles is 'peaceful resolution of conflicts among Member States of the Union through such appropriate means as may be decided upon by the Assembly'. The PSC is the current 'appropriate means' by which the AU attempts to resolve conflicts. The PSC was inaugurated in May 2004, after the entry into force of its Protocol. The PSC Protocol establishes an African Standby Force (ASF) with a mandate to intervene in a member state in respect of grave circumstances or at the request of a member state in order to restore peace and security.

The ASF shall also provide humanitarian assistance to alleviate the suffering of civilian populations in conflict areas and support efforts to address major natural disasters. The ASF shall perform other functions as the PSC or AI Assembly might direct, including observation and monitoring missions and other types of peace support missions. It shall also engage in deployment missions in order to prevent 1) a dispute or a conflict from escalating; 2) an ongoing violent conflict from spreading to neighbouring areas or states; and 3) the resurgence of violence after parties to a conflict have reached agreement.

Finally, it shall engage in peace building, including post-conflict disarmament and demobilisation.

AMIS and its Mandate

AMIS was established April 2004; it was then called the Ceasefire Commission (CFC). Its mandate consisted of planning, verifying and ensuring the implementation of the rules and provisions of the N'djamena Agreement; defining the routes for the movement of forces in order to reduce the risks of incidents; requesting appropriate assistance with de-mining operations; receiving, verifying, analysing and judging complaints related to possible violations of the ceasefire; developing adequate measures to guard against such incidents in the future; and determining clearly the sites occupied by the combatants of the armed opposition and verifying the neutralisation of the armed militias. The badly drafted CFC Agreement also provided for an AU Monitoring Mission as the operational arm of the cfc. It provided for Military Observers (MILOBS), which 'may be lightly armed'. The AU Monitoring Mission was to be deployed on the basis of the commitment of the Sudanese government, JEM and SML/A—the principal antagonists in the Darfur crisis—to ensure the protection and safety of the MILOBS.

AMIS initially comprised 80 military observers and a protection force of 600 troops. The PSC enlarged this number to 3320 in July 2004 and, on 20 October 2004, the force level was beefed up to around 7000 personnel, made up of 686 military observers, 4890 troops, and 1176 civilian police. The PSC further increased the force level on 28 April 2005 to its current total authorised strength of 6171 military personnel and 1560 civilian police, because of the 'precarious security situation and persistent attacks against civilians'.

As modified, AMIS's mandate is to monitor and observe compliance with the N'djamena Agreement and all such agreements in the future; to assist in the process of confidence building; and to contribute to a secure environment for the delivery of humanitarian relief, and beyond that, to the return of IDPS and refugees to their homes, in order to assist in increasing the level of compliance of all parties with the N'djamena Agreement and to contribute to the improvement of the security situation throughout Darfur. It is also authorised to 'protect civilians whom it encounters under imminent threat and in the immediate vicinity, within resources and capability, it being understood that the protection of the civilian population is the responsibility of the GoS [Government of Sudan]'. Even this new mandate is less robust than expected, probably because of a lack of capacity and of prudential calculations about the overall prospects for peace in Sudan. Nevertheless, the Security Council expressed its support for AMIS and urged UN member states 'to provide the required equipment, logistical, financial, material, and other necessary resources'.

The first phase of AMIS's deployment ended in June 2005, with total personnel of 2635, comprising 452 military observers, 1732 troops, 40 CFC members/ international support staff, 413 civilian police personnel and 12 members of the Darfur Integrated Task Force (DITF). The second phase was scheduled to end in August 2005, with deployment of 6171 military personnel, with an appropriate civilian component including up to 1560 civilian police. The third phase was a follow-up mission, with projected personnel of 12 300. Instructively, Rwanda—a country that had experienced the horrors of genocide—was the first African state to contribute troops towards the AMIS. Similarly, as of 26 July 2005, 'three (3) days before the deadline established by the AU plan of deployment' of enhanced AMIS, Rwanda had completed the deployment of its first battalion of 680 troops in Darfur and 'made itself ready to start the deployment of its second Battalion'.

AMIS was scheduled to withdraw from Sudan by the end of September 2006 after the expiration of its current mandate. Its term has now been extended until the end of 2006, a temporary concession that the PSC managed to obtain from the government during the September 2006 UN General Assembly meeting in New York. The Arab League reportedly pledged to fund the interlude, while the UN would provide logistics and other material support. Al-Bashir insisted that he would not accept a UN force designed to place 'Sudan under mandate, a sort of trusteeship'. Thus, a patient that submits to global medication in Southern Sudan insists on a dangerous self-medication on its Western frontier, notwithstanding that the disease has deepened into a septic abscess. Khartoum's rhetoric is obviously short on logic and long on mass psychology, but it has so far cowed the Security Council and prevented it from taking robust action to end the genocide.

A Preliminary Evaluation

AMIS is the first continental experiment at peacekeeping under the AU legal framework. What has been its achievement for the short period of its operation in Darfur? Certainly, AMIS serves as a moral presence and encourages a modicum of restraint in Sudan. However bad things presently look in Darfur, they could have been far worse without AMIS. The Security Council itself acknowledges AMIS's role in reducing large-scale organised violence in Darfur. AMIS has also been able to offer limited protection to aid workers, which has enabled the delivery of essential humanitarian assistance, without which the genocide would have been worse. Ultimately, success at peacekeeping is judged by the probability of ending a crisis and achieving a lasting peace. Thus, even when all allowances have been made, AMIS is not the firewall that will stop unremitting atrocities in Darfur.

AMIS has failed in Darfur because it has been incapacitated by numerous weaknesses, including problems of command and control, logistical support, operational practice and a lack of funds. Its patently inadequate budget has largely been supported from the outside—by the EU, the UK and Germany, with the USA providing some logistics. The UN also provides some strategic support, through its Assistance Cell in Addis Ababa. Nevertheless, AMIS remains grossly incapacitated and is 'watching helplessly while civilians are slaughtered'. The terms and conditions under which it operates have largely been negotiated with, if not defined by, the Sudanese government, thereby compromising one of the cardinal rules of peacekeeping—objectivity and impartiality. According to Krizner, 'The African Union [Mission in Sudan] is not motivated. Culturally they don't identify with the Muslim population in the region. They have little sympathy for Darfurians. And, ultimately, they are controlled by the government in Khartoum. When they receive reports of Janjaweed attacks they wait for days before investigating'.

AMIS does not have the ability even to resist attacks against its members, let alone the refugees it is supposed to protect. A group of AMIS contingents was taken hostage by one of the rebel factions in October 2005; four were killed, others were released a day later. A few days later the UN withdrew its non-essential aid workers from west Darfur, acknowledging that it could not protect even its own staff. The government is still conducting offensive military over-flights in north Darfur and troop deployments to north, south and west Darfur, in direct violation of the DPA. Darfur has been subjected to renewed aerial bombing that brings greater misery to a population that has already endured much pain and anguish.

Although the AU is reportedly expanding its peacekeeping operation by 4000 to bring the force level of AMIS to 11 000 by the end of 2006, the failure to make a serious impact on the security situation in Darfur has created a 'categorical imperative' for the deployment of UNMIS. A promise of protection becomes destructive where real force is not available to back up the offer. To save face, the AU insists on playing a lead role in the overall Darfur peace process, 'including the conduct of the Abuja Peace Talks and the Darfur—Darfur dialogue and consultation provided for by the Declaration of Principles (DOP) signed in Abuja on 5 July 2005, as well as in the implementation of existing and future agreements between the parties'. Africa is not bereft of a sense of irony.

In retrospect, is there really a need for a new peacekeeping force in Darfur? Is it not possible for the global community to reinforce AMIS by further enhancing its mandate, strengthening its mobility, providing more funding and better equipment for it to deal with the crisis? The present writer finds fallacious the claim that the AU and its member states cannot assemble and finance an effective African force to keep the peace in Darfur. If a few West African states were able to prevent anarchy in Liberia and Sierra Leone, under the auspices of the Economic Community of West African States Monitoring Group (ECOMOG), common sense show that a continental organisation of 53 member states should be able to mobilise and deploy a credible force in Darfur, with necessary logistical support. There is simply no political will among states that make up the AU.

UNMIS and Resolution 1706

The spiralling violence and displacement in Darfur led senior UN officials and human rights NGOS to warn of an imminent humanitarian catastrophe, compelling the Security Council to adopt Resolution 1706. An earlier attempt at bolstering the peacekeeping efforts in Darfur was Resolution 1590, which established UNMIS to support implementation of the Comprehensive Peace

Agreement (CPA) between the Sudanese government and the Sudan People's Liberation Movement/Army (SPLM/A) in Nairobi, Kenya on 9 January 2005. The CPA brought to an end the 30-year-long civil war in Southern Sudan that led to two million deaths and four million displacements. It allows the south to determine, in a referendum to be conducted in six years from 2005, whether to remain in a united Sudan or to set up an independent state, based, obviously, on the inherent right of peoples to self-determination. 'When a people', says Soyinka, 'have been subjected to a degree of inhuman violation for which there is no other word but genocide, they have the right to seek an identity apart from their aggressors'.

Resolution 1590 authorised UNMIS to have up to 10 000 military personnel and an appropriate civilian component, including up to 715 civilian police personnel. It requested UNMIS to 'closely and continuously liaise and coordinate at all levels with the . . . [AMIS] with a view towards expeditiously reinforcing the efforts to foster peace in Darfur, especially with regards to the Abuja peace process and the [AMIS]'. On 16 May 2006 the Council adopted Resolution 1679, which called on the AU and UN to agree upon requirements necessary to strengthen the capacity of AMIS to enforce the security arrangements of the Darfur Peace Agreement, 'with a view to a follow-on [UN] operation in Darfur'.

In July 2006 the UN Secretary-General presented a report on Darfur to the Security Council. The report described the main elements of the DPA and identified the implementation priorities. It also identified some risks and challenges involved in deploying a UN peacekeeping force in Darfur; elaborated on support the UN could offer to AMIS to enhance its ability to protect civilians and implement the Agreement; proposed a mandate and mission structure for a UN operation in Darfur; and provided details on various components of the proposed mission and their specific functions. Finally, the report recommended 'a large, agile and robust military force' that entails 'high troop density to provide wide area coverage; high mobility to move forces rapidly in response to developing crises; and robust military capability to deter and defeat spoilers'.

The DPA was intended to instil some new dynamics into resolving the Darfur conflict, but it faces formidable challenges. To start with, the DPA has not received support from IDPS and many others affected by the conflict. Two of the parties involved in the Abuja talks—the UNMIS and the Abdelwahid faction of the SLM/A—remain outside the DPA, despite extension of the signing deadline to 31 May. Only the government delegation and the SLM/A faction led by Minni Minawi signed the Agreement. The lack of unanimity prevents the Cease-fire Commission and the Joint Commission—two mechanisms established by the DPA—from making real progress on implementation. Elements opposed to the DPA have reportedly mobilised sections of Darfurians against the Agreement. Rebels have further split into factions, attacking government locations, all of which provides the government with a ready excuse for continuous attacks and air raids, 'under the pretext that the civilian population had to be protected'. Current attacks follow long-standing patterns of destruction, forced displacement and violence against civilians.

The remainder of this section examines UNMIS's mandate for Darfur and the principles underpinning Resolution 1706.

UNMIS's Mandate

Resolution 1706 defines the mandate of UNMIS in Darfur. It authorises the expansion of the existing UNMIS by up to 17 300 military personnel and an appropriate civilian component including up to 3300 civilian police personnel and up to 16 Formed Police Units. UNMIS's mandate is to support implementation of the DPA and the N'djamena Agreement. Consequently, it 'shall take over from AMIS responsibility for supporting the implementation of the [Agreements] upon the expiration of AMIS' mandate but in any event not later than 31 December 2006'. Specifically, UNMIS shall monitor and verify implementation of the Agreements by the parties; observe and monitor the movement of armed groups and redeployment of forces in areas of UNMIS deployment; investigate violations of Agreements and report them to the Ceasefire Commission; co-operate and co-ordinate, together with relevant actors, with the Ceasefire Commission through provision of technical assistance and logistical support; and maintain a presence in key areas, including buffer zones, camps and demilitarised zones, in order to promote the re-establishment of confidence and deter violence.

UNMIS shall also monitor trans-border activities of armed groups along the Sudanese borders through regular ground and aerial reconnaissance activities; assist with development and implementation of a comprehensive and sustainable programme for disarmament; assist parties, in co-operation with other actors, in preparations for, and conduct of, referendums provided for in the DPA; and assist parties, in co-ordination with the AU, in promoting understanding of the DPA and the role of UNMIS, through an effective public information campaign.

UNMIS is to co-operate closely with the Chair of the Darfur–Darfur Dialogue and Consultation (DDDC), through technical support and co-ordination of other UN agencies to this effect, and assist parties to the DDDC to adopt an all-inclusive approach to reconciliation and peace building; assist parties to the DPA in promoting the rule of law (including an independent judiciary) and the protection of human rights; and ensure an adequate human rights and gender presence, capacity and expertise within UNMIS to carry out human rights promotion, civilian protection and monitoring activities that pay attention to the needs of women and children. Finally, UNMIS is to facilitate and co-ordinate the voluntary return of refugees and IDPS and provide humanitarian assistance through the establishment of necessary security conditions in Darfur; contribute towards international efforts to protect, promote and monitor human rights in Darfur and co-ordinate efforts towards protecting civilians, especially vulnerable groups; assist parties to the Agreements with humanitarian de-mining assistance, technical advice, co-ordination and mining awareness programmes; and assist in addressing regional security issues, including through the establishment of a multidimensional presence in key locations.

Significantly the Security Council, acting under Chapter VII of the UN Charter, authorises UNMIS to use 'all necessary means' it deems within its capabilities to: protect UN personnel, facilities, installations and equipment; ensure the security and freedom of movement of UN personnel, humanitarian workers, assessment and evaluation commission personnel; prevent disruption of the implementation of the DPA by armed groups, without prejudice to the responsibility of the GoS; protect civilians under threat of physical violence; and seize or collect arms or related materials whose presence in Darfur is in violation of the Agreements and the measures imposed by resolution 1556, and to dispose them as appropriate.

The Security Council is now known to be evasive when invoking Chapter VII, and Resolution 1706 is reflective of this ambivalence. The reluctance to identify the precise legal basis for its resolutions has led to arguments regarding the legal basis of Security Council operations, since different articles of Chapter VII give different legal outcomes. However, the particular article envisaged could be discovered from the wordings of each resolution. Resolution 1706 authorises UNMIS 'to use all necessary means', a phrase that appears in Article 42 of the UN Charter. This provides that, where non-forceful measures prove inadequate in restoring international peace and security, the Council can 'take such action by air, sea, or land forces as may be necessary to maintain or restore international peace and security', including 'demonstrations, blockade, and other operations by air, sea, or land forces of Members of the [UN]'. It may be concluded that Resolution 1706 represents a robust mandate for UNMIS, albeit in the context of peacekeeping. . . .

Conclusion: Playing Dice with Lives

Almost everyone agrees that Darfur is a humanitarian catastrophe—the worst in recent memory, according to the UN—and that its magnitude requires sustained assistance and engagement by the global community. It is also not in doubt that the Sudanese government cannot be trusted to guarantee the security of lives in Darfur, being a participant in the mayhem. As Polgreen has noted, 'one of the assumptions of the [DPA] was that the government had control over the Arab militias and the power to disarm them. This is based on a deeper assumption that the interests of Darfur's Arabs would be tended to by Khartoum. Neither is turning out to be true.'

Although Darfur has pushed the moral sensibilities of the global community beyond limits, it still hibernates between sympathy and apathy. During the recent 34-day carnage in Lebanon—between the Hezbollah guerrillas and Israel—Darfur literally drifted to the margins of public discourse. As in Iraq, death has become too commonplace to matter. As in Rwanda, the world watches while the catastrophe worsens. The Security Council is busy playing dice with lives, holding endless closed-door meetings and passing countless, often self-serving, but utterly meaningless resolutions. These failings in stopping mass atrocities across the globe cast a shadow over the UN's policing mechanism. The Security Council's hesitancy to take robust actions to suppress Africa's often brutal conflicts has led to missed opportunities to stem bloodshed and damage to the economic and social fabric of many countries, as happened with the UN's ambivalence in the Democratic Republic of Congo in 1997. The Council, says the UN High-level Report, 'has not always been equitable in its actions, nor has it acted consistently or effectively in the face of genocide or other atrocities. This has gravely damaged its credibility.' Wedgwood likens the Council to 'the US Senate in the late 18th century—an often opaque body delivering often opaque results'.

The signals emitting from the AU are even more depressing—and some-times laughable. Pursuant to a decision taken at the AU Assembly's January 2006 Khartoum Summit, al-Bashir is preparing to assume leadership of the AU in January 2007. That exceptionally absurd decision reads:

> The leaders expressed their appreciation for the initiative taken by HE President Omar Hassan Al-Bashir to accept the postponement of his term of Chairmanship for the [AU] until 2007. The leaders consider this gesture to be a true reflection of the great sense of responsibility and leadership demonstrated by President Al-Bashir. The leaders agreed after extensive consultations that the Sudan will assume the Chairmanship of the Union in the year 2007.

When that happens, when a tyrant who speaks mainly the language of violence, hatred and division takes over the mantle of leadership of a conti-nental organisation whose goals include the promotion of peace and security, then al-Bashir will become a vendor of peace and the protagonist of an African renaissance! It will be interesting to see 'how best' the AU under Chairman al-Bashir will 'engage the Sudanese authorities and other stakeholders . . . to expedite the peace process in Darfur'. Such political undercurrents show that group solidarity matters more in Africa than the protection of human and peoples' rights. Caught up in this crossfire, this pincer movement, are mil-lions of refugees and IDPS who face the torture of hunger and misery daily and whose future remains bleak. These victims of ethnic hatred are crying out for compassion and rescue, whatever the helmet of rescuers, green or blue.

The global community should stop playing dice with Darfur lives and should end its fruitless megaphone diplomacy in Sudan. 'The situation in Darfur', says the *Minnesota Daily*, 'is a tragedy of epic proportions, and the world's conscience is on trial'. Organising endless peace talks in Abuja and adopting countless resolutions in New York—with a tsunami of publicity—are no longer sufficient; they never were. Darfur requires a muscular multilateral-ism, because it is a contest between terror and resistance. Western states, including the EU, have the capacity to put real pressure on the Sudanese gov-ernment to end the killing in Darfur, but they have chosen to play Pontius Pilate. These states should recall their troubled history—including the two bru-tal world wars of the 20th century—and realise that tyranny knows neither colour nor race.

POSTSCRIPT

Are African-Led Peacekeeping Missions More Effective than International Peacekeeping Efforts in Africa?

The debate about African peacekeeping initiatives is not simply about military effectiveness. Some see it as an abdication of Western responsibility in Africa, or an unwillingness to intervene due to a combination of past failures and stereotypes about conflict in Africa.

In the case of the United States, two watershed events for American peacekeeping efforts in Africa were the failed military intervention in Somalia in 1993 and the lack of intervention during the Rwandan genocide in 1994. In the twilight of the first Bush administration in 1992, the United States intervened militarily in Somalia to dispense food aid that was not being effectively distributed due to the presence of armed militias. The American force was then reduced under the new Clinton administration and made part of a UN operation with a mandate to protect the delivery of humanitarian assistance and disarm the warring factions. Following the deaths of 26 Pakistani soldiers, the United States sent in army rangers and delta force commandos to try to capture a particularly problematic warlord named Mohammed Aideed. Then in October 1993, 18 U.S. soldiers were killed and 50 wounded in a street war that also cost the U.S. military two Black Hawk helicopters. With the sight of a dead U.S. army ranger being dragged through the streets of Mogadishu on international television, then president Bill Clinton ordered the withdrew of all U.S. troops. This debacle is now commonly referred to as "crossing the Mogadishu line." It resulted in a new U.S. Presidential Directorate (#25) stating that the United States should not become involved in a war unless there was a clear national interest and the conflict could be won.

The events in Somalia had a chilling effect on U.S. interest in addressing the humanitarian crisis in Rwanda in 1994. Following the death of Rwandan President Juvenal Habyarimana in a mysterious plane crash in April 1994, the systematic elimination of Tutsis and moderate Hutus was begun by hard-line elements in the military and Habyarimana government. With most expatriates having left the country, and the meager UN force ordered to protect itself, it is estimated that over a million Tutsis and moderate Hutus were murdered while hundreds of thousands fled the country as refugees. Following these atrocities, the minority Tutsis amassed their forces and began a process of retribution. While the situation in Rwanda eventually was quelled, the inaction of the U.S. and other foreign powers has been roundly condemned.

The specter of Somalia and Rwanda continue to haunt U.S. peacekeeping efforts in Africa today, with a fear of failure lingering from the first case, and the regret of inaction from the latter.

One response of the United States has been to support the development of an African peacekeeping force so that it no longer needs to intervene on the African continent. Some feel that this is an abdication of responsibility, or worse yet, an unwillingness to intervene because of stereotypes about Africans and the nature of ethnic conflict. In his essay "The Politics of Naming: Genocide, Civil War, Insurgency" (*London Review of Books*, March 2007), the prominent African intellectual and native of Uganda, Mahmood Mamdani, is critical of the language used to describe the conflict in Darfur as compared to similar atrocities in Europe. Yet, he is also leery of a humanitarian intervention by the major powers in Darfur, Sudan. He argues that a lasting peace cannot be built on such interventions and is rather more supportive of the African Union's efforts to broker power-sharing arrangements.

Contributors to This Volume

EDITOR

WILLIAM G. MOSELEY is an associate professor of geography, and coordinator of the African studies program, at Macalester College in Saint Paul, Minnesota, where he teaches courses on Africa, environment, and development. He received a B.A. in history from Carleton College, an M.S. in environmental policy and an M.P.P in international public policy from the University of Michigan, and a Ph.D. in geography from the University of Georgia. He has worked for the U.S. Peace Corps, the Save the Children Fund (UK), the U.S. Agency for International Development, the World Bank Environment Department, and the U.S. State Department. His research and work experiences have led to extended stays in Mali, Zimbabwe, Malawi, Niger, Lesotho, and South Africa. He is the author of over 30 peer-reviewed articles and book chapters that have appeared in such outlets as *Ecological Economics*, the *Geographical Journal*, the *Geographical Review*, *Applied Geography,* and *Geoforum*. He also has written pieces for the popular press that have been published in the *International Herald Tribune*, the *Christian Science Monitor*, the *Philadelphia Inquirer*, the *San Francisco Chronicle*, the *Minneapolis Star Tribune*, and the *Chicago Sun Times*. He is the lead author of several edited collections, including *African Environment and Development: Rhetoric, Programs, Realities* (Ashgate, 2004), *The Introductory Reader in Human Geography: Contemporary Debates and Classic Writings* (Blackwell, 2007), and *Hanging by a Thread: Cotton, Globalization and Poverty in Africa* (Ohio University Press, 2008).

AUTHORS

FUAMBAI AHMADOU, originally from Sierra Leone, is an anthropologist and post-doctoral fellow in the department of comparative human development at the University of Chicago. Dr. Ahmadou studies male and female initiation rites in Africa and has published numerous book chapters on the subject.

ANITA ALBAN is an external lecturer of health economics at the Institute of Public Health at the University of Copenhagen. Her research interests include cost-effectiveness of HIV/AIDS and TB interventions in Africa and Asia, access to drugs for poor communities, and mathematical models of health care in developing countries.

KOFI ANNAN, originally from Ghana, was the seventh Secretary General of the United Nations. He received a Nobel Peace Prize in 2001, and has advocated for peace, human rights, and HIV/AIDS research within the international community. He has worked extensively in peacekeeping negotiations and more recently in fighting terrorism.

JOEL D. BARKAN is a professor of political science at the University of Iowa and senior consultant on governance at the World Bank. His research interests include democratization, macro-economic reform in developing countries, and electoral processes.

THOMAS J. BASSETT is a professor of geography and affiliate of the Center for African Studies at the University of Illinois, Urbana–Champaign. His research interests include Third World development, African agrarian systems, political ecology, and the history of cartography. He is the author of *The Peasant Cotton Revolution in West Africa: Côte d'Ivoire, 1880–1995* (Cambridge University Press, 2001), and co-editor (with D. Crummey) of *African Savannas: Global Narratives and Local Knowledge of Environmental Change in Africa* (James Curry and Heinemann, 2003). He also has penned numerous journal articles and book chapters that have appeared in such outlets as the *Annals of the Association of American Geographers, Africa,* and the *Review of African Political Economy.*

MICHAEL BRATTON is a professor of political science and African studies at Michigan State University. His research interests include comparative politics, public administration, and African politics. He is the author or coauthor of *The Local Politics of Rural Development: Peasant and Party-State in Zambia* (University Press of New England, 1980), *Governance and Politics in Africa* (Lynne Rienner Press, 1992), and *Democratic Experiments in Africa: Regime Transitions in Comparative Perspective* (Cambridge University Press, 1997).

PADRAIG CARMODY is a lecturer in Geography at the Trinity College Dublin in Ireland. His research focuses on the effects of globalization and economic liberalization on African countries. He has published numerous articles about poverty alleviation, development strategies and economic liberalization and is the author of *Tearing the Social Fabric: Neoliberalism, Deindustrialization, and the Crisis of Governance in Zimbabwe* (Heinemann, 2001).

JUDITH CARNEY is a professor of geography at the University of California in Los Angeles. She is the author of numerous peer-reviewed articles that have appeared in such outlets as the *Journal of Ethnobiology, Progress in Human Geography,* and *Human Ecology.* Her book, *Black Rice: The African Origins of Rice Cultivation in the Americas* (Harvard University Press, 2001), won the African Studies Association's Herskovits Award in 2002.

KEVIN M. CLEAVER is director of Agriculture & Rural Development of the World Bank and heads the World Bank Board of Rural Sector Managers. His interests include environmental issues, agricultural policy and adjustment, forestry, and natural resource management. His publications include *A Strategy to Develop Agriculture in Sub-Saharan Africa and a Focus for the World Bank* (1993), *An Agricultural Growth and Rural Environment Strategy for the Coastal and Central African Francophone Countries* (1992), and *Conservation of West and Coastal African Rainforests* (1992).

MARCUS COLCHESTER is the director of the Forest Peoples Programme of the World Rainforest Movement. His primary work has involved securing the rights to land and livelihood of indigenous peoples. He has been a fellow in the Pew Fellows Program in Conservation and the Environment, an associate editor for *The Ecologist* magazine, and honorary advisor on Development in the Amazon to the Venezuelan government.

ANDREW CREESE works at the World Health Organization's Essential Drugs and Medicines Policy Department as a senior health economist. His interests include health systems financing, economic evaluation, and pharmaceutical policy issues. He has worked in Ghana and Malawi, as well as other African nations.

LIZ CREEL is a population specialist and senior policy analyst at the Population Reference Bureau.

SUNDAY DARE is a Nigerian journalist and a former Nieman Fellow at Harvard University. Dare's career has focused on investigative reporting of political corruption, military dictatorships, and human rights violations. He is a member of the Washington-based International Consortium of Investigative Journalists, an organization composed of leading investigative journalists from around the world.

JARED DIAMOND is professor of physiology and biogeography at the University of California at Los Angeles (UCLA). His research interests include biogeography, and geography and human society. He is best known for his Pulitzer Prize-winning book, *Guns, Germs and Steel: The Fates of Human Societies* (W. W. Norton, 2005), and its follow-up, *Collapse: How Societies Choose to Fail or Succeed* (Penguin Books, 2006).

TIM DOCKING is an African Affairs Specialist with the United States Institute of Peace. Docking is a political scientist who has provided congressional testimony. He also has published numerous book chapters and articles on peace and governance.

KATHERINE FLOYD is a health economist in the Stop Tuberculosis Department at the World Health Organization.

ARTHUR A. GOLDSMITH is professor of management at the University of Massachusetts, Boston. He is the author of *Building Agricultural Institutions: Transferring the Land-Grant Model to India and Nigeria* (Westview, 1990).

DAVID C. GOMPERT is an adviser for Refugees International and a senior fellow at the RAND Corporation, a nonprofit research and policy institution. He served as senior adviser for national security and defense for the Coalition Provisional Authority in Iraq in 2003 and 2004, and worked extensively for the State Department and National Security Council. As a researcher, he published books on international affairs, national security policy, and information technology.

ROBIN M. GRIER is an associate professor of economics and area coordinator for Latin American studies at the University of Oklahoma. She has published numerous articles in journals such as *Economic Inquiry* and *Public Choice*. Her areas of specialization include international finance, development, and Latin American economics.

LORNA GUINNESS is a lecturer in the health policy unit at the University of London's School of Hygiene and Tropical Medicine. She previously worked as an economist for UNAIDS. Her research interests include economic evaluation, health systems, HIV/AIDS, sexual health, and sexually transmitted diseases.

JULIE HEARN is a lecturer in the Department of Politics and International Relations at Lancaster University. She has undertaken research in Uganda, Ghana, and South Africa on a collaborative DFID-funded research project, "Foreign Political Aid, Democratisation and Civil Society in Africa." She has published numerous articles in such outlets as the *Review of African Political Economy, Third World Quarterly,* and *Africa World Review.*

DUNCAN HEYWARD was a Carolina rice planter during the early twentieth century and also served as the governor of South Carolina for four years from 1903–1906.

PHILIP J. HILTS teaches journalism at Boston University. He has reported for the *New York Times* and the *Washington Post* for over 20 years. His interests are in health and science, and has authored six books on these subjects.

HUMAN RIGHTS WATCH is a nonprofit organization supported by contributions from private individuals and foundations worldwide. The organization is the largest of its kind based in the United States. Human Rights Watch researchers conduct fact-finding investigations into human rights abuses in all regions of the world. They then publish these findings in dozens of books and reports every year. The aim is to generate extensive coverage in local and international media that will help to embarrass abusive governments in the eyes of their citizens and the world.

LUCY JAROSZ is associate professor of geography at the University of Washington. Her research interests include food and agriculture, rural poverty and inequality, rural development, and environmental change. She has conducted fieldwork in Madagascar and South Africa. Her articles have appeared in such outlets as the *Journal of Rural Studies* and *Antipode*.

DOROTHY LOGIE is a general practitioner and active member of Medact (an organization of health professionals challenging barriers to health). She is the founder of the Scottish Borders Africa AIDS group.

PAUL E. LOVEJOY is the Canada research chair in African Diaspora History and a distinguished research professor of history at York University in Toronto, Ontario, Canada. His research interests include the trans-Atlantic slave trade, diaspora studies, and slavery in Africa. He has published more than 20 books on these topics, including *Transformations in Slavery: A History of Slavery in Africa* (Cambridge University Press, 2000).

OLIVER MAPONGA is Economic Affairs Officer in the Southern Africa Office of the United Nations Economic Commission for Africa. His research interests include small-scale mining, mining investment regulations, regional mineral economics, and environmental management in the minerals industry.

ROBERT MATTES is an associate professor of political studies and director of the democracy in the Africa Research Unit in the Centre for Social Science Research at the University of Cape Town. He is also cofounder and codirector of Afrobarometer (a survey of Africans' attitudes towards issues including democracy and markets) and an associate with the Institute for Democracy in South Africa. His research interests include the development of democracy/democratic political culture in Africa and the impact of race and identity on politics in South Africa. He is the author of *The Election Book: Judgment and Choice In the 1994 South African Election* (Idasa, 1996).

PHILIP MAXWELL is professor and head of the Department of Mineral Economics and Mine Management at the Western Australian School of Mines at Curtin University of Technology. His recent research interests include the regional economic impacts of mining and mineral commodity markets. He is the coauthor of three textbooks and has authored or coauthored more than 70 articles, book chapters, discussion papers, or monographs.

THANDIKA MKANDAWIRE, originally from Malawi, is the director of the UN Research Institute for Social Development. From 1986 through 1996, he was executive secretary of the Council for the Development of Social Science Research in Africa (CODESRIA), headquartered in Dakar. He is an economist who has published extensively on structural adjustment, democratization, and social sciences in Africa.

MICHAEL MORTIMORE is a geographer who taught at Nigerian universities between 1962 and 1986, and subsequently was a research associate at Cambridge University and the Overseas Development Institute. He currently is with Drylands Research. He has performed research and published numerous books on the topic of environmental management by small holders in the dry lands of Africa. He is the author of *Roots in the African Dust: Sustaining the Drylands* (1998) and the coauthor of *Working the Sahel: Environment & Society in Northern Nigeria* (1999) and *More People, Less Erosion: Environmental Recovery in Kenya* (1994).

SIDDHARTHA MUKHERJEE is a Senior Resident in internal medicine at Massachusetts General Hospital and a Clinical Fellow in Medicine at Harvard Medical School. He has written articles for *The New Republic* and has been a guest on WBUR, Boston's NPR affiliate.

JOHN MURTON is with the Foreign and Commonwealth Office of the British government, and is currently serving as the British High Commissioner to the Republic of Mauritius.

FRANCIS Y. OWUSU, originally from Ghana, is an associate professor of geography at Iowa State University. His research interests include sustainable development, urban and community development, environmental planning, and policy. He is the director of the Africa Specialty Group of the Association of American Geographers and a member of the Global Development Network.

LYDIA POLGREEN is a journalist for the *New York Times*. She is the West African bureau chief, based in Dakar, Senegal. She received a George Polk Award, awarded annual by Long Island University, in foreign reporting for her coverage of ethnic violence in Sudan's Darfur region.

ROBERT I. ROTBERG is director of the Program on Intrastate Conflict and Conflict Resolution at Harvard University's John F. Kennedy School of Government. He is also president of the World Peace Foundation, and has taught political science and history at both Harvard and the Massachusetts Institute of Technology. His research focuses on political and economic issues of developing countries, especially Africa and Southeast Asia. He has authored *The Founder: Cecil Rhodes and the Pursuit of Power* (Oxford University Press, 1988) and *The Rise of Nationalism in Central Africa* (Harvard University Press, 1965).

MICHAEL ROWSON is the assistant director of Medact (an organization of health professionals challenging barriers to health) and coauthor of *Do No Harm: Assessing the Impact of Adjustment Policies on Health* (2002).

GÖTZ A. SCHREIBER was the principal economist in the World Bank's West Central Africa Department. More recently he has worked on Central Asian issues for the World Bank. His areas of interest include macroeconomic policy, human resources, agricultural and rural development, and natural resource management.

RICHARD A. SCHROEDER is an associate professor of geography, and former chair of African studies, at Rutgers University. He is the author of *Shady Practices: Agroforestry and Gender Politics in the Gambia* (1999) and *Producing Nature and Poverty in Africa* (co-editor) (2000). He has published numerous articles in outlets such as the *Annals of the Association of American Geographers, Economic Geography,* and *Africa*.

GERALD E. SCOTT is an associate professor of economics at Florida Atlantic University. His research interests include debt, development, and structural adjustment in Sub-Saharan Africa. He has published articles in journals such as the *Atlantic Economic Journal* and *American Economist.*

ROBERT SNYDER is faculty in the department of biology at the College of the Ozarks. He has worked with environmental programs in Illinois, consulted for the Environmental Protection Agency, and spent six years in Rwanda engaged in agricultural development related to natural resources. His research interests include food production, sustainable resource use, and international development.

CAROL B. THOMPSON is a professor of political economy at Northern Arizona University. Her research interests include international political economy, environment, and Southern Africa. She is on the executive board of the Association of Concerned Africa Scholars, and has testified in U.S. Congressional hearings about policy toward Africa. Her books include *Biopiracy of Biodiversity—Global Exchange as Enclosure* (Africa World Press, 2007).

JOHN THORNTON is a professor of history and African American Studies at Boston University. His research and teaching have focused on Africa and the Middle East. His books include *The Kingdom of Kongo: Civil War and Transition, 1641–1718* (University of Wisconsin Press, 1983), *Africa and Africans in the Formation of the Atlantic World, 1400–1680* (Cambridge University Press, 1992; second expanded edition, 1998), and *The Kongolese Saint Anthony, Dona Beatriz Kimpa Vita and the Antonian Movement, 1684–1706* (Cambridge University Press, 1998).

MARY TIFFEN is a historian and socio-economist at Drylands Research. She is interested in long-term change and development, interdisciplinary research, and social and economic interactions with technology. She authored *The Environmental Impact of the 1991–92 Drought on Zambia: Report* (1994) and *The Enterprising Peasant: Economic Development in Gombe Emirate, North East Nigeria* (1976). She coauthored *More People, Less Erosion: Environmental Recovery in Kenya* (1994).

NSONURUA UDOMBANA, originally from Nigeria, is associate professor and director of the Human Rights Center, Central European University, Budapest. His research interests include international law, human rights, and the African judicial process. He has published many articles. He is the author of *Human Rights and Contemporary Issues in Africa* (Malthouse Press, 2003).

UNITED NATIONS ENVIRONMENTAL PROGRAMME is based in Nairobi, Kenya. Their mission is "to provide leadership and encourage partnership in caring for the environment by inspiring, informing, and enabling nations and peoples to improve their quality of life without compromising that of future generations."

ALI ZAFAR is an economist at the World Bank. He specializes in macroeconomic policy, public finance, and international trade in South Asia and

Sub-Saharan Africa. He advises developing country governments on macroeconomic and fiscal issues. His research focuses on the growing role of China in the world economy, post-conflict economic recovery, exchange rate issues, and poverty reduction in Africa.

KOLI BI ZUELI is an associate professor at the Institute of Tropical Geography, University of Cocody in Abidjan, Ivory Coast. His interests include West Africa, development, the environment, and cultural and political ecology.